The Use of Color
in
History, Politics, and Art

The Use of Color in History, Politics, and Art

Edited by Sungshin Kim

UNIVERSITY of
NORTH GEORGIA
UNIVERSITY PRESS

Dahlonega, Georgia

Copyright © 2016 University of North Georgia Press

All rights reserved. No part of this book may be reproduced in whole or in part without written permission from the publishers, except by reviewers who may quote brief excerpts in connection with a review in newspaper, magazine, or electronic publications; nor may any part of this book be reproduced, stored in a retrieval system, or transmitted in any form or by any means electronic, mechanical, photocopying, recording, or other, without written permission from the publisher.

Fair Use Notice: Images and figures used in this work are protected under copyright and used under "fair use" defined in section 107 of the Copyright Act 1976 where allowance is made for "fair use" for purposes such as criticism, comment, news reporting, teaching, scholarship, education, and research.

Published by:
University of North Georgia Press
Dahlonega, Georgia

Printing Support by:
BookLogix
Alpharetta, GA

Cover design by Sungshin Kim and Corey Parson.

Cover Art courtesy of Sarah Claussen, *Continuous Flow,* Encaustic on Wood Panel, 24" x 48", 2012.

ISBN: 978-1-940771-08-3

Printed in the United States of America, 2016
For more information, please visit ung.edu/university-press
Or email ungpress@ung.edu

Table of Contents

Introduction   v
    Sungshin Kim

Part I   Color and Political Power

1. Painting on a White Foundation: Color, Countenance, and Performance in the *Analects* and *Han Feizi*   3
    Thomas Radice

2. Color, Adornment, and Social Conflict: Fashioning Cultural Identity in Ancient Greece and Rome   23
    Michael Proulx

3. Color Symbolism in the Turko-Mongolian World   51
    Timothy May

4. Lawful Colors and Color of Law in Late Tudor England   79
    Renee Bricker

5. From Dun to White: Forts, Power, and the Politics of Restoration in the United Arab Emirates   103
    Victoria Hightower

6. The Colors of American Diplomacy   123
    Christopher Jespersen

Part II   Color and Representation in Art and Literature

7. Metachromatics: The Historical Division Between Color and Line/Form as Analytic   143
    Robert Machado

8. Jean-Léon Gérôme and the Color of Flesh   187
    Pamela J. Sachant

9. "Whiteness" and Identity in Jean Rhys's *Wide Sargasso Sea* and Michelle Cliff's *Abeng*   201
    April Conley Kilinski

Part III   Color in Contemporary Discourse and Debates

10. Pink is the New Green: Raising Little Shoppers from Birth   225
    Amy Hagenrater-Gooding

11. Understanding Color, Race, and Identity through the (Body) Politics of Barack Obama   243
    Celnisha L. Dangerfield

12. Aversion to the Color Gray: The Monochromatic Nature of Turkish Domestic and Foreign Policy   265
    Jonathan S. Miner

About the Contributors   287

Introduction

Sungshin Kim

As ubiquitous as colors are to human perception, a long tradition exists of dismissing them as superficial. In the classic opposition with form, color (in the general, abstract sense) does indeed appear to be the recessive element, as something that can never exist independently on its own. Yet an alternative aesthetic tradition could be assembled in which overt colors have been highly valued, often exactly as a liberation from the dominant tradition: signifying the primitive, the childlike, or the sensual. When Yves Klein calls color "enslaved by line that becomes writing," he posits it against the rule of logos.

These oppositions hint at the potential of color to provide a point of departure for the exploration of structures of thought. The essays in this collection all explore how color—whether as abstract notion or considering particular colors—can provide clues to the interpretation of concrete historical formations, works of art and literature, or the specifics of a political situation. Made up of historians, scholars of art, literature, and popular culture, as well as political scientists, the authors of this volume were asked to engage color as it emerged in their specific domains of research, which range broadly from the politico-ethical thought of classical China to the shopping malls of the present. This volume is thus not a history of the use of color or its theorization, but a demonstration of the role color can take in the analysis of culture (including political culture) and its products.

The essays collected here started as contributions to the 2012 Arts and Letters Conference on "The Significance of Color," held at the University of North Georgia. Presented in expanded and often revised form, they illustrate the particular strength of different disciplines while laying out their case to a broader audience. The best way to introduce them might be a reflection on color from the perspective of my own field, as a historian.

The most obvious way to historicize color would be as part of the history of taste. For instance Michel Pastoureau has traced the ascent of blue, from a color that was rarely used in ancient art to the one that most people in the West, at least according to surveys, now call their favorite.¹ But it turns out, this rise started with the use of blue as a non-color (like black and white, but also grey, today), embraced by elites during the crisis of the late Middle Ages as an other-worldly hue that could stand for the abnegation of temptation.

But the rise and fall of colors is also a history that has to be told in a material key, involving man's relationship with nature as well as the transformation of economic forces. Imperial purple in the Ancient Mediterranean world depended on the sea snails from which this pigment was extracted, as Michael Proulx mentions in his contribution. In the Medieval West, the dyeing industry was surrounded by mystery not just due to the wonder of transformation itself, but also because the dyeing guilds were very protective of their trade secrets.

The desire for certain hues has even been linked to exploitation. One of the most bizarre examples must be that of "mummy brown," a deep brown used by Western painters from the sixteenth to the nineteenth centuries, which was produced by the grinding up of Egyptian mummies, relying on a centuries-long trade in these embalmed corpses. Upon learning the details of the process, the Pre-Raphaelite artist Edward Burne-Jones abandoned the color, ceremonially burying his last tube. In our own times, as Amy Hagenrater-Gooding reminds us in this volume, the color pink is almost completely intertwined with the apparatus of mass consumption that employs and reproduces its gendered connotation.

So colors do have a history, shaped by cultural, socio-economic and technological change. But can we historicize color not just in terms of the twists in fortune of specific colors and their changing meanings, but also in what it has meant to perceive colors in the first place?

To help throw light on this question, I would like to contrast how color was appreciated in two distinct historical periods. First, the high Middle Ages, which Herman Pleij in his *Colors Demonic and Divine* describes as an epoch when color reached its cultural prime, during which aristocratic and urban culture saw a mania for the use of bright colors, often in the most stark combinations, on materials that ranged from such textiles as linen and silk to leather, wood and furs, and, of course, in the illumination of manuscripts. Even in architecture, usually thought of as almost entirely concerned with form, color was central to the Gothic, in which colored light captured by stained glass played a crucial role.²

Beyond this explosion of hues, Pleij also argues that color was more meaningful then than it is today. Colors were potentially meaningful signs as part of the God-given order of Creation for fallen man to interpret. So red came to be associated with blood, but this was in the first place the blood of Christ, shed for the salvation of mankind. In this search to interpret the divine order, everything could be linked to everything else, in a system-building that might look arbitrary to us. Colors could be associated with the four elements, seasons, temperaments, etc., although no consensus was ever reached that codified such systems.

---

1   *Blue: The History of a Color* (Princeton: Princeton University Press, 2001).

2   Herman Pleij, *Colors Demonic and Divine: Shades of Meaning in the Middle Ages and After*, trans. Diane Webb (New York: Columbia University Press, 2004), esp. 5-6, 13.

This way of seeing—the search for association— also meant that colors could be used by their bearers to express values or emotional states. In the verses and plays of aristocratic culture, the Virtues, personified by women, were often distinguished by the colors of their dress. So Fidelity would be dressed in black, Honor in gold, Chastity in white, Constancy in blue, Protection in green, and Love in red. Courtly literature also shows the use of color to signal the stages of the passions in romance. Here green could stand for hope, white for faith in a happy outcome, blue for steadfastness, brown for modesty, gold for fulfillment and black for mourning for a lost love. But in all these cases, a large number of combinations circulated so the precise meaning of colors could appear interchangeable. Pleij even cites a play in which colors themselves figure as characters, quarreling about their own meaning and value.[3]

To put this medieval use of color in comparative perspective, I turn to comments made by Fredric Jameson on modern—nineteenth century—art, in his intervention into affect theory.[4] In the medieval examples sketched above, we find colors organized into a system with each of them expressing a clearly *named* value or emotion: fidelity, hope, mourning. This is not changed by the fact that the exact assignment of a specific meaning to each color was often rather arbitrary. Color was used in the Middle Ages to express a clearly circumscribed state of feeling or even the essence (as in the case of the Virtues) of their bearers. Compared to such named emotions, Jameson notes a very different logic when it comes to modern affects, with "Baudelaire's description of a painted street sign [as] 'a green so delicious it hurts'; or Flaubert's remark that all of *Salammbô* (1862) was written to convey a certain bilious shade of yellow."[5]

These colors do not convey the clearly named and reified emotions we saw in medieval literature, but rather a bodily state on a (much less precise) sliding scale. That is how Jameson distinguishes modern affects, with an entirely new attention to the body, from the older systems of emotions that had been in circulation. In our examples of medieval art, colors stood for emotions that were in themselves stable and essential. The body did not play a role in them, except as a frame to display them on. But for Baudelaire and Flaubert, colors could work upon one's bodily state, truly changing how one felt. Contrasting Pleij and Jameson demonstrates how color can function as a clue to deeper cultural formations, in this case showing different ways in which color related to subjectivity.

***

Part One of this collection brings together studies on the role of color in historically different political cultures. The first two essays in this volume are explorations in ancient political thought. Thomas Radice uses the Chinese term *se*, whose translations include "color," as his starting point for a study of ritual in Ancient Chinese political thought in which he reveals certain commonalities

---

3   Ibid., 10, 14, 23-4, 28-9.

4   As developed in his "Wagner as Dramatist and Allegorist," in *The Ancients and the Postmoderns* (London: Verso, 2015).

5   Ibid., 39.

across opposed philosophical schools, as well as a more active role prescribed for the ruler. Michael Proulx's work focuses on the antique Mediterranean, where he shows how colors like purple, or more precisely the associations attached to them, figured in the representation of political and religious communities. Timothy May's study here is the first fully devoted to color symbolism in the Turko-Mongolian cultures of Central Asia (advancing also some new hypotheses along the way). In the next piece, by Renee Bricker, color serves as a window of changes and continuities in sixteenth-century English culture. The remaining two pieces of Part One consider color in the twentieth century, offering an arresting contrast between cultural imaginations of the local and the global. In the first, Victoria Hightower looks at the role of color in the construction of political authority and the invention of tradition in the United Arab Emirates, while Christopher Jespersen's essay on US international history studies the use of color to signify or imagine global, world-encompassing, threats.

Part Two turns to color in the arts, and is opened by Robert Machado with a theory-based exploration of the way in which color is expressed in verbal and visual media. Then Pamela Sachant looks at the use of flesh tones in the work of nineteenth-century French painter Jean-Léon Gérôme, as the starting point for a discussion of the aesthetic ideals of this period and their transgression. Finally, April Conley Kilinski studies the power of color symbolism in the representation of race, perhaps the most charged expression of color in modern history. Her lens is an intertextual reading of the novels of Jean Rhys and Michelle Cliff, drawing on Postcolonial theory.

The final section consists of three essays that deal with contemporary politics and culture. Amy Hagenrater-Gooding offers a critical reading of the use of pink in contemporary consumer culture. Celnisha L. Dangerfield looks at the representation of Barack Obama during his first years in office from the angle of communication studies. Jonathan Miner brings us to contemporary Turkey, where the color gray is his starting point for an overview of the contradictions in Turkish politics.

***

I am grateful to the College of Arts and Letters of the University of North Georgia, especially its Dean, Chris Jespersen, for his financial support and even more for suggesting the topic of color. Many thanks are also due to my fellow committee members, Tanya Bennett, Álvaro Torres-Calderón, Paul Dunlap, and Eugene Van Sickle, who helped organize the 2012 UNG Arts and Letters Conference. I fondly recall the visit of Victor Mair and Paula Roberts to Dahlonega to participate in the conference—it was a priceless reunion. Further, I also want to express my gratitude to Tanya Bennett and Joyce Stavick in the English department at UNG and to Jon Mehlferber in Visual Arts for offering their expertise. Andy David graciously provided resources from the UNG Music department.

In preparing this volume, I was fortunate to have colleagues at the Department of History, Anthropology, and Philosophy at UNG who encouraged me with their good humor. I would also like to give special acknowledgment to the members of the University of North Georgia Press, BJ Robinson, Corey Parson, and Amy S. Beard, for their dedication to this project. Many thanks are due to the reviewers of each chapter for their comments. Finally I give my affectionate thanks to Kurt for providing wide-ranging references and insights throughout the process.

Part I

Color and Political Power

1

Painting on a White Foundation: Color, Countenance, and Performance in the *Analects* and *Han Feizi*

Thomas Radice

Confucius[1] taught his students many things about ritual, but sometimes they repaid the favor, if only accidentally.[2] One example is *Analects* 3.8:

> Zixia 子夏 asked, "'Artful dimples of her smile, beautifully well-defined eyes, white on which to adorn'–what does this mean?" The Master replied, "The painting comes after the white." Zixia then asked, "Do rituals also 'come after?'" The Master said, "You stimulate me, Zixia! It is you with whom I can begin to talk about the *Odes*!"[3]

The *Odes* (*Shijing* 詩經), a collection of early Chinese poetry, was an important authoritative text for Confucius, for he believed it held the key to self-cultivation, if only one could interpret it correctly.[4] Here, however, it is Zixia

---

[1] I would like to thank the participants of the 2012 North Georgia Arts and Letters Conference for their helpful comments on my original presentation, especially Victor Mair, Sungshin Kim, and Eli Alberts. I also thank the two anonymous referees, who challenged me to clarify my ideas.

[2] Confucius (or Kongzi 孔子, ca. 551 – 479 B.C.E.) was one of the most famous (if not *the* most famous) thinker in early China. He lived in a period of great social and political upheaval, which eventually resulted in China fragmenting into several autonomous states in the Warring States period (ca. 480 – 221 B.C.E.). Confucius taught mostly about morality and politics (without much of a distinction made between them). He wrote nothing, but his sayings were collected by his disciples (and his disciples' disciples) in a text called the *Analects* (*Lunyu* 論語), which also includes sayings attributed to some of his disciples. Because of the numerous issues pertaining to authorship and date of composition in this text, it is nearly impossible to discern the sayings of the historical Confucius from later additions. Consequently, I use the name, "Confucius," in this essay mainly as a way of referring to the contents of the *Analects* without assuming that Confucius actually said any of it.

[3] *Lunyu jishi* 論語集釋, ed. Cheng Shude 程樹德 (Beijing: Zhonghua shuju, 1990), 5.157–159. Unless stated otherwise, all translations in this essay are my own. For this passage, compare translations in D.C. Lau, trans., *The Analects* (New York: Penguin, 1979), 68 and Edward Slingerland, trans., *Confucius: Analects with Selections from Traditional Commentaries* (Indianapolis, IN: Hackett, 2003), 19-20.

[4] For more passages on Confucius's emphasis on studying the *Odes*, see *Analects* 2.2, 8.8, 13.5, 16.13, 17.9, and 17.10. For a broader discussion of the significance of the *Odes* in the thought of Confucius and other Warring States thinkers, see Paul R. Goldin, "The Reception of the *Odes* in the Warring States Era" in *After Confucius: Studies in Early Chinese Philosophy* (Honolulu: University of Hawai'i Press, 2005), 19–35.

who points out a very fundamental aspect of rituals (*li* 禮),[5] though it is a seemingly irrelevant passage about a woman putting on makeup before a wedding. But as it turns out, the woman's makeup–or, more specifically, its application–is a perfect metaphor for rituals. The key line in the poem is the last one (though it is actually absent in the received version of the *Odes*[6]). Confucius clarifies for Zixia that the line implies a temporal sequence: first the white powder, then the paint "afterwards" (*hou* 後). Zixia then somehow makes the intellectual leap to rituals occurring *after* something else. Commentators tell us that before the woman applies the colors to her face, there first must be a white foundation–which, in turn, will make the colors more striking.[7] In the same way, then, rituals come after something else, which make them better or more effective in some way.

This color metaphor highlights more than just how someone should perform a ritual. The significance of the "brightness" or "dullness" of colors is that they are perceived as such by others. Likewise, ritual performances are also observed and evaluated by others who evaluate their success or failure. This essay analyzes this phenomenon by discussing "performance," paying particular attention to the performer/audience relationship. Analysis of audience reception of performances, in particular, highlights an important aspect of early Confucian politics, one that reveals an underlying connection between the thought of Confucius and that of someone normally thought to be diametrically opposed to him, Han Feizi 韓非子.[8] Though there are clear differences between the two, they share a desire to discern the truth about political "actors" and a deep skepticism about most people's ability to do so.

The "Color" of Performance

Rituals were fundamental to the way Confucius envisioned religion and politics, but they also were part of a larger process of self-cultivation that ideally resulted in becoming "humane" (*ren* 仁), "virtuous" (*de* 德), or a "gentleman"

---

5 *Li* is a complex term in early Confucianism. It can refer to a formal religious ritual, but it also refers to aspects of more mundane social intercourse. As such, it has been translated in various ways, including "etiquette" and "propriety." For a good discussion of the development of *li* in the period discussed in this essay, see Masayaki Sato, *The Confucian Quest for Order: The Origin and Formation of the Political Thought of Xunzi* (Leiden: Brill, 2003), 163–236. In order to avoid confusion, in this essay, I consistently translate *li* as "ritual" conceived in the broad sense to include all the formalities and banalities encompassed in this term. To this end, I define "ritual" as Ronald Grimes does: "Ritual is embodied, condensed, and prescribed enactment," which he further explains as something separate from ordinary action that is stylized, and requires "unpacking" for outsiders to make sense of it. See his "Religion, Ritual, and Performance" in *Religion, Theatre, and Performance: Acts of Faith*, ed. Lance Gharavi (New York: Routledge, 2012), 38.

6 The passage that Zixia quotes is from Ode 57. For a full translation, see Arthur Waley, trans., *The Book of Songs: The Ancient Chinese Classic of Poetry*, edited with additional translations by Joseph R. Allen (New York: Grove Press, 1996), 48–49.

7 *Lunyu jishi*, 5.158.

8 Unlike the *Analects*, the *Han Feizi* is composed of longer essays on various topics, most of which are believed to have been composed by the historical Han Feizi (d. 233 B.C.E.). He is often associated with "Legalism" (*fa jia* 法家), a term that did not exist until the first century B.C.E. Because of the diversity of views contained in the texts associated with "Legalism," I deliberately avoid the term in this essay, preferring to avoid over-generalizations in the form of "Confucianism vs. Legalism." For a discussion of the problems of "Legalism," see Herlee G. Creel, "The *Fa-chia* 法家: 'Legalists' or 'Administrators'?" in *What is Taoism? And Other Studies in Chinese Cultural History* (Chicago: University of Chicago Press, 1970), 92–120 and Paul R. Goldin, "Persistent Misconceptions about Chinese 'Legalism,'" *Journal of Chinese Philosophy* 38.1 (2011), 88–104.

(*junzi* 君子) – all terms used throughout the *Analects* to denote the ideal individual.⁹ At one point, for example, when he was asked about "humaneness," Confucius described it as "overcoming oneself and returning to ritual" (*ke ji fu li* 克己復禮), and when asked for more clarification, he told his disciple not to do anything that was not in accordance with ritual (*fei li*非禮).¹⁰ Zixia's insight in 3.8 shows that ritual performance, if it really is intended to "overcome oneself," cannot be merely a matter of moving in a prescribed fashion. He makes this point more directly in 17.11:

> The Master said, "'Rituals! Rituals!,' they say. Is this to say 'jade and silk?' 'Music! Music!,' they say. Is this to say 'bells and drums?'"¹¹

The comment on music clarifies the previous one about ritual because it is easier to understand how the simple presence of bells and drums does not constitute music. Any random striking of bells and drums does not constitute music either. The production of authentic music through these instruments requires some special skill in the performer. Likewise, though jade and silk are important "props" in a ritual, they are not substitutes for what a person does with them.

Regarding what might come "before" the ritual that leads to a proper performance, passages describing filial piety (*xiao* 孝) provide a good indication about what is required.¹² For example, in 2.7, Confucius complains that people equate filial piety with "nourishment" (*yang* 養) for their parents. That is, they think that the simple act of keeping their parents alive is sufficient for fulfilling their filial duties. But Confucius sees this as no better than caring for dogs and horses. As he says, "without respect (*jing* 敬) what's the difference?"¹³ This feeling of respect must, in some sense, come "before" the filial actions in order for them to be truly filial. Confucius makes a similar point in 1.11:

> When his father is alive, observe the son's intentions; when his father is dead, observe his actions. If for three years he does not change the ways of his father, he can be called filial.¹⁴

Most commentators focus on the latter part of the passage regarding the actions of the son after his father's death, but it is the beginning of the passage that is more intriguing. Commentators explain that because a son cannot "act on his

---

9   Much like *li*, these terms are not easily translated into English. *Ren*, for example, is often translated as "benevolence" or simply "Good;" *junzi* has been translated also as "noble person" or "superior person."

10 *Analects* 12.1; *Lunyu jishi*, 24.817–821. To emphasize the importance of ritual in all forms of behavior, Confucius actually specifies not to "look" (*shi* 視), "listen" (*ting* 聽), "speak" (*yan* 言), or "move" (*dong* 動) unless it is in accordance with ritual.

11 *Lunyu jishi*, 35.1216; compare translations in Lau, *Analects*, 145 and Slingerland, 205.

12 According to *Analects* 2.5, when Confucius was asked about filial piety, he eventually replied with explicit appeal to ritual practices: "When one's parents are alive, serve them according to ritual; when they die, bury them according to ritual, and sacrifice to them according to ritual." *Lunyu jishi*, 3.81.

13 *Luyu jishi*, 3.85.

14 Ibid., 2.42; compare translations in Lau, *Analects*, 60 – 61 and Slingerland, 5.

own" (*zi zhuan* 自專), one must "observe his intentions" (*guan qi zhi* 觀其志").[15] The notion of proper intentions is similar to the requirement of respect expressed in 2.7, but here the issue is not simply how to perform filial duties properly, but also how to evaluate others' performances. Exactly how one observes the intentions of others is not explained (even by the commentators), but returning to the issue of "color" provides a clue to what Confucius had in mind. For example, 2.8 reads:

> Zixia asked about filial piety. The Master said, "The countenance is what is difficult. When there is work to be done, the young take on the burden; when there is food and drink, they are placed before the elders–is this what it means to be filial?[16]

The word, *se* 色, in addition to "countenance," can mean "color," "beauty," and even "sex"—all uses found in the *Analects*, and all having to do in some sense with appearance. This passage, like 2.7, invokes the issue of empty, mechanical behavior toward parents, but here Confucius requires a visible expression on the part of the child. One must provide wine and food, but one must do so with the correct expression that indicates to others that the individual is acting with the proper motivation. If one's countenance, for example, demonstrates that one is performing the action begrudgingly, then the ritual is not performed successfully. The intention is, so to speak, "written all over one's face."

Nowhere in the *Analects* is the issue of one's face so significant than in Book 10, which traditionally has been interpreted as specific observances of Confucius himself (though most modern commentators believe that it is mostly a collection of descriptions of superior people in general). Most passages in the *Analects* that discuss ritual focus more on the general importance of it for moral and/or political success. By contrast, Book 10 rarely delves into abstractions, and remains thoroughly in the specific behavior of the performer, so much so that whatever quotations of Confucius it contains are of secondary importance. The real significance is in what he did and how he did it.

The impact of Confucius's facial expressions is showcased in four of the eighteen passages in this book (3, 4, 5, and 25). These passages, in addition to describing his actions, specify that Confucius "changed his countenance."[17] Each of these passages begins with setting up a specific context (such as "when his ruler called upon him to receive a guest," "when entering the duke's gate," "when grasping a jade tablet," "when he saw someone mourning," and "when fine food was placed before him"), resulting in Confucius's altering his facial expression. The context provided by the narrator provides a certain situation to which Confucius responds, but it is also general enough to indicate that actions of Confucius are not entirely original. The level of generality in the context implies that Confucius performed the described behavior, not only in that particular instance, but rather *whenever* he encountered that situation. Consequently, we can describe Con-

---

15 *Lunyu jishi*, 2.44. See also *Analects* 2.10, in which Confucius says that, when evaluating the character of others, one must "observe their motives" (*guan qi suo you* 觀其所由); *Lunyu jishi*, 3.92.

16 *Lunyu jishi*, 3.88; compare translations in Lau, *Analects*, 64 and Slingerland, 10.

17 In passages 3, 4, and 5, the operative term used is *bo* 勃; in 25, it is *bian* 變.

fucius's "performance" in a more formal sense. Confucius's actions are what Richard Schechner calls "restored behavior," which he insists is "the main characteristic of performance."[18] As Schechner puts it, "Performance means: never for the first time. It means: for the second to the nth time. Performance is 'twice-behaved behavior.'"[19] Restored behavior is repeated for a particular context, even rehearsed. It is meant to cover a broad range of activities that can fall under the concept of performance, from theatrical events to religious rituals, to forms of social interaction–all of which are distinct from ordinary behavior.

Conceiving early Confucian ritual performance as restored behavior also informs the way others have described the aesthetic dimensions of Confucian ethics. Herbert Fingarette, Karyn Lai, and Amy Olberding, for example, have all used the analogy of a musical performance to describe ritual performance in the *Analects*, especially in the way a performer exhibits the elements of a masterly or virtuoso performance, and even the development of such virtuosity as a metaphor for self-cultivation.[20] The notion of restored behavior actually implies much of both the aesthetics of a musical performance and the skills required for an adept one, since musical performance qua performance is a form of restored behavior. Analyzing ritual as restored behavior, however, is more firmly situated in human behavior, and virtuosity is displayed through one's own body rather than through an external instrument. Therefore, a closer analogy to describe a ritual performer would be an actor rather than a musician, which has the advantage of better accommodating Confucius's specific requirements of (and personal example as) an ideal performer, especially the expressive function of the face.[21]

Regardless of whether one is a musician or an actor, in the act of performing there is always an audience. As Marvin Carlson writes, "Performance is always performance *for* someone, some audience that recognizes and validates it as performance even when, as is occasionally the case, that audience is the self."[22] The audience in Book 10 of the *Analects* is clearly not Confucius only, and its presence is revealed through the text's narrative technique. For example, though the specific facial expressions that Confucius makes are never described in any detail, the implication in each passage is that his face expressed some sense of sincerity, reverence, or sympathy. However, it is a distinct feature in all the passages in Book 10 that the feelings of Confucius are never described. There are no passages in which Confucius is said to have "felt pity" or "felt a deep sense of respect." These attributes are merely implied through a surface description of what he did and

---

18   Richard Schechner, *Between Theater and Anthropology* (Philadelphia: University of Pennsylvania Press, 1985), 35.

19   Ibid., 36.

20   See Herbert Fingarette, *Confucius–the Secular as Sacred* (New York: Harper Torchbooks, 1972), 53–54; Karyn Lai, "Confucian Moral Cultivation: Some Parallels with Musical Training" in *The Moral Circle of the Self: Chinese and Western Approaches*, ed. Kim-chong Chong, Sor-hoon Tan, and C.L. Ten (Peru, IL: Open Court, 2003), 107–139 and "*Li* in the *Analects*: Training in Moral Competence and the Question of Flexibility," *Philosophy East and West* 56.1 (2006), 72–76; Amy Olberding, *Moral Exemplars in the Analects: The Good Person is That* (New York: Routledge, 2012), 125–135. Much of what Olberding describes as "personal style" on pp. 112–125 actually fits well with what I describe as "theatricality" below.

21   This is not to deny the importance of music in early Chinese ritual. For a detailed discussion of the connection between music and formal rituals in early China, see Lai "Confucian Moral Cultivation."

22   Marvin Carlson, *Performance: A Critical Introduction*, second ed. (New York: Routledge, 2004), 5.

how he appeared when he did it, as if it truly were something witnessed or seen. These exclusively visual descriptions of Confucius's behavior are not insignificant. Though all passages in the *Analects* were written by people other than Confucius, the passages in Book 10 go into great detail about what specifically the author saw Confucius do–and, presumably, do well. The author, then, is a spectator to the action, describing Confucius's restored behavior to the reader.[23]

This connection between the actions of the performer and the reactions of the audience is what Willmar Sauter calls "theatricality."[24] Sauter distinguishes the actions of a performer as "exhibitory," "encoded," and "embodied." An exhibitory action is the mere appearance of a performer in front of an audience, which can also indicate a person's mental status as a performer (e.g., confident or nervous).[25] A performer's actions, including gestures and vocal actions, are encoded in that they follow certain cultural patterns and aesthetic norms.[26] And finally, these actions are embodied when they are intended to signify some meaning to another person (i.e., the audience).[27] All of these actions overlap in practice, which can be demonstrated through an example from the *Analects*. In 10.25, when Confucius encountered someone in mourning, he "changed (his countenance)" (*bian* 變), and the passage later mentions that in a similar situation, he leaned forward on the crossbar of his carriage (*shi zhi* 式之). To follow Sauter's analysis, Confucius's physical appearance (i.e., his physical presence) in the situation is a basic exhibitory action in showing himself–either intentionally or unintentionally–to his audience (i.e., the mourners and the narrator).[28] His actions of changing his countenance and bending forward in his carriage are encoded in that they are considered appropriate for his specific cultural circumstance and they follow certain aesthetic norms as dictated by ritual. Ultimately, these actions are embodied in that they signify Confucius's sympathy and respect to both the mourners and any onlookers.

But the performer is only half of the theatricality equation. Sauter outlines three levels of "theatrical communication" to correspond to the three types of actions of the performer in order to understand the spectators' reception of a performance. Exhibitory actions communicate at the "sensory" level in that they cause "both automatic responses, which only gradually are processed into understandable cognitive knowledge, and persistent feelings that remain active during an entire performance."[29] Encoded actions communicate at the "artistic" level and require a certain competency on the part of the spectator to transform the pleasure of the experience into an intellectual evaluation of the performer's

---

23   The reader, in turn, becomes another kind of "spectator" of Confucius's performance.

24   Willmar Sauter, *The Theatrical Event: Dynamics of Performance and Perception* (Iowa City: University of Iowa Press, 2000), 50.

25   Ibid., 53-54. It should be noted that the "mental state" that Sauter has in mind is different from the performer's intentions, which will apply to embodied actions. These exhibitory actions are similar to what might be called "stage presence."

26   Sauter, 54.

27   Ibid., 56.

28   Later on in this essay, I distinguish how the people Confucius encounters and the narrator form different types of audiences.

29   Sauter, 59.

skill.³⁰ Lastly, the "symbolic" level corresponds to embodied actions in which the audience recognizes the meaning of the actions that the performer is trying to convey. For all of these levels of communication, however, Sauter insists that the spectators themselves bring as much to the performance as the performer. As he puts it, "Since prior experiences, producing expectations, preferences, and prejudices have a strong impact on both emotional and cognitive reactions during and after the performance, they become part of the actual theatrical experience and can be dealt with as direct responses to the performer."³¹ These subjective experiences are significant in understanding how an audience "observes the intentions" of a performer–indirectly and, perhaps, imperfectly.

Gentlemen, Village Worthies, and Uncultivated Audiences

To understand the significance of Confucius's own idea of spectators' reception of ritual performance with regard to their personal experiences, it is first necessary to discuss what he saw as a pervasive performance problem. As much as Confucius stresses the importance of an expressive countenance for ritual performance, he also expresses a strong distrust for such overt expressions in one's actions. Take, for example, 1.3:

> The Master said, "Clever words and a fine-looking countenance are rarely signs of humaneness."³²

Confucius here acknowledges the very real possibility of hypocrisy–that people may attempt to "put on a good face," but their performance is not founded upon the proper feelings of respect or other moral intentions. It is all spectacle with no substance. Likewise, in 11.21, Confucius questions whether someone who speaks in a serious manner is really a gentleman (*junzi* 君子) or merely "appears" or "has the countenance" (*se*) of one. Thus, Confucius exposes a problem for his stress on ritual performance: the performers must express (especially through the face) their sincerity, but some people try to express sincerity without really having it.

What is far worse, however, is that others are so easily duped by such people, so much so that receiving popular acclaim, according to Confucius, is hardly a sign that one is virtuous. For example in 12.20, his disciple, Zizhang 子張, asks about the criteria for referring to someone as "distinguished" (*da* 達), and when Confucius asks Zizhang what he thinks being "distinguished" means, Zizhang describes it as being "well-known" (*wen* 聞). However, Confucius insists that these two notions are far from equivalent, and differentiates the two as follows:

> Distinguished people have an upright temperament and love rightness. They examine the words (of others) and observe their countenances, and anxious-

---

30 Ibid., 59-60.

31 Ibid., 58.

32 *Lunyu jishi*, 1.16; compare translations in Lau, *Analects*, 59 and Slingerland, 2. This passage in repeated in 17.17 and a similar point is made in 5.25.

ly defer to others. They will surely be distinguished in their states and their families. Those who are well-known may have countenances that indicate humaneness, but their actions are far from it, and remain without any self-doubt. They will be well-known in their states and in their families.[33]

There are a few things that become apparent here. First, Confucius's own disciple makes a serious mistake in confusing fame with distinction. Second, people who are merely "well-known" can become so basically by "faking" it. That is to say, they have the proper appearance, but their actions in some sense do not meet the criteria of humaneness. Finally, someone who is truly distinguished is not only moral, but also a good observer of others' countenances, and therefore is perceptive to the reaction of others, and perhaps even the morality of others.

One can see how all three of these issues are related when one investigates in more detail the notion of true self-cultivation vis-à-vis the lack of such cultivation in much of society. For example, the mistake that Zizhang makes is not isolated to 12.20. Elsewhere in the *Analects*, Confucius insists that his disciples not necessarily follow popular opinion regarding the evaluation of someone else's character. In 13.24 and 15.28, Confucius tells his disciples to be more discerning than the average person. In 13.24, in particular, Confucius insists that instead of looking to see whether everyone (*jie* 皆) in a village loves (*hao* 好) a certain person, it is better to see if all the "good" (*shan* 善) people love him. Thus, some people are simply better judges of character than others.

These passages clarify a basic element of Confucius's political theory–the attraction of virtue. As Confucius says very famously in 2.1:

> One who rules by virtue can be compared to the pole star, which stays in its place while the other multitude of stars revolves around it.[34]

Likewise, at the end of 12.19, Confucius says,

> The virtue of the gentleman is like the wind; the virtue of the uncultivated person is like the grass. When the wind blows over the grass, the grass must bend.[35]

These passages indicate that popular opinion can be a sign of one's superior cultivation,[36] especially since in other passages, Confucius insists that the un-virtuous person has the opposite effect. As he says in 13.6, after noting the ease that the ones who have corrected their character (*shen zheng* 身正) can rule over the people, he says "As for those who do not correct their character, though they issue orders, they will not be followed" (*qi shen bu zheng, sui ling bu cong* 其身不正，雖令不從。)[37]

---

33 *Lunyu jishi*, 25.868–869; compare translations in Lau, *Analects*, 116 and Slingerland, 134–135.
34 *Lunyu jishi*, 3.61; compare translations in Lau, *Analects*, 63 and Slingerland, 8.
35 *Lunyu jishi*, 25.866; compare translations in Lau, *Analects*, 115–116 and Slingerland, 134.
36 Similar ideas are expressed in *Analects* 2.19 and 12.22.
37 *Lunyu jishi*, 26.901.

But clearly this is not the full story. As Confucius insists in 15.28, people are not necessarily repulsed by an uncultivated person. A virtuous person may have great charisma,[38] but a less cultivated person may have a similar appeal. It is in this context that the saying, "The village worthy is the thief of virtue" (*xiangyuan de zhi zei ye* 鄉原德之賊也),[39] illustrates what must have been a serious problem for Confucius: someone who could be considered by many to be virtuous, and yet not actually be virtuous.

This problem leads to the second issue indicated by 12.20 – that people can put on a countenance that some others perceive to represent genuine intentions, but these intentions are not really there. Mencius (Mengzi 孟子)[40] elaborates on this notion of the "village worthy" during a conversation with Wan Zhang 萬章, one of his disciples. In 7B.37, Mencius distinguishes Confucius's feelings about the "village worthy" from those who are "wild" (*kuang* 狂) and those who are "timid" (*juan* 獧). Both the "wild" and the "timid" are inferior to those who follow the mean of the Way (*zhong dao* 中道) by not achieving this mean. As Kwong-loi Shun points out, both "wild" and "timid" individuals try to improve themselves, but the "village worthies" already feel satisfied with their self-cultivation.[41] Mencius imagines them saying, "To be born in this era is to be of this era – to be good is enough."[42] However, Mencius explains that the danger of the village worthy is not in mere complacency or mediocrity, for as Wan Zhang indicates, they are quite popular with other people. It is here that Mencius has a difficult time explaining precisely what is noticeably wrong with the village worthy:

> If you try to criticize them, there is nothing to hold up; if you try to pin them on something, there is nothing to pin. They are in agreement with the current customs and connected with this corrupt era. They reside in what resembles devotion and trustworthiness, and their actions resemble honest purity. The multitude is pleased with them, and so they are self-assured, but you cannot enter the Way of Yao and Shun[43] with them. Thus, they are called "thieves of virtue." [44]

This explanation shows that the "village worthies" are not mere hypocrites who

---

38 Philip J. Ivanhoe aptly translates *de* as "moral charisma," which he describes as "the natural attraction one feels toward morally great individuals." See his *Confucian Moral Self Cultivation*, second ed. (Indianapolis, IN: Hackett, 2000), xiii.

39 17.13; *Lunyu jishi*, 35.1219.

40 Mencius, a major Warring States thinker, lived during the fourth century B.C.E., and supposedly was trained by Confucius's grandson. He saw himself as transmitting the ideas of Confucius, but he also elaborated on them in original ways. His ideas are contained in a text that bears his name. Like the *Analects*, the *Mencius* was not written by the person to whom it is attributed, and the passages are not in ordered according to topic. However, the passages tend to be longer than those in the *Analects*, and most of them are snapshots of conversations that Mencius had with various individuals, including kings, his disciples, and other thinkers with opposing viewpoints.

41 Kwong-loi Shun, *Mencius and Early Chinese Thought* (Stanford, CA: Stanford University Press, 1997), 178.

42 *Mengzi zhengyi* 孟子正義, ed. Jiao Xun 焦循 (Beijing: Zhonghua shuju, 2004), 29.1029. Compare translations in D.C. Lau, trans., *Mencius* (New York: Penguin, 1970), 203 and Bryan W. Van Norden, trans., *Mengzi with Selections from Traditional Commentaries* (Indianapolis, IN: Hackett, 2008), 195.

43 Yao 堯 and Shun 舜 were legendary sage kings, considered by many Warring States thinkers to be great moral exemplars.

44 *Mengzi zhengyi*, 29.1031; compare translations in Lau, *Mencius*, 203 and Van Norden, 195.

say one thing and do another, either consciously or unconsciously. They follow accepted norms, and perhaps do so whole-heartedly, which makes them difficult to criticize. But Mencius insists that there is a higher standard, and despite the praise they receive from most people, there are others (such as Mencius and Confucius) who can discern who is a truly cultivated person.

Mencius then elaborates on this problem by quoting Confucius:

> I hate a resemblance that is false. I hate weeds for fear that they will be confused with grain sprouts. I hate flattery for fear that it will be confused with rightness. I hate glibness for fear that it will be confused with truthfulness. I hate the tunes of Zheng 鄭 for fear that they will be confused with proper music. I hate purple for fear that it will be confused with vermillion. I hate the village worthies for fear that they will be confused with the virtuous.[45]

The qualification of "false" (*fei* 非) that is added to "resemblance" (*si* 似) in the beginning of this passage is not redundant or insignificant. The only instances of this term in the *Analects* are in Book 10 in reference to what Confucius himself "appears" to be doing.[46] But presumably, what Confucius "resembles" to be in those passages is "true" (*shi* 是) or genuine; that is, one can trust the surface appearance to be a sign of his true character. Of the series of false resemblances that follow, it is the last three that are the most significant, for a very close variation is also found in *Analects* 17.18. They also point to an interesting connection between aesthetic and moral performance and judgment. At first glance, Confucius makes a transition from the aesthetic (color and music) to the moral (the "village worthy"). However, in the case of music, Confucius finds the tunes of Zheng to be licentious and therefore immoral, not merely less beautiful than other music.[47] But more importantly, given the above discussion about the theatrical aspects of morality through ritual performance, one can more clearly discern how moral criticism can be intertwined with aesthetic criticism in more complex ways. Rather than some forms of art leading its audience to either moral or immoral behavior, moral activity as performance affects its viewers in ways that are aesthetic. People are drawn to the morality of others in the way they gravitate toward a style of music or a particular color. In Sauter's terms, people who form an audience for ritual performances respond to the morality of the performer on the sensory—and especially the artistic and symbolic—levels as responses to the performers' theatrical communication.

But to further understand the aesthetic responses of the audience to ritual performances, it is helpful to introduce one way Schechner analyzes audiences. He distinguishes two general types of audiences: "integral" and "accidental." In the simplest terms, "an accidental audience comes 'to see the show' while the integral audience is 'necessary to accomplish the work of the show,'"[48] but Schechner also

---

45　*Mengzi zhengyi*, 29.1031; compare translations in Lau, *Mencius*, 203 and Van Norden, 195.

46　*Analects* 10.1 and 10.4.

47　Zheng was one of the major states during the Warring States period. For Confucius's criticism of the music of Zheng, see *Analects* 15.11.

48　Richard Schechner, *Performance Theory*, revised ed. (New York: Routledge, 2003), 220; Schechner continues,

insists that the boundaries between the two are not always firm.[49] Audiences can shift from "accidental" to "integral" and vice versa. Moreover, what makes Schechner's distinction applicable to the Confucian context is how he applies these audiences to rituals and "aesthetic theater" (performances that are intended primarily to provide aesthetic enjoyment for the audience)[50] to form four broad categories: integral-aesthetic, integral-ritual, accidental-aesthetic, and accidental-ritual.[51]
For any ritual, the integral audience includes the main participants. In the case of Analects 10.25 discussed above, the integral audiences are the mourners to whom Confucius responds with his own ritual behavior.[52] Sometimes, however, as in every case in Book 10 and other descriptions of Confucius's ritual behavior, rituals have accidental audiences–spectators who do not have a special connection to what is taking place before them.[53] In 10.25, Confucius behaves in response to the mourner, but as noted above, his behavior is also witnessed by the narrator, who is presumably not a mourner. The narrator is part of an accidental audience and his[54] experience of the ritual is different from the mourner's, because he is witnessing the larger spectacle. As such, his experience is similar (though not identical) to an accidental-aesthetic audience in that he perceives the aesthetic features–or, in Sauter's sense, the theatricality–of the ritual. The main difference from a purely aesthetic performance is that for Confucius and Mencius, the theatricality of Confucius's ritual performance is also a fundamental part of his exemplary moral behavior, which then also draws the audience toward moral cultivation.

But again, as Sauter insists, the audience response to a performance has much to do with the audience members themselves. The above discussion has revealed a similar perspective from Confucius and Mencius, but with significant differences. Sauter's description of the performer/audience relationship makes no value judgment about the performer or the audience with regard to any kind of "cultivation," whether moral or aesthetic. For example, since Sauter's conception of theatricality depends on communication between the performer and spectator, he speaks favorably of instances when performers alter their actions in order to re-establish engagement with the audience if it is lost.[55] Such manipulation of a performance that caters specifically to the audience is not something that Confucius condones, and he repeatedly insists cultivated individuals should be very concerned about the lack of recognition they receive from others.[56] One reason for this rigid

---

"Or, to put it another way, the accidental audience attends voluntarily, the integral audience from ritual need. In fact, the presence of an integral audience is the surest evidence that the performance is a ritual." As shown below, however, Schechner also acknowledges how non-ritual performances can have integral audiences.

49   Schechner, *Performance Theory*, 220.
50   This form of theater can include modern Western-style theater, non-Western theater, and performance art.
51   Ibid., 221.
52   The mourners, of course, are also performers in their own ritual, in which Confucius is part of the integral audience.
53   One example that Schechner uses is "tourists watching a ceremony" (p. 221).
54   Though the sex of the narrator is never specified, I am using "he" and "his" in order to avoid the cumbersome "he or she" and "his or her," and because the authors and editors of the *Analects* were most likely men.
55   Sauter, 61. Sauter notes examples of accommodating an audience that cannot understand the spoken language of the performance and also accommodating a very young audience. In both instances, the performers respond to the spectators who either fall asleep or leave their seats during the performance.
56   See for example *Analects* 1.16, 4.15, 14.30, and 15.19.

perspective on performance is that, for Confucius, members of (accidental-ritual) audiences fall within a range between the cultivated and uncultivated. The uncultivated spectators are mainly the common people, who lack the necessary expertise, and who are drawn to the words and facial expressions that seem to indicate authentic morality. By contrast, cultivated spectators can point out that there are better examples of morality elsewhere, or simply that a given moral performance is lacking in some way. This special perception informs Confucius's insistence that "only the humane person is able to love others and hate others."[57] To use the color metaphor in 3.8, uncultivated spectators see what seem like "brilliant colors" in a person's makeup, but cultivated spectators do not because they have experience with what truly brilliant colors look like.

In addition to appreciating a narrower range of performances, cultivated spectators also are not merely passive observers. Their "expertise" in judging performers is not analogous to theater critics, who may boast a wide range of theatrical experiences that therefore qualify them to distinguish truly "great performances." Rather, as cultivated spectators, they are also cultivated performers themselves. This issue is exhibited most strikingly in the recently excavated Guodian 郭店 version of "The Five Aspects of Conduct" (*Wu xing* 五行):[58]

> Humane thoughts: [they] are essential; being essential, you will have keen insight; having keen insight you will be at ease; being at ease you will be gentle; being gentle you will be happy; being happy your demeanor is pleasant; having a pleasant demeanor you can be intimate; being intimate you will be loving; loving your countenance will be jade-like; having a jade-like countenance you will be formed; being formed you will be humane.[59]

This passage shows a progression from something unobservable (one's thoughts) to the observable (one's countenance), which in turn leads to the full description of being "humane." In this way, then, one can begin to surmise how one's face allows others to "observe one's intensions." The passage that immediately follows,

---

57 4.3; *Lunyu jishi*, 7.230.

58 A version of this text (along with other texts) written on silk was originally discovered in 1973 in a tomb that dates to 168 B.C.E. It was discovered at Mawangdui 馬王堆 in the province of Hunan 湖南. In 1993, an earlier version of this text written on bamboo slips (again, with other texts) was discovered in a tomb that dates to around 300 B.C.E. It was discovered in Guodian in the province of Hubei 湖北. Since many parts of the slips had deteriorated over such a long period of time, and since whatever was used to tie them together had deteriorated completely, scholars have tried to figure out how they should be ordered. Nearly everything about these texts is still hotly debated by scholars–from the order of the slips to the proper transcription into modern Chinese characters to how exactly these texts fit into Warring States intellectual history. Nevertheless, there is a general consensus that these texts are very important, and will revolutionize how we understand the Warring States period. The original compilation of these texts was published in *Guodian Chumu zhujian* 郭店楚墓竹簡 (Beijing: Wenwu, 1998). For a good overview of the significance of these texts and other excavated manuscripts, see Edward L. Shaughnessy, *Rewriting Early Chinese Texts* (Albany: State University of New York Press, 2006). For an interpretations of how Guodian manuscripts (particularly, the "Five Aspects of Conduct") help us better understand Warring States intellectual history, see Mark Csikszentmihalyi, *Material Virtue: Ethics and the Body in Early China* (Leiden: Brill, 2004) and Kenneth W. Holloway, *Guodian: the Newly Discovered Seeds of Chinese Religious and Political Philosophy* (New York: Oxford, 2009). All translations from "The Five Aspects of Conduct" in this essay are Holloway's. He follows the transcription of Li Ling 李零 from his *Guodian Chujian jiaoduji* 郭店楚簡校讀記 (Beijing: Renmin daxue chubanshe, 2007). Below, I cite page numbers to Li Ling's transcription, but also indicate the original slip number provided in *Guodian Chumu zhujian*.

59 Holloway, 133; Li Ling, 101; slips 12–13.

however, provides an interesting qualification to what appears to be revealed in the face:

> Wise thoughts: [they] are extended; having extended [your thoughts] you will comprehend; once you comprehend you will not forget; not forgetting you will have keen vision; having keen vision you will perceive an outstanding person; being able to perceive an outstanding person you will have a jade-like countenance; having a jade-like countenance you will be formed; being formed you will be wise.[60]

As with the previous passage from this text, there is a connection between thoughts and facial expressions, but here the process toward a "jade-like countenance" (*yu se* 玉色) includes the ability to "perceive an outstanding person" (*jian xianren* 見賢人). In this context, "outstanding" (*xian* 賢) should be understood as exceptional morality, something similar to the notion of "humaneness" in the previous passage. Therefore, what one "perceives" (or more literally "sees") are the very qualities that lead to having a "jade-like countenance." To read this in the context of the *Analects*, though all people may be influenced by a person with a true "jade-like countenance," the only people who can truly perceive superior cultivation are people with an identical level of cultivation themselves. In the absence of such a superior individual, less cultivated spectators will most likely be attracted to others with "non-jade-like" countenances and not seek out someone better. Given that Confucius thought such outstanding individuals were rare in society,[61] it is all the more apparent that the inability of the majority of society to perceive an inauthentic performance would concern him. Hence, "the village worthy is the thief of virtue," not only because he deceives others into thinking he is virtuous, but also because most people are incapable of demanding a better performance from someone who really is virtuous.

Performing Politics in the *Han Feizi*

In the Warring States period, there was no one less impressed with the common people than Han Feizi, who explicitly rejected the idea of "gaining the hearts of the people" (*de min zhi xin* 得民之心)[62] through the kind of moral charisma described in the *Analects* and other early texts. According to Han Feizi, the common people had "the minds of little children" (*ying'er zhi xin* 嬰兒之心),[63] by which he meant that they did not really know what was good for them, and were in no place to evaluate what the ruler did for his state. The ruler was like a parent who cared for his children in such a way that the children may "yell and scream incessantly, because they do not understand that the little pain they suffer now will bring great benefit later."[64]

---

60 Holloway, 133; Li Ling, 101; slips 14–15.
61 See *Analects* 15.4 and 6.29.
62 *Han Feizi jijie* 韓非子集解, ed. Wang Xianshen 王先慎, (Beijing: Zhonghua shuju, 1998), "Xian xue" 顯學, 50.463.
63 Ibid., "Xian xue," 50.464.
64 Adapted from Burton Watson, trans., *Han Feizi: Basic Writings* (New York: Columbia University Press, 2003),

As such, Han Feizi was critical of the Confucians for their insistence on the inviolable connection between morality and politics. His view was not that there was no morality, only that it had little place in politics. If anything, moral duties conflicted with political loyalty.[65] Moreover, he believed that the words of so-called "outstanding" (*xian*) people were too mysterious for ordinary people to comprehend.[66] And since few people ever seemed to master moral behavior, it was impractical to assume that one could populate a state's government with virtuous people.[67] As a result, rather than promoting a political theory based on the morality of ritual performance, Han Feizi recommended the establishment of a clear set of laws (*fa* 法) that all people could understand. He even made an analogy to make-up, similar to what is found in *Analects* 3.8:

> Appreciating the beauty of Maoqiang or Xishi will not improve one's appearance, but if you use rouge, gloss, powder, and eye-paint, you will become twice as attractive as you were to begin with. Talking about the humaneness and righteousness of the former kings will not improve your government, but clarifying one's laws and regulations and determining rewards and punishments will be the rouge, gloss, powder, and eye-makeup of the state. Thus, the enlightened ruler is quick to apply real aids, reluctant to praise the former kings, and does not speak of humaneness and righteousness.[68]

Despite the rejection of moral government–and its foundational ritual performances–the writings of Han Feizi do not express a rejection of performance. In fact, his essay, "The Way of the Ruler" (*Zhu dao* 主道),[69] describes an elaborate performance that the ruler must perform for his ministers, who, according to Han Feizi, want only to manipulate him. Han Feizi recommends that the ruler remain "empty" (*xu*虛) and "still" (*jing*靜).[70] These two notions, which are especially prominent in the *Laozi*,[71] are a means for the ruler to hide his true desires (*yu* 欲)

---

129. This idea contrasts sharply with the notion of "the father and mother of the people" (*min zhi fu mu* 民之父母 or *min fu mu* 民父母) that appears in other Warring States texts, which denotes a more "loving" relationship between the ruler and the people.

65   Han Fei tells two stories of men who faced a choice between fulfilling their filial duties or fulfilling their duties to their ruler, chose the former. The first, a man named Honest Gong (Zhi Gong 直躬) turned his father into the authorities for stealing a sheep, and was subsequently executed for unfilial behavior. The second was a man who was a member of the military in the state of Lu 魯, who repeatedly retreated from combat because his elderly father would have no one to care for him if his son died in battle. Confucius praised this man and recommended him for an official position in the government. Han Fei sees such both the condemnation of Honest Gong the praise of the son from Lu as examples of how morality does not make for a strong government. See *Han Feizi jijie*, "Wu du" 五蠹, 49.449. For another version of the "Honest Gong" story, see *Analects* 13.18.

66   *Han Feizi jijie*, "Wu du," 49.450.

67   Ibid., "Wu du," 49.451.

68   Ibid., "Xian xue," 50.462; compare translation in Watson, *Han Feizi*, 128.

69   Unlike the *Analects*, the *Han Feizi* is composed of longer essays on various topics, most of which are believed to have been composed by the historical Han Feizi. An overview of textual issues can be found in Jean Levi, "Han fei tzu 韓非子," in *Early Chinese Texts: A Bibliographical Guide*, ed. Michael Loewe (Berkeley, CA: Society for the Study of Early China, 1993), 115–124.

70   *Han Feizi jijie*, "Zhu dao," 5.26.

71   The *Han Feizi* actually contains the earliest partial commentary on this text in two chapters: "Jie lao" 解老 and "Yu lao" 喻老. For a discussion of the relationship between the *Han Feizi* and the *Laozi*, see Tae Hyun Kim, Other *Laozi* Parallels in the *Hanfeizi*: An Alternative Approach to the Textual History of the *Laozi* and Early Chinese

and will (*yi* 意) from his ministers. As Han Feizi says, "If the ruler reveals his desires, his ministers will engrave themselves [*zi jiang diao zhuo* 自將雕琢] (accordingly)…If the ruler reveals his will, his ministers will change their exterior [*biao* 表] (accordingly)."[72] Given the above discussion of the "The Five Aspects of Conduct," the metaphor of "engraving" oneself becomes all the more significant in that one can imagine ministers attempting to mimic a "jade-like countenance" that agrees with the given desires of the ruler. To combat this under-handed tactic, Han Feizi advises rulers to do exactly what Confucius hates: resemble something that they are not (*si er fe* 似而非).[73] As Han Feizi puts it, "See but appear not to see; hear but appear not to hear; know but appear not to know."[74] But all of these actions are *re*actions, such that Han Feizi, in guiding a ruler's performance, is really guiding his role as an audience engaged in a process of theatricality with his minister. Unlike the Confucian gentleman, Han Feizi's minister as performer will always play to his audience to receive a positive response, so the ruler as audience must appear contrary to what is true in order to get at the truth about his ministers.

This combative relationship between ruler and minister becomes all the more apparent in another of Han Feizi's essays, "The Difficulties of Persuasion" (*Shuo nan* 說難). Though the act of persuasion is not quite a ritual in the Confucian sense, it is restored behavior in that there are certain protocols to be followed. Han Feizi states in the beginning that what is difficult about persuasion is not anything to do with one's knowledge or abilities, but rather in knowing the "mind" (*xin* 心) of the person one is persuading.[75] In full accordance with his warnings to the ruler in the previous essay, Han Feizi admonishes the minister to tailor his advice carefully to the specific attributes and desires of the ruler/audience before him.[76] In this way, the ruler functions as both an integral audience–without whom there is no "persuasion"–and an accidental audience–who (hopefully) responds to the specific exhibitory, encoded, and embodied actions of the minister that are tailored to what the ruler finds appealing. In other words, knowing the mind of the ruler informs the proper aesthetic necessities of the performance.

Though in many respects, the notion of "persuasion" (*shuo* 說) is distinctly verbal, Han Feizi emphasizes its visual aesthetics in a closing anecdote about a minister named Mi Zixia 彌子瑕, who was beloved by the ruler of Wei 衛. On one occasion, Mi heard about his mother's illness, and used the ruler's carriage to go visit her. On another occasion, when Mi and the ruler were walking through an orchard together, Mi bit into a peach and then decided to share it with the ruler. On both these occasions, the ruler of Wei praised Mi Zixia–first for his filial

---

Thought," *Sino-Platonic Papers* 199 (2010), 1-76. See also Philip J. Ivanhoe, "Han Feizi and Moral Self-Cultivation," *Journal of Chinese Philosophy* 38.1 (2011), 31–45.

72 *Han Feizi jijie*, "Zhu dao," 5.26

73 Han Feizi does not actually use this phrase, but the same meaning is implied in the passage quoted below.

74 *Han Feizi jijie*, "Zhu dao," 5.28; compare translation in Watson, *Han Feizi*, 17.

75 *Han Feizi jijie*, "Shuo nan," 12.86.

76 For another analysis of the relationship between these two essays, see Paul R. Goldin, "Han Fei's Doctrine of Self-Interest" in *After Confucius: Studies in Early Chinese Philosophy* (Honolulu: University of Hawai'i Press, 2005), 58–65. My performance analysis of these essays elaborates on tension that Goldin sees between these two essays.

devotion to his mother, and second for his generosity. Over time, however, Mi Zixia's looks faded (*se shuai* 色衰),[77] and as a result, the ruler's love for him followed suit, resulting in Mi's being accused of a crime against the ruler. The ruler of Wei then interpreted Mi's actions differently. Taking the ruler's carriage to visit his mother was considered theft, and the sharing of a peach was an offensive act of offering the ruler a half-eaten peach.

For this reason, it is no wonder that Han Feizi associates ministers with concubines. As Han Feizi notes about concubines in particular, their beauty fades (*mei se shuai* 美色衰) by age thirty, though the ruler's "fondness for sex" (*hao se* 好色) is still strong, even at age fifty.[78] The ruler's inevitable longing for younger, more beautiful companions is why, Han Feizi asserts, the women of the palace "hope for the (early) death of their ruler" (*ji qi jun zhi si* 冀其君之死).[79] Mi Zixia serves as an instructive example of this point. Much like a young concubine, his good looks allow him to enjoy great favor, but the inevitable decline of his appearance leads to his equally inevitable demise. Though Han Feizi's comparison between ministers and concubines serves as a warning to rulers, the story of Mi Zixia is a warning to ministers, who, unlike concubines, have the potential to make up for the loss of their natural beauty through a new aesthetic appeal of skillful performance, one that establishes a theatrical dynamic between the minister and his ruler.

In another tale of warning, Han Feizi tells the story of Mr. He 和氏 who offered an unpolished piece of jade to a ruler of Chu 楚.[80] The ruler had someone examine it, but this person insisted that it was merely a rock. Thinking Mr. He was trying to deceive him, the ruler ordered Mr. He's foot to be amputated as punishment. When the next ruler of Chu took the throne, Mr. He tried offering the same piece of jade again, but met the same disbelief, anger, and punishment from the ruler (his other foot was amputated). It was only after Mr. He wept profusely and lamented that his genuine gift of jade was repeatedly mistaken as a fraud, and the ruler subsequently ordered someone to polish it, that the jade was finally recognized as such.

There are two notable aspects of this story. The first is that Han Feizi uses Mr. He's jade as an example of a truly good idea presented by a potential advisor, which means that his bleak scenario of mutual mistrust between a ruler and his ministers is mitigated by his belief that some people do have more worthy advice to offer a ruler than others. After all, Han Feizi himself was someone who desired to serve a ruler, and insisted that his views were much more effective than those of others. The story of Mr. He, in fact, is really a message to most Warring States rulers, who, according to Han Feizi, generally fail to recognize when worthy ideas are presented to them. Thus, while Han Feizi may think that the common people have the "minds of little children," he really has little faith in the abilities of rulers to understand what is best for their states.

---

77 Ibid., 12.94.

78 Ibid., "Bei nei" 備內, 17.115.

79 Ibid. For more on the connection between sex and power in the *Han Feizi*, see Paul Rakita Goldin, *The Culture of Sex in Ancient China* (Honolulu: University of Hawai'i Press, 2002), 41–42.

80 *Han Feizi jijie*, "He shi" 和氏, 13.95–97. For a full translation of this story, see Watson, *Han Feizi*, 81–82.

The second notable aspect of this story is that good ideas are not enough. Mr. He's wisdom needed for its appearance to be altered in order for its value to be recognized. Han Feizi, like Confucius, is not content with relying solely on what the audience (i.e., the ruler) finds pleasing because the audience cannot be trusted as the best perceivers of good policies. Unlike Confucius, however—and in addition to the obvious rejection of moral government—Han Feizi does not recommend that would-be ministers remain content, even if the value of their ideas is not acknowledged. Mr. He is the prime example of the danger of taking such a position in Warring States politics. According to Han Feizi, he should have "engraved" (*diao zhuo* 雕琢) himself, much like the ministers depicted in "The Way of the Ruler," for at least he had something substantive to offer beyond a skilled and aesthetically pleasing performance. Performance, then, is a necessary "add-on" that simply responds to what Han Feizi sees as a bleak political situation in the late Warring States in which rulers must constantly be wary of manipulation and ministers must constantly be wary of being accused of such manipulation.

If Han Feizi, like Confucius, has a concept of a qualified individual coupled with a distrust of popular opinion, who is the "village worthy?" The term, *xiangyuan*, does not appear in this text. However, in his essay, "Eminence in Learning" (*Xian xue* 顯學), Han Feizi accuses the Confucians and Mohists[81] as the root cause of disorder. More precisely, disorder results from the rulers who apply the ideas of the Confucians and Mohists in their states. Much like the common people of the *Analects*, who become seduced by the performances of the less-than-virtuous, rulers become seduced by the performances of unqualified advisors. And to make matters worse, rulers patronize members of both traditions, despite their contradictory advice. As a result, Han Feizi believes these rulers cannot help but drive their kingdoms into chaos.[82]

Such a pessimistic outlook on Warring States politics is why "The Way of the Ruler" and "The Difficulties of Persuasion" are two essays that offer no content knowledge for either the ruler or the minister. Both essays are purely about "methods" of performance. Although Han Feizi clearly believes that some ideas are better than others (and therefore, some individuals are wiser than others), he believes it is unlikely that a knowledgeable advisor will gain an audience with a perceptive and capable ruler. The most likely scenario would be a meeting between an unknowledgeable advisor and an unperceptive and incapable ruler. In such an event, the best both can hope for is to escape death. Performance, then, is a survival strategy for a world in which "jade-like" wisdom is, indeed, a rare jewel.

Conclusion

In the late nineteenth century, James Legge translated *Analects* 9.18 as follows: "The Master said, 'I have not seen one who loves virtue as he loves beauty

---

81   The Mohists were the intellectual descendants of Mozi 墨子, a thinker who lived during the fifth century B.C.E. He disagreed vehemently with many of the details of Confucius's political philosophy, but agreed with his general principle that the best government was a moral government.
82   *Han Feizi jijie*, "Xian xue," 50.548.

(se)."[83] One might criticize this translation as an example of Victorian prudishness, for Legge acknowledges in his notes that se here means "sensual pleasure."[84] A more direct rendering of this passage, then, would be "I have never seen someone who loves virtue as much as sex."[85] However, from the above discussion, it seems that Legge's translation may be particularly apt for the broader meanings of se in the text. One might imagine Confucius wishing that more people recognized true virtue than its attractive, yet inferior, resemblance that stems from a skilled performance by someone with an expressive countenance. Moreover, one can see how Han Feizi might agree with at least part of this saying. Though surely he would not be concerned with loving virtue, he would wish more people (i.e., rulers) would recognize those people with truly worthy ideas, rather than be distracted by the fine appearance and performance of charlatans. Thus, both Confucius and Han Feizi wished more audiences recognized and appreciated the "painting on a white foundation" rather than the less vivid "colors" without this foundation, although what Confucius and Han Feizi each recognized as "white" differed considerably.

Bibliography

Bodde, Derk. "Sex in Chinese Civilization," *Proceedings of the American Philosophical Society*. 129.2 (1985): 161-172.

Carlson, Marvin. *Performance: A Critical Introduction*. 2nd ed. New York: Routledge, 2004.

Cheng Shude 程樹德, ed. *Lunyu jishi* 論語集釋. Beijing: Zhonghua shuju, 1990.

Creel, Herlee G. "The *Fa-chia* 法家: 'Legalists' or 'Administrators'?" in *What is Taoism? And Other Studies in Chinese Cultural History*. 92-120. Chicago: University of Chicago Press, 1970.

Csikszentmihalyi, Mark. *Material Virtue: Ethics and the Body in Early China*. Leiden: Brill, 2004.

Fingarette, Herbert. *Confucius–the Secular as Sacred*. New York: Harper Torchbooks, 1972.

Goldin, Paul Rakita. *The Culture of Sex in Ancient China*. Honolulu: University of Hawai'i Press, 2002.

_____. "The Reception of the *Odes* in the Warring States Era." In *After Confucius: Studies in Early Chinese Philosophy*. 19-35. Honolulu: University of Hawai'i Press, 2005.

---

83   *Lunyu jishi*, 18.611. James Legge, trans., *Confucian Analects, The Great Learning, and The Doctrine of the Mean* (Oxford: Clarendon, 1893; reprint, New York: Dover, 1971), 222. This passage is actually numbered 9.17 in Legge's translation.

84   Legge refers the reader to his note about *se* in 1.7 on pp. 140–141.

85   For more on the meaning of *se* as "sex," see Derk Bodde, "Sex in Chinese Civilization," *Proceedings of the American Philosophical Society* 129.2 (1985), 161–162.

_____. "Han Fei's Doctrine of Self-Interest." In *After Confucius: Studies in Early Chinese Philosophy*. 58-65. Honolulu: University of Hawai'i Press, 2005.

_____. "Persistent Misconceptions about Chinese 'Legalism,'" *Journal of Chinese Philosophy* 38.1 (2011): 88-104.

Grimes, Ronald. "Religion, Ritual, and Performance." In *Religion, Theatre, and Performance: Acts of Faith*, ed. Lance Gharavi. 27-41. New York: Routledge, 2012.

Guodian Chumu zhujian 郭店楚墓竹簡. Beijing: Wenwu, 1998.

Holloway, Kenneth W. *Guodian: the Newly Discovered Seeds of Chinese Religious and Political Philosophy*. New York: Oxford, 2009.

Ivanhoe, Philip J. *Confucian Moral Self Cultivation*. 2nd ed. Indianapolis, IN: Hackett, 2000.

_____. "Han Feizi and Moral Self-Cultivation," *Journal of Chinese Philosophy* 38.1 (2011): 31- 45.

Jiao Xun 焦循, ed. *Mengzi zhengyi* 孟子正義. Beijing: Zhonghua shuju, 2004.

Kim, Tae Hyun. "Other *Laozi* Parallels in the *Hanfeizi*: An Alternative Approach to the Textual History of the *Laozi* and Early Chinese Thought," *Sino-Platonic Papers* 199 (2010): 1-76.

Lai, Karyn. "Confucian Moral Cultivation: Some Parallels with Musical Training" in *The Moral Circle of the Self: Chinese and Western Approaches*, edited by Kim-chong Chong, Sor-hoon Tan, and C.L. Ten. 107-139. Peru, IL: Open Court, 2003.

_____. "*Li* in the *Analects*: Training in Moral Competence and the Question of Flexibility," *Philosophy East and West* 56.1 (2006): 72-76.

Lau, D.C., trans. *Mencius*. New York: Penguin, 1970.

_____. *The Analects*. New York: Penguin, 1979.

Legge, James, trans. *Confucian Analects, The Great Learning, and The Doctrine of the Mean*. Oxford: Clarendon, 1893. Reprint, New York: Dover, 1971.

Levi, Jean. "Han fei tzu 韓非子." In *Early Chinese Texts: A Bibliographical Guide*, edited by Michael Loewe. 115-124. Berkeley, CA: Society for the Study of Early China, 1993.

Li Ling 李零. *Guodian Chujian jiaoduji* 郭店楚簡校讀記. Beijing: Renmin daxue chubanshe, 2007.

Olberding, Amy. *Moral Exemplars in the Analects: The Good Person is That*. New York: Routledge, 2012.

Sato, Masayaki. *The Confucian Quest for Order: The Origin and Formation of the Political Thought of Xunzi*. Leiden: Brill, 2003.

Sauter, Willmar. *The Theatrical Event: Dynamics of Performance and Perception*. Iowa City: University of Iowa Press, 2000.

Schechner, Richard. *Between Theater and Anthropology.* Philadelphia: University of Pennsylvania Press, 1985.

————. *Performance Theory*. Rev. ed. New York: Routledge, 2003.

Shaughnessy, Edward L. *Rewriting Early Chinese Texts*. Albany: State University of New York Press, 2006.

Shun, Kwong-loi. *Mencius and Early Chinese Thought*. Stanford, CA: Stanford University Press, 1997.

Slingerland, Edward, trans. *Confucius: Analects with Selections from Traditional Commentaries*. Indianapolis, IN: Hackett, 2003.

Van Norden, Bryan W., trans. *Mengzi with Selections from Traditional Commentaries*. Indianapolis, IN: Hackett, 2008.

Waley, Arthur, trans. *The Book of Songs: The Ancient Chinese Classic of Poetry*, edited with additional translations by Joseph R. Allen. New York: Grove Press, 1996.

Wang Xianshen 王先慎, ed. *Han Feizi jijie* 韓非子集解. Beijing: Zhonghua shuju, 1998.

Watson, Burton, trans. *Han Feizi: Basic Writings*. New York: Columbia University Press, 2003.

2

Color, Adornment, and Social Conflict: Fashioning Cultural Identity in Ancient Greece and Rome

Michael Proulx

Color[1] and its association with adornment were often a focal point of social conflict in the ancient Mediterranean world. Competing societal interests used color and fashion to mark cultural boundaries, providing for an opportunity to explore the contentious social and cultural histories of Greece and Rome through the prism of color, dress, and cultural identity. Central to the construction of each civilization's early communal identity was a discourse of virtue based on material simplicity, modest modes of self-expression, and personal restraint. From the fifth to first centuries BCE, conservative Greek and Roman elites staunchly opposed the influx and popularity of vibrant colors and personal adornment. By the third century BCE, use of color throughout the Mediterranean basin was rampant, and by the second century CE, Christian bishops sought to separate their communities from the popular fashions of their day by promoting natural colors that mirrored a belief in sacred values of modesty and purity. However, after efforts to suppress vibrant color and adornment failed, colors such as purple were adopted into a developing Christian worldview and were even used for sacred meanings. At the same time, a remarkable development occurred: black, a color with initially negative connotations, emerged with powerfully positive meanings. Examining the process by which these transformations occurred and tracing the tension between elite criticisms of color and adornment in the ancient Mediterranean world can provide insight into how communal identity, often shaped within the context of cultural tension, was in constant flux, transforming societies in new and unexpected ways.

---

1   I want to thank the organizers of the 2012 Humanities Conference at the University of North Georgia for assembling a diverse group of scholars on a provocative topic of important relevance. Dr. Sungshin Kim deserves special recognition for her work and guidance bringing the proceedings to its current form. My hope is that this contribution may be of some use for non-specialists. I am grateful to the article's reviewers. Their comments and suggestions saved me from numerous mistakes. Any remaining errors are wholly my own. Lastly, I want to thank Julie Higbee for her patience and support. This contribution is dedicated to her.

Ancient Near East and Greece

For ancient Mesopotamian cultures predating ancient Greece and Rome, color symbolized characteristics of one's relationship with the divine world. The region's access to natural resources provided ample supplies of pigment deriving from diverse resources,[2] and people in the ancient Near East produced a rich pallet of color schemes including silver, gold, purple, sapphire blue, orange, jasper, turquoise, lapis lazuli, and others. These colors in particular were associated with worship of divine entities such as Ishtar, Ahura Mazda, and Yahweh,[3] and were vital symbols that connected the temporal sphere with the divine. The Greek historian Herodotus recorded a spectacular description of the colors painted on the walled fortification of the Median city at Ecbatana, in modern western Iran. Herodotus described what he believed to be an elaborate urban defensive system that included seven circular walls, each interior wall higher than the wall beyond it. Each wall was painted a specific color: the sequence from outer wall to inner wall was white, black, crimson, blue, red, silver, and finally, gold.[4] Modern scholars doubt this, as it is highly probable that Herodotus recorded a second-hand account of a Babylonian temple. The walls were actually the structural rectangles of a ziggurat, which ascended in smaller sequential order of seven levels, and its purpose was religious, not defensive.[5] An example can be found at the Temple of Nebuchadnezzar at Birs Nimrud in modern Iraq, where the foundation is approximately 272 square feet with a height of twenty-six feet. The color schemes of each level correlated with planetary bodies in the ascending order from the foundation to the summit: Saturn (black), Jupiter (orange), Mars (red), Sun (gold), Venus (yellow), Mercury (blue), and the Moon (silver).[6] The symbolism of these colors was vital for Nebuchadnezzar, whose intention is inscribed on the ziggurat: "I invoke Marduk, King of the Heavens and Earth, that this, my work, may be preserved for me under your care, in honor and respect. May Nebuchanezzar, the royal architect remain under your protection."[7] Thus, color served to help communicate the divine reverence and devotion that would ensure favor from the gods. These colors, however, were not reserved exclusively for the gods, as popular consumption of ornate hues such as purple spread throughout the ancient Near East.

It is not known exactly when purple appeared as a desired color for popular use in the Mesopotamian world. Evidence suggests that by 1500 BCE purple dye emerged as a valued commodity traded between the Phoenician coast and the Eastern Tigris River region.[8] The Levantine coast, particularly in the area of Tyre,

---

2 Robert Finlay, "Weaving the Rainbow: Visions of Color in World History," *Journal of World History 18*, no.4 (2007): 413-414.

3 Finlay, "Weaving the Rainbow," 414, with Robert Steven Bianchi, "Symbols and Meanings," in *Gifts of the Nile: Ancient Egyptian Faience*, ed. Florence Dunn Friedmann (New York: Thames & Hudson, 1998), 22-31.

4 Herodotus, *Histories*, 1.98-99.

5 Henry C. Rawlinson, "On the Birs Nimrud, or The Great Temple of Borsippa," *The Journal of the Royal Asiatic Society of Great Britain and Ireland* (1855): 1-34, esp. 18 n. 1.

6 Rawlinson, "On the Birs Nimrud," 17-18.

7 Ibid., 32.

8 Meyer Reinhold, *History of Purple as a Status Symbol in Antiquity* (Brussels: Latomus, 1970), 9. Reinhold remains the best survey for the topic of purple in the ancient world.

provided a regular industry of purple production. Ancient coastal people harvested the native shellfish species *Bolinus brandaris* for its unique secretions that turned purple when exposed to the air. The laborious nature of production added significantly to its value; a quarter-million shellfish were necessary to manufacture a single ounce of dye.[9] Its exclusive nature reserved this color for elites in the Tigris and Euphrates region. With the rise of Persian dominance over Mesopotamia in the fifth century BCE, use of certain colors including purple by Persian elites spread as a result of efforts to communicate Persian authority within the Mesopotamian context and beyond.

By the sixth century BCE, purple had become the symbol of Persian royalty. When Cyrus the Great (r. 559 BC – 530 BCE) restricted use of purple for the imperial family alone,[10] he began the long tradition of wearing a purple robe over a purple tunic with a white vertically-centered stripe.[11] The politics of purple exclusivity were coupled with the practice of providing gifts of purple robes and attire for regional governors who shared authority with the Great King.[12] For Greeks, Persian ostentatious display of power through color stood in stark contrast to their own modest material culture and the values associated with it.

Greeks viewed vibrant colors emanating from Persia with caution. Things "Babylonian" were *poiklos*—"multicolored,"[13] a distinction that underscores the stark contrast between material abundance of eastern values and Greek culture. Athenians were sensitive to their limited resources for the production of luxury goods. The rough island landscapes of the Aegean simply could not compete with the resource-rich lands of the Persian Empire. As one example of the Greek culture of modesty and material restraint, political rivals of the great democratic leader Pericles (d. 429 BCE) denounced his design and decoration of the Parthenon, complaining that it was as ostentatious as a vainly-dressed temple prostitute.[14] Such reactions to perceived non-Greek material culture and adornment underscore a particular Greek worldview from the earliest periods of their recorded history.

Herodotus (c. 484–425 BCE) first documented Greek perceptions of the cultures and lands east of the Aegean. While his grand work, *The Histories*, provides an important account of the Persian Wars (499-449 BCE) with the stated intent to explain the origins of the wars, it also provides a provocative glimpse into Greek perceptions of their Persian neighbors. For Herodotus, cultural differences made conflict inevitable. Greek virtues of freedom were checked by the balance of reason and democratic institutions; Persians were driven to monarchy and the corrupt influence of *hubris* that stems from tyrannical tendencies. Herodotus

---

9   Lloyd Jensen, "Royal Purple of Tyre," *Journal of Near Eastern Studies* 22.2 (1963): 104-118; Philip Ball, *Bright Earth: The Invention of Colour* (London: Viking Press, 2001), 225.

10   Reinhold, *History of Purple*, 18.

11   Xenophon, *Cyrus*, 8.3.

12   Xenophon, *Cyrus*, 8.2, 3.1; with Reinhold, *History of Purple*, 19.

13   Finlay, 419, with Margaret Miller, *Athens and Persia in the Fifth Century BC: A Study in Cultural Receptivity* (Cambridge: Cambridge University, 1997) and Edith Hall, *Inventing the Barbarian: Greek Self-Definition through Tragedy* (Oxford: Clarendon Press, 1989).

14   Plutarch, *Life of Pericles*, 1.211.

constructed the principles of his ethnographic thesis through a series of dialogues and reported events. In each episode, Persian rulers suffer from a negative trait stemming from the Greek idea of *eros*—uncontrollable desire.[15] In the pages of *The Histories*, Persian kings Cyrus the Great, Cambyses II (r. 530-522 BCE), Darius I (r. 522–486 BCE), and Xerxes (r. 486-465 BCE) long to expand their authority over all people. Their efforts, as Herodotus composed in great detail, inevitably led to *eris* or "strife" with surrounding people and within their own ranks. The cost to each of these rulers was enormous.[16] Cyrus was slain during his invasion of modern Kazakhstan, inhabited by the nomadic Massagetae and led by their queen Tomyris.[17] Cambyses II reportedly went insane after his campaigns against Carthage, the Ammonians (in modern Libya), and Ethiopia ended in various catastrophes. He killed a brother out of political jealously, and killed one sister he had married in order to marry another of his sisters. He eventually died of a self-inflicted knife wound to the thigh, in the exact location where previously he had stabbed an Egyptian sacred calf.[18] Darius suffered a humiliating defeat by Greeks at the Battle of Marathon (c. 490 BCE) and died thereafter while trying to suppress rebellion in Egypt.[19] Having lost his brother and a large number of ships to an Athenian navy that was smaller than his own, Xerxes lost his entire army while trying to retreat from Greece. His disastrous invasion of Greece cost Persia the entire northern Aegean.[20] Each of these episodes broadcasts the powerful values that Herodotus's Greek audience would understand; *eros* was a fatal trait of monarchies, the worst form of government, given the egalitarian values of Greek-style democracies.

The critical comparison Herodotus made with these examples of Persian rulers is that, despite greater brute force, monarchy forced the group to follow the predilections of one man. For Herodotus, this was the vital difference between civilized and barbarous nations. In the *Histories,* Herodotus's nomadic barbarians were ruled by kings; when Cyrus assembled the tribal armies of this empire to launch an invasion against the Scythians, he summoned their kings.[21] This link between the royal government of Persia and the royal governments of barbarian tribes provided Herodotus with a crucial element of his rhetoric: the Persians were symbolically barbarians.[22] Greeks were the only free people because they restricted individual power, whereas the 'barbaric' Persians were enslaved by the desires of the ruler, just as barbarian nations were. The democratic virtues of restraint, Herodotus proposed, guarded against such individual folly with reasoned debate and greater concern for the collective community. Herodotus's link between monarchy, individual power, *eros, hubris,* and ornate material culture appears in subtle ways, and purple became the ultimate symbol of personal and social corruption.

---

15 For the following see François Hartog, *The Mirror of Herodotus: The Representation of the Other in the Writing of History*, trans. Janet Lloyd (Berkeley: University of California, 1988), 209-381.

16 Hartog, *The Mirror of Herodotus*, 330-340.

17 Herodotus, *Histories*, 1.205-214, with Hartog, *The Mirror of Herodotus*, 331.

18 Herodotus, *Histories*, 3.17-26, 3.29-31, 3.64-66.

19 Herodotus, *Histories*, 7.1-4.

20 Ibid., 8.70-8.108, 8.126-129.

21 Ibid., 4.102, 4.106, 4.159; with Hartog, *The Mirror of Herodotus*, 324.

22 Hartog, *The Mirror of Herodotus*, 323-324.

In one famous account, the Persian ruler Cambyses's ambitious attempt to expand his empire south of Egypt failed partly because of the royal association with ornate material culture. Herodotus reported that before Cambyses launched his invasion of Ethiopia, he wanted to assess the sophistication and abilities of his opponents. A covert Persian ambassador brought gifts to test the Ethiopian king's reactions. Among the gold jewelry, perfume, and wine that the Persian ambassadors exhibited before the king was a purple robe.[23] The response of Herodotus's Ethiopian king was that he saw through the ruse; he rejected the items, mocking the society that produced the purple robe as a sign of vanity. In this story, Ethiopian humility and simplicity represented superior virtue in the face of Persian cultural refinement and opulence. An infuriated Cambyses launched his offensive into southern Egypt, but, plagued by logistical difficulties, it disintegrated within a week. The debacle was proof that excessive material culture debilitated Persian society. This anecdotal story stands in high relief to the modest nature of Greek material culture that Herodotus offers.[24]

The cautionary tone of moderation is a common theme in Herodotus because Persian use of color became synonymous with excess and effeminacy. After the decisive battle of Plataea in 479 BCE, which effectively ended the Persian Wars, Greek forces were stunned by the lavish gold and silver furniture, adornments, and brightly-colored tapestry abandoned on the battlefield by the retreating Persian king, Xerxes. At the victory banquet, the Spartan king, Pausanias, toasted the Greeks by mocking Xerxes as one who suffered from "foolishness... who, with such provisions for life came to take away from us our possessions which are so pitiful."[25] Again, Herodotus draws a distinction between Persian material wealth and Greek modesty and simplicity and Greece's resulting moral and physical superiority. Ironically, despite the sardonic tone of his ridicule, Pausanias proceeded to divide the spoils from the treasure among the eager hands of the Greek soldiers.

While this promoted Greek strength, it also illustrated the tension among the elite Greek society struggling to maintain cultural identity in the midst of great change in the eastern Mediterranean. Greeks sometimes resisted Persian influence overtly, but they also accepted and even embraced it in other ways. Notably, cultural exchange with the Persians could not be avoided despite the intention of some Greek elites like Herodotus.

For all the attention paid to political conflicts between the Greeks and Persians, relations were not always antagonistic in their long history together. For example, in the sixth century BCE, Greek artisans and engineers were involved in the construction of Persian capitals under Cyrus the Great and Darius II.[26] Another revealing example is Aeschylus's tragedy *The Persians,* which recounts the day that news of Xerxes' disastrous expedition against Athens at the Battle of Salamis

---

23 Herodotus, *Histories*, 3.20-25. The Ethiopian king is unnamed.

24 James S. Romm, *The Edges of the Earth in Ancient Thought* (Princeton: Princeton University, 1992), 55.

25 Herodotus, *Histories*, 9.82.3.

26 Trudy S. Kawami, "Greek Art and Persian Taste: Some Animal Sculptures from Persepolis," *American Journal of Archaeology* 90.3 (July, 1986): 259; with D. Stronach, *Pasargadae* (Oxford, 1977), 22; A.B. Tilia, *Studies and Restorations at Persepolis and Other Sites of Fars II* (IsMEO Reports and Memoirs 18, Rome, 1976), 3; M. Roaf, "Sculptures and Sculptors at Persepolis," *Iran* 21 (1983): 150

(480 BCE) reached the Persian capital at Persepolis. While the play reaffirms the importance of Greek values, as exemplified by the divine punishment Xerxes receives for his *hubris*,[27] it is told from the Persian perspective. Long passages recount the carnage in vivid detail and invoke empathy for the tremendous loss of Persian lives and property.[28] The deep sorrow that Aeschylus wanted his Greek audience to feel for their enemy could be successful only if Greek suspicion of Persian culture was tempered by the long periods of peaceful coexistence. These patterns of cultural exchange also reached philosophical planes.

Plato made a passing but telling reference to coloring statues in *Republic*. At one point in the dialogue, he reveals a penchant for Persian culture. Using Socrates as his interlocutor, Plato incorporates purple as a metaphor for the supreme idea of perfection. He writes: "Suppose that we were painting a statue, and someone came up to us and said, 'Why do you not put the most beautiful colors on the most beautiful parts of the body—the eyes ought to be purple, but you have made them black.'"[29] To illustrate the importance of preparing society to achieve the supreme ideal, Plato combines the metaphor of dyeing colors with cultivating virtue:

> You know, I said, that dyers, when they want to dye wool for making the true sea-purple, begin by selecting their white color first; this they prepare and dress with much care and pains, in order that the white ground may take the purple hue in full perfection. The dyeing then proceeds; and whatever is dyed in this manner becomes a fast color, and no washing either with lyes or without them can take away the bloom. But, when the ground has not been duly prepared, you will have noticed how poor is the look either of purple or of any other color...
>
> Yes, he said; I know that they have a washed-out and ridiculous appearance.[30]

The essence of Plato's idea of perfection in the metaphor is purple, and its value can be diminished to a "ridiculous" state; it is an example of a remarkable shift in cultural taste that acknowledges the ready acceptance of popular fashion, given previous aversions to Persian cultural models. Such representation in Plato's imagination reveals how Persian influence of purple permeated some elite values despite a history of stereotypes and disdain for all things Persian.

During the fifth century BCE Greeks began to develop a taste for vibrant colors. By 420 BCE, luxurious purple clothing and multicolored vases were in great demand in Athens, the very seat of resistance to Persian ways.[31] Alexander the Great (d. 323 BCE) began synthesizing Macedonian fashions with Persian imperial dress and customs, namely wearing a purple head band interwoven with white that was stitched to a Macedonian felt hat dyed purple, and adopting a Persian

---

27   See Edith Hall, *Inventing the Barbarians: Greeks Self-Definition through Tragedy* (Oxford: Clarendon, 1989).
28   Aeschylus, *The Persians*, lines 58-64,133-139, 249-285, 302-330, 515-596, 964-1003.
29   Plato, *Republic*, 4.420.
30   Ibid., 4.429.
31   Reinhold, *History of Purple*, 25; with András Alföldi, "Gewaltherrsher und Theaterkönig," in *Late Classical and Medieval Studies in Honor of Albert Mathias Friend, Jr.* (Princeton, 1955), 40.

royal tunic worn with a purple robe.[32] Alexander's Persian-styled clothing caused some consternation, however. His demand that his own Macedonian companions perform the Persian practice known as *proskynesis*, which involved prostrating before the king, invoked the dismay of this senior command and ridicule of elite Greek society.[33] For Greek historians, such outrageous acts were in line with Alexander's belief that he was a god.[34] In essence, emulating Persian royal customs was akin to madness.

Regardless of negative reactions, the *Diadochoi*, the Hellenistic successor kings of Alexander, followed his policies of adopting Persian customs and imperial dress. Eumenes of Cardia (d. 316 BCE), Alexander's former secretary and general, gave his own personal bodyguard purple robes and purple felt hats, a military dress requirement that sought to distinguish them plainly from his regular Macedonian guard.[35] No fewer than eight Hellenistic kings and rulers incorporated Persian purple into their style of rule.[36] As Greek rulers, soldiers, travelers, colonists, craftsmen, and tradesmen traversed and settled into the vast territories of the Hellenistic kingdoms, the rhetoric of Greek opposition to Persian things, so clear just a century earlier, came to embrace the more utilitarian values promoted by Hellenistic philosophies like Stoicism and Epicureanism, values that espoused one to endure hardships of the world rather than overcome them and to seek moderation and balance instead of outright intolerance. After Alexander, the boundary between Greek and Persian material customs had been blurred, and the sharpness by which Greek culture had so stridently opposed eastern ways was now blunted.

The Roman *Mos Maioru*m and Greek Corruption

As in the Greek world of the fourth and fifth centuries BCE, this dichotomy of rejecting yet desiring color and adornment was equally acute and varied. Roman tradition had long despised purple for its overt representation of Etruscan royal authority to which Romans had submitted for nearly 300 years. Once the city gained its independence from its Etruscan overlords in 509 BCE, however, sensitivity to purple decreased. Brutus the Liberator, whom Roman tradition credits with leading the revolt, supported purple dress for religious festival days and triumphal processions.[37] In this way, ancient Roman tradition held that the elite patrician class defended the *mos maiorum* or "way of the elders." Modesty and simple dress reflected the inner *pietas* or "duty" of a patrician's character, which emphasized constant vigilance to uphold the traditions of the family and the state.

Restraint in dress was a key signifier that expressed *pietas* values, and the senatorial class often set the tone for the rest of society. Roman sensibilities were

---

32 Quintus Curtius Rufus, *The History of Alexander*, 45.2; Rienhold, 28.

33 Diodorus Siculus, 17.77.5; *Plutarch, Life of Alexander*, 44.1; Brian Bosworth, "Alexander and the Iranians," *The Journal of Hellenic Studies* 100 (1980): 1-21.

34 Arrian, *Anabasis,* 3.3-4; Plutarch, *Alexander* 27.8-10.

35 Plutarch, *Life of Eumenes*, 8.7; with Reinhold, *History of Purple,* 31.

36 Reinhold, *History of Purple,* 33, fn. 8.

37 Dionysius of Halicarnassus, 4.74; with Reinhold, *History of Purple,* 39-45 for the following.

so attuned to it that the great Jewish revolutionary Judah Maccabee (c. 165 BCE) reportedly was astonished by the drab garments worn by the Roman senators; they lacked the purple robes or diadems worn by the Hellenistic monarchs against whom the Maccabees had revolted.[38] Common Roman decorum regarding avoidance of ornate dress also struck fear in the hearts of eastern rulers who wore purple. When a Roman delegation visited Prusias II (r. 182-149 BCE), the Hellenistic king of Bithynia (in modern day northern Turkey), he removed his Alexander-styled white and purple diadem and purple dress to avoid offending the senatorial ambassadors who wore simple tunics and Roman shoes.[39] It was this type of modesty that Roman elites were expected to display.

An example of such decorum can be found in the sentiments of a staunch defender of Roman tradition, Cato the Elder (234-149 BCE). Distinguished for not owning any embroidered Babylonian tapestry, he stridently defended a Roman law known as the *Lex Oppia* (197 BCE). It had restricted women from wearing more than half an ounce of gold and prohibited them from wearing multi-colored garments with purple because such ornamental display was viewed as insensitive to Roman military sacrifice and seditious against the natural social order.[40] Created during the dark days of the Second Punic War, when Hannibal of Carthage defeated several Roman armies, the law struck against cultural vanity. Cato argued that the wealthy suffered from a "disease" of "self-indulgence," with their tastes for refined products. Their wanton selfishness drove poorer Romans to envy what they could not afford. As a result, poorer husbands would feel distraught and trapped by their wives, who would torture them to provide what their friends' husbands could. Civil discord would develop from personal greed and rivalry, thereby destroying civil unity.[41] However, not all Romans held themselves to such high standards of *pietas*.

Popular forces countered Cato's demand for personal austerity. The tribune Lucius Valerius proposed a legal reversal, arguing that women ought to have some measure of equality with men. The historian Livy presents a fantastic story of an "army of women" flooding the streets of Rome in protest, many journeying in from the countryside and surrounding towns.[42] Having reached the senate house, they shut down legislative debate and eventually besieged the homes of key senators until the law was repealed. Even with this popular force in favor of ornamentation, however, conservative forces remained suspicious of those who wore purple because they believed it reflected severe personal defects such as pride, immorality, and even treason.

Roman historians utilized purple as a rhetorical tool to illustrate that popular historical figures could be blamed for upsetting Roman civil order. Plutarch, writing more than a century after the fact, used purple to explain the mass political violence associated with the assassination of the tribune reformer Tiberius Gracchus (d. 133 BCE). Groups linked to senatorial interests killed Gracchus

---

38   I Maccabees 8.14, with Reinhold, 40.

39   Diodorus Siculus, 31.15.2, with Reinhold, 40.

40   Livy, *History of Rome*, 34.1-8. The *Lex Oppia* was repealed in 195 BCE. Patricia A. Johnston, "Poenulus 1, 2 and Roman Women," *Transactions of the American Philological Association* 110 (1980): 143-159.

41   Livy, *History of Rome*, 34.4.

42   Livy, *History of Rome*, 34.2.

and many of his supporters because he proposed legislation that was viewed as both offensive and threatening to the senate.[43] The slaughter that erupted in the streets of Rome as a result was partially driven by a rumor that Gracchus had once touched a purple robe he received as a gift from a Hellenistic king.[44] Another anecdote recalls 100 years of civil war in the first century BCE between patrician and plebeian political forces that can be associated with the reported wearing of a purple robe into the senate house by the Plebeian consul Marius the day after he had celebrated a triumph in Rome.[45] Protocol dictated that conquering generals be allowed to wear the robe only during the procession through the city and to remove the garment after the ceremonies. In the minds of conservative patricians, Marius's transgression exposed deep character flaws, flaunting pride, and blind ambition. The overreach excited anti-monarchical sensibilities upon which the Roman state was founded, and fear of a resurgent Estruscan-style monarchy loomed in the collective patrician memory. Any association with royal symbols could be enough to taint one's reputation.

Such sensibilities and rhetoric extended into the last decades of the Roman Republic, and Cicero used associations with monarchy as a common slur against his political enemies. Among Cicero's provocative allegations of corruption and abuse of power against the infamous Roman governor Verres was the possession of purple bedspreads that he had distributed among his friends.[46] A few years later, he castigated fellow conspirators who associated with Catiline, a senator who plotted the overthrow of the Roman state in 63 BCE as individuals who "hover around the Forum, [and] gleam in purple."[47] The senators were so fearful of a return to monarchy that they permitted Cicero to condemn many of these individuals to be strangled without trial.

Caesar himself was linked to the dangerous color by the historian Plutarch in foretelling ways. When he invaded Egypt in 49 BCE during the battle of Pharos, the famous lighthouse in the harbor of Alexandria, Caesar was forced to abandon his ship and swim to safety under a hail of arrows and missiles with important papers in one hand, and, ostensibly, a purple robe clenched in his teeth so that they would not fall into the hands of the Egyptian forces.[48] A few years later, during the heady pastoral festival of the Lupercalia, Marc Anthony mischievously offered to crown Caesar with a diadem, as he sat wrapped in a triumphal purple gown.[49] Caesar dodged his confidant's attempts several times; eventually the diadem was placed upon one of Caesar's statues. Although the celebrating crowd applauded each time Caesar refused Anthony's gesture, the guardians of the *mos maiorum*

---

43 The wars against Carthage and the Greek east placed undue pressure on the citizen soldiery of the Republic. Large numbers of citizens lost their farms as a as a result of long campaigns away from home. The loss of property rendered them homeless and thus ineligible for service. Many flocked to the city of Rome for redress. Tiberius sought to settle these veterans on conquered state property known as the *ager publicus*. This move ran afoul with senatorial interests in managing these resources.

44 Plutarch, *Life of Tiberius Gracchus*, 14.

45 Plutarch, *Life of Marius*, 12.5.

46 Cicero, *Against Verres*, 2.2.72, 2.5.31, 2.5.86, 2.5.13, 4.26.59.

47 Cicero, *Against Catiline*, 2.5; 4.12.

48 Plutarch, *Julius Caesar*, 49; Suetonius, *Julius Caesar*, 64.

49 Plutarch, *Marc Anthony*, 12.

found the scene maddening. Later, some tribunes removed the diadem from the statue only to find themselves deposed from their office by Caesar himself.

In the attempt to understand the political motivations of Tiberius Gracchus, Verres, Catiline, Caesar, and the political violence tied to them, Roman chroniclers employed the stigma of purple to explain why society should remain vigilant over traditional virtues. Personal character flaws, not Roman values, were to blame for turbulent times. It was much easier for conservatives to explain how men, who enjoyed immense public support, could succumb to corrupting eastern values, rather than accept the sweeping cultural changes underway. Yet despite these cases in which purple was used to explain moral failing, many aristocratic Romans were never as austere as conservatives like Cato, Plutarch, and Cicero had wished them to be.

Roman elite sensibilities had long favored purple. Even though Roman tradition reviled any political individual who applied purple to raise his status, social norms for elites as a group were flexible. Romans had adopted elements of Etruscan administration and cultural practices such as the *toga praetexta* with its purple borders, or the *latus clavus*, a broad purple or crimson stripe embroidered on the toga fringes.[50] These markings distinguished individuals from the Plebeian class as well as from those of their own patrician status, just as their Etruscan overlords had done. By the early third century BCE when Roman authority extended into the Hellenistic world, wearing purple for official and private use was prevalent. As a result of imperial expansion, immense treasure and wealth poured into Italy, bringing with it an influx of Hellenistic influences.[51] Roman adoption of ornate display of status was, in many ways, keeping with the long practices extending from the Persian plateau to the Mediterranean basin. This is evident in the Roman practice of giving gifts of purple robes and tunics to royal foreign dignitaries, as well as senators distinguishing themselves from others by wearing scarlet shoes.[52]

With the widespread presence of colors from the Persians and Greek east, austere Roman traditions could not diminish popular taste for adornment. Beauty books were bountiful throughout Roman history. The second-century CE physician, Galen (c. 129-200), noted that books on heightening one's personal appearance, from hair dyeing to cosmetics, were as numerous as medical books, emphasizing the great care and cost Romans expended to present themselves in public.[53] The face required special attention. To remove unwanted facial hair, exotic concoctions of animal blood, fish gall and livers, leeches, and frogs were blended with oil or vinegar and appropriately smeared. Various chalks, white paint, or white lead were applied to whiten the skin, after which *splenia*, or small plaster beauty patches shaped into stars or crescent moons, were attached to hide unwanted blemishes. To present a complete cranial array, dyeing one's hair red, golden yellow, or black was desirable for both men and women.[54]

---

50   Reinhold, *History of Purple*, 39.

51   Ibid., 40.

52   Reinhold, 42, with P. C. Sands, *The Client Princes of the Roman Empire under the Republic* (Cambridge, 1908), 75-76; R.J.A. Talbert, *The Senate of Imperial Rome* (Princeton: Princeton University, 1984), 219-210.

53   Galen, 5.12, with Ortha Wilner, "Roman Beauty Culture," *The Classical Journal* v.27.1 (1931): 37.

54   Wilner, "Roman Beauty Culture," 27, 31-33.

Notwithstanding the popularity of self-adornment with color display, many critics denounced these beautification practices. Julius Caesar himself was a target, drawing negative attention for his habit of wearing a wreath to conceal a receding hairline.[55] The poet Martial (c. 40-102 CE) ridiculed the culture of make-up, writing: "The face you show the world is laid at night/ Not in your bed but in your hundred rouge-pots."[56] The satirist Juvenal (c. 55-138 CE) lampooned the "plague" and "infection" of elites who were consumed with the finery of their status, painted eye lids, curled and netted hair, lavish gowns, and tunics of checkered purple and blue.[57] In his "Third Satire," he mocked the new elite of Rome, depicting them as the "purple-clad gentry" who wear "painted headdresses," and ornate "Greek-fangled slippers, and dinner coats..." in contrast to himself as a traditional Roman farmer wearing rugged boots.[58] Some viewed the proliferation of materialism as an ominous sign; Pliny the Elder (d. 79 CE) was despondent over the boundless popularity of bejeweled cups and marbled walls, believing that the future of the Roman state hung in the balance. He characterized with revulsion the intense scarlet and purple imported from India as flowing like the "blood of dragons and elephants."[59]

Color as a metaphor for corruption was also used to warn of potential dangers in the power of oratory. Cicero and Quintilian described persuasive speech as "rhetorical colors" which could be applied to discourse as "drapery or colors" that exaggerates or obfuscates truth.[60] For Juvenal, reality itself was threatened. He disparaged the trending culture of flattery and sophistry introduced by Greek orators who were "experts in flattery, and will praise the talk of an illiterate, or the beauty of a deformed, friend, and compare the scraggy neck of some weakling to the brawny throat of Hercules."[61] The rhetorical abilities of Mark Anthony (d. 30 BCE), who became a symbol of Roman debauchery with Cleopatra, were characterized as flamboyant Greek sophistry for their "Asiatic taste" and "empty flourishes and unsteady efforts for glory."[62]

As these examples show, Roman critics had the ability to project their cultural woes and insecurities onto the Greeks. And yet, despite attempts to restrict the community from cultural synthesis with the east, popular desires found ways around conservative Roman values, for much of the criticism over the proliferation of color and personal ornamentation can be linked to broader liberal social movements occurring in the first century BCE.

Emerging independent expressions and behaviors of a new generation of Roman women help to illustrate the dichotomy of tradition and change. Until the first century BCE, Roman husbands had long enjoyed relaxed scrutiny for

---

55 Suetonius, *Life of Julius Caesar*, 45.
56 Martial, *Epigram* 11. 37, in Wilner, "Roman Beauty Culture," 31.
57 Juvenal, *The Second Satire*, 2.64-82.
58 Juvenal, *The Third Satire*, 3.322, 81, 58-80.
59 Pliny, *Natural History*, 33.7, 35.261, 35.299, with Finlay, "Weaving the Rainbow," 421.
60 Cicero, *De Inventione*, 1.4-5; *De Oratore*, 42.199; Quintilian, *Institutio Oratoria*, 8.4.28; 4.2.88-95.
61 Juvenal, *The Third Satire*, 86.
62 Plutarch, *Life of Mark Anthony*, 2.482.

their sexual indiscretions, but the growth of the empire altered that imbalance in gender relations. The vast sums of wealth, foreigners, and slaves that poured into Rome as a result of conquests in the Greek east relaxed the social mores of many in high status. Newly affluent Romans wishing to display their status hosted lavish banquets attended by courtesans, often drawn from the new populations of foreigners, freedwomen, and slaves, many of whom offered sexual favors to Roman men. Within this heady atmosphere of empire and entertainment culture, Roman women who possessed wealth, owned property, and could divorce their husbands increasingly began to challenge traditional gender expectations by pursuing their own desires, including sexual fulfillment from men outside of their marriages.[63] By the end of the first century BCE, these "new women" caught the attention of Catullus, Propertius, Ovid, and Plautus, who penned poems and plays about older noblewomen chasing younger men, husbands prostituting their wives, and dowry-wealthy women purchasing the attention of men.[64] The changing sexual mores were so common that Plutarch advised newly wedded men to keep their young wives entertained, lest they seek other men to satisfy their desires.[65]

Concern over deteriorating values reached the highest levels of government by the time Augustus established his authority over the Republic in 27 BCE. So many men and women had delayed marriage that he sought legal measures to encourage a return to social decorum. The 'moral reforms' issued by Augustus (c. 18-9 BCE) sought to uphold the *mos maiorum*: marriage was regulated to match proper social groups together; adultery became a public crime punishable by exile or death; the unmarried were prohibited from inheriting money or property (widowed men and women were given one and two years respectively to remarry); widows who had produced three living children were not required to remarry, and inheritances were taxed for those without children.[66] Each of these provisions redirected Romans to core values of *pietas*: duty to the family and the state. But Augustus's attempts to reform lax individuals were largely unsuccessful, even as the emperor's own household was shaken by a "new woman."

Augustus's married daughter, Julia (c. 39 BCE-14 CE), had a reputation for living an extravagant life punctuated by promiscuity and risqué dress. Anecdotal stories record her independent spirit: Julia reportedly had "flocks of lovers" and had nocturnal sexual rendezvous in the Roman Forum—even on the Rostra, the

---

63   On legal rights of Roman women, see Susan Treggiari, *Roman Marriage*: Iusti Coniuges *From the Time of Cicero to the Time of Ulpian* (Oxford: Clarendon, 1991), 323-364, 435-480. On the independent nature of Roman noblewomen, see Elaine Fantham, "The 'New Woman': Representation and Reality," in *Women in the Classical World* (New York: Oxford University, 1994), 280-292; R.A. Bauman, *Women and Politics in Ancient Rome* (London: Routledge, 1992), 78-90.

64   Fantham, "The 'New Woman': Representation and Reality," 285; E. Green, *The Erotics of Domination: Male Desire and Mistress in Latin Love Poetry* (Baltimore: Johns Hopkins, 1998), 105-106; T. Crisafulli, "Representations of Feminine: The Prostitutes in Roman Comedy," in *Ancient History in a Modern University: The Ancient Near East, Greece, and Rome*, ed. T.W. Hillard, R.A. Kearsley, C.E.V Nixon, A.M. Nobbs, (Grand Rapids: Eerdmans, 1998), v. 1, 223.

65   Plutarch, "Advice to Bride and Groom," 140B.

66   *Lex Iulia de Maritandis Ordinibus* regulated marriage; *Lex Iulia de Adulteriis Coercendis* criminalized adultery; *Lex Papia Poppaea* penalized the unmarried; *Lex Iulia de vicesima hereditatum* taxed inheritances for the childless.

public platform on which senators addressed the citizen assemblies;[67] Augustus frequently counseled Julia to moderate her luxurious mode of life and her choice of extravagantly-dressed friends, but when he registered his displeasure after she appeared at a gladiatorial show with men much younger who were dressed in ornate styles, Julia replied, "these men will be old when I'm old." After someone commented on her unabashed promiscuity, she described herself as "a ship careful not to take on too many passengers."[68] Whether these stories can actually be attributed to Julia is not of concern here, for they show that a tradition about this imperial "new woman" had reached iconic levels long after her fall from grace.

In 2 BCE, Augustus ordered Julia's arrest for her part in an embarrassing sexual scandal that involved several leading senators and aristocrats. He banished her to a small island where she lived in solitary confinement without access to wine or other luxury.[69] The sternness of Augustus's justice shocked many in Rome, triggering several popular protests and petitions for her release.[70] Public disapproval was so vocal that Augustus convened public assemblies to justify his actions, upon which he cursed the citizens with his wish that they have daughters like Julia. While Augustus resisted outright repeal of his judgment, he did transfer Julia's interment after five years to the southern Italian city of Rhegium, where she lived under less stringent conditions. However, when her husband Tiberius succeeded Augustus as emperor in 14 CE, he reinstated the severe penalty of restricting Julia to solitary confinement in a single room without any company until her death, which was rumored to have been by starvation.[71]

The episode of Julia Augusta is most revealing for the emerging cultural realities represented by Roman "new women." This generation of women openly embraced a lifestyle of independent thought and action that included material goods and sexual liberation. At every level of their lives, color and adornment were the expressions of their independence. Their continued presence in Roman society emphasizes the fact that the concerted effort by some elites to maintain their sense of *pietas* was, in some sense, a bygone reality. On one level, one must seriously consider how these popular reactions against Augustus and repeated appeals for clemency influenced his familial right to punish a family member. On another level, these reactions directed against the government expose how popular sentiment regarding women's freedoms had worked on the traditions of the *mos maiorum*. Although Tiberius reasserted his legal right to punish his wife for adultery, Suetonius recorded the actions of the two emperors differently. Whereas Augustus was remembered as a father who was plagued by the familial misfortunes of the untimely death of his heirs and of the presence of independent-minded women, Tiberius was infamous for his associations with savage political

---

67   Seneca, *On Benefits*, 6.32.1.

68   Macrobius, *Saturnalia*, 2.5.1-10.

69   Suetonius, *Life of Augustus*, 65.3. Julia's solitary confinement was on the Island of Ventotene, near Naples. Augustus was so disturbed by Julia's sexual independence that he forbade any man to visit her without his approval and even then, he required a full report of visitor's build, complexion, and any noticeable scars.

70   Ibid.

71   Ibid.

violence, cruelty, and sexual perversions.[72] For Suetonius, a clear distinction had been made: though "new women" may have been an undesirable social element for some, they were clearly accepted by popular Roman sentiment. Nevertheless, Julia's fate and the fate of other women at the hands of their husbands and fathers expose deep patrician anxieties linked to popular non-conformist culture.[73]

As with the Greek traditionalists before them, Roman conservatives resisted but ultimately had to give way to the insatiable appetite for color and adornment and the status it conveyed. By the second-century CE, private use of purple in the Roman world was at its highest; in some areas such as Egypt, use of bright colors was nearly universal in all levels of society.[74] Still, at the height of its consumption, another sector criticized purple, this time early Christians who applied new meanings to color and status in the Mediterranean world.

Color and Morality in Early Christianity

Early Christian leaders promoted a culture of modesty and decorum as had their Roman elite predecessors. Partly, this message of modesty targeted the Roman "new women," who, by the first century CE, formed a significant portion of influential converts to the new faith. Despite their conversions, many of these women retained some of their previous behavior. Within the early Christian community, then, messages drawing a distinction between standards of Roman status and the more modest and humble Christian values began to appear. Efforts to reign in lavish dress, drinking, and promiscuity, while fostering self-control, cultivating respect of others, and patience were specific goals of some New Testament letters extolling new women to "dress themselves in orderly adornment with propriety and modesty, not with braided hair or gold or pearls or flashy clothes."[75] Perhaps no one did more to construct a framework for Christian restraint and modesty against materialism than the Bishop of Alexandria, Clement (c. 150-215).

Clement's *Paedagogus*, or "The Instructor," written about 200 CE, attacked adornment of material culture with vehemence. Silver and gold were "only deceptions of the vision."[76] Impractical and "senseless" as items for display, the precious metals required excessive resources to obtain. They were difficult to acquire and keep safe, and were not adapted for regular use. According to Clement, Christian perfection required that one be "stripped of arrogance and fading display of things" that were not practical for many tasks. The "stupidity of luxury" prevents one from seeing that earthenware bowls and lamps work as well as those made of costly silver and gold, a servant's bed works the same as an ivory couch, and a goat

---

72   Suetonius, *Life of Augustus*, 65.1-2; Suetonius, *Life of Tiberius*, 61-66, 75; Tacitus, *Annals*, 6.51.

73   Elaine Fantham, *Julia Augusti: The Emperor's Daughter* (London: Routledge, 2006), 1-32, 124-134; For Augustus' view of sexual indiscretion see, Judith Ginsberg, *Representing Agrippina: Constructions of Female Power in the Early Roman Empire* (New York: Oxford University, 2006), 123-130; with Bruce Winter, *Roman Wives, Roman Widows: The Appearance of New Women and the Pauline Communities* (Grand Rapids: Eerdmans Publishing, 2003), 21-31.

74   Reinhold, *History of Purple*, 53-54.

75   1 Timothy 2:9. For similar references see 1 Timothy 5:11-15, 1 Corinthians 11:2-16, , Titus 2:3-5; see Winter, *Roman Wives, Roman Widows*, 77-119, 123-130, 141-167.

76   Clement, *Paedagogus*, 2.3.

skin covering is as sufficient to keep warm as a purple bedspread.[77] For his model, Clement turned to Jesus, writing that the Christ ate from common bowls and reclined on the ground: "He [Jesus] did not bring a silver foot bowl from heaven."[78] The bishop went so far as to condemn the methods of production of gold and silverware; poisonous fumes and billows of smoke were unhealthy for the workers and the environment. Gold and silver objects and jewelry may have been useless in Clement's judgment, but color adornment on the body was especially disconcerting because it altered the natural state of God's design for the body.

Though the state of sin entered into by Adam and Eve in the Garden of Eden could not be undone, Clement believed that humans could attempt to limit their separation from God by resisting temptation in all forms. Living simply and resisting material adornment and excess was important for remaining as close to the divine as possible and not increasing the schism between God and humans. In essence, with each application of rouge on the lips and white powder on the face, for every layer of brightly-colored clothing worn on the body and sparkling jewelry dangling from the ears or clamped on the wrists and fingers, one increased the distance between humankind and God. Like Adam and Eve expelled from Eden in shameful sin, Christians in Clement's community unknowingly continued to walk away from paradise by embracing popular forms of material culture. In this way, unlike earlier Greek and Roman calls for traditional modesty, Clement's rhetoric has a distinct quality of morality with the burden of salvation attached to it. Thus, the function of simple clothing and wares, unprocessed by costly dyes and metals, was vital because these items were believed to create a more divine condition by halting one's march toward damnation.

Proclaiming that simple dress and neutral colors directed one toward the righteousness of God was only one component of Clement's rhetoric; another part revealed that extravagantly dressed Christians might be servants of evil. For Clement, simple clothing reflected truth, while colored garments shimmered with deception that corrupted the divine plan. Clement wrote:

> What are we to imagine ought to be said of the love of ornament, and dyeing of wool and variety of colors... and still more, of artificial hair and wreathed curls, of the staining of the eyes... and painting with rouge and white lead, and dyeing of the hair and the wicked arts that are employed in such deceptions?[79]

In other words, personal adornment distracts from the 'truth' of a person. For Clement, applied color on the body and dress served no useful purpose except to "inflame greedy eyes... for mischievous voluptuousness." Purple dress, in particular, was "stupid and luxurious," used only by "crafty women and effeminate men" who were "insane" for the purpose of "inflaming the lusts."[80] Augustine (354-430), Bishop of Hippo, wrote of such a seductive hold that colors had upon him:

---

77 Ibid.
78 Ibid.
79 Ibid., 2.9.
80 Ibid., 2.11.

> The eyes delight in fair and varied forms, and bright and pleasing colors. Let these not take possession of my soul! ...The pleasures of sight affect me all the time I am awake. There is no rest from them given me... For daylight, that queen of the colors, floods all that we look upon everywhere I go during the day. It flies about me in manifold forms and soothes me even when I am busy about other things, not noticing it. And it presents itself so forcibly that if it is suddenly withdrawn it is looked for with longing, and if it is long absent the mind is saddened.[81]

These concerns about the deceptive nature of processed color and destroying God's natural design suggest a subtle image of Adam and Eve's temptation by demonic forces. The first man and woman may have been tricked by the serpent in the Garden of Eden, but both were weakened and made vulnerable by desire. Clement's provocative message here was that people were willingly deceiving each other, thereby participating in the destruction of souls. Without proclaiming it directly, Clement accused those who wrapped themselves in the culture of material adornment and engaged in the sexual behavior associated with it of being servants of the demonic. This very simple but very profound step to becoming an agent of the Devil was of dire concern for many Christians.

Within the Christian ascetic movement in particular was an emphasis on resisting physical forms of temptation. In many ways, popular asceticism emerged in Egypt as a rejection against the perceived decadent lifestyles and cultural status quo of many new converts to Christianity after the Emperor Constantine legalized and supported the faith in 313.[82] No longer was Christianity an opposing movement with outsider status, but it was integrated into Roman life more broadly. To ascetics, cultural practices such as beautification with color and adornment were deliberate means of temptation by embracing the material world and drifting away from God.

Ascetic holy men and women appear as popular Christian heroes because of their reputation for renunciation of sexual activity and material culture. They adopted a radical lifestyle, wearing rough dress often made from coarse materials, and maintaining rituals of physical self-chastisement and self-denial of food and rest through lengthy prayer vigils.[83] Tradition held that ascetics used the powers gained by these rituals to heal the sick and battle the embodiment of temptation—demons.[84] Perhaps not surprisingly, some of these demons were personified

---

[81] Augustine, *Confessions*, 10.51.

[82] Traditional Roman practices that countered Christian theological morality remained constant long after Constantine. See, Ramsay MacMullen, "What Difference Did Christianity Make?" *Historia: Zeitschrift für Alte Geschichte*, v. 35.3 (1986): 322-343; W.V. Harris, "Child-Exposure in the Roman Empire," *The Journal of Roman Studies*, v. 84 (1994): 1-22; Elizabeth Clark, "Antifamilial Tendencies in Ancient Christianity," *Journal of the History of Sexuality*, v. 5.3 (1995): 356-380; Joshua Tate, "Christianity and the Legal Status of Abandoned Children in the Later Roman Empire," *Journal of Law and Religion*, v. 24.1 (2008/2009): 123-141.

[83] See Peter Brown, *The Body and Society: Men, Women, and Sexual Renunciation in Early Christianity* (New York: Columbia University Press, 1988).

[84] For general background see, Peter Brown, "The Rise and Function of the Holy Man in Late Antiquity," *The Journal of Roman Studies*, v. 61 (1971): 80-101; Patricia Cox Miller, *Biography in Late Antiquity: A Quest for the Holy Man* (Berkeley: University of California, 1983); Susanna Elm, *"Virgins of God": The Making of Asceticism in*

as those who would have represented the outer world, or uncivilized 'other' to Egyptians—their neighbors to the south, the Ethiopians.[85] In Christian hagiography, darker skinned Ethiopians came to symbolize sexual temptation. The *Life of Anthony*, hagiography's earliest ascetic model, provided the first occurrence. Anthony of Egypt (c. 350), was most strongly tested by an Ethiopian boy who represented a demon of fornication.[86] Hereafter, Ethiopians became stock symbols of demonic fornication in the hagiography of ascetic monks. Stories include those of a monk who was tempted by dreams of an Ethiopian girl as she gathered corn; demons who appeared as Ethiopian women to arouse a monk into fornication; and a monk who succumbed to delirium when a demon, disguised as an Ethiopian woman, pierced him with an arrow infused with sexual desire—the bow and arrow were signature weapons of Ethiopian women.[87]

The portrayal of black people as sexualized beings, or dangerous 'others,' had been present in parts of the Roman world before the fourth century. In Rome, during the first three centuries, when "new women" were raising concerns about lax sexual morals, some upper-class Roman women were known to engage in sexual relations with lower status black men. This behavior was seen as a particular social breach by critics whose negative attitudes about sexual activities with unprivileged black people appear in the contemporary poetry of Martial, Juvenal, and Claudian.[88] These anxieties related to inappropriate associations were further intensified by regional security concerns in Egypt. Egyptian and Roman authorities also expressed fear of a tribal raiding group known as the Blemmyes, who roamed the regions of southern Egypt attacking Roman military outposts, villages, and trade routes since Augustus gained control of Egypt after defeating Cleopatra and Marc Anthony in 31 BCE. These nomads had become associated generally with black Africans and, by extension, Ethiopians who lived farther south.[89] Though the Roman cultural ridicule and fear of eroticized blackness and power is complex, each of these early depictions of black people lacks any depiction of the demonic.

It is within this unique context of Roman cultural associations of blackness with sexual promiscuity and fear that early Christian language of salvation and sin synthesized spiritual negativity with blackness.[90] The symbols of light in opposition to darkness were potent images to that effect. Notwithstanding the copious references to light and darkness in the Hebrew Testament, early Christian writings employ the dichotomy of light and darkness in terms of behavior,

---

Late Antiquity (New York: Oxford University, 1996).

85   Lloyd A. Thompson, *Romans and Blacks* (Norman: University of Oklahoma Press, 1987), 57-85. Thompson produces a foundational work examining the complexity of Roman identity, ethnic rhetoric and discourse.

86   Anthanasius, *Life of Anthony*, 6.

87   Palladius, *Lausiac History*, 23; John Cassian, *On Impurity*, 1.67; Palladius, "Of Fornication," in *Apophthegmata Patrum*, 579; cited in Gay L. Byron, *Symbolic Blackness and Ethnic Difference in Early Christian Literature* (New York: Routledge, 2002), 46-47. On Ethiopian weapons, see Strabo, *Geography*, 17.2.3.

88   Thompson, *Romans and Blacks*, 26-49, esp. 26-31.

89   Byron, *Symbolic Blackness and Ethnic Difference in Early Christian*, 82-84.

90   Thompson, *Romans and Blacks*, 112-113; David Brakke, "Ethiopian Demons: Male Sexuality, the Black-Skinned Other, and the Monastic Self," *Journal of the History of Sexuality*, v. 10.3/4, Special Issue: Sexuality in Late Antiquity (2001): 501-535.

emphasizing that one should be alert, sober, and watchful in order to prepare for the coming daylight of God.[91] In the charged rhetoric of darkness as representing distance from God, early Christian communities in Egypt, North Africa, Palestine, and Asia Minor first commonly called the Devil "the Black One" (Greek: *ho melas*). The anonymous first-century writer of the "Epistle of Barnabas" (c. 70-115 CE) employed the rhetoric of "the Black One" to emphasize the internal vices and sins threatening communal salvation.[92] Fourth-century Egyptian monk Macarius synthesized these notions in his homilies, saying that Christians were the "sons of light" pitted against the false apostles of the "children of darkness."[93] By declaring membership as the "sons of light," Egyptian Christians like Macarius claimed to be the representatives of God's light, and by extension, God's authority on earth. Thus, the discourse of black demonology grew in the Egyptian Christian mind partly from these symbolic representations of positive and negative forces in Egypt.

Despite the negative Christian association with black, it became, at the same time, a symbol of redemption. Repentance is a central theme of the Christian message. The term appears no less than twenty-one times in the Gospels.[94] Without it one cannot prepare for the coming of God, but just how one repents for sins of the past was not clearly defined. Caring for the needy, proclaiming the Christian message, and trying not to commit more sin may be 'visible' actions of repentance, but they might be temporary states of repentance in the sense that each act ends. In a very distinct way, color provided that opportunity for continuous self-expression of atonement. In another way, early Christianity revealed a complex set of Egyptian Christian anxieties regarding spiritual purity and salvation in which black was both a symbol of vice and sin but also a powerful color of atonement.[95] The third-century theologian Origen (c. 182-254) referred to blackness and Ethiopians in symbolic terms to represent all communities of the Christian church without the demonic negative traits.[96] Cyril, the bishop of Alexandria (c.376-444), wrote that all people were symbolically Ethiopians because their "dark minds are not yet illuminated by God's grace."[97] Similarly, the Christian writer Jerome (c. 347-420) explained blackness as a symbolic transitory state shared by all:

> At one time we were Ethiopians in our vices and sins. How so? Because our sins had blackened us. But afterwards we heard the words: "Wash yourselves

---

91 John 12:36; Ephesians 5:8; 1 Thessalonians 5:1-11. For a provocative interpretation of Biblical uses of 'light,' see Norman R. Petersen, *The Gospel of John and the Sociology of Light: Language and Characterization in the Fourth Gospel* (Valley Forge, PA: Trinity Press International, 1993), chapters 3-4.

92 "Epistle of Barnabas" 4:9, 18:1-2, 19:1-12, 20:1-2, with Byron, *Symbolic Blackness and Ethnic Difference in Early Christian*, 60-69.

93 Macarius, *Spriritual Homilies,* 2.1-5; with Thompson, *Romans and Blacks*, 112.

94 Matthew 3:2, 3:8, 3:11, 4:17, 11:20, 21:32; Mark 1:4, 1:15, 6:12; Luke 3:1, 3:3, 3:8, 5:32, 13:3, 13:5, 15:7, 16:30, 17:3, 17:4, 24:47. No mention of the doctrine appears in the Gospel of John.

95 David Brakke, *Demons and the Making of the Monk: Spiritual Combat in Early Christianity* (Cambridge: Harvard University, 2006), 127-181.

96 Byron, *Symbolic Blackness and Ethnic Difference in Early Christian*, 72-75.

97 Cyril, *Glaphyra, Explanatio in psalmos, fragments on Kings,* in *Patrologia Graeca* 69, col. 1188, cited in Thompson, *Romans and Blacks,* 112.

clean!" And we said: "Wash me, and I shall be whiter than snow." We are Ethiopians, therefore, who have been transformed from blackness into whiteness.[98]

The duality of blackness appears in its symbolizing original sin as well as redemption. In these examples, black represented two sides of the possible. On the one hand, it represented the sinfulness of humankind. Conversely, it remained a vital link to salvation in that all individuals were considered to be in a fallen, or 'blackened,' state. The color black served as a tactile visual reminder of the need for humility and repentance, which was essential for salvation. Thus, by extension, wearing dark clothing could provide one with a potent symbol that expressed one's repentance and served as an example of spiritual transformation. By donning black robes and tunics, holy individuals could live in a continuous state of humility before God, bound in each moment of spiritual salvation by the dark garment wrapped around the body or draped upon the head. In this fashion, monks wore black to live in a state of continual repentance while serving as examples for the greater community.

Pragmatically, black also fulfilled the values of material simplicity promoted by Clement. Garment production required no extravagant expense, thereby being more natural than the cost of producing purple, white, or other colors. Accordingly, devout Christians did not need to conform to popular fashion because an economic alternative to spiritual resonance existed. Dressing in black clothes provided another benefit for Christians: for those who could not endure the rigorous demands of an ascetic lifestyle, dark clothing could be an accessible form of piety with which Christians could display their devotion. In essence, black clothing provided opportunities for more Christians to distinguish themselves with sacred status through the association of color and repentance.

Application of dark tones became symbols of holiness outside of Egypt as well. When the monastic movement emerged and captured the popular imagination of Roman culture in the fourth-century, it offered different images of holiness than had been used in early Roman Christianity. In Italy, the bishop Martin of Tours (d. 397) reportedly smeared black and grey ashes over his face and body in ritual to entice divine aid.[99] While fifth-century official episcopal vestments were white, the bishop's daily garment was a simple *paenula* or sleeveless woolen cloak, dyed brown or black.[100] This integration of dark colors into the Roman Christian lexicon and use occurred at the same time that purple and other vibrant colors were being given Christian meanings as Christianity was adopted by the Roman state.

The Late Roman World and Beyond

When Christians were persecuted, they found deep meaning in disengaging themselves from the material world in preparation for a heavenly state to come;

---

98   Jerome, "Homily 18 on Psalm 86," in *St. Jerome: Homilies on Psalms* (Westminster, 1964), 140; with Byron, *Symbolic Blackness*, 55-57.

99   Sulpicius Severus, *Dialogues*, 3.6.

100 Jane Hayward, "Sacred Vestments as They Developed in the Middle Ages," *The Metropolitan Museum of Art Bulletin*, v. 29.7 (1971): 299-309, esp. 301.

however, the impulse to separate from the material world became less pressing when the religion unified with the state. Previous taboo colors flourished in the period between the emperors Constantine, who ended persecution in 313, and Theodosius I, who declared Christianity the religion of the Roman state in 380. Purple and the brilliant colors associated with ornate dress, once considered suspect, were enthusiastically used by a greater percent of the population and the state apparatus. Perhaps no single factor did more to silence the polemics against purple than the popular desire to express Christian virtues through imagery. Churches built under Constantine's rule were lavishly decorated with multicolored marble, mosaics, and paintings applied with brilliant colors, in particular silver and purple, reflecting the popular vogue of the period.[101] Traditional imperial color symbols extended to images of the divine itself: purple was adapted to iconic mosaics and paintings of Jesus, Mary, and angels.[102] Eventually, these new sacred colors were associated with the emerging leaders of the late Roman world—the bishops. Apart from the tradition of darker tones for clergy, between the ninth and tenth centuries, liturgical priestly vestment became increasingly ornate and codified with bright colors.[103] This transformation of color values reveals an important element foundational to early Christian identity. Persecution had helped define what a true Christian was, and opposition to its values had identified and solidified cultural boundaries. However, unification of the state with Christianity undermined these first-century invectives. With fewer cultural distinctions between the two, there was no need to oppose the use of bright colors and adornment.

By the fifth century, previous Roman aversions to other questionable eastern tastes were also in transition. New fashion trends that were non-Roman in origin swept through the eastern and western Roman provinces. In telling examples of cultural transference, despite war with and continual threat from Persia, the Roman Emperor Justinian (r. 527-565) and all emperors thereafter adopted the distinctive imperial Persian soft scarlet-red shoes embroidered with pearls in an eastern style.[104] Barbarian attire was in high demand. Hunnic-styled bright tunics, shirts, trousers, and shoes won over all levels of Constantinople's population.[105] The Byzantine historian Procopius described the notorious socio-political gang called the "Blues" as wearing the flamboyant Hunnic shirt, known for its loosely constructed body tucked into the trousers and its ballooning sleeves with tight cuffs, exaggerating the man's physique so that it would appear more muscular.[106] The Blues also sported long mustaches and beards in the "Persian style," while wearing their hair in Hunnic fashion—cut short on the forehead to the temples and grown long and flowing in the back.[107]

---

101   Cyril Mango, *The Art of the Byzantine Empire, 312-1453* (Toronto: University of Toronto Press, 1986), 3-18; with Ramsay MacMullen, "Some Pictures in Ammianus Marcellinus," *Art Bulletin* 46 (1964): 69-90.

102   Reinhold, *History of Purple*, 65; with R. Delebrueck, *Die Spätantike Kaiserornat*, in *Die Antike* 8 (1932): 20-21.

103   Hayward, "Sacred Vestments," 301.

104   Jean Ebersolt, *Les Arts Somptuaries de Byzance: Étude sur L'Art Impérial de Constantinople* (Paris: Ernest Leroux, 1923), 39.

105   Ebersolt, *Les Arts Somptuaries de Byzance*, 38.

106   Procopius, *Secret History*, 7.11-14.

107   Ibid., 7.8-10.

Eastern influences were not limited to men. Brilliantly decorated mosaics of the empress Justina with her male and female entourage displayed at the Basilica San Vitale in Ravenna, Italy, depict a dazzling array of gowns in gold, red, violet, blue, green, yellow, white, and brown. Pearl jewelry and footwear were worn in distinct Persian designs.[108] Presumably as a result of the popularity of the new imperial style, the Emperor Heraclius (r. 610-641) sponsored Persian weavers in Constantinople to support the demand for colored textiles.[109] Increased need for purples and reds required control of production resources. Although the imperial court of Constantinople retained the high-grade Tyrian purple for itself, a broader section of the population had access to lower quality dyes derived from widely available and inexpensive fruit and vegetable sources.[110] By the fifth century, use of color and adornment had been integrated into the cultures throughout the Mediterranean world and were no longer resisted or viewed with suspicion.

In the first millennium BCE, color and adornment were the most visible elements that expressed a society's cultural identity. Efforts to define and maintain these cultural boundaries throughout the history of ancient Greek and Roman civilizations reveal processes of cultural change over time. Initially, conservative Greek and Roman leaders criticized the ever-present influences of Persian sophistication prominently displayed through color and adornment. Yet the consuming interests of a multitude of individuals who adorned themselves in gleaming colors present a paradox; cultures can adopt in curious ways that which they appear to reject. Greek and Roman communal self-identification and cultural development were dependent upon those neighboring traditions which were contrived as decadent and corrupt. Yet slow revolutions altered the carefully constructed values of each. For the ancient Greeks, the rhetoric of modesty and restraint promoted virtues of egalitarian principles emblematic of Greek-style democracies; however, elites adopted a taste for the resource-rich and brilliantly-colored Persian Empire. Cultural transformation in Rome was, in part, driven by a new generation of independent-minded individuals in the first century BCE who sought their own pleasures through material expression. In a rapidly expanding empire, patricians trying to maintain the *mos maiorum* and *pietas* values were undermined by the "new women" of their own social class. Modest fashion and personal adornment blurred the old social distinctions. As Christianity moved from outsider status to a state religion, a curious inversion of values took shape. Purple, a color that had been maligned by Greek, Roman, and Christian leaders alike had been incorporated into the religion's liturgical needs. Simultaneously, the ancient color of royalty was joined by another color that both repelled and worked on the Christian mind: along with purple, black could not be regulated or restricted, and it conveyed its own powerful spiritual message. Modesty and extravagance in color and adornment came to co-exist in the popular Mediterranean culture of the public sphere and private search for salvation.

---

108   Ebersolt, *Les Arts Somptuaries de Byzance*, 36-38, 42.

109   John Gage, *Color and Culture: Practice and Meaning from Antiquity to Abstraction* (New York: Little Brown, 1993), 62; with Ebersolt, *Les Arts somptuaries de Byzance*, 125, 143, and C. Delvoye, "Les Tissus Byzantines," *Corsi d'arte Ravennata e Bizantina* 16 (1969), 126-127.

110   Reinhold, *History of Purple*, 58-61.

Bibliography

Ancient Sources in Translation

Aeschylus, *Persians*. Vol. 1. Translated by Alan. H. Sommerstein. Loeb Classical Library 145. Cambridge, MA: Harvard University Press, 2009.

Arrian. *Anabasis*. Vol. 1. Translated by P.A. Brunt. Loeb Classical Library 236. Cambridge, MA: Harvard University Press, 1976.

Athanasius. "Life of Anthony." In *Life of Antony, Select Writings of Athanasius*. Translated by H. Ellershaw, Library of Nicene and post Nicene Fathers 2.4. New York, 1924, reprint. 1957, 195-221.

Augustine. *Confessions*. Translated by R S Pine-Coffin. New York: Penguin Books, 1961, reprint 1985.

Cicero. *Against Catiline*. New York : St. Martin's Press, 1964.

_____. *Against Verres*, vol. 7-8, Loeb Classical Library. Cambridge, MA: Harvard University Press,

_____. *On the Composition of Arguments*. In *The Orations of Marcus Tullius Cicero*, vol. 4, translated by C.D. Yonge. London: George Bell & Sons, 1888, 241-380.

_____. *De Inventione* (*On Invention*). Translated by H. M. Hubbell. The Loeb Classical Library 386. Cambridge, MA: Harvard University Press, 1949.

_____. *De Oratore.* (*On the Orator*). Books 1-2. Translated by E. W. Sutton and H. Rackman. The Loeb Classical Library 348. Cambridge, MA: Harvard University Press, 1942. Revised, 1948.

Clement of Alexandria. *Paedagogus*. Translated by Simon P. Wood. *Christ the Educator*. New York: Fathers of the Church, Inc., 1954.

Quintus Curtius Rufus. *The History of Alexander*. Translated by John Yardley. Penguin Classics, 1984.

Diodorus Siculus. *Library of History.* Vol. 8. Translated by Bradford Welles. Loeb Classical Library 422. Cambridge, MA: Harvard University Press, 1963.

Dionysius of Halicarnassus. *Roman Antiquities*. Vol. 2, Translated by Earnest Cary. Loeb Classical Library 347. Cambridge, MA: Harvard University Press, 1939.

Galen. *Method of Medicine.* Vol. 2. Translated by Ian Johnston. Loeb Classical Library 517. Cambridge, MA: Harvard University Press, 2011.

Herodotus. *Histories*. (*The Persian Wars*). Vol. 1-4. Translated by A. D. Godley. Loeb Classical Library 117-120. Cambridge, MA: Harvard University Press, 1925.

Hippocrates. *On Airs, Waters and Places*, 23. Vol.1, Translated by W.H.S. Jones. Loeb Classical Library 147. Cambridge, MA: Harvard University Press, 1923.

Homer. *Iliad.* Vol. 1. Translated by A.T. Murray. Loeb Classical Library 104. Cambridge, MA: Harvard University Press, 1919.

_____. *Odyssey.* Vol. 1. Trans. Translated by A.T. Murray. Loeb Classical Library 104. Cambridge, MA: Harvard University Press, 1919.

Jerome. "Homily 18 on Psalm 86." In *St. Jerome: Homilies on Psalms.* Westminster, 1964, 140.

Juvenal. *Satires.* (*Juvenal and Persius*). Translated by Susanna Morton Braund. Loeb Classical Library 91. Cambridge, MA: Harvard University Press, 2004.

Livy. *History of Rome.* Vol. 9. Translated by Evan T. Sage. Loeb Classical Library 295. Cambridge, MA: Harvard University Press, 1935.

Macarius. *Spiritual Homilies,* 2.1-5. In *Fifty Spiritual Homilies of St. Macarius the Egyptian.* Translated by A.J. Mason. New York: The MacMillan Company, 1921.

Macrobius. *Saturnalia,* 2.5.1-10. Translated by Robert A. Kaster. Loeb Classical Library 510. Cambridge, MA: Harvard University Press, 2011.

Martial. *Epigram.* Vol. 1. Translated by D.R. Shockleton Bailey. Loeb Classical Library 480. Cambridge, MA: Harvard University Press, 1993.

Plato. *The Republic.* Vol. 1. Loeb Classical Library 237. Cambridge, MA: Harvard University Press, 2013.

Pliny. *Natural History.* Vol. 9. Translated by H. Rackham. Loeb Classical Library 394. Cambridge, MA: Harvard University Press, 2013.

Plutarch. "Advice to Bride and Groom." *Moralia.* Vol. 2. Translated by Frank Cole Babbitt. Loeb Classical Library 222. Cambridge, MA: Harvard University Press, 1928.

_____. "Life of Alexander." *Parallel Lives,* Vol. 12. Translated by Bernadotte Perrin. Loeb Classical Library 99. Cambridge, MA: Harvard University Press, 1919.

_____. *"Life of Julius Caesar."* *Parallel Lives.* Vol. 12. Translated by Bernadotte Perrin. Loeb Classical Library 99. Cambridge, MA: Harvard University Press, 1919.

_____. "Life of Eumenes." *Parallel Lives.* Vol. 13. Translated by Bernadotte Perrin. Loeb Classical Library 100. Cambridge, MA: Harvard University Press, 1919.

_____. "Life of Marius." *Parallel Lives.* Vol. 101, Translated by Bernadotte Perrin. Loeb Classical Library 101. Cambridge, MA: Harvard University Press, 1920.

_____. "Life of Pericles." *Parallel Lives.* Vol. 3. Translated by Bernadotte Perrin. Loeb Classical Library 65. Cambridge, MA: Harvard University Press, 1920.

———. "Life of Tiberius Gracchus." *Parallel Lives*. Vol. 10. Translated by Bernadotte Perrin. Loeb Classical Library 102. Cambridge, MA: Harvard University Press, 1921.

———. "Life of Marc Anthony." *Parallel Lives*. Vol. 9. Translated by Bernadotte Perrin. Loeb Classical Library 101. Cambridge, MA: Harvard University Press, 1920.

Polybius. *Histories*, vol. 4. Translated by W.R. Paton. Loeb Classical Library 159. Cambridge, MA: Harvard University Press, 2011.

Procopius. *Secret History*. Translated by Richard Atwater. New York: Covici Friede; Chicago, Il: P. Covicii, 1927, reprinted, Ann Arbor, MI: University of Michigan Press, 1961.

Quintilian. *Institutio Oratoria (The Orator's Education)*. Vol. 2-3. Translated by Donald A. Russell. Loeb Classical Library 125, 126. Cambridge, MA: Harvard University Press, 2002.

Strabo. *Geography*. Vol. 8. Translated by Horace Leonard Jones. Loeb Classical Library 267. Cambridge, MA: Harvard University Press, 1932.

Suetonius. "Life of Julius Caesar." *Lives of the Twelve Caesars*. Vol. 1. Translated by J.C. Rolfe. Loeb Classical Library 31. Cambridge, MA: Harvard University Press, 1914.

Sulpicius Severus. *Dialogues*. Translated by B.M. Peebles. In *The Fathers of the Church. A New Translation* 7. Washington (D.C.): Catholic University of America Press, 1949, 179-427.

Tacitus. *Annals*. Books 4-6, 11-12. Translated by John Jackson. Loeb Classical Library 312. Cambridge, MA: Harvard University Press, 1937.

The "Epistle of Barnabas." In *The Apostle Fathers*. Edited by J.B. Lightfoot and J.R. Harmer; 2nd edition by Michael W. Holmes. Grand Rapids, MI: Baker Book House, 1992.

Xenophon. "Cyrus." *Cyropaedia*. Vol. 1-2. Translated by Walter Miller. Loeb Classical Library 51-52. Cambridge, MA: Harvard University Press, 1914.

Scholarship

Ball, Philip. *Bright Earth: The Invention of Colour*. London: Viking Press, 2001.

Bauman, R.A. *Women and Politics in Ancient Rome*. London: Routledge, 1992.

Bianchi, Robert Steven. "Symbols and Meanings." In *Gifts of the Nile: Ancient Egyptian Faience*. Edited by Florence Dunn Friedmann, 22-31. New York: Thames & Hudson, 1998.

Bolton, Herbert E. "The Black Robes of New Spain." *The Catholic Historical Review* 21, no. 3 (1935): 257-282.

Bosworth, Brian. "Alexander and the Iranians." *The Journal of Hellenic Studies* 100 (1980): 1-21.

Brakke, David. "Ethiopian Demons: Male Sexuality, the Black-Skinned Other, and the Monastic Self." *Journal of the History of Sexuality* 10, no. 3/4, Special Issue: Sexuality in Late Antiquity (2001): 501-535.

——. *Demons and the Making of the Monk: Spiritual Combat in Early Christianity*. Cambridge: Harvard University Press, 2006.

Brown, Peter. "The Rise and Function of the Holy Man in Late Antiquity." *The Journal of Roman Studies* 61 (1971): 80-101.

——. *The Body and Society: Men, Women, and Sexual Renunciation in Early Christianity*. New York: Columbia University Press, 1988.

Byron, Gay L. *Symbolic Blackness and Ethnic Difference in Early Christian*. New York: Routledge, 2002.

Clark, Elizabeth. "Antifamilial Tendencies in Ancient Christianity." *Journal of the History of Sexuality* 5, no. 3 (1995): 356-380.

——. "Ascetics, Class, and Gender." In *Late Ancient Christianity: A People's History of Christianity*. Vol. 2. Edited by Virginia Burrus. Minneapolis, MN: Augsburg Fortress, 2010.

Cox Miller, Patricia. *Biography in Late Antiquity: A Quest for the Holy Man*. Berkeley: University of California Press, 1983.

Crisafulli, T. "Representations of Feminine: The Prostitutes in Roman Comedy." In *Ancient History in a Modern University: The Ancient Near East, Greece, and Rome,* edited by T.W. Hillard, R.A. Kearsley, C.E.V Nixon, A.M. Nobbs, 222-229. Grand Rapids: Eerdmans, 1998.

Delebrueck, R. "Die Spätantike Kaiserornat." *Die Antike* 8 (1932): 20-21.

Delvoye, C. "Les Tissus Byzantines." *Corsi d'arte Ravennata e Bizantina* 16 (1969): 126-127.

Ebersolt, Jean. *Les Arts somptuaries de Byzance*: Étude sur L'Art Impérial de Constantinople. Paris: Ernest Leroux, 1923.

Elm, Susanna. *"Virgins of God": The Making of Asceticism in Late Antiquity.* New York: Oxford University Press, 1996.

Fantham, Elaine. "The 'New Woman': Representation and Reality." In *Women in the Classical World.* New York: Oxford University Press, 1994.

——. *Julia Augusti: The Emperor's Daughter*. London: Routledge, 2006.

Finlay, Robert. "Weaving the Rainbow: Visions of Color in World History." *Journal of World History* 18, no. 4 (2007): 414.

Gage, John. *Color and Culture: Practice and Meaning from Antiquity to Abstraction.* New York: Little Brown Press, 1993.

Gardner, J. W. "Blameless Ethiopians and Others." *Greece and Rome* 24, no. 2 (1977): 185-193.

Ginsberg, Judith. *Representing Agrippina: Constructions of Female Power in the Early Roman Empire*. New York: Oxford University Press, 2006.

Green, E. *The Erotics of Domination: Male Desire and Mistress in Latin Love Poetry*. Baltimore: Johns Hopkins, 1998.

Hall, Edith. *Inventing the Barbarian: Greek Self-Definition through Tragedy*. New York: Clarendon Press, 1989.

Harris, W.V. "Child-Exposure in the Roman Empire." *The Journal of Roman Studies* 84 (1994): 1-22.

Hartog, François. *The Mirror of Herodotus: The Representation of the Other in the Writing of History*. Translated by Janet Lloyd. Berkeley: University of California, 1988.

Hayward, Jane. "Sacred Vestments as They Developed in the Middle Ages." *The Metropolitan Museum of Art Bulletin* 29, no. 7 (1971): 299-309.

Hendrix, Elizabeth A. "Painted Early Cycladic Figures: An Exploration of Context and Meaning." *Hesperia: The Journal of the American School of Classical Studies in Athens* 72, n. 4 (Oct-Dec., 2003): 405-446.

Isaac, Benjamin. "Proto-Racism in Graeco-Roman Antiquity." *World Archaeology* 38, no. 1 (2006): 32-47.

Jensen, Lloyd. "Royal Purple of Tyre." *Journal of Near Eastern Studies* 22, no. 2 (1963): 104-118.

Johnston, Patricia A. "Poenulus 1, 2 and Roman Women." *Transactions of the American Philological Association* 110 (1980): 143-159.

Kawami, Trudy S. "Greek Art and Persian Taste: Some Animal Sculptures from Persepolis." *American Journal of Archaeology* 90, no. 3 (July, 1986): 259-267.

Lesky, A. "Aithiopika," *Hermes* 87 (1987): 27-38.

MacMullen, Ramsay. "What Difference Did Christianity Make?" *Historia: Zeitschrift für Alte Geschichte* 35, no. 3 (1986): 322-343.

Mango, Cyril. *The Art of the Byzantine Empire, 312-1453*. Toronto: University of Toronto Press, reprint 2000.

Miller, Margaret. *Athens and Persia in the Fifth Century BC: A Study in Cultural Receptivity*. New York: Cambridge University Press, 1997.

Petersen, Norman R. *The Gospel of John and the Sociology of Light: Language and Characterization in the Fourth Gospel*. Valley Forge, PA: Trinity Press International, 1993.

Rawlinson, Henry C. "On the Birs Nimrud, or The Great Temple of Borsippa." *The Journal of the Royal Asiatic Society of Great Britain and Ireland* (1855): 1-34.

Reinhold, Meyer. *History of Purple as a Status Symbol in Antiquity*. Brussels: Latomus, 1970.

Romm, James S. *The Edges of the Earth in Ancient Thought*. Princeton, NJ: Princeton University Press, 1992.

Sands, P. C. *The Client Princes of the Roman Empire under the Republic.* Cambridge, 1908.

Talbert, R.J.A. *The Senate of Imperial Rome.* Princeton, NJ: Princeton University Press, 1984.

Tate, Joshua. "Christianity and the Legal Status of Abandoned Children in the Later Roman

Empire," *Journal of Law and Religion* 24 no. 1 (2008/2009): 123-141.

Thompson, Lloyd A. *Romans and Blacks*. Norman, OK: University of Oklahoma Press, 1987.

Treggiari, Susan. *Roman Marriage*: Iusti Coniuges *From the Time of Cicero to the Time of Ulpian*. Oxford: Clarendon, 1991.

Vercoutter, Jean. Jean Leclant, Frank Snowden, and Jehan Desanges, *The Image of Black in Western Art I: From the Pharaohs to the Fall of the Roman Empire.* Cambridge, MA: Harvard University Press, 1976.

Wilner, Ortha. "Roman Beauty Culture." *The Classical Journal* 27, no. 1 (1931): 37.

Winter, Bruce W. *Roman Wives, Roman Widows: The Appearance of New Women and the Pauline Communities*. Grand Rapids: Eerdmans Publishing, 2003.

3

Color Symbolism in the Turko-Mongolian World

Timothy May

Color has played an important role in identity in Inner Asia for centuries, if not millennia.[1] Color in Inner Asia has marked direction, social status, royal titles, and even sacral identity. It is clear that not all colors are equal, and in the following specialized vocabulary, only a few colors of the spectrum are included. The key colors in the Turko-Mongolian world have been, in no particular order, *köke, kökö; khöke* (blue), *tsagaan, chaghan,* or *aq* (white*), shar, shara,* or *shira* (yellow), *altan* (gold), *kara* (black), and *kizil, ulaghan* or *ulaan* (red). The significance of the meanings of these colors has subtly altered over the centuries, yet each of the specialized colors denoted multiple categories of symbolism in the sacral and socio-political realms. While each category will be reviewed, the primary focus here will illustrate the use of these terms in connection to Turko-Mongolian polities and conclude with a discussion of the color application to one particular empire, whose appellation has eluded our understanding but was acknowledged by other Turko-Mongolian polities.

Although both Turks and Mongols came from Mongolia, they spoke different languages, albeit with a similar grammatical structure and, increasingly, shared many loan words. Linguists consider them, along with Tungusic (e.g. Manchu and other languages), to be part of the Altaic language family. In addition to related languages, the Turks and Mongols shared culture, primal religions (e.g. shamanism), and socio-political structures. Differences existed, but a Turk could exist in the Mongolian world and a Mongol could exist in the Turkic world without culture shock. Furthermore, with the rise of the Mongol Empire, greater mingling of Turks and Mongols occurred and resulted in the Turkicization of parts of the Mongol empire such as in the western regions (Central Asia, the Pontic and Caspian steppes, and in the Middle East), while in the eastern regions the Turkic population became more Mongolian. It is this intermingling of Turkic and Mongolian culture and ethnicity that is known as Turko-Mongolian.

---

1   This research was made possible with the generous support of Scott Jacobs. Any errors, of course, remain my own.

Although the sacral meaning cannot be completely divorced from the socio-political or even directional meaning of a color, this work will first investigate the sacral meaning of colors among Turko-Mongolian cultures and then the socio-political. A preliminary discussion of the sacral meaning of color is necessary as it influenced their perspective of the world, not only in a temporal sense, but also in terms of religion and culture, which intertwined with the socio-political meanings. This will then clarify the names of certain color-coded Turko-Mongolian states.

Sacral Meanings

Each color had a sacral meaning related to the traditional cosmology of the Turkic and Mongolian tribes of the Mongolian plateau: cosmos/heaven (blue), air (white), fire (red), water (black), earth (yellow).[2] The exact sacral significance of these colors evolved over time often due to outside influences such as Buddhism.

Blue

In terms of sacral meanings, *köke* or blue has been considered an auspicious and sacred color among most Inner Asia peoples for centuries. The Turkic empire that arose in Mongolia in the sixth century, after overthrowing the Ruruan (circa 375-552 CE), became known as the Köke or Gök Turk (Blue Turk). The color referred to their auspicious status due to Heaven or Tengri's favor. The Mongols, like all steppe polities before them, also considered blue an auspicious color, which is evinced in much of their cultural legacy. The familiar Chinese porcelain that frequently appears in white with blue designs became the dominant form of porcelain during the Yuan dynasty (1265-1368).[3] The Mongols introduced to China Persian artists who were acquainted with the Iranian use of cobalt blue dye in ceramic tiles. With this exchange, the dark blue design marked a transition in Chinese porcelain, reflecting the sacral nature of the color blue for the Mongols.[4] This sacral nature is also evident in the primary god of the Mongols, *Köke Möngke Tengri* or the Blue Eternal Heaven.[5] A visit to the steppes of Mongolia makes this appellation quite apparent. Furthermore, in the epic folklore, the Mongols consider themselves descendants of the offspring of a blue-grey wolf (*börte chino*) and a (*qo'ai maral*) fallow or white doe.[6] While the word to describe the wolf,

---

2   Munkh-Erdene Lhamsuren, "The Mongolian Nationality Lexicon: From the Chinggisid Lineage to Mongolian Nationality (From the seventeenth to the early twentieth century)," *Inner Asia* 8 (2006): 72. Also see Klaus Sagaster, *Die Weisse Geschichte (Čaɣan teüke)*, Asiatische Forschungen (Wiesbaden: Otto Harrassowitz, 1976).

3   James Millward, *The Silk Road: A Very Short Introduction* (Oxford: Oxford University Press, 2013), 105-106. Millward points out that the Tang Dynasty first used blue and white pottery, but the technique was different as the Tang artists painted cobalt blue over a white slip. The Yuan era pottery (and afterwards) painted the cobalt dye directly on the *kaolin* clay, glazed it and then fired the piece at a very high temperature. The Tang period blue and white ware does not appear to have been quite as popular either.

4   Timothy May, *The Mongol Conquests in World History* (London: Reaktion Books, 2012), 249. For more details on the Yuan era porcelain, see Yuka Kadoi, *Islamic Chinoiserie: The Art of Mongol Iran*, Edinburgh Studies in Islamic Art (Edinburgh: Edinburgh University Press, 2009), 39-73.

5   Walther Heissig, *The Religions of Mongolia*, trans. Geoffrey Samuel (Berkeley: University of California Press, 1980), 47-48.

6   *The Secret History of the Mongols*, § 1. There are various translations of *The Secret History of the Mongols*, with the 2003 edition by Igor de Rachewiltz being the most authoritative. The following editions in English and

börte, differed from *köke,* the color association is still clear because the animal is associated with *Tengri,* as *börte* describes the night sky.[7] At the same time, the animal is grounded in realism: blue wolves do not exist, yet a blue-grey wolf seems plausible, thus allowing for the heavenly connection with the sky. The entire *Secret History of the Mongols* is laden with heavenly symbolism to reinforce the idea that the rise of Chinggis Khan was the will of Tengri and was set in motion long before his birth.[8]

During the Second Conversion era, in which Buddhism became the dominant religion among the Mongols in the sixteenth and seventeenth centuries, additional uses of the sacral color blue appeared with Buddhist connotations.[9] Although the traditional heavenly symbolism remained, it was bolstered by Buddhist influences. With the Second Conversion, Chinggis Khan entered the Buddhist pantheon as Vajrapani. As Elisabetta Chiodo explains,

> The symbolic colour of Vajrapani and the Vajra Family is blue. The colour symbolism in Mongolian cosmology place the blue Mongols at the center of the empire established by Činggis [sic]. As a matter of fact, Galdan writes in his *Erdeni-yin erike* that the Mongols are called Blue Mongols because Činggis is an incarnation of the blue Vajrapani.[10]

Here we see a Buddhist interpretation of color symbolism applied to pre-Buddhist color symbolism. For the Mongols, blue was the color that represented the center and it came to represent the Mongol people.[11]

The new application of blue is demonstrated in the naming of a new city built in the sixteenth century. The Tümed Mongol ruler, Altan Khan (1508-1582), who will be discussed below, built a capital city in the steppes of southern Mongolia (comprising much of modern Inner Mongolia), naming it Kökö Khoto or the Blue City—modern Hohhot in Inner Mongolia, PRC. The city became a center of Buddhism, ruled by a Buddhist ruler endorsed by the Dalai Lama and was a haven for members of the millenarian White Lotus sect who, somewhat ironically, viewed

---

Mongolian have been consulted. Igor de Rachewiltz, trans. and ed., *The Secret History of the Mongols* (Leiden: Brill, 2003), Urgunge Onon, trans. and ed., *The Secret History of the Mongols: The Life and Times of Chinggis Khan* (London: Routledge, 2001); Francis W. Cleaves, trans. and ed., *The Secret History of the Mongols* (Cambridge, MA: Harvard University Press, 1982). In Mongolian, Sh. Gaadamba, ed., *The Secret History of the Mongols* (Ulaanbaatar: Ulsiin Xevleliin Gazar, 1990). As existing original copies of *The Secret History* only exist in Ming era documents and rendered into Chinese from the Mongolian in phonetic Chinese characters, one must also include Igor de Rachewiltz's rendering of the *The Secret History* back into its original Middle Mongolian: Igor de Rachewiltz, *Index to the Secret History of the Mongols* (Chippenham, UK: Curzon Press, 1997). In some later accounts, Börte Chino and his wife are humans with the names of Blue-Grey wolf and Fallow Deer.

7   Lawrence Krader, *Formation of the State* (Englewood Cliffs, NJ: Prentice Hall, 1968), 90.
8   Rachewiltz, *The Secret History of the Mongols,* 225.
9   Not all scholars are in agreement that Buddhism died out in Mongolia with the collapse of the Yuan Empire. Although the Mongols lost China in 1368, the Northern Yuan continued in Mongolia until 1634. For more on the dissenting view on the Second Conversion see Dominique Dumas, "The Mongols and Buddhism in 1368-1578: Facts-Stereotypes-Prejudices," *Ural Altaische Jahrbücher* 19 (2005): 167-221.
10 Elisabetta Chiodo, "The Black Standard (*qara sülde*) of Činggis Qayan in Baruun Xüree," *Ural-Altaische Jahrbücher* 15 (1997/1998): 254. For more on Vajrapani and the association with Chinggis Khan, see Sagaster, *Die Weisse Geschichte, passim.*
11 Henry Serruys, "Mongol Altan 'Gold'='Imperial'", *Monumentica Serica* 21 (1962), 377.

the Ming Dynasty as an unjust and oppressive government.[12] The color associated with the city not only represented the sacral and auspicious nature of the city as a capital, but also the city's association with Buddhism. Furthermore, as blue also indicated the center, it denoted that Köke Khoto was the political center of Altan Khan's polity. Through Chinggis Khan, the auspicious color of Eternal Blue Sky is stripped of its pre-Buddhist and shamanic sacral significance and wedded to a Buddhist symbolism, thereby providing greater meaning to the name of Altan's capital, Köke Khoto. This is evident as Altan Khan built Yeke Zuu, or the Grand Temple, a large monastery just to the south of the city, cementing his commitment to Buddhism. Furthermore, the blue carried connotations from the Yuan period as the color of the Mongol royalty, giving Altan Khan some pretensions as the premier Mongol prince. Finally, the blue color also symbolized the peace between the Mongol and Chinese residents inhabiting the city.[13]

Blue carried over into Buddhism among the later Mongols with the *khadag* or blue silk scarf which was often given as an offering and used as prayer flags. White *khadag*s are also used, but blue seems to predominate and carry more importance. Curiously, the blue *khadag* is used in shamanic practices as well at öböös or rock cairns placed at spiritual nexus points; this began as shamanic ritual, but entered Buddhist practice as well.[14] In Buddhism, the *öböös* purpose transformed from a shamanic rite into offerings accompanied by Buddhist prayers and practices. Rather than an animal sacrifice, other gifts were given to the gods and other spirits such as stones and *khadag*s with prayers written on them.[15]

Yellow

Shar or *shira* (yellow) carried significance with a sacral meaning in medieval Inner Asia, but gained greater importance with the rise of Buddhism in Mongolia. The Tibetan variant of Buddhism introduced by the Gelugpa monks and spread through the efforts of the Altan Khan and the Dalai Lama became known as the *Shar Sashiin* or Yellow Faith due to the saffron colored robes and headpieces that the monks wore. Yellow, despite its association with the Buddhist Gelugpa sect, carried sacral meanings prior to the arrival of Gelugpa Buddhism in Mongolia. It was considered a heavenly color, perhaps connected with a solar spirit. The *Secret History of the Mongols,* reveals that Bodonchar, the ancestor of the Mongols, and two of his brothers are the offspring of Alan Goa (a mortal) and a "shining yellow man" who entered Alan Goa's yurt through the smoke-hole and left the tent as a *shira noqai* or yellow dog (perhaps in more than one way).[16] This connects the Borjigin Mongols, the clan of Chinggis Khan, to heaven. Igor de Rachewiltz, argues that the *cheügan shira gü'ün* or shining yellow man is a personification of

---

12   The Red Turban movement that overthrew the Mongol Yuan dynasty emerged from the White Lotus. The White Lotus society was of Chinese origin, thus the color appellation has no relevance to Inner Asian color symbolism.

13   Isabelle Charleux, "De la ville bleue a la metropole grise: Fondation, protection et destruction de Kökeqota (Huehaote)," *Etudes mongoles et siberiennes* 35 (2004), 71.

14   Dorji Banzarov, "The Black Faith, of Shamanism Among the Mongols," trans. Jan Nattier and John R. Krueger, *Mongolian Studies* 7 (1982): 67.

15   Banzarov, "The Black Faith", 68.

16   *SHM,* §21.

Heaven (*tengri*) and that yellow is the color of gold (*altan*), which is the "symbol of supreme power and leadership."[17] There is no disputing the meaning of *altan*, more of which will be discussed below, but one must question whether yellow is gold in this instance. *Altan* does not appear to have other sacral meanings, particularly in conjunction with Tengri, the sky god. Yellow, however, being the color of the sun does make sense in this instance.[18] While the sun is found in the heavens, it is not part of it in the mythology; rather, it exists as a distinct entity or object, like the moon. Clearly, the Mongols viewed *shira* and *altan* as distinct colors with equally distinct meanings. Furthermore, after the Second Conversion, yellow gained more importance through its association with Jambhala, the Buddhist god of wealth, or the *sang-un ejen* or Lord of the Treasury.[19] Texts associated with Jambhala refer to him as the Yellow Jambhala, as in the *Shira jambala-yin sang* (Yellow Jambhala's Treasury) and *Ene sara jimbhala-yin takil ene bui* (This is the offering of the Yellow Jambhala).[20] Yellow itself is not the color of wealth, but carries meaning from Indo-Tibetan iconography. Nonetheless, the color associated with the god in the Buddhist iconography transfers sacral importance to the color in society, just as the association with Vajrapani gave new and different importance to blue.

Gold

The sacral meaning of *altan* or gold blended with its socio-political importance. Henry Serruys firmly established that the meaning of *altan* was a synonym for "imperial" among the Mongols. A custom developed in which everything connected to the emperor was referred to as *altan*, particularly when dealing with Chinggis Khan. This custom began in the era of the Mongol Empire, but coalesced during the Yuan Dynasty (1265-1368). Evidence found in the *Secret History of the Mongols* suggests that it may have begun shortly after his death. The word *altan* is used for virtually everything belonging to Chinggis Khan, including his person, his family, government, and more.[21] In the *Secret History* there are several references to this such as *altan terme* (golden tent)[22], *altan bosoqa* (golden threshold)[23], *minu altan amin* (my golden life).[24] Later inscriptions confirm that the *Secret History* was not unique. The Sino-Mongolian inscription of 1362, found in Gansu, Chinggis Khan is referred to as *altan beye* (golden body) and *altan chirai* (golden face) which are metaphors for "the imperial person" and "the imperial presence" respectively.[25]

---

17   Igor de Rachewiltz, ed., *The Secret History of the Mongols,* vol. 1 (Leiden: Brill, 2003), 263-264.

18   Also see Paul Pelliot, *Histoire secrete des Mongols,* restitution du texte mongol et traduction française des chapitres I à VI (Paris: Librairie d'Amérique et Orient 1949), 124, n.1; Rachewiltz, *Secret History,* 265.

19   Elisabetta Chiodo, *The Mongolian Manuscripts on Birch Bark from Xarbuxyn Balgas in the Collection of the Mongolian Academy of Sciences, Part I,* (Wiesbaden: Harrasowitz Verlag, 2000),148. Jambhala also served as the protector of the northern quarter of the world.

20   Chiodo, *The Mongolian Manuscripts on Birch Bark*, 148.

21   Serruys, 357-358.

22   *SHM,* § 184, 185, 187.

23   *SHM,* § 137

24   *SHM,* § 233.

25   Serruys, 358.

Black

The sacral meaning of *kara* or black has changed over time. It has often served as the color of warning or danger. The *tuq* or standard of horse tails that stood before the khan's *ger* was black during times of war. In the early modern period, *kara* or black assumed a more spiritually ominous meaning. During the Second Conversion to Buddhism among the Mongols, shamanism became known as the *kara shashiin* (*kara shasin* or *kara sajin* in the vertical script) or the Black Faith, connoting that it was "crude and unenlightened."[26] Prior to the Second Conversion, shamanism was never known as this; rather, shamanism simply existed although there were divisions within shamanic practice. Through the Buddhist lens, though, black developed a negative connotation in association with evil, and the oppression of shamans and shamanic practices was legalized. Possession of spirit placings or *ongons* consulting a shaman, and the use of shamanic charms were all punishable by fines according to the Mongol-Oirat Regulations of 1640.[27]

Black and White carried some meaning in shamanism prior to this in terms of connections with the spirit world, but it was not quite a cosmic duality of good and evil in a Manichaean sense. It had more to do with types of spirits and their proclivity to assist humans in the mundane world. *Kara* spirits tended to be more malevolent, but this is not to say that they were evil. Black flags were also used to warn of danger due to illness, often caused by the presence of *kara* spirits. John of Plano Carpini, the Franciscan monk who traveled to the Mongol capital at Karakorum in the 1240s on behalf of Pope Innocent IV (r. 1243-1256), observed that, if anyone was sick beyond care, the Mongols placed a spear with a black cloth outside their *ger* or yurt. No one was to enter the tent. If one even came into the vicinity of that tent, that person was forbidden from entering the *orda* or camp of the chief or emperor until the new moon, thus allowing a period of purification.[28] No one entered except a shaman and, occasionally, a relative. This arrangement worked on two levels. The person dying was clearly beyond the aid of a shaman and thus the isolation prevented the black spirit from possibly possessing another person, as in the Inner Asian shamanic world illnesses were caused by spirits. On another level, as germ theory did not exist in the thirteenth century, this period of isolation also prevented contagion from spreading.

The duality of spirits necessitated specialists with skills beyond a shaman's normal repertoire, leading to the rise of *chaghan böge* (white shamans) and *kara böge* (black shamans). White shamans dealt with good spirits and were more effective at gaining the spirits' assistance in matters of importance. Black shamans, however, dealt with evil spirits, particularly those of evil shamans, in the sense of warding them off. Unfortunately, they sometimes succumbed to the temptations that came with the power to control these spirits. Curiously, the white shaman wore robes that were primarily blue (associated with heaven), while the black sha-

---

26   Dorji Banzarov, "The Black Faith, of Shamanism Among the Mongols," trans. Jan Nattier and John R. Krueger, *Mongolian Studies* 7 (1982): 56.

27   Valentine A. Riasanovsky, *Fundamental Principles of Mongol Law* (Bloomington, IN: Indiana University Press, 1965), 191.

28   John of Plano Carpini, "History of the Mongols", trans. A Nun from Stanbrook Abbey, in Christopher Dawson, ed., *The Mongol Mission* (London: Sheed and Ward, 1955), 12.

man wore white robes. The sacral color attributes that designated them as black or white indicated the origin of the spirits that they engaged. The type of shaman one became was also determined by one's ancestral spirits. If one's ancestral spirits were predominantly white, one became a white shaman, and black spiritual ancestors made one a black shaman.[29] White spirits, according to the Buriat Mongols, originated in the west, while black spirits came from the east and were usually associated with plagues and illness or chthonic spirits, who were always dangerous. Ancestral spirits were also divided into black and white, with further delineation based on greater or lesser status, usually based on their status in the mundane world.[30] Hence a khan would be a powerful spirit, whether black or white. In addition to the lesser spirits analogous to the Arabian *jinn,* more powerful beings known as *tengri* existed. These should not be confused with the *Köke Möngke Tengri,* which was the Supreme Being. The lesser *tengri* were lesser gods, of which ninety-nine existed with fifty-five white, benevolent *tengri* and forty-four black, malevolent *tengri*.[31] Some association with good and evil also entered the sacral meaning, simply as the kinder and helpful spirits were white, while malevolent spirits were black. At the same time, the *kara böge* was feared by the populace not so much as a person, but as one who wielded power. A black shaman was imbued with immense power, as the *kara* spirits were so dangerous to control. Indeed, the *kara böge* could call upon the *kara tengri* to protect his tribe from outside evil as well as secure their power in war.[32] This delineation between the two types of shaman was strict. One could not be a gray shaman. As Klaus Hesse indicates,

> The white shamans venerated the white spirits, the black the black spirits exclusively, and the white shamans who called upon or venerated the black spirits lost their right in venerating and calling the white spirits; the black shamans did not dare to call upon the white spirits because of their fear of the revengeful and terrifying black spirits.[33]

White spirits, however, were easier to coerce into helping. One such being was the White Old Man or *Chaghan Ebügen*. Although he was a shamanic figure, his popularity and importance was so great among Mongols that he carried over into Buddhism, although no canonical text includes him.[34] The White Old Man appeared as he was described: an old man with white hair, white clothing, and a dragon staff that was clearly the same as a shaman's staff. The *Chaghan Ebügen* was the personification of creative power, but he could also destroy. With a blow

---

29 Klaus Hesse, "A Note on the Transformation of the White, Black and Yellow Shamanism in the History of the Mongols," *Studies in History* 2, 1 (1986): 22.

30 Hesse, "A Note on the Transformation of the White, Black and Yellow Shamanism," 21-22.

31 Hesse, "A Note on the Transformation of the White, Black and Yellow Shamanism," 21. The number 9 is an auspicious number for the Mongols and could manifest in a variety of ways, such as nine beings, nine gifts, nine punishments, or often replicated as triplicated triplets. See Larry W. Moses, "Triplicated Triplets: The Number Nine in the *Secret History of the Mongols,*" *Asian Folklore Studies* 45 (1986): 287-294.

32 Hesse, "A Note on the Transformation of the White, Black and Yellow Shamanism", 22.

33 Hesse, "A Note on the Transformation of the White, Black and Yellow Shamanism", 22.

34 Walther Heissig, *The Religions of Mongolia,* tran. Geoffrey Samuel (Berkeley: University of California Press, 1980), 78.

from his staff he could kill or spread illness among livestock.[35] Nonetheless, as the Lord of the Earth and the Waters, he was also protector of the good and punisher of the wicked—a position which the Buddha confirmed during an induction into the Buddhist pantheon.[36] Considering the combination of his role as a protector with duties to ward off evil, his ability to spread disease, and his white robes, one may wonder if the *Chagan Ebügen* was originally a *Kara Böge* or Black Shaman in a previous incarnation.

Like black, white also carried other sacral meanings. Just as the black *tuq* signaled war, a white *tuq* signaled peace, auspicious occasions, and good fortune.[37] When Temüjin ascended the throne as Chinggis Khan in 1206, a white *tuq* was present, signifying not only the peace that now reigned in Mongolia with the defeat of all opponents, but also the auspicious occasion of Temüjin's rule.[38] The existence of separate standards to indicate peace or war was not merely a pragmatic tool, but reflected the spiritual reality as well. White and black spirits known as *sülde* (protector spirits) dwelt within the *tuq*, which were also thought to be the genius of their particular clan. The usual custom was to sacrifice an important prisoner to the *kara tuq sülde* after a victory to thank the *sülde* for his protection and assistance in battle.[39] To the outside observer, this appeared as a sacrifice to the banner, but in reality it was to the spirit dwelling within the *tuq*. Because of the confusion, outsiders often referred to the *tuq* by using the term *sülde*. The *tsaghaan* or *chaghan tuq sülde* represented not only a period of peace, but also the well-being of the tribe. Prayers to the *chaghan sülde* also included requests for protection.[40]

After Chinggis Khan died, his spirit became more than simply an ancestral spirit: it transformed into a demi-god that carried over into Buddhism in the sixteenth century. As such, he served as the *sülde* not only of his clan, the *altan uruq* (Golden Kin) or the Borjigin, but also of the entire Mongol Empire. Thus his *sülde* inhabited both the *tsaghaan* or *chaghan tuq* and the *kara tuq* of war.[41] As the *tengri* of the *chaghan tuq sülde,* Chinggis Khan received prayers requesting his protection, at least one of which included a request to destroy the enemies of Buddhism. In addition, the *chaghan tuq sülde* was viewed as the support of the state—literally a pole or pillar which upheld the purpose of the state and thus merited veneration.[42] As the *kara sülde* was one of war, it is not surprising that prayers to Chinggis Khan as the *kara sülde tengri* include requests to destroy enemies and

---

35   Heissig, *The Religions of Mongolia,* 77.

36   Sanj Altan, "An Oirad-Kalmyk Version of the "White Old Man" Sutra found among the Archives of the Late Lama Sanji Rabga Möngke Baqsi," *Mongolian Studies* 29 (2007): 13-26.

37   Elisabetta Chiodo, "The White Standard (čaɣan tuɣ sülde) of the Čaqar Mongols of Üüsin Banner," *Ural-Altaische Jahrbücher* 16 (1999/2000): 241.

38   He Qiutao, *Sheng wu qin zheng lu (Bogda bagatur bey-e-ber tayilagsan temdeglel)*, trans. Arasaltu (Qayilar, PRC: Obor Monggol-un Soyul-un Keblel-un Qoriy-a, 1985), 39.

39   Hesse, "The Transformation of White, Black and Yellow Shamanism", 24. Also see Heissig, *The Religions of Mongolia,* 87 for an invocation to the *kara sülde* which includes instructions for a sacrifice to it.

40   Heissig, *The Religions of Mongolia,* 85.

41   Heissig, *The Religions of Mongolia,* 59-64; 84-85.

42   Chiodo, "The White Standard," 232-233.

towns.⁴³ Although it was a pre-Buddhist rite, during the Second Conversion era and well into the Qing Empire, lamas performed the veneration rites to the banners and certain clans, known as *tuqchinar*, were assigned to care for the *tuq* every day.⁴⁴ While the *chaghan tuq sülde* received veneration from all Mongols, only lamas and the family of Chinggis Khan (*altan urug* or Golden Kin) worshipped the *kara tuq sülde*. Even in the modern era, outsiders are prohibited from viewing the rites, unlike the rites connected with the *chaghan tuq sülde*, although with the latter, non-Mongols may be prohibited from participating in the rites.⁴⁵

During the Second Conversion shamanism of any sort became illegal and shamans were persecuted with fines, maltreatment, and even death. Some shamans resisted by becoming lamas and practiced what Hesse calls yellow shamanism—"an amalgamation of lamaistic and shamanistic beliefs and practices."⁴⁶ As Buddhism in Mongolia was very syncretic, some shamanic practices were readily adopted by the lamas as evinced with the aforementioned *öböös*. In addition, some shamanic prayers were used with the tengris transformed into incarnations of lamas or members of the Buddhist pantheon.⁴⁷ The Buddhist lamas did not dare interfere with the deified Chinggis Khan but simply incorporated him into the Buddhist pantheon of god as the incarnation of the deity Vajrapani.⁴⁸ In the worship of the kara tuq sülde, Chinggis Khan not only manifests as Vajrapani, but also as a fierce protective deity known as Dharmapala.⁴⁹ Even the black shamans with their terrifying tengris could find some refuge as lamas who paid particular attention to the vengeful gods and boddhisattvas of Buddhism. Even with this form of Yellow shamanism, which could be rightly viewed as syncretic Buddhism, the Buddhist church could never fully eradicate shamanism, particularly the black shamans. It appears that while white shamans who dealt with healing, astrology, and other more benign forms could be replaced by the *shara shajin* or Yellow Faith of Buddhism many people still found the services of the *kara böge* necessary and their functions not fulfilled through lamas. Indeed, some of the prayers reflect that the kara böge served as an underground resistance to Buddhism, and people asked for the *kara tengri* to avenge them by destroying greedy lamas and perhaps an overly oppressive religion as many viewed it by the twentieth century:

> Oh thou, who thou comest to eat 90 monks
> And returnest to eat 100,000 monks.
> Oh thou, who thou comest riding the frenzied wolves
> And feedest the fire with the Kanjur and Tanjur.⁵⁰

---

43 Heissig, *The Religions of Mongolia*, 85-86.
44 Chiodo, "The White Standard", 235, 238.
45 Chiodo, "The Black Standard," 252-253.
46 Hesse, "A Note on the Transformation of White, Black and Yellow Shamanism", 18.
47 Walther Heissig, *The Religions of Mongolia*, 40-42.
48 Hesse, "A Note on the Transformation of White, Black and Yellow Shamanism", 28.
49 Chiodo, "The Black Standard", 253.
50 Hesse, "A Note on the Transformation of White, Black and Yellow Shamanism", 29.

Oddly enough, it is because of the lingering shamanic resentment and anger about the arrival of Buddhism and persecution of shamanic rite and practitioners, combined with a growing alienation of the believers from Buddhist Sangha's avarice and domination of the quotidian over the centuries that allowed a new faith to then successfully persecute the Yellow Faith. The new faith's practitioners successfully tapped into the latent hostility of many and painted the *shara shajin* as an exaggerated version of the Mongolians' view of the Buddhist monasteries. The new faith also came with a color, *ulaan* or the red of communism.

Directional

The cardinal directions were also associated with colors. For the most part, Inner Asian groups used common directional names for the points of the compass; however, color directional meanings provided symbolism in connection to a socio-political meaning. As Christopher Atwood explains,

> In Mongolian chronicles of the seventeenth century, the world described appears divided into realms or countries (*ulus*), each with its own customs, languages, and traditions of rule. Neither political disunity within a realm nor a realm's incorporation into a larger empire disrupted this sense of a historically continuous domain. A vivid illustration of this country-consciousness lies in the numerical and color schemes which Mongolian historians used to order these realms in space. One common trope in these chronicles was that of the "five colors and four aliens" (*tabuen öngge dörben khari*) which together made up the "nine great realms" (*yisün yekhe ulus*). These nine great countries were distributed in terms of the four cardinal directions plus the center and each identified with a particular color. Invariably at this time, the "great blue Mongol realm" (*yekhe khökhe Monggol ulus*) was placed in the center. To east lay the white Solonggos and Bitüüd realms, meaning roughly Korea and Manchuria. To the south was the red Khitad and Khiliyed realms-Khitad is the name for the realm of China. To the west lay the black realms of Tibet (or Tanggud) and Tajik, while to the north lay the yellow realms of Sartuul (Sarts or Central Asian oasis dwellers) and Tokmak (a city in present-day Kyrgyzstan, but probably indicating the Turkic nomads of Central Asia as a whole). In their political narrative, of course, the chronicles focus on the Mongols in relation to particular realms.[51]

This orientation, however, was not fixed and changed over time, perhaps due to better geographic knowledge or a more accurate understanding of power. For instance, the Mongolian chronicler Injannashi (1837-1892) moved Mongolia from the center to the northern lands (*khoitu gajar*) and included not only Mongolia, but also Manchuria and Kazakhstan. The color blue also moved to the north. Replacing it in the center came the red (south) Chinese and China, resuming

---

51   Christopher P. Atwood, "National Questions and National Answers in the Chinese Revolution; Or, How do You Say Minzu in Mongolian?," *Indiana East Asian Working Papers Series on Language and Politics in Modern China* 5 (July 1994), 44.

China's own historic view as the Middle Kingdom during the Qing period (1636-1912).[52] According to Atwood, Injannashi, who lived in what is now the Inner Mongolia Autonomous Region, PRC, "revolutionized the Mongols' understanding of their own past in his 'Blue Chronicle of the Rise of the Great Yuan Dynasty' (*Yekhe yuwan ulus-un mandugsan törü-un khökhe sudur*)."[53] Not only did he move Mongolia and blue to the north, but he also reduced the number of colors used to four and increased the alien people to five. Thus the color-coded world-view now consisted of the blue Mongols to the north, red Chinese to the south (but also China as the Middle Realm or Kingdom—*Dumdadu ulus*), white Korea to the east, and black Tibetans to the west. The alien people were no longer other people, but legendary groups such as Dog-headed people, etc. His changing view also reflected a shift in Qing attitudes—in the late eighteenth century, the Manchu rulers of the Qing dynasty paid increasing attention to their most populous subjects, the Han Chinese, rather than the Mongols, who received considerable attention and favoritism in the first century and a half of the Qing Empire. This was most apparent during Injannashi's lifetime, when Inner Mongolia was opened to Han immigration, eventually outnumbering the Mongols and causing considerable tensions which continue today.

Yet other systems of color with directional meanings existed. In the medieval era and before among the Turks, black meant north and white represented west.[54] Blue was in the east, gold in the center, and red to the south. This may have played a role in the names of certain geographical locations. For instance, the Kizil Kum Desert, or Red Sand desert in Turkic languages, is not named for the color of the sand. The latter appears to be a standard sand color. Its location, however, in what is now Kazakhstan, Turkmenistan, and Uzbekistan was south of the steppes and thus the Gök Turk Empire. While it is not certain, the location of the desert in relation to the steppes may have played a role in its name.

Other geographical features were known by their colored names. The Seljuk Turks who dominated the Middle East for the eleventh century referred to the Mediterranean as the White Sea (Aq Deniz) and to the Black Sea, well as the Black Sea (Kara Deniz). Indeed, the later was known to the Ancient Greeks as the Pontus Euxeinos which translated as Black or Dark Sea. The origin of the nomenclature, however appears not to be Greek but rather Scythian. Greeks who traded and colonized the coast adopted the color terminology as it sounded similar to a Greek word for "inhospitable", which was probably based on their own experiences there[55] The actually use of Pontos Euxeinos or Black Sea was rare, however an only appears in a verse by Euripides in his *Iphigenia Taurica*.[56] More frequently, the Black Sea was simply known as the Pontos or The Sea. More standard usage

---

52   Atwood, 53-54; Lhamsuren, 72-73.

53   Atwood, 51-52.

54   Omeljan Pritsak, "Qara. Studien zur türkischen Rechtssymbolic," in *Studies in Medieval Eurasian History* (London: Variorium Reprints, 1981), 255, 259.

55   François de Blois, "The Name of the Black Sea", pp, 1-8, in Maria Macuch, Mauro Maggi, and Werner Sundermann, eds *Iranian Languages and texts from Iran and Turan: Ronald E. Emmerick memorial volume* (London: Harrassowitz), 1.

56   De Blois, 2.

of the Black for the sea north of Anatolia does not appear in the sources until the mid-thirteenth century when a Byzantine treaty mention it. The Latin version of the treaty glosses it as *Mari Nigro*. The usage spread and in the fourteenth century Arab writers also adopted it—*al-bahru al-'aswad*.[57]

François de Blois attributes the expanded and sustained usage to the Mongols who dominated the region, although the Seljuks of Rūm, who ruled much of Anatolia from the Battle of Manzikert (1071) in which they defeated the Byzantines to the Battle of Köse Dagh (1243), when the Mongols defeated the Seljuks, may have also used the term. However, even though the Byzantines controlled much of the cost, even after the loss of Constantinople to the Fourth Crusade, 1204, appear not to have used the term until the 1260s. There are some issues with this as the Mongols also controlled the Pontic Steppes, the region north of the Black Sea. Thus for the Mongols there, the Black Sea should have been Red. There is no indication that this worked. It is clear, however, that the name Kara Deniz became the standard name during the Ottoman era (c. 1350 to 1922) and why it is the current name.[58] There is no indication that the Red Sea is Red because of color symbolism, although it was south of the Ottoman territories so to speak.

Socio-Political

Although Inner Asian pastoral nomads tended to be fairly egalitarian in terms of gender, nonetheless a clear divide existed between the aristocracy and non-aristocracy. Generally speaking, the nobility were known as the white-boned or the *chaghan yasun*, while the commoners were the *kara yasun*, or black-boned. The idea of the white-boned referring to the nobility pre-dates the Mongol empire but the concept underwent a drastic change with the rise of Chinggis Khan. His social revolution restructured the aristocracy of the steppe so that only Chinggisids (his descendants and those of his brothers) were considered aristocracy. As Lawrence Krader explains,

> Here the nobility was termed cagan [sic] yasun, likewise meaning white bone, and the commoners qara [sic] yasun, also black bone. Both the Turks and the Mongols conceive a 'bone' as the expression of the principle of kinship by virtue of common descent in the male line. Sons of brothers are related in the bone, and the conception is extensible indefinitely to include myriads of such agnatic kin. The genealogical table of Chingis Khan's descent extends over twenty-four generations, back to the mating of a wolf the color of the night sky, and a white doe. The descendants of this line were kin by virtue of a common bone.[59]

Prior to this all nobles were considered white-boned while commoners were considered black-boned. With the transition to a Chinggisid-dominated aristocracy,

---

57 De Blois, 4.
58 De Blois, 4.
59 Krader, *Formation of the State*, 90.

only the Chinggisids remained white-boned and did so for centuries. Others, however, did modify the idea including in non-nomadic areas such as Russia. It appears to have occurred in the twelfth century as the Kievan Rus' expanded into the black lands or *chernozem* referring to the black soil regions of the Pontic steppes. According to Jerome Blum, "The peasants who lived on this land were known from the twelfth century on (and possibly earlier) as the 'black people.'"[60] The "black people" were free peasants and did own land, although they also could work the land of the boyars. During the era of early Muscovy, the Russian nobility appear to have adopted the Turko-Mongol concept of white nobility and black commoners from their period as Mongol subjects. It is not too surprising, particularly as many Russians forged genealogies to trace their ancestry to Chinggis Khan. Also one must consider that many Tatars (as the Turkicized Mongols were known) entered the Russian aristocracy as Moscow expanded. To be certain, not all of the old steppe elite did so, as it usually required conversion to Orthodox Christianity, but sufficient numbers did to cause a switch in Russian identity. While this became more prevalent after the Mongol conquests, the fact that the peasants in the steppe were referred to as the "black people" makes it quite possible that the practice began with contact in the Pontic steppes with the Kipchaks who nomadized the *chernozem* in the twelfth century.

While black was associated with being common or the non-noble, one should not conflate this to mean the ordinary herdsmen alone because this included all segments of society outside of the Chinggisids. Indeed, in the *Secret History of the Mongols,* we find examples of aristocracy referring to themselves as *kara,* but who made reference to other body parts rather than the bone, where one part of the soul resided. In one scene in the *Secret History of the Mongols,* we find Chinggis Khan's uncles Altan, Quchar, and Sacha Beki making obeisance to him, saying

> If we disobey your commands, part us from our goods and our noble wives, and cast our black heads on the ground![61]

qala cinu busi bolqa'asu qari siri-dece qatun eme-dece manu qaqaca'ulju qara teri'ü manu kösör-tür gejü[62]

In this context, head (*teri'ü*), has a double meaning. It means not only a body part but also carries the meaning of a leader or the head of a group. The normal word for the physical body's head is *toloyai* (modern—толгой). Here the black heads refer to both their physical head, but also their roles as leaders. By referring to their *qara* or *kara teri'ü,* Chinggis Khan's uncles are acknowledging a subordinate status to him. Furthermore, by saying that Chinggis Khan should cast their heads to the ground, it is implied he should execute them—perhaps by behead-

---

60   Jerome Blum, *Lord and Peasant in Russia from the Ninth to the Nineteenth Century* (Princeton: Princeton University Press, 1961), 93.

61   My translation. It should be noted that later, they did disobey his commands and he did take their goods. They were executed, not by beheading, but having their spines broken.

62   Igor de Rachewiltz, ed., *Index to the Secret History of the Mongols* (Richmond, UK: Curzon Press, 1997), §123.

ing. Due to taboos on spilling the noble blood on the ground, the uncles again acknowledge an inferior status.

As evinced by the example of Chinggis Khan's uncles, being *kara* should not be viewed as a derogatory term, as it included the highest ranking generals as well as what might be considered the minor nobility—former tribal elites or those leaders of non-Chinggisid blood. While the Khan might be theoretically all powerful, he nonetheless ruled through the minor nobles and needed to consult them. This dependency became greater with the continued balkanization of the Mongol world. The leading black nobles were the so-called *karachi* beys.[63] The *actor nomenis* suffix of *-chi* added to *kara* transforms the color term into "one who performs the black (duties)," or the non-royal duties. Again, while the *karachi* were not the rulers, they still wielded considerable power and influence as clan leaders and advisers to the ruler. Furthermore, as demonstrated in the Crimean Khanate in the sixteenth and seventeenth centuries, the khan could not always control the *karachi* nobles. Thus the khan had to develop a good relationship with them. While he had greater authority, when the khan was weak, the *karachis*—particularly if they stood together—could ignore the authority of the khan.

The dual color coded social hierarchy continued beyond the Mongol Empire. Among the Kazakhs, who emerged as an ethnonym in the fifteenth century, the sultans or *tore* were Chinggisid princes and considered "white boned" (*ak söyek*) and were outside the normal clan system of the Kazakhs. The majority of the Kazakhs Chinggisids traced their lineage to Baraq Khan and his sons, Janïbek and Kirāy, who formed the Kazakh confederation. A hierarchy existed among the Chinggisids. At the top were the khans who ruled over the *zhüzes* or major confederations of the Kazakhs. The khans' sons used the title of sultan and often ruled individual tribes within their respective fathers' *zhüz*. Their descendants, who did not become sultans or khans, were called *töräs*. They ruled clans, at least as a figurehead if not in reality. Even so, they held diplomatic duties and dispensed justice. Although the Chinggisids were usually the only "white" nobility, on occasion other groups emerged. In many parts of Central Asia were the *Khojas* or *Khwājas*, Muslim religious leaders who were considered *sayyids* or descendants of the Prophet Muhammad and intermingled Yasavi sufis who proselytized and converted much of Central Asia to Islam.[64]

The "black boned" (*kara söyek*) included not only the common nomads but also an aristocracy of elites who were at first elected based on their charisma, military prowess, wealth, or influence. These positions gradually became hereditary in most cases. Even so, the "black boned" elite consisted of two categories. The first were the *batyr* or hero and the second were the *bii*, which translates as "judge." Their title, however, did not limit their role or power which depended on their own abilities and charisma.[65] Nevertheless, their power and authority could even

---

63   Uli Schamiloglu, "The Qaraci Beys of the Later Golden Horde: Notes on the Organization of the Mongol World Empire," Archivum Eurasiae Medii Aevi 4 (1984): 283-297.

64   Allen J. Frank, "The Qazaqs and Russia," in *The Cambridge History of Inner Asia: The Chinggisid Age*, ed. Nicola di Cosmo, Allen J. Frank, and Peter B. Golden (Cambridge: Cambridge University Press, 2009), 366; Shirin Akiner, *The Formation of Kazakh Identity* (London: The Royal Institute of International Affairs, 1995), 15-16.

65   Akiner, 15-16; Frank, 366.

rival that of the white boned and they became the leaders of several clans. In some circumstances, their authority was greater as they dealt directly with clan affairs, unlike the Chinggisid sultans who were outside of the clan system. Thus, the *kara* groups, by any name, wielded considerable authority and power throughout history. While they were not necessarily rivals to the *chaghan* or *aq,* the *kara* could fill a vacuum when the white boned no longer served a purpose.

Yet *kara* could also be used as a derogatory term in describing status. This manifests most apparently in a number of writings by the eighth Jibzundamba Khutugtu (1870-1924), the highest ranking incarnate lama in Mongolia. In these bulls issued towards the end of the Qing dynasty, he propagated anti-Chinese and anti-Manchu ideology while exhorting the Mongols to be true to the Yellow Faith. In one such bull, he wrote, "You, my Northern Khalkhas! The Manchu people abandon spears and saddle-pads when the black Chinese (*Qara* [sic] *kitad-i*) arrive. You lived cursing my religion and the assemblies. It is said that you turned away from my teaching. That is why you will suffer by falling into the hands of the enemy of the wrong side."[66]

In a bull from 1892, the Bogd Gegen or Jibzundamba Khutugtu had declared himself to be the protector and savior of all Mongols, not only the Khalkha in northern Mongolia (Mongolia today) where he dwelt in Urga (modern Ulaanbaatar), but also in parts of Inner Mongolia.[67] In this section, from the "Prophecy of the Holy Gegen," the Jibzundamba Khutugtu castigates the Mongols for swaying from the Buddhist faith, specifically the Gelugpa sect.[68] Furthermore, in his statement about the Manchus, the rulers of the Qing Empire, he indicates that they have become weak because they now associate with the Chinese. By referring to the Chinese as "black," the Jebtsundamba Qutuqtu has created a binary world in which *kara* is no longer simply non-Chinggisid in the Mongolian world, but non-Mongolian. Therefore, the Mongols at all levels of the social hierarchy are inherently *chaghan,* or white, and must not be dominated by the Chinese. Thus, in the eyes of the Jibzundamba Khutugtu, all of the Mongols are Chinggisids.[69] Yet, while he elevates all of the Mongols to the level of the Chinggisids, the Jibzundamba did not dilute the significance of the *chaghan yasun* identity. Quite the contrary: as the original incarnation of the Jibzundamba Khutugtu was a Chinggisid, the eighth Jibzundamba Khutugtu held the Chinggisids in high regard, although he was of Tibetan origin.

This idea becomes most apparent in the "Epistle of the Eighth Jibzundamba Khutugtu" which reads,

> The god, Khan Qormusta has sent me, and this is his order: Because he has the sufferings of the numerous Mongols before his eyes, and because the memory of the three kinds of lineages, that of the five permanent virtues, the life-style of the wise and good ones have become absolutely unknown

---

66   Alice Sarközi, *Political Prophecies in Mongolia in the 17th-20th centuries,* Asiatische Forschungen (Wiesbaden: Otto Harrassowitz, 1992), 124. Also see p. 120 for the Mongolian text.
67   Lhamsuren, 79.
68   The date of this prophecy is uncertain, but appears to be from the early 1890s.
69   Lhamsuren, 79.

at various times, a change of time has become unavoidable—that is why he sent me. This is the decree of Heaven (*tnger-yin*): The black-headed Chinese became many (*qara terigüten irgen ulaγan bolayad*) and they have reached the extremes of disorder, that is why the compassionate Buddha should remember the many Mongols who believe with faith in the religious teaching...There will be an unimaginable amount of suffering. Black-headed Chinese become many (*qaran terigüten irigen olan bolγad*); they do not love the religion of Buddha and they have reached the extremes of disorder, so that it is impossible to not to accept the well-established law of the predecessors as an example and not to follow the order of Heaven.[70]

This is followed by a call to boycott Chinese goods and Chinese people altogether. The Jibzundamba Khutugtu informs the Mongols that if they follow this advice, they will "be without misery and will not taste bitter sufferings, and from now on you will be without troubles, and will live in very great wealth and abundance—it is certain."[71] He also warns them that if they live and dress like the Chinese, then they will die together with the Chinese. Furthermore, he admonishes them to remember that "You are the white bone human descendants (*chaghan yegüden yasutan*) derived from four Emperors of the Yuan" (the Chinggisid Dynasty that ruled East Asia from 1265-1368).[72]

Here the Jibzundamba links all Mongols with the Chinggisids through the Yuan Dynasty, which ruled East Asia, including all of what comprised the Qing Empire. By invoking the Yuan and not just Chinggis Khan, the Jibzundamba implicitly indicates that the Mongols should rule over the Chinese and not the opposite. Furthermore, the Jibzundamba Khutugtu refers to the Chinese as *qaran terigüten irigen olan* or the "many black-headed people." The Chinese or *kitad* are not even specifically mentioned in certain passages; instead, they are referred to in another fashion. As with the scenario from the *Secret History of the Mongols*, in which *teri'ü* (Middle Mongolian) equates not to the head of a body, but to the head—or leader—of a group, making it a play on words, *terigüten* is simply the Classical Mongolian adjectival form of *terigün*, which means "head, chief, beginning, first, chief, foremost."[73] The adjectival form of *terigün* modifies *irgen*. In Middle Mongolian, the term meant "people" or specifically non-Mongolian groups. By the late Qing period, the word could still refer to people, but normally it served as a modifier to indicate a specific group, such as *Sart irgen* (Central Asian people). Another meaning evolved in which *irgen, irigen,* or *iregen* equated to Chinese, reflecting the dualistic view of the Mongols towards Chinese merchants and settlers in Mongolian lands. Referring to them as the *qara teirgüten irigen* in such a matter implies that the Chinese are claiming some leadership or ruling authority, thus attempting to usurp the rightful authority of the *chaghan*

---

70   Sarközi, 129-130. See also 127-129 for the original Mongolian text. In the phrase "The black-headed Chinese", the original Mongolian shows *qara terigüten irgen ulaghan* or the black-headed red people. Here the red refers to the China in the directional sense.

71   Sarközi, 131. See 129 for the original Mongolian text.

72   Sarközi, 128.

73   Ferdinand D. Lessing, *Mongolian-English Dictionary* (Bloomington, IN: The Mongolia Society, 1995), 805.

yasutan, or white boned people, which would violate the very order of the universe as the Jibzundamba Khutugtu indicates.

Another issue exists, however. In the first statement that the "Black Headed people became many", the phrase is transliterated as *"qara terigüten irgen ulayan bolayad"*.[74] The second occurrence is transliterated as *"qaran terigüten irigen olan bolyad"*.[75] The first three words are not problematic. *Qara* and *qaran* mean black with the latter with the "n" being a variable stem attached to the adjective. *Terigüten* and *irgen* also bear no issues and combined with *qara* translates as the "black-headed people". Issues arise with *ulayan* and *olan*. *Ulayan* means red. Sarközi equates it with *olan* in her transliteration, indicating that she thought the scribe simply made a mistake.[76] However, I am not fully convinced that this was a mistake as *ulayan* is two letters longer and three motions longer when written in the classical Mongolian script. It is unlikely that one would make this sort of error, particularly when *olan* or "many" is written perfectly in another passage in the same prophecy. As stated earlier, here the Chinese are not referred to as the *Kitad*, the normal Mongolian term but through the metaphor of *"qara terigüten irgen"*. Yet, in the same manuscript the Chinese are referred to in other fashions as well.

The first variance is by referring to them as the *"siralduyusan olan iregen"* or literally, the "yellow many people" or more properly the "many yellow people" with the *-lduysan* prefix being a compound prefix of the reciprocal voice *-ldu* and the preterite participle or *nomen concretum -ysan*.[77] In the *Epistle by the 8th rJeb-bcundam-pa Khutukhtu to the Khalkha and other Mongol tribes*, the Jibzundamba issued the order, "from the beginning of the first of the fourth month of this year ride to the south and clear away the yellow Chinese population".[78] The use of yellow to describe the Chinese is interesting and unclear in the symbolism of the color. It is unlikely that it is tied to idea of the "Yellow Peril" made famous by Kaiser Wilhelm in 1895 as the *Epistle* was written in 1892.[79] Perhaps it is tied to yellow being the elemental color for the earth as the Chinese were viewed largely as farmers tied to the land rather than being nomads? Regardless, the phrasing is clearly derogatory. More frequently in the document the Chinese are called *Kitad*, which is the normal term for the people of China. The Kitad originally referenced the Khitan, an Inner Asia people who spoke a Mongolian language, who established the Liao Dynasty (960-1125) that ruled over northern China and much of Mongolia.

The *Epistle* reveals great concern that the Mongolians will become assimilated by the Chinese now entering both Mongolia and present day Inner Mongolia Autonomous Region, PRC. Both regions were part of the Qing Empire (1636-1911). The concern with the ever increasing population is demonstrated by the terms *qaran terigüten irigen olan* or the "many black-headed people" and *"siralduyusan olan irgen"* or "the many yellow people". This returns to my earlier point regard-

---

74 Sarközi, 127.
75 Sarközi, 128.
76 Sarközi, 127.
77 Gronbech and Krueger, 25 and 37.
78 Sarközi, 131.
79 For more on the Yellow Peril, see Christopher Jespersen, "The Colors of American Diplomacy" in this volume.

ing the first use of *qara terigüten irgen* in this *Epistle*. Clearly the scribe knew the orthography of *olan*. While there are some inconsistencies among other words, such as irgen (irgen, irigen, iregen) it reflects more archaic spellings that includes one additional motion in writing the word. Transitioning from *olan* to *ulayan* however, requires a more conscious effort. The use of *ulayan* was intentional. So with this in mind, the passage "*qara terigüten irgen ula*yan bolayad" reads as "the black-headed people became red". It is a play on words that fits in the Jibzundamba Khutugtu's concern that the Han Chinese (ethnic Chinese) are claiming some leadership or ruling authority not only vis-à-vis the Mongols but the Manchus as well. As discussed previously, the black-headed are non-royal, but by indicating they became *ulayan,* the Chinese have claimed the color of the south or more importantly the Middle Kingdom in Injannashi's (who died in 1892) schema. The use of *ulayan* carries even more weight as red is an auspicious color in Chinese culture akin to the use of blue among the Mongols. Thus through this color symbolism, the Jibzundamba Khutugtu expresses his concern that the Chinese are ascending and may eventually replace the Mongolians as the rightful rulers of Mongolian lands.

While the Jibzundamba Khutugtu's employment of *ulayan* is a new use of color, in Inner Asia, color was also used in the identity of states. The most obvious was the Jochid Ulus or Kipchak Khanate, more commonly known now as the Golden Horde. Scholars refer to this territory as the Jochid Ulus: an *ulus* is a Mongolian word used to designate the Mongolian people and it gradually came to refer to a "state" or "realm," while the Jochid appellation refers to Jochi, the eldest (and perhaps illegitimate son) of Chinggis Khan.[80] This territory was Jochi's patrimony. Islamic states commonly referred to it as *Bilad al-Qifjaq*, or the land of the Kipchaks. Even after the Mongol domination of the Pontic and Caspian Steppes, Kipchak Turks comprised the majority of the population. It was also known as the *Ulugh Ulus*, or Great or Big Ulus. In the Russian sources it appeared as *bol'shaia orda*, or Great Horde.[81] Over time, and beginning in the late sixteenth century, Russian sources referred to the territory as the Golden Horde or *Zlataia Orda*. The exact reason why the Russians referred to it as such is unclear, although a persistent legend that Batu, the son of Jochi, had a tent made of gold cloth, existed. There is some credence to this, as the Mongols had a fondness of *nasij*, or cloth of gold, and a few Mongol khans and khatuns (or queens) received tribute from vassals that sometimes included fabrics, and on one occasion, even a chapel, which was a cloth of gold. It is more likely that the Russian bookmen were simply following the example that the Mongols used in referring to the camp of the Great Khan (or the Khan at the time), as the *altan ordo*, or Golden Camp.[82] Yet, it was not necessarily golden because the material of the khan's tent was most likely made with felt. Rather, at its very basic level, *altan* means imperial as stated earlier. This may have simply come from the idea that the emperor's possessions were

---

80   See Munkh-Erdene Lhamsuren, "The Mongolian Nationality Lexicon", *passim. Irgen* is the usual word for people, but as Munkh-Erdene Lhamsuren demonstrates, it was used for non-Mongol groups. *Ulus* was always used to reference the Mongols.

81   Peter B. Golden, "Migrations, ethnogenesis," in *Cambridge History of Inner Asia: The Chinggisid Age*, ed. Nicola di Cosmo, Allen J. Frank, and Peter B. Golden (Cambridge: Cambridge University Press, 2009), 114.

82   The English word "horde" is derived from *orda* and *ordo,* the Turkic and Mongolian words for camp.

altan, or golden. Just as Chinggis Khan's tent was the *altan terme*, or golden tent, so also the residence of the Khan of the then independent Golden Horde would have been *altan* as well as his camp, or *orda*.

Typically, the emperor of China (or at least that part of China that had ties and influence in the steppes of Mongolia) was known as the *Altan Khan*. This included the ruler of the Jin Empire (1124-1234) and the Qing Emperors (1636-1911). The Mongols themselves did not readily use this title. Their rulers were not known as Altan Khan even after conquering the Jin and Song Empires in 1235 and 1276, respectively. Among the Mongols, the first use of Altan Khan was when a Chinggisid prince named Altan became the khan of the Tümed Mongols in the sixteenth century. The status of his title was later increased by favor shown by the Dalai Lama; nonetheless, the only reason why his title became Altan Khan was that Altan was his name. It should be noted that his twin sister was named Möngge or silver.

The connection with imperial status pre-dated the Mongols as well. The Jin Dynasty that ruled northern China from 1125 to 1234 took the name Jin, as it meant "Golden" in Chinese. The Jin, however, were not of Han ethnicity, but rather were Jurchen, a Tungusic group from Manchuria, and thus Inner Asian. Because they ruled not only the Chinese, but also other Inner Asian groups in southern Mongolia and northern Mongolia, the use of color symbolism assisted them in establishing their legitimacy in distant areas beyond the Gobi desert in addition to their authority over nomads closer to their borders.

Although the Mongols used *altan* to refer to the Jin Emperor, and it may have simply been a direct translation of "Jin," the Mongols employed *altan* as imperial less frequently for non-Mongol and non-Chinggisid states. Its usage also depended on proximity to other powers. Henry Serruys noted that during the fifteenth and sixteenth centuries, Mongols in southern Mongolia (Inner Mongolia, PRC), referred to the Ming emperor as *altan beye* (golden person), but the Khalka in northern Mongolia and others farther away from the Ming referred to the Ming as *shira* or yellow, but never *altan*.[83]

Returning to the imperial orda, it was therefore referred to as the *altan orda* or *altan ordu,* even if it was not in the center of the state. Thus the central camp, where the khan resided, was the Golden Horde, although there are some problems with the etymology, as indicated above. It is certain that the Golden Horde did not use that term to refer to itself, particularly during the time of the Mongol Empire, as it was subordinate to the Mongol ruler in Mongolia. Unfortunately, much of what we know about this polity is derived from outside sources because the archives and chancellery housed in Sarai and New Sarai were destroyed by the Emir Timur (Tamerlane) in his war against the Golden Horde khan, Toqtamish, in the late fourteenth and early fifteenth centuries. Indeed, Timur's depredation signaled the death knell for the state, as it never fully recovered and became a shadow of its former self.

But how did the so-called Golden Horde refer to itself? It does not appear to be the Golden Horde, for at no point was it an imperial center, although it was

---

83 Serruys, 371-373.

ruled (as all Mongol polities were) by a Chinggisid prince. Nonetheless, the Jochid line which was descended from Jochi, probably an illegitimate child of Chinggis Khan, was not a contender for the Great Khan's throne. The extant Mongolian sources always refer to the Jochid domains as the Ulus Jochi. The Islamic sources usually refer to it as the kingdom of the Kipchaks (*al-mamālīk al-qibjāq*) or the land of the Kipchaks (*Bilad al-Qifjaq*) in reference to the fact that the rulers dominated the Kipchak Steppe which stretched from the Dniester to Ural Rivers, thus comprising the Pontic and Caspian steppes.[84] In addition, the majority of the population of this khanate was Kipchak Turks. The issue is further complicated because the Ulus Jochi or Golden Horde was divided into two major branches ruled by two of Jochi's sons: Batu (d. 1255) and Orda.

Batu received the western portion which was often referred to as the Aq Orda (White Horde), while Orda's territory in the east was the Köke Orda (Blue Orda). The use of the Turkic, and not Mongolian terminology is intentional and also fits the directional color symbolism that was in use at the time as mentioned earlier. Turkic became the dominant language of the Golden Horde territories because of the large number of Kipchak Turkic nomads. Mongolian was used in the upper levels of the court, but Turkic became the *lingua franca*. Generally speaking, when scholars refer to the "Golden Horde," they are actually referring to the Aq Orda or "White Horde" although for most of their history the White and Blue patrimonies were united, with the Köke Orda vying for independence in 1368 under the leadership of Urus Khan. His efforts were ultimately thwarted by Toqtamish Khan, who also originated from the Köke Orda, with the support of his patron, Emir Timur, or Tamerlane.

Situated in western Siberia between the Ural and Irtysh Rivers, the first ruler of the Köke Orda was named Orda, the eldest son of Jochi. It never gained the importance of the Aq or Chaghan Orda (White Horde) which lay to the west of the Ural River. The Köke Orda appears to have been subordinate to it, as they could not mint their own coins and they also participated in the campaigns of the Aq Orda.[85] Nonetheless, the Köke Orda remained important, particularly in the fur trade as the Siberian tribes. After the fragmentation of the so-called Golden Horde, meaning, in this instance, the Golden Horde authority over all of the other *ordas* in the region, the Köke Orda ceased to exist. Instead, it became known as the Sibir Khanate, based on the fact that its capital was the town of Sibir (modern Tobolsk); it is also the origin of the name Siberia. Ultimately, however, the Sibir Khanate or Köke Orda ceased to exist with the expansion of Muscovy, which conquered it in the late sixteenth century.

Yet why were these regions referred to as White and Blue? A traditional explanation is that they reflect the Right and Left wings or hands of Jochi's patrimony. The orientation was always facing south, making the right the White side while the left was Blue. This orientation stems from the era of the Xiongnu in Mongolia and

---

84   Ibn Fadl Allah al-'Umarī, *Kitāb Maṣālik al-abṣā wa mamālik al-amṣār: Mamālik bayt Jinkiz Khān*, ed. K Lech (Wiesbaden: Otto Harrassowitz Verlag, 1968), 70.

85   Istvan Vasary, "The Jochid Realm: the western steppe and Eastern Europe," in *The Cambridge History of Inner Asia: The Chinggisid Age* ed. Nicola di Cosmo, Allen J. Frank, and Peter B. Golden (Cambridge: Cambridge University Press, 2009), 82.

was used throughout Turko-Mongolian states since then, including the Gök Turk Empire. As previously stated, the west-east (Aq-Köke) orientation also fit the directional color schema, but it is not certain if the usage was based on direction.

One must not exclude that the names carried a sacral color contextual meaning. The sources do not clarify if it is a sacral meaning of auspicious or heavenly nature, or if Köke was used as a directional meaning such as center. The latter would carry meaning only if Köke meant north or east. Directionally, white can mean west or east, depending on the symbolism schema. In relation to the position of *Yeke Monggol Ulus* or the Great Mongol State of Chinggis Khan and his successors, the Köke Orda was in the center of the empire. Still, this cannot be accepted as it does not change the fact that the Aq Orda was west of it which does not fit the use of color in which *köke* means center. And the west-east interpretation only makes sense in a Jochid exclusive context, yet these terms to described the house of Batu and Orda by other Chinggisids in other parts of the Empire. A better understanding of the meaning of the Blue and White Hordes might be gleaned by examining another historical example—that of Kara Khitai.

The connotation of this status carried over in reference to other empires as well. The Liao Dynasty collapsed in 1125 with the invasions of the Inner Asian Tungusic Jurchen from Manchuria, which then created the Jin Empire. Led by Yelü Dashi (r. 1131-1143), some of the Liao fled westward, first to strongholds in Mongolia, but then farther west into present day Kazakhstan and Kyrgyzstan. There they established what the Chinese sources referred to as the Western Liao. Steppe groups, however, referred to the Western Liao by another name, Kara Khitai. Khitai, from which the early modern term for China—Cathay—was derived, referred to the ruling class of the Western Liao or Kara Khitai—Khitans. The Khitans were another Inner Asian group of perhaps proto-Mongolian origins judging from philological evidence. As such, and because the refugees who established Kara Khitai in the Central Asia steppes were of Inner Asian origin and not of the royal family but a cadet branch, the Turkic and Mongolian peoples in the Mongolian steppe referred to them as the Kara Khitai, noting their Inner Asian ancestry as well as their non-royal status. It should not be assumed, however, that the Kara Khitans were not viewed as important or powerful. Kara Khitai became a hegemonic power in Central Asia and perhaps even used the name Kara Khitai as this title enters Persian and Arabic sources as well. Considering the large number of Turks also moving into the Middle East in the twelfth century, perhaps displaced by the rise of Kara Khitai, the term may have also been introduced to the Middle East by the Turkic nomads or by Muslims dwelling under the rule of the Buddhist Khitans.

This concept has not been considered by scholars dealing with the Kara Khitai. Indeed, the most recent and authoritative study of the Kara Khitai by Michal Biran of Hebrew University, does not suggest that Kara means non-royal.[86] She does, however, consider the numerous Chinese appellations for Kara Khitai, which included *Xi Liao* (Western Liao) as well as *Dashi guo, Dashi Linya guo*—all of which denote the kingdom's founder, Yelü Dashi. Yelü was the family

---

86 Michal Biran, *The Empire of the Qara Khitai in Eurasian History: Between China and the Islamic World* (Cambridge: Cambridge University Press, 2005), 215-217.

name of the Khitan royal family, while Dashi was a title which may be translated as Grand Preceptor.[87] Biran suggests that this might have been inspired by the Islamic practice of associating kingdoms with the name of their founders such as the Abbasids, Seljuks, etc.[88] But because it was not a Muslim kingdom, this claim is tenuous at best, particularly when the Chinese also referred to the Kara Khitai by other names, which Biran also notes, such as *Da Qidan* (Great Khitans), *Xi Qidan* (Western Khitans), and even *Dashi Qidan* (Dashi's Qidan) or the *Hei Qidan* (Black Khitans).[89] As Biran says, the Khitans did indeed refer to themselves as *Hala Qidan* (Kara Khitan) in their own documents. Kara Khitan is also mentioned in Korean, Mongol, and Persian sources in the thirteenth and fourteenth centuries, and the name carried over to a successor state founded in the early thirteenth century in Kirman in modern Iran.[90] What is curious, though, is that Kara Khitai is not mentioned in the Islamic sources before the Mongol invasions. Prior to this, the Muslim sources (Arabic and Persian), simply refer to it as Khita (Khitā or Khiṭā), which referred not only to Kara Khitai, but also the Liao Dynasty.[91]

Biran does investigate why the Kara Khitai were called the Kara or Black Khitai. She recognizes that Kara carries directional significance among Inner Asian societies and says that it refers to North based on the medieval Altaic schema. She ascribes an additional meaning that Kara carried prestige because it had been used with other groups such as the early medieval Turkic Karakhanid dynasty in Central Asia (who became Khitan subjects) and she offers it as the equivalent of *Da* or Great in Chinese. Ultimately, Biran dismisses the directional meaning, as did Doerfer in his linguistic studies, and Wittfogel and Feng in their studies on the Liao and Kara Khitai. Biran concludes that, although Kara Khitai meant Black Khitai during the Mongol period, it is not clear if *Hala* originally meant Black or only Great in Khitan when the empire was founded.[92] Nonetheless, the directional meaning here could apply. As previously stated, black or *kara* did refer to west in one Mongolian chromatic framework of Inner Asia. As the Khitans fled east, among other Inner Asia groups, they could easily have been identified as the Kara (or West) Khitai. This was a useful method of identifying them, as large numbers of Khitans remained behind as subjects of the new Jin Empire. Yet this explanation may simply be circumstantial.

Kara Khitai, however, was not the first empire to be described by a color term. The Kara Khitans conquered the Karakhanids (840-1212). It is clear that the Chinese dynasties did not refer to the previous Central Asian empire, the Karakhanids (Black Khans) as *Halahan* or *Kalahan*, which are modern Chinese terms for the Karakhanid Empire. The Song sources occasionally used *Heihan*, which is the literal translation of Black Khans. Most of the Chinese sources refer to them as Dashi, which Biran explains as deriving from "the Arabic *nisba* of the 'Ṭāy Tribe

---

[87]   K. A. Wittfogel and Feng Chia-sheng, *History of Chinese Society: Liao* (Philadelphia: The American Philosophical Society, 1949), pp. 643 and 648. This title continued to be used by the rulers.

[88]   Biran, 215.

[89]   Biran, 215-216.

[90]   Biran, 216.

[91]   Biran, 216.

[92]   Biran, 217.

(*ṭāzī*) that eventually developed into the term Tajik. In Chinese it originally meant Arabs or Arabia. Gradually it included the subjects of the Arab empire, including Persians and later Turks. Eventually the term signified Muslims in general."[93] But Biran's explanation that *Dashi* corresponds with the *Tajik* (*ṭāzī*) in relation to the Karakhanids is problematic. The Chinese were not alone in describing the Arabs as Tajik. Eighth-century Turkic runic inscriptions on the Tonyuquq and Küli Chor stelae refer to the Arabs of Central Asia as *täzik*.[94]

Here is a more plausible etymology: both Biran and Liu Yengsheng note that a number of Chinese scholars claim that—based on a passage in the *Song shi* and another in the *Liao Shi*[95]—the Karakhanids were founded by Uighurs after the collapse of their empire in Mongolia in 840. Peter Golden and others, however, link them more to the Karluk Turks and ultimately to the Ashina clan of the Gök or Köke Turks.[96] In either case, the founders were not directly from the royal line but either a cadet line or another aristocratic family that did not have claim to sovereign power. In this manner, the *kara* in Karakhanid means the same as *kara* did for Inner Asians in Kara Khitai. While Michal Biran is certainly correct in that we cannot assume what the Khitans meant by Hala or Kara, as an Inner Asian society, the concept of Kara as a social marker did resonate with the Khitans and others. It did not signify that their power was lesser (indeed, many rulers in Mongolia and the other steppes held the Khitan Gurkhan in high esteem), but that it was different and not that of the royal line.

Because the directional meanings do not make sense in the context of Kara Khitai, Karakhanid empire, Köke Ordo, or the Aq Ordo—along with the fact that there has never been a Red Ulaghan Ordo—the directional meanings of the colors do not apply to color-coded state names. In the Inner Asian tradition, color names associated with kingdoms carried sacral and social values, such as auspicious (*köke*) and imperial (*altan*), as well as the denoted social rank such as noble (*aq or chagan*) and non-noble or non-royal (*kara*). While the Aq Orda and Köke Orda may have been divided along traditional methods of right and left, the colors meant that the Aq Orda was the Noble Orda and the Köke Orda was the Auspicious Orda. This referred to its rulers as not only being of the *chaghan yasun*, since all of the Chinggisids in the Golden Horde were, but it also denoted authority over all others in the Jochid patrimony. For the Köke Orda, it was the Auspicious Orda, reflecting not only the grandeur of the *Köke Möngke Tengri* but also the favored color of the Mongols. Finally, while West Khitai would function well for Kara Khitai, its regional predecessor and vassal, the Kara Kha-

---

93 Michal Biran, "Qarakhanid Studies: A View from the Qara Khitai Edge," *Cahiers d'Asie Centrale* 9 (2001), 79.

94 Volker Rybatzki, *Die Tonuquq-Inschrift* (Szeged: Universitas Szegediensis de Attila József nominata, 1997), 69-70. Also see H.W. Bailey, *Indo-Scythian Studies: Khotanese Texts VII* (Cambridge: Cambridge University Press, 2009). My thanks to Victor Mair and Peter Golden for bringing my attention to this. Ross and Thomsen translate Tazik as Sogd people, referring to Sogdia, which corresponds to the same region and refer to a sedentary/non-nomadic people. See E. Denison Ross, "The Tonyukuk Inscription: Being a Translation of Professor Vilhelm Thomsen's final Danish rendering," *Bulletin of the School of Oriental Studies*, 6/1 (1930): 42.

95 Biran, "Qarakhanid Studies: A View from the Qara Khitai Edge," 79; Liu Yensheng, "A century of Chinese research on Islamic Central Asian history in retrospect," *Cahiers d'Asie Centrale* 9 (2001): 119. Wang Riwei appears to be the first Chinese scholar to suggest this origin in his writings of 1935 and 1936.

96 Peter Golden, "The Karakhanids and early Islam" in *The Cambridge History of Early Inner Asia*, ed. Denis Sinor (Cambridge: Cambridge University Press,1990), 351.

nid Empire indicates that Kara meant it was a state from a *kara* branch of the royal clan.

Although the sacral and socio-political meanings of colors are intertwined, their application to polities often results in meanings that are less obvious. Considering the names of the capitals and cities of the Turko-Mongolian steppe empires, such as Karakorum and Karabalaghasun, the translations of Black Sands and the Black City do not necessarily provide lucid meanings of their names. That, however, is a topic for another study.

Bibliography

Akiner, Shirin. *The Formation of Kazakh Identity*. London: The Royal Institute of International Affairs, 1995.

Altan, Sanj. "An Oirad-Kalmyk Version of the "White Old Man" Sutra found among the Archives of the Late Lama Sanji Rabga Möngke Baqsi." *Mongolian Studies* 29 (2007):

Atwood, Christopher P. "National Questions and National Answers in the Chinese Revolution; Or, How do You Say Minzu in Mongolian?" *Indiana East Asian Working Papers Series on Language and Politics in Modern China* 5 (July 1994). http://www.indiana.edu/~easc/publications/doc/working_papers/Issue%205%201994%20July%20IUEAWPS%20Judge,%20Atwood.pdf

Bailey, H. W. *Indo-Scythian Studies. Khotanese Texts VII*. Cambridge: Cambridge University Press, 2009.

Banzarov, Dorji. "The Black Faith, of Shamanism Among the Mongols." Trans. Jan Nattier and John R. Krueger. *Mongolian Studies* 7 (1982): 53-92.

Biran, Michal. *The Empire of the Qara Khitai in Eurasian History: Between China and the Islamic World.* Cambridge: Cambridge University Press, 2005.

_____. "Qarakhanid Studies: A View from the Qara Khitai Edge." *Cahiers d'Asie Centrale* 9 (2001): 77-89.

Blum, Jerome. *Lord and Peasant in Russia from the Ninth to the Nineteenth Century.* Princeton: Princeton University Press, 1961.

Charleux, Isabelle. "De la ville bleue a la metropole grise: Fondation, protection et destruction de Kökeqota (Huehaote)." *Etudes mongoles et siberiennes* 35 (2004): 69-116.

Chiodo, Elisabetta. *The Mongolian Manuscripts on Birch Bark from Xarbuxyn Balgas in the Collection of the Mongolian Academy of Sciences, Part I.* Wiesbaden: Harrasowitz Verlag, 2000.

_____. "The Black Standard (*qara sülde*) of Činggis Qaɣan in Baruun Xüree," *Ural-Altaische Jahrbücher* 15 (1997/1998): 250-254.

_____. "The White Standard (čaγan tuγ sülde) of the Čaqar Mongols of Üüsin Banner." *Ural-Altaische Jahrbücher* 16 (1999/2000): 232-244.

Cleaves, Francis W., trans. and ed. *The Secret History of the Mongols.* Cambridge, MA: Harvard University Press, 1982.

De Blois, François. "The Name of the Black Sea". Pp. 1-8. In Maria Macuch, Mauro Maggi, and Werner Sundermann, eds., *Iranian languages and texts from Iran and Turan: Ronald E. Emmerick memorial volume.* Wiesbaden: Harrassowitz, 2007.

Dumas, Dominique. "The Mongols and Buddhism in 1368-1578: Facts-Stereotypes-Prejudices." *Ural Altaische Jahrbücher* 19 (2005): 167-221.

Frank, Allen J. "The Qazaqs and Russia." In *The Cambridge History of Inner Asia: The Chinggisid Age*, pp. 363-379. Ed. Nicola di Cosmo, Allen J. Frank, and Peter B. Golden. Cambridge: Cambridge University Press, 2009.

Gaadamba, Sh., ed. *The Secret History of the Mongols.* Ulaanbaatar: Ulsiin Xevleliin Gazar, 1990.

Golden, Peter B. "Migrations, ethnogenesis." In *Cambridge History of Inner Asia: The Chinggisid Age*, pp. 109-119. Ed. Nicola di Cosmo, Allen J. Frank, and Peter B. Golden. Cambridge: Cambridge University Press, 2009.

_____. "The Karakhanids and early Islam." In *The Cambridge History of Early Inner Asia,* pp. 343-370. Ed. Denis Sinor. Cambridge: Cambridge University Press,1990.

He Qiutao. *Sheng wu qin zheng lu (Bogda bagatur bey-e-ber tayilagsan temdeglel).* Trans. Arasaltu. Qayilar, PRC: Obor Monggol-un Soyul-un Keblel-un Qoriy-a, 1985.

Heissig, Walther. *The Religions of Mongolia.* Trans. Geoffrey Samuel. Berkeley: University of California Press, 1980.

Hesse, Klaus. "A Note on the Transformation of the White, Black and Yellow Shamanism in the History of the Mongols." *Studies in History* 2, 1 (1986): 17-30.

Kadoi, Yuka. *Islamic Chinoiserie: The Art of Mongol Iran.* Edinburgh Studies in Islamic Art. Edinburgh: Edinburgh University Press, 2009.

Krader, Lawrence. *Formation of the State* . Englewood Cliffs, NJ: Prentice Hall, 1968.

Lessing, Ferdinand D. *Mongolian-English Dictionary.* Bloomington, IN: The Mongolia Society, 1995.

Lhamsuren, Munkh-Erdene. "The Mongolian Nationality Lexicon: From the Chinggisid Lineage to Mongolian Nationality (From the seventeenth to the early twentieth century)." *Inner Asia* 8 (2006): 51-98.

Liu Yensheng. "A century of Chinese research on Islamic Central Asian history in retrospect." *Cahiers d'Asie Centrale* 9 (2001): 115-129.

May, Timothy. *The Mongol Conquests in World History*. London: Reaktion Books, 2012. Millward, James. *The Silk Road: A Very Short Introduction.* Oxford: Oxford University Press, 2013.

Moses, Larry W. "Triplicated Triplets: The Number Nine in the *Secret History of the Mongols*." *Asian Folklore Studies* 45 (1986): 287-294.

Onon, Urgunge, trans. and ed., *The Secret History of the Mongols: The Life and Times of Chinggis Khan* London: Routledge, 2001.

Pelliot, Paul. *Histoire secrete des Mongols,* restitution du texte mongol et traduction française des chapitres I à VI. Paris: Librairie d'Amérique et Orient 1949.

Plano Carpini, Jean de. "History of the Mongols". Trans. A Nun from Stanbrook Abbey. In Christopher Dawson, ed., *The Mongol Mission*. London: Sheed and Ward, 1955.

Pritsak, Omeljan. "Qara. Studien zur türkischen Rechtssymbolic". Pp. 239-63. In *Studies in Medieval Eurasian History*. London: Variorium Reprints, 1981.

Rachewiltz, Igor de, trans. and ed. *The Secret History of the Mongols.* Brill's Inner Asian Library. Leiden: Brill, 2003.

_____. *Index to the Secret History of the Mongols.* Chippenham, UK: Curzon Press, 1997.

Riasanovsky, Valentine A. *Fundamental Principles of Mongol Law* .Bloomington, IN: Indiana University Press, 1965.

Ross, E. Denison. "The Tonyukuk Inscription: Being a Translation of Professor Vilhelm Thomsen's final Danish rendering." *Bulletin of the School of Oriental Studies,* 6/1 (1930): 37-43.

Rybatzki, Volker. *Die Tonuquq-Inschrift* . Szeged: Universitas Szegediensis de Attila József nominata, 1997.

Sagaster, Klaus. *Die Weisse Geschichte (Čayan teüke)*. Asiatische Forschungen. Wiesbaden: Otto Harrassowitz, 1976.

Sarközi, Alice. *Political Prophecies in Mongolia in the 17th-20th centuries.* Asiatische Forschungen. Wiesbaden: Otto Harrassowitz, 1992.

Schamiloglu, Uli . "The Qaraci Beys of the Later Golden Horde: Notes on the Organization of the Mongol World Empire." *Archivum Eurasiae Medii Aevi* 4 (1984): 283-297.

Serruys, Henry . "Mongol Altan 'Gold'='Imperial'", *Monumentica Serica* 21 (1962): 357-378.

al-'Umarī, Ibn Fadl Allah. *Kitāb Maṣālik al-abṣā wa mamālik al-amṣār: Mamālik bayt Jinkiz Khān*. Ed. K Lech. Wiesbaden: Otto Harrassowitz Verlag, 1968.

Vasary, Istvan. "The Jochid Realm: the western steppe and Eastern Europe." In *The Cambridge History of Inner Asia: The Chinggisid Age*, pp. 67-85. Ed.Nicola di Cosmo, Allen J. Frank, and Peter B. Golden (Cambridge: Cambridge University Press, 2009.

Wittfogel, Karl. A. and Feng Chia-sheng. *History of Chinese Society: Liao*. Philadelphia: The American Philosophical Society, 1949.

4

Lawful Colors and Color of Law in Late Tudor England

Renee Bricker

To comprehend the uses of color in law assumes that a full color spectrum is visually perceptible.[1] Without that ability, neither literal nor rhetorical uses of color make sense. The starting point of this essay is the physical event of color of law which began with hues on the banners of feudal and royal court officials. By the sixteenth century, England's authorities still boasted colorful banners, but color had long since made a shift from visible sign to speech. That rhetorical slide of color from visual experience to metaphor and analogy was critical to its conceptual appearances in legal discourse. No longer were the banners themselves essential to representing official status when individuals presented themselves "under color of law." "Under color" was malleable enough to identify a number of offenses, including "under color of loyalty" and "under color of religion." Color, therefore, had transformed from physical sensory perception to verbal signifier. What was color? How did early modern English people understand color as function and category? Color's flexibility and contingency become more apparent when one considers historical accounts. An anecdote that sketches the instability of color and light and shows its provisional nature will help to explain both its steady regulation and verbal utility.

At the London Assizes in March 1538, widow Johanna Thorpe was a defendant in a suit brought by her neighbor William Ermystede that concerned, among other things, her window with "four lights toward his garden" that allowed Thorpe to see into it.[2] Her view, Ermystede contended, ought to be eliminated; the court agreed, but allowed Thorpe some light. At her own expense, she was ordered to install a loupe so that her view of the garden would be obstructed though some light might still enter her home. The alternative, the court determined, was that

---

[1] Appreciation and gratitude are extended to Carole Levin and Eric Ash for reading earlier drafts of this essay; their comments have been invaluable. Thanks are due especially to this volume's editor, Sungshin Kim, whose patience and sharp editorial guidance have steered this to completion. Of course deficits of argument and style that remain are mine. Original spellings in sources quoted below have been retained.

[2] Four lights means four openings. London Assizes. 129. [B.124] (fn. 16) 29 March 1538.

the window should be "clean stopped up."³ In the next century, Sir Isaac Newton told the Royal Society that color was one of the "oddest…operations in Nature," produced as it was from transparent light.⁴

Property disputes over access to light—color's *sine qua non,* according to Newton—arose in an increasingly congested London. Though its answer may seem obvious, could there be a *right* to light? That the question emerged at all in sixteenth century England reveals that access to light was not at all something to be assumed. Yet without light, there could be no experience of color. Without an experience of color, or without "the *event* of color," its capacity as a tool for persuasion—a competence that is visual, rhetorical, and rooted in the senses—is nonexistent.⁵ Johanna Thorpe and her neighbor may be set aside at this point as a useful reminder that because light and access to light were not assured, color's persuasive powers were contingent upon other conditions.

The event of color both a sensory experience and as legal concept in Elizabethan England was provocative, unstable, and malleable, all of which made it potentially threatening. As with the trajectory of color of law, this essay proceeds from actual color, regulated by Tudor sumptuary laws from the reigns of Henry VIII through Elizabeth I, to the rhetoric of color in law in the pamphlet debate between Sir William Cecil and William, Cardinal Allen. The final section regards the 1584 Bond of Association that united subscribers by oath to avenge even the attempted assassination of Queen Elizabeth. The bond was soon after regarded as pushing, even exceeding, limits of legality, and so was superseded by a subsequent Parliamentary act. In what follows, color as an investigative tool for analysis—Tudor sumptuary laws and rhetorical use in law—are mined speculatively for clues about the volatile and fragile nature of the Elizabethan regime's goal to create and preserve political and social stability.

Tudor History in Broad Strokes

Henry VII seized the throne through military success at Bosworth Field in 1485, ending what has become known as the War of the Roses. Henry himself did not have a strong claim to the English Crown, but his marriage with claimant Elizabeth of York, besides united the two warring dynasties, which reinforced the legitimacy of Henry's monarchy. The repercussions of the establishment of the Tudor dynasty help to explain the uncertainty that underlay some of the statutory responses and proclamations issued by later Tudor monarchs.

The marital vexations of his son, Henry VIII, are well known and can be better explained when framed within the context of solidifying the Tudor dynasty. Henry's quest for a male heir led to six marriages in all (his last wife, Catherine Parr, surviving him), and culminated with the third Act of Succession

---

3   London Assizes. 129. [B.124] (fn. 16)

4   Robert Finlay, "Weaving the Rainbow: Visions if Color in World History," *Journal of World History* 18 (December 2007): 431.

5   Robert Pasnau, "The event of color," *Philosophy Studies*142 (2009): 353–369. William M. Reddy, *The Navigation of Feeling: A Framework for the History of Emotions* (Cambridge: CUP, 2001), 4. Citing Brent Berlin and Paul Kay, *Basic Color Terms,* Reddy says that perception of color and its interaction with light shapes language, not the other way around.

in 1539 that established his last will and the line of succession. Yet this Act ensured that his youngest daughter and final heir, Elizabeth I, inherited a clouded title because it maintained her illegitimate birth while restoring her to the line of Tudor succession. When her sister Mary became queen, Mary rectified this question of legitimacy for herself only. For reasons that can only be guessed, Elizabeth chose to ignore the legal status of her illegitimate birth so it remained in force for her from accession in November 1558 until her death in 1603. Two related conditions complicated Elizabeth's monarchy: religion and her cousin, Mary, Queen of Scots.

This was the era of the European religious reformations, and Henry VIII threw in his lot with Protestants when efforts to obtain a divorce from his first wife, Katharine of Aragon (Mary's mother), were frustrated by Pope Clement VII. After his divorce, he married Elizabeth's mother, Anne Boleyn, thus making Elizabeth *the* child of the English reformation. Henry VIII's divorce from Katharine of Aragon, and Anne Boleyn's, subsequent execution did not change this. When she became queen Elizabeth's first task was to cement the Church of England and establish the monarch as its leader. Two Acts of Parliament achieved this officially; however, a process of Protestantization of the English people, many of whom remained Catholic, characterized the course of the Queen's reign.[6] Mary, Queen of Scots, Elizabeth's cousin and heir, was a Catholic with legitimate birth status and ambitions of being named to the English succession. These circumstances made her a lightning-rod for the disaffected in England. Religious conflicts on the continent and subsequent divided loyalties, along with perceptions of Elizabeth's vulnerability to assassination all demanded address. One tactic of the central Elizabethan regime was to regulate behavior through sumptuary laws that encompassed commerce and military provisions.

Lawful Colors

The 1570s and 1580s, the middle decades of Elizabeth I's nearly forty-five year reign, were fraught with political fears of invasion, assassination, and treason believed to emanate from threats both internal and external, manifesting particularly in Catholics.[7] Clothing colors and fabrics achieved visual communication between segments of the commonwealth to advance or proclaim "public ends."[8] Apparel regulations were thus a way for the center of the regime to assert its own version of what commonwealth meant, or should be, to further public good. Scholars frequently emphasize social organization as the main goal of sumptuary legislation; but, this oversimplifies or obscures its other objectives.[9] Examination

---

6   See Christopher Haigh, "The English Reformation: A Premature Birth, A Difficult Labour and a Sickly Child," *The Historical Journal* 33 (June1990): 449-459.

7   I am using Corey Robin's definition of political fear as distinctive from other types of fear. "By political fear, I mean a people's felt apprehension of some harm to their collective well-being—the fear of terrorism, panic over crime, anxiety about moral decay—or the intimidation wielded over men and women by governments or groups. What makes [these] types of fear political rather than personal is that they emanate from society or have consequences for a society." Corey Robin, *Fear: The History of a Political Idea* (Oxford: Oxford University Press, 2004), 2.

8   Peter Lake and Steven Pincus, *The Politics of the Public Sphere in Early Modern England,* Politics, Culture and Society in Early Modern Britain (Manchester: Manchester University Press, 2012), 5.

9   Kim M. Phillips, "Masculinities and the Medieval English Sumptuary Laws," *Gender & History* 19 (April 2007), fn.5.

of sumptuary laws reveals that specifying colors, such as restrictions on the use of scarlet, crimson, blue, and purple, was a starting point of regulation that reached into commerce, industry, military, national security, and status. Restrictions applied to color and fabric together, so that the two were not considered separately.[10] Therefore, cloth figures prominently in what follows. Sumptuary laws then may be mined effectively to reconsider developments in late Tudor society outside the narrow circumference of dress and appearance. After definition of commonwealth, this section proceeds to the apparel regulations themselves to conclude with a discussion of legal color of office and retainers.

In his elaboration of a commonwealth's divisions, Sir Thomas Smith explained, "we in England divide our men commonly into foure sortes, gentlemen, citizens and yeoman artificers, and labourers."[11] This continued his concept of civil society according to the Great Chain of Being that articulated four elements, four humors, and four divisions among ranks of people in Tudor England.[12] However, it is one thing to claim that clearly understood categories for people existed in a society; it is another matter altogether to create and maintain the boundaries between them. Color worked both through visual language and physical perception to produce an effort, if not the outcome, to achieve that demarcation. That a spate of royal proclamations specified dress and color according to rank while also enforcing regulations of apparel betrays a conflict between an idealized version of social organization and the reality of untidy lived experiences. In other words, people must have been capitalizing on the economic developments of the day that included the creation of credit, increased commerce, and trade in order to purchase goods according to what they might afford regardless of rank.[13]

Social historian Keith Wrightson describes a vibrant, complex economic world in sixteenth century England. Commercial activity in the mid-sixteenth century reveals fissures in early modern English economic life that pitted prevalent thought about what was right according to God's law on one side with the enthusiasm for enterprise and consumption on the other. In 1563 Parliament passed a bill forbidding the sale of apparel on credit to people whose yearly income was under £200. This prevented—or was meant to prevent—people from living beyond their means while others profited from that behavior.

Yet the Usury Act of 1571 indicated limited compromise by repealing earlier Tudor statutes that prohibited loans. Instead it allowed these at fixed interest rates

---

10 Charlene Elliott, "Purple Pasts: Color Codification in the Ancient World." *Law & Social Inquiry* 33 (2008): 187. "Hunt's observation, that "it is easy to assert a status claim by donning a purple robe," underscores the absolute importance of color *and cloth*."

11 Sir Thomas Smith, *De Republica Anglorum* (*DRA*). *The maner of gouernement or policies of the Realme of Englande*. 1583. STC 22857, 20.

12 The seminal exposition of this idea is Arthur O. Lovejoy, *The Great Chain of Being: The Study of the History of an Idea* (Cambridge: Harvard University Press, 1976). For its understanding to Elizabethans, see Eustace W. Tillyard, *The Elizabethan World Picture* (New York, Vintage Books, 1959).

13 "[Those] who could specialise profitably in market gardening, fruit growing or small-scale dairying…could help small tenants survive even prosper, sharing to a lesser degree the rising real incomes and increased consumption of the yeomanry." Keith Wrightson, *Earthly Necessities: Economic Lives in Early Modern Britain*, The New Economic History of Britain (New Haven and London: Yale University Press, 2000), 140, 189.

with certain restrictions.[14] "The sayde Statute now revyved shalbe most largely and strongly construed for the repressing of Usurie, and against all p[er]sons that shall offend against the said Statute...directly or indirectly."[15] In other words, not loans themselves but restraining excessive profit from them was the intent of this latest statute. Elizabeth's principal secretary, Lord William Cecil, Baron Burghley, sat in the Parliament's House of Lords by this time. There, as in the Queen's Privy Council, he pursued what Wrightson calls a "dual strategy" to preserve political stability while encouraging "the orderly development of economic" growth.[16] Not only did regulation of clothing, materials, and acceptable colors of clothes designate people's position in society, but also these legal actions point toward a perceived need to protect people from their own spending inclinations and to restrict merchants from profiting unfairly. Direct government intervention in commercial activity, at least in this area, struck a note of paternalism toward consumption as well. It is evidence of the strategy of William Cecil to maintain the ideal of commonwealth while encouraging economic initiative.[17]

Through government regulations, a visual system of order was created with what may be taken to be uneven success at enforcement, judging from successive insistent proclamations. People were also directed to purchase domestic goods so that apparel proclamations during these middle decades of the reign regulated commercial markets. Together these created a political economy of color that reveals contested social arenas and disrupted social organization through visual politics and a language of perception that demonstrated who complied with apparel statutes and who did not. Increased trade, population growth, and the Usury Act suggest increased demand for consumer goods among all but the poorest people, who were not a distinct group until the later part of the century.[18] This was also a period of economic transition that preserved earlier notions of commonwealth as it sought to balance changes in manufacturing, trade, and income patterns. Regulation of clothing and colors was one tactic taken to realize that strategy.

The 1570s and 1580s were a time of increased effort to regulate dress, but it began just under one year after Elizabeth's accession with the Proclamation Against Excess in Apparel, issued late October 1559. These proclamations reiterated statutory prescriptions of what kinds of materials and colors were permitted or forbidden according to social rank. For example, statutory repetitions of color prohibitions continued to stipulate that "scarlet, crimson or blue" was allowed only for those ranked "dukes, marquises, earls or their children, baron, and knights of the order."[19] At the same time, members of the Queen's Privy Council agreed to articles "for reformation...in abuses of apparel" in their own households and among their own servants.[20] This step fit with the common belief that the

---

14   4 *Statutes of the Realm* 543 (1547-1624), Statutes of Queen Elizabeth, 13 Eliz., c. 8. https:Heinonline.org. This statue repealed 37 Hen. 8, c. 12, and 5/6 Ed. 6, c.17; Wrightson, 156.

15   4 *Statutes of the Realm* 542 (1547-1624) Statutes of Queen Elizabeth, 542, 13 Eliz., c. 8, §6.

16   Wrightson, 156.

17   See Wrightson above.

18   Wrightson, 148-9.

19   *TRP*, 464. Enforcing Statutes of Apparel. I Eliz. I.

20   *Calendar of State Papers, Domestic: Edward, Mary and Elizabeth, 1547-80*. Letter entries dated and num-

lower classes imitated the upper classes so that, to paraphrase Wrightson, emulation influenced consumption practices.[21]

According to the proclamation, this imitation was a detriment to the consumers' material well-being because it impelled people to attempt to live above their income. Not only this, but also excess consumption threatened tax revenues:

> [W]here there is mention made of values of yearly livelihoods and goods, the best account thereof is to be made by the taxations of this last subsidy, so as if any will be excused by pretense of his livelihood or substance to offend, it is as meet that he answer to the prince in subsidy for that value, as seek defense to break any good law.[22]

The next year another proclamation followed that was intended to "repress the inordinate gains" of those engaged in manufacture of items for wear. Together these convey the regime's effort to stratify groups of people, but also intervention to limit profits that might be earned unfairly by manufacturers. One reason to curtail profits might be found in the restrictions that limited choices, not only by degree of noble rank, but also by annual income in an effort to protect the "meaner sort" from poor purchase choices. Thus multiple ends could be achieved. People were compartmentalized into social categories through visual recognition while economic mobility was curbed. This suggests that the regime protected consumers from the greed of retailers and manufacturers, as well as from personal ambition and taste.

Another reason to monitor profit and consumption was military provision. There were no standing armies in sixteenth century England, as in most of Christian Europe.[23] In England, everyone was expected to participate in national defense. Critical to the defense effort was maintaining horses. An apparel proclamation issued in 1562 addressed specifically this issue:

> [H]er majesty findeth like cause to have two other great enormities daily increasing in this her realm to be speedily reformed, for which there do remain in force good laws. The one is the monstrous abuse of apparel almost in all estates, but principally in the meaner sort. The other is the decay and disfurniture of all kinds of horses for service within the realm

The proclamation acknowledged that "the decay of horses within the realm" was due in part to stealing and selling them outside the country. However, this was also a consequence of neglect in breeding and maintenance within the realm. The solution, enforcing the laws, involved the mobilization of local sheriffs and the creation of special commissions to conduct a census of horses throughout the kingdom.

The proclamation established methods of proceeding. Men were to account for their occupations and incomes, and these were to be checked against the sub-

---

bered 1559 Oct. 20.12, and Oct. 20.13.
21 Wrightson, 299.
22 *TRP,* 464. Enforcing Statutes of Apparel, Westminster, 21 October 1559, I Elizabeth I. Larkin and Hughes, 136-8.
23 Jeremy Black, *War in Early Modern World, 1450-1815* (London: Routledge, 1998), 18.

sidy rolls for compatibility in order to discern tax deceit. Moreover, "if personas shall not have...horses according to the statute, by reasons of their wives apparel" they were expected to comply by the proclamation deadline or face the penalties. Therefore, living within one's means meant that households should be able to keep horses, which were important for national defense, and that the laws pertaining to apparel were obeyed. If wives dressed beyond the means of the annual household income, they did so in violation of the law. Blithely spending money on clothes rather than on horses needed for defense threatened national security. It also revealed possible tax fraud because a discrepancy might exist between an assigned value according to the subsidy roll and available funds.

The steady regulation of apparel suggests that it was perceived as an important deterrent against threats of fraud and other criminal behaviors. Order and disorder were connected to color and cloth in the proclamations because wearing proscribed dress had the potential for criminal misrepresentation. If they could muster the funds, English women and men who belonged to lower social ranks might manage to buy clothing intended for their social superiors, perhaps even passing themselves as belonging to a higher rank. So, too, people of higher rank could pretend to be otherwise. Such pretense was not limited to using color deceptively since it included dress itself, with respect to costume and fabric.

People did in fact dress to deceive. Not only was it dangerous to dress outside of one's own rank in light of penalties one might incur, but such misrepresentation also posed dangers to others. By violating dress prescriptions, high-ranking people could perpetrate a fraud or hide treason. In 1569 Thomas Percy, Earl of Northumberland, and Charles Neville, Earl of Westmoreland, were declared traitors for their part in the Northern uprising of the Catholic nobility and their supporters in England. Northumberland was captured "wandering alone disguised in simple apparel."[24] Because of the discovery of a treasonous plot that year between Thomas Howard, Duke of Norfolk and English detainee Mary, Queen of Scots, 1571 was an especially busy year for proclamations concerned with treason, traitors, and actions intended to modulate behaviors.

Universities were commanded to suppress "irregularities of the students respecting apparel," through directives sent to the Vice-Chancellor at Cambridge and Heads of Houses at Oxford.[25] In recognition of potential deceit, a 1571 proclamation announced a bill passed in Parliament against priests entering the realm disguised variously as servants or mariners.[26] Disguised priests and malefactors of all sorts made dress a matter of national security. Ten years later Jesuit Edmund Campion was apprehended disguised as a "roister," according to a Protestant polemic, or as a jewel merchant, according to Catholic accounts.[27]

---

24   *CSP, Dom.*, 1569. Dec. 25. Durham 51. George Freville to [Sir William Cecil].

25   *CSP, Dom.* 1566. Nov. 11. Cecil to Dr. Beaumont.

26   "House of Commons Journal. Vol. 1: 27, April 1571," *Journal of the House of Commons*, vol. 1, 1547-1629 (1802), 86. *CSP, Dom.* 1571. "60. Bill against "Disguised Priests," or Professors of the Romish religion, being found in England, disguised in the apparel of serving men, or mariners; and for the punishment of gypsies remaining in England."

27   William Cecil, *The Execution of Justice*, 1583 (*STC*, 4903), C.i. "[T]he other named Edmund Campion... who was found out being disguised like a roister," and cited in Thomas M. McCoog, "The Flower of Oxford": The

In his 1583 purtinanical pamphlet, *Anatomie of Abuses,* Phillip Stubbes proceeded from the declaration that "pride is the principal abuse," with apparel being one of its symptoms.[28] Composed as a dialogue, the question was posed of how pride in apparel can occur. Stubbes answered,

> [W]earyng of Apparell more gorgeous, sumptuous and precious than our state calling or condition of lyfe requireth, wherby, we are puffed up into Pride, and infroced to thinke of our selves, more than we ought...this sinne of excesse in Apparell, remayneth as an example of evyll before our eyes, and as a provocative to sinne, as Experience daylye sheweth.[29]

Clothing, Stubbes asserted, was a gift from God to hide the shame and filth of original sin and for warmth. He argues that velvets, silks, damasks, and satins might be worn in foreign countries because in those lands, people are drawn to the luxurious materials from lack of simpler goods like wool.[30]

Every private person should dress as his "station and condition of life requireth," while those who occupy offices of law should dress in a style worthy of their offices, "thereby to strike a terrour and feare into the harts of the people."[31] Stubbes's pamphlet was a success, enjoying subsequent printings in his time.[32] Its popularity conveys the position that the genre of moralistic writing warned of disaster to those whose behavior was sinful and was a "reflexion of life and thought" in late sixteenth century England.[33]

The conjunction of religion with consumption patterns to prevent or limit economic excess, while beyond the scope of this essay, merits mention. Though the royal proclamations and the parliamentary statutes on apparel are mute on religion, likening material excess with godliness, Stubbes shows, was a feature in popular literature. In Stubbes's pamphlet, Philoponus answers Spudeus saying that clothing is a gift from God. "First, that sin was the cause why our apparel was given us. Secondly, that God is the author, and giver therof. Thirdly, that it was give[n] us to cover our shame...not to feed the insatiable desires of me[n]s wa[n]to[n] and luxurious eies."[34] But Stubbes had other issues besides sin, and his warnings through Philoponus against excess invoke economic protection as well as social order through visible cueing.

Color is only one component of this cueing, and its pursuit leads to the broader issues connected with imported materials. Stubbes emphasized do-

---

Role of Edmund Campion in Early Recusant Polemics," *The Sixteenth Century Journal* 24 (Winter, 1993): 899. "In disguise as a traveling jewel salesman from Dublin, on June 25, 1580, Edmund Campion crossed into England, a country that he had abandoned for religious reasons nine years earlier."

28   Phillip Stubbes, *The Anatomie of Abuses*, STC 23376.357.05, 10. Terry P. Pearson, "The Composition and Development of Phillip Stubbes's "Anatomie of Abuses" *The Modern Language Review* 56 (July 1961): 321-332.

29   Stubbes, Bv.

30   Stubbes, C.ii.

31   Stubbes, C.ii.

32   Pearson, 326.

33   Pearson, 323.

34   Stubbes, C.iiii.

mestic textiles and restrictions of purchase of foreign wares in order to avoid self-impoverishment:[35]

> [W]her there is store of other clothing there hath been geven, less store of silks, velvets, satens, damasks, and such like: and wher there is plenty of them, there is no clothing else, thus the Lord did deale for that every country ought to contente themselves, with there owne kind of attire: except necessytie force the contrarie…Simplicitie and Christian sobrietie, both of apparel and maner of lyvinge, we should not onely please God…[but] enriche our Cuntry."[36]

Woad and madder, substances necessary for producing blue and red dyes, were locally available in England.[37] Yet their abundance—even surplus, especially of woad—hurt prices. The Crown explicitly restricted sowing woad to address this problem declaring,

> that a late attempt of breaking up and tilling of very fertile grounds to sow woad is upon a late [recent] private and inordinate gain practiced, to the manifest grief of her people in divers places…that the excessive gain found thereby, without regard to the public weal, is like both to continue and increase this attempt, to the great damage of the commonweal.[38]

With global expansion, imported dyestuffs became a greater economic issue as the sixteenth and seventeenth centuries advanced because of access to New World sources for producing colors.[39] Because dyes were luxury items, richer colors than those that could be obtained from woad or madder signaled a level of opulence more appropriate to the aristocracy. Therefore, restrictions on colors of apparel protected status by limiting access to its outward signs.[40]

Division of social and political ranks identifiable by color could be a potent way to maintain order because once seen and identified, transgressors could be punished. At least this was the intent. That several apparel proclamations followed one another over successive decades questions their effectiveness. Men and women, it seems, required periodic and escalating reminders about what they could and could not wear. The regime responded with increased efforts to involve and mobilize groups of people across the social spectrum as the 1560s advanced, and through the 1570s. As the regime navigated the 1580s, that action intensified.

---

35 Stubbes, C.ii.

36 Stubbes, C.iii.

37 Jane Schneider, "Peacocks and Penguins: The Political Economy of European Cloth and Colors," *American Ethnologist* 5 (August 1978): 401-1.

38 *TRP*, "678. Prohibiting Sowing of Woad, Richmond, 14 October 1585, 27 Elizabeth I," 516-7.

39 Herman Van Der Wee, "The Western European Woollen Industries, 1500-1750," Ch. 8 in *The Cambridge History of Textiles*, vol. I (Cambridge: Cambridge University Press, 2003), 400.

40 Schneider writes, "Dyestuffs…were luxury items in the long-distance trade that linked Europe and Asia," 421.

Colors of Law

The apparel regulations discussed above show that color could be used to preserve social order by visibly categorizing people. Likewise, color organized difference. In the instance of sumptuary laws, the prescribed categories of social groupings were materially constructed so that membership and its trespass could be seen right away. Comparable to this, in conditions of direct violence such as military combat, color functioned as a means to sort groups of people according to whether they were allies or enemies. Color plainly proclaimed one's loyalty.[41] The remainder of this essay, beginning with colors of office, takes up the rhetorical use of color. In legal discourse the linguistic use of color achieves what it seems to do because of people's prior sensory experience of color in offices of law.

Examples of the use of colors in banners to announce allegiance or authority of office are readily found. In fact, these are so common that they can be overlooked. Pausing to consider these displays draws attention to how color manifests a visual language that is effective because it appeals to the power of emotion to inspire fidelity or to deceive.[42] The colors of banners were calling cards that also served to incite or inflame onlookers who understood their meanings in an emotive event of color, that is through the physical experience of color that also evoked emotional reaction.

Henry VII contended with two Yorkist uprisings during Parliament sessions in March 1486.[43] When Parliament assembled for the second time in December, it enacted the statute against unlawful retainers in effect from 1487, the third year of Henry VII's reign.[44] That proclamation declared,

> any farmer or tenant...retained by any person or persons contrary to the statutes, by livery, badge, token, oath, indenture or promise, or goes to any field, gathering or assembly wearing any man's livery, badge or token except the king's...that all grants and leases made to him...then be entirely void and of no effect.[45]

The context is significant for knowing why this measure was undertaken. The uprisings, a series of actions to challenge the authority of the Crown and specifically Henry VII's sovereignty, are connected to what G.R. Elton describes as the "familiar story" of the "overmighty subject."[46] A member of the nobility with too

---

41   In his typology of violence, Johan Galtung defines direct violence according to categories of survival, well-being needs, identity, and freedom, to specifically include killing and maiming. His formulation of violence also suggests that regulations of apparel, through directly effecting identity needs, could be interpreted as a form of direct and structural violence. Johan Galtung, "Cultural Violence," *Journal of Peace Research*, vol. 27, no. 3 (1990): 292.

42   Reddy, 321fn. 5.

43   Rosemary O'Day, *The Longman Companion to the Tudor Age* (London and New York: Longman, 1995), 47.

44   O'Day, 120. Parliament assembled in 1487 from 9 November until 18 December.

45   Chris Given-Wilson (general editor); Paul Brand, Seymour Phillips, Mark Ormrod, Geoffrey Martin, Anne Curry, Rosemary Horrox (editors), "Henry VII: November 1487," *Parliament Rolls of Medieval England*, British History Online, http://www.british-history.ac.uk/report.aspx?compid=116565.

46   G. R. Elton, *The Tudor Constitution*, 2nd ed. (Cambridge: Cambridge University Press, 1982), 31.

many men retained in his service was a nobleman at risk of being "overmighty," thus threatening the power and authority of the Crown.[47] Retainers were the followers of a particular lord who swore him allegiance and service, even when doing so meant opposing the dominant allegiance owed to the monarch.[48] In return, retained men received gifts from their lord, including offices, land, and money, as well as his endorsement should the retainer be confronted with a lawsuit.[49] The banner, badge, or livery of a lord showed others that a man was retained in service to a lord who also claimed his allegiance. If falsely retained, that is, if illegally displaying the colors of a particular office or a nobleman in violation of restrictions, such retainers were also prepared to deceive others, whether ordinary folk or another nobleman.

Whereas apparel regulations ascribed certain colors to specific social ranks, the act against retainers targeted colors as signs of potentially disloyal servants aligned with overly ambitious nobility, who were themselves potential traitors. Limiting retainers reduced the likelihood of treason, and it restricted the forces available to a single nobleman. In the visual economy of emotion, color signaled rank, and it also signaled legitimacy of office, for example, and of allegiances. The 1487 Act Against Retainers, enforced again in 1572 by a royal proclamation, shifted discussion of color from its utility to mark boundaries of social rank and loyalty to its conceptual employment in "under color of law."

False retainers illustrated abuse of the colors of office through wearing clothing and signs, "livery, badges, or other tokens." Such unlawfully retained servants "plainly hinder justice and disorder the good policy of the realm by maintenance of unlawful suits and titles and by stirring up and nourishing of factions, riots and unlawful assemblies, the mothers of rebellion."[50]

Both the proclamation and the statute it sought to enforce prescribed punishments and a limited period for informing the Crown—forty days for Henry VII, twenty for his granddaughter. Both also identified similar problems with unlawfully retained servants, including damage to Crown properties and unlawful assembly. When situated within the contexts of the recent uprisings in York, in Henry's case, and the persistent threats, real and imagined, of English Catholics at home and abroad for Elizabeth, controlling crowds through limiting servants and imposing punishments for violating that limitation are understandably interpreted as a regime's central effort to enforce Crown allegiance. Signifiers such as the special clothes and tokens associated with specific officers were the focus of enforcement. Illegally retained servants indicated official status through specific signs and colors such as blue or crimson, and by association with those on whose behalf they acted. Such people were poised to act against the law, so that one violation of law made possible a further violation. Retainers of those without authorization to expand their household staff are examples of how the literal use of color in "color of office" presumed the power of actions done "under the color

---

47 The term "Crown" is shorthand here for the authority and power of the monarchy as institution.
48 Elton, 31.
49 Elton, 31.
50 Paul L. Hughes and James F. Larkin, eds., *Tudor Royal Proclamations*, vol. 3, *The Later Tudors, 1588 – 1603* (New Haven and London: Yale University Press, 1969), 350.

of law" might signal legitimacy to others. It is this latter category of color that the remainder of this essay addresses.

Under Color of Law

Color used as a rhetorical strategy in proclamations and treatises accomplished, or at least tried to address, explicit goals through legal discourse. As a tool for analysis, color as textual expression, rather than sensory experience, compels combining and comparing documents that at first sight may not seem to have a clear connection. For example, proclamations against false retainers, concealed lands, disguised priests, and excess in apparel may seem unrelated to one another. Yet, seen with color as the common denominator, these each confront overlapping problems of allegiance, loyalties through enforced sociopolitical order realized by using color in the language of law. As a rhetorical strategy, 'color' described behavior associated with loyalties or character, as in "colourable argument," or "to colour their own cruelty."[51] Color also had specific legal uses as in 'colors of office,' or 'under color of law' and the distinction between the two categories is in the rhetorical shift of color as a designation of lawful to false authority.

Color used descriptively rather than in contrast to the formula of its legal expression shows its widened use as a metaphor for unlawful actions committed by non-officials.[52] To further explain this shift from literal to linguistic, it is useful to summarize the trajectory of the expression, *under color of law*. First, color had a literal connotation with specific offices of government, such as administrative and judicial posts like sheriffs and court officers. These officers were retained or otherwise acted officially according to the colors associated with their posts. In this way, people would know that the person with whom they were confronted, or to whom they might appeal, were acting with proper authority of office. English legal historian T. F. Plucknett observes that, by Richard II's reign in the late fourteenth century, "color of law" appeared with a meaning altered to respond to the specific problem of people deceitfully presenting themselves according to the colors of a particular office.[53] By the sixteenth century, as review of the documents under discussion here shows, color in legal discourse had become a metaphor deployed as a rhetorical strategy, rather than to indicate the literal appropriation or misuse of colors.

The deployment of 'color of law' was explicit in Lord Burghley's pamphlet, *Execution of Justice in England*, and in William, Cardinal Allen's riposte, *A True, Sin-*

---

51 Richard Verstegan, "Letters and Despatches of Richard Verstegan (c.1591-1640)," ed. by Anthony G. Petti, *Catholic Record Society*, no. 52 (London, 1959): 1.2.2, 1.5.7.

52 Steven L. Winter, "The Meaning of "Under Color of Law"," *Michigan Law Review* 91 (December 1992): 331. Legal discourse came to demonstrate "the reliance on a metaphor-under color of law-to mediate the application of legal restrictions on the exercise of state power." Nodes of this shift are represented in this essay's discussion of color and law.

53 Theodore F. T. Plucknett, *A Concise History of the Common Law*, Fifth Edition (London: Butterworth and Co., 1956), 412,fn.2. Plucknett also writes that color came to be used to refer to the defective title of the plaintiff alleged by the defendant in property matters. "It soon became the practice…to give feigned colour of a purely fictitious character; this raised a fictitious question of law not amounting to the general issue, and served as an excuse for leaving the whole case to the court [sic].", 412-3.

cere, and Modest Defense of English Catholics.⁵⁴ Both Burghley and Allen used the phrase to attack opponents and to depict offensive conduct. It is these two texts, therefore, that are examined next, first chronologically and then comparatively.

The Execution of Justice in England was a response to foreign reactions and criticism of the regime's handling of English Catholics, specifically the torture and subsequent execution of Jesuit Edmund Campion in 1582.⁵⁵ In formulating his defense of official government action, Burghley constructed an argument that used color, among other things, to describe the Jesuit's actions, and those of perceived traitors who were also Catholic. The thrust of Burghley's argument was that the Jesuits were *not* punished for religion, or for matters of conscience. Because Pope Pius V issued a bull of excommunication against Elizabeth in 1570, her Catholic subjects were released from obedience to her and indeed obligated to support an invading Catholic power when the time seemed right to do so.⁵⁶ The papal bull encouraged "trouble to the realm by stirring rebellion," according to Burghley.⁵⁷ Therefore, while the bull presented "occasion to doubt" the intentions of those found wandering about, they were not charged "in their consciences or otherwise, by any inquisition to bring them into danger of any capital law, so as no one was called to any capital or bloody question upon matters of religion."⁵⁸ English law, Burghley maintained, did not condemn matters of conscience—the crimes committed by the Jesuits were treason and sedition. Their religious affiliation was mere coincidence. This position is well understood by Tudor historians. Using color for historical analysis drives investigation of how Burghley constructed a legal argument meant to persuade a foreign audience, the fulcrum of which was the rhetorical strategy of color in legal discourse.

The *Execution of Justice* began with the assertion that it was commonplace that "all offenders…great and small…make defense of their lewd and unlawful facts by untruths and by coloring and covering their deeds…" to claim that their actions were misunderstood for something else.⁵⁹ This strategy was that of 'coloring' one's actions and it represents a rhetorical shift in the legal use and meaning of color. Everything that followed proceeded from the assertion that accused people protested their crimes in order to achieve two goals: impunity, and the desire to continue to pursue those illicit activities. Burghley sought to persuade protesting audiences that, had the executed Jesuits not been caught, prosecuted, and executed, their real intentions would have materialized in further

---

54 Hereafter these will be referred to as *The Execution of Justice*, and *A Modest Defense* spelled according to Allen's text rather than as in the modern edition edited by Robert M. Kingdon cited above. Cecil is the acknowledged and accepted author of *The Execution of Justice*, though the treatise was originally published anonymously.

55 *The Execution of Justice in England by William Cecil and a True, Sincere, and Modest Defence of English Catholics by William Allen*, ed. and intro. by Robert M. Kingdon (Ithaca, NY: Cornell University Press, 1965).

56 A papal bull is an encyclical issued by the pope with his seal meant to direct, advise, and announce. *New Advent Catholic Encyclopedia*, http://www.newadvent.org/cathen/03052b.htm.

57 William Cecil, Baron Burghley, "The Execution of Justice in England," Bii, *STC* 4903.

58 Cecil, Bii. The "bloody question" asked whether as English Catholic, one would support a foreign Catholic invader or stand by the English Protestant Queen. It was a question that pitted conscience of religion against national allegiance and loyalty.

59 Cecil, A.ii.

criminal action to the detriment of the realm and the Queen. In short, he strove to convince his readers that the executions were utterly necessary. This required that Burghley assert that religion had no part in these prosecutorial events, which were all conducted properly according to English law.

To reinforce this point, Burghley cited another case of two men accused, convicted, and executed for piracy and other "treacheries," who also "liked the Bishop of Rome [because he was] in favor of their treason," yet did not "color their offenses."[60] Instead, they did "flatly to animate them [their intentions in order] to continue their former wicked purposes" of leading an armed rebellion against the Queen of England. Only after confronted with charges did they "pretend" or color, that is use alternate language to describe their offences as something other than rebellion.[61] This exemplifies the way color is used in the next few passages and is consistent with its legal development over the next two centuries of English common law.[62]

What the treatise does not say is as important as what it does say. The Jesuits were never referred to specifically as priests, nor indeed as Catholics. Instead the argument focused on their allegiance to the Bishop of Rome and adherence to the papal bull that encouraged treason; charges were confined specifically to "maintaining of the Popes…foresaid authorities and Bull…and for no other causes or questions of religion were these persons condemned."[63] In this way, the argument omitted religion or liberty of conscience in order to maintain the construction of the Jesuits' crimes as treason, while their protests to the contrary were depicted as mere color of religion in the pamphlet which considered these only a pretext:

> "[T]rue it is, that when they were charged and convinced of these pointes of conspiracies and treasons, they would still in their answers colourably pretend their actions to have been for religion: but in deed and truth they were manifested to be for the procurement and maintenance of the rebellions and wars against her Majesty and her realm."[64]

The pamphlet continued with dehumanizing characterizations of the Jesuits in order to depict them as inhuman, thus deserving their punishments. This also served to explain their "unnatural" opposition to their lawful queen:[65] "[I]f these kind of vermin were suffered to creep by stealth into the Realm, and to spread their poison within the same, howsoever when they are taken, like hypocrites,

---

60   Cecil, A.iii. This refers to Thomas Stuckley and events in Ireland, which remained Roman Catholic at this time. Ireland was an especially dangerous place from the perspective of the central English regime because of its island position making it a potentially strategic departure point for military invasion. That Ireland resisted English efforts to Protestantize it escalated the threat it posed.

61   Cecil, A.iii.

62   Plucknett, 412-13.

63   Cecil, B.iii.

64   Cecil, B.iii.

65   In a variety of Elizabethan sources, such as proclamations against sedition, seminaries abroad and Jesuits including this present treatise on loyalty and allegiance, treason and behaviors deemed contrary to lawful obedience to the sovereign and the English government were regularly characterized in language that cast obedience to their sovereign as lawful and natural.

they colour and counterfeit the same with possession of devotion in religion."[66] In this excerpt, and that quoted above, color is used to imply that actions appear legal though interpreted otherwise.

With final force, Burghley asserted that, "there is no doubt by Gods grace (her Majesty being so much given to mercy and devoted to peace) but all colour and occasion of shedding the blood of any more of her natural subjects of the this land…should utterly cease."[67] Color in law, at this time, had three distinct meanings: the literal, the plausible, and the pretext, or rhetorical, whereby one action was presented as an altogether different one.[68] The color metaphor Cecil employed conveyed that continued direct violence could not be defended as lawful or justified when undertaken by parties outside of the regime. There was no way to make acceptable the unacceptable deed.

In defending the regime's fatal conviction of English Jesuit Edmund Campion, Cecil deployed color to make alternate points to explain or condemn. When turning next to William, Cardinal Allen, color is used as metaphor and analogy to attack and rebut, rather than in the legal contexts used by Cecil. Attention to color in these contexts means also attending to rhetorical strategy and the power of ideas in what was propaganda for sympathy or condemnation as each side used similar conceptual frameworks of language in different ways to achieve equivalent ends.

William Allen was ordained a priest in 1565 and founded the seminary at Douai in 1568 specifically to train priests for England, the first of whom returned in 1574.[69] Allen undertook the foundation of the seminary specifically to respond to what he identified as the Elizabethan strategy for elimination of English Catholicism through attrition of its senior clergy.[70] His solution was to train new priests to send back to England to minister to its Catholic population. Anne Dillon summarized the essence of the contention between the central English government and that of Catholics in terms of the questions about whether one could be a faithful Catholic while simultaneously remaining a loyal subject. Dillon answered that question by examining the construction of Catholic martyrdom; focusing on the rhetorical use of color expands that answer to address *how* each argument was advanced.

Printed in 1584, the year after the publication of Cecil's pamphlet, Allen's *A True, Sincere and Modest Defense of English Catholics*, directly confronted the question of loyalty and faithfulness to counter-argue that Campion and the priests tortured and executed with him were martyred. He insisted that they died for their faith, not because they were guilty of treason. Allen began with a direct assault on the author of the *Execution of Justice*: "And yet this good writer [Cecil]…to colour their cruelty towards Catholic gentlemen, setteth down the

---

66   Cecil, B.i.

67   Cecil, E. IV.

68   By 'plausible' color of law could also mean that there might be some basis for the claim at issue. This area is not under discussion in this essay. "The defective title which the defendant attributes to the plaintiff is called 'colour', and in earlier cases [before the fourteenth century] it seems that is really did represent the facts," Plucknett, 412.

69   Anne Dillon, *The Construction of Martyrdom in the English Catholic Community, 1535 – 1603*, St. Andrews Studies in Reformation History (Aldershot: Ashgate, 2002), 11-12.

70   Dillon, 11.

matter as though cases on Cons[c]ience, Religion or of the Sea Apostolic were but in some degrees, in some little part punished."[71] This passage used color as analogy to characterize the duplicitous meaning of the regime's actions. Elsewhere in his pamphlet, Allen deployed the legal use of color to convey the potential for an argument's plausibility: "[i]n the first Parliame[n]t of her Majesty's reign, it was indeed in a manner thrust upon her against her will: because otherwise there could have been no color to make new laws for change of Religio[n]."[72] That is, without Parliament's insistence, Allen argued, there could not have been legal ground for changes in religion.

For Allen's purposes, colors served several functions: as legal terminology, as metaphor or analogy, and as a sense of government legerdemain, or downright untruth:

> For Princes and communities in disorder have a thousand pretences, excuses, and colours, of their unjust actions: they have the name of authority, the shadow of laws, the pens and tongues of infinite at their commandment: the may print or publish what they like, suppress what they list: whereof private men, be they never so wicked or good, have not so great commodity.[73]

He drew attention to the disparity between what a government and a private individual may do. The government may distort its actions using the considerable tools at its disposal, including the laws, statutes, and proclamations it can create and promulgate as well as the propaganda to influence their reception. These were not available to private citizens. By muting counter explanations, censorship, according to Allen, completed the scope of official powers to make an official pronouncement of what may have occurred, and why. He characterized such acts using the language of light, shadow, and color. This recalls Reddy's understanding of color and emotion discussed above, particularly how the language of light and color work to persuade an audience through emotional appeal.

Allen carefully chose examples to represent a range of offending behaviors in order to demonstrate that Protestants commit treason, and also that people in positions of authority, regardless how illegitimately they do so, use those instruments of office to promote their desired version of events:

> When the last Duke of Northumberland, for the like ambitious purpose [to usurp the Crown like Richard III in his previous example], would have disabled and defeated traitorously both the noble daughters of his own Sovereign and Master: and by the title of his daughter in law, possessed himself of the Crown: what number of pamphlets and edicts were published on the s[udden], for colouring of that foul treachery and intolerable treason?[74]

---

71 William Cardinal Allen, *A True, Sincere, and Modest Defense of English Catholics*, STC (2nd. ed.) 373, 54.
72 Allen, 8.
73 Allen, 4.
74 Allen, 4.

It is worth pausing to reflect on Allen's choice of Northumberland as an example.[75] The Duke of Northumberland was John Dudley, father of Elizabeth's favorite, Robert Dudley, Earl of Leicester. The significance of Allen's use here is the co-incidence of Leicester's position in Elizabeth's inner circle notwithstanding that his father had tried to intercept and prevent her eventual succession. Moreover Northumberland, an antipapist, had committed what Allen characterized as "foul treachery and intolerable treason," but he colored his treason by trying to cover his actions with the shade of legitimacy.[76]

According to Allen, Northumberland misused the utilities of the state, its edicts and propaganda, to portray the revolt as a lawful transition of sovereignty. By extension, Allen also implied that the current regime was similarly misusing government apparatuses to falsely accuse English Catholics and the executed Jesuits of treason. To make this point, Allen denounced the government by clarifying its claim that the Catholic clerics were involved with the "Irish quarrel," perhaps encouraging Irish resistance to the English Crown. When torture failed to reveal anything, "they sticked [sic] not to rack father Campion extremely for search on that point," in order to "give more colour" to the claim of Irish involvement.[77] In the history of English common law, to color an argument once meant that it might have substance.[78] In this case, retreat from further torture gave credence to claims of Irish involvement, according to Allen.

The Bond of Association, produced and circulated in October 1584, the same year as Allen's *Modest Defense*, completes the trajectory of color from sensory to rhetorical event in legal terminology. The bond, a device drawn from medieval English law and feudalism, was a solution to the perceived problem of the threat of assassination of the English monarch coupled with an undefined succession in that event.[79] It was intended to mobilize the nation, or at least particular Protestant segments of what had become the increasingly diverse human landscape of the English polity, through its successful operation "under color of law."[80] An extralegal device—that is, outside of law though not technically illegal—its inclusion shifts this inquiry to consider an instrument that succeeded in the goal to mobilize.

Historian J. E. Neale, among others, characterized the bond as "lynch law," but this is inadequate—and inaccurate—particularly when reconsidered "under

---

75   Allen referred to the rebellion in 1553 whereby the Duke had arranged marriage between his youngest son and Lady Jane Grey, heir after Henry VIII's children, because she had a claim to the English Crown through her mother and her relation to the Tudors. Had he succeeded for more than the nine days it took Henry's eldest daughter, Mary, to quash the revolt and seize her rightful inheritance, he would have retained power and furthered Protestantism.

76   Thomas Percy, Earl of Northumberland, also discussed in this essay in connection with the 1569 Northern rebellion, was Catholic while John Dudley, Duke of Northumberland associated with the 1553 rebellion was Protestant.

77   Allen, 20.

78   Plucknett, 412.

79   Bracton Law, 233, 244. English translation Copyright (c) 1968-1977 by the President and Fellows of Harvard College. Latin text Copyright (c) 1922-1942 by Yale University Press. Javascript presentation software, CGI scripts, and text-conversion software Copyright (c) 1998, Legal Information Institute,Cornell Law School. http://bracton.law.harvard.edu/index.html

80   Carole Levin, "Bond of Association," in *Historical Dictionary of Tudor England, 1485-1603*, Ronald H. Fritze, editor-in-chief (New York and London: Greenwood Press, 1991), 62-3.

color of law."[81] Lynch law is defined as punitive action taken by *unofficial* persons against someone suspected, or accused of, a crime.[82] The bond does not fit this rubric for three reasons. First, members of the Queen's Privy Council who had legal training conceived and drafted it. They were its first subscribers, and the invitation to join was more an expressed expectation of others to subscribe.[83] Second, the Privy Council sent the bond to lords lieutenant for wider circulation, directing them to obtain subscriptions throughout the realm.[84] It was distributed by men with the actual colors of office, invested with civil or ecclesiastical authority, and the local arrangements for disseminating the bond were left to them.[85] This meant that the bond was circulated with the trappings of law. In this way, there was nothing at all unusual about its dissemination. Other royal directives through proclamations, including those on apparel, had also been distributed through local officials. The central government depended on local apparatus for executing orders. In proclamations issued to enforce statutes of apparel, for example—though any proclamation would suffice to make the same claim —"all the articles…shall be put into execution…by all manner of magistrates and officers."[86]

Third, through the ritual of subscriptions, men of the bond were themselves invested with authority by an oath that empowered them to murder. The men of the bond solemnly vowed, "that with our whole powers, Bodies, Arms, Lands and Goods, and with our children and servants…[to] pursue, and suppress all manner of persons that Shall by any means intend and attempt anything dangerous or hurtful" to the Queen.[87] Joined by oath and seal in a society committed to a collective venture of violence, under the color of law, they subscribed to "withstand, offend and pursue as well by force of arms, as by All other means of revenge… And…never desist from all manner of Forcible pursuit against such persons to the uttermost extermination of them."[88] This hot language was cooled in March 1585, tempered by parliamentary statute, the Queen's Safety Act.[89]

Sir Thomas Digges in his treatise, "What Daungers May Ensue," addressed to Parliament in November 1584, raised objections that echoed legal constructions expressed in other legal documents, including the proclamations for apparel.[90] Digges was motivated by what he characterized as "poyntes wherein mens

---

81   Referencing J.E. Neale, for an example, Cressy and Levin independently cite Neale's characterization of the Bond as "lynch law." David Cressy, "Binding the Nation: The Bonds of Association, 1584 and 1696," in Tudor Rule and Revolution, D. J. Guth and J. W. McKenna, eds. (Cambridge: CUP, 1982), 218; Carole Levin, *Historical Dictionary of Tudor England, 1485-1603*, Ronald H. Fritze, ed. (London and New York: Greenwood Press, 1991), 63.

82   Lynch law has a specific legal meaning as "a term descriptive of the action of unofficial persons, organized bands, or mobs, who seize persons charged with or suspected of crimes, or take them out of the custody of the law, and inflict summary punishment upon them, without legal trial, and without the warrant or authority of law." *Black's Law Dictionary*.

83   David Cressy, "Binding the Nation: the Bonds of Association, 1584 and 1696," in *Tudor Rule and Revolution: essays for G. R. Elton from his American friends* (Cambridge: Cambridge University Press, 1982), 220.

84   Cressy, 218, 220-1.

85   Cressy, 221.

86   TRP, "542. Enforcing Statutes of Apparel," 282.

87   SP12/173/83. "19 October 1584, Corrections to Bond Draft by Sir Francis Walsingham."

88   SP12/173/83.

89   Levin, 63.

90   Sir Thomas Digges, "The Daungers that may ensue by the Othe of Association hereafter if it be not qualified

consciences are wounded, and myndes greeved by this Othe." First among these points was the vow made for children and servants "whose hartes and actions are not in the power of Father or Masters to rule."[91] This component of the oath would not have seemed objectionable immediately because it was not unusual for fathers and masters to be held responsible for those under them. Even in the apparel proclamations, men were held accountable for household members. In 1562 excess in wives' apparel was identified in a proclamation as one cause why a man might be unable to provide a horse for national defense according to the requirements of another statute.[92] Moreover, by 1580 another proclamation enforcing statutes of apparel directed that fathers and masters act upon those under them:

> [S]pecial charge to all those who bear office within the said house to see due observation of the same…according to their degrees, that they do respectively see the same speedily and uly executed in their private household and families…and each man in his own household for their children and servants…likewise to cause the said orders to be straightly kept by all lawful means they can.[93]

Digges objected to what was a commonly held practice of legal responsibility for servants and children when the stakes were as high as murder and treason. People felt pressured to conform by subscribing, as refusal to do so could look like guilty intent, and if the promises of the bond seemed strong, they might have also seemed legal.

The enthusiastic response to the bond was due, no doubt, to a desire to show the wider community personal loyalty to the Queen. Crown allegiance and the display of personal loyalty were the results, not the precipitating causes, of subscription, however. Among the ingredients that may demonstrate their influences here are ideas of early modern masculinity and duty. Assuming that none, or only a minimal number, of the men who subscribed—and there were thousands—were homicidal, it is reasonable to presume instead that these men believed they were doing something legal sanctioned by the Crown and presented under color of law with the full force of authority. The conviction that the pledge to commit murder without trial, based on suspicion alone, and despite its direct contradiction to English common law and criminal procedure, must have convinced subscribers because it had all the appearances of legality, the pretext of law.

The formula and ritual of subscription added to its legal appearance. Men assembled to participate in the sometimes elaborate legal rituals: signing, setting their seal, and swearing the oath of association. Moreover, the capacity of ritual to create, not merely reflect, the very conditions it encourages by subscription to the bond affected the semblance of law.[94] Fraudulence of color of office was precisely

---

by a convenient Act of Parliament," Lansdowne Manuscripts, 98/4.
91 Digges, Lans. MSS., 98/4.
92 *TRP,* 494. Enforcing Statutes of Apparel, Westminster, May 1562, 3 Elizabeth I, 192.
93 *TRP,* 646. Enforcing Statues of Apparel, Westminster, February 1580, 22, Elizabeth I, 455.
94 David I. Kertzer, "Ritual, Politics, and Power," in *Readings in Ritual* Studies, Ronald L. Grimes, ed. (Upper Saddle River, NJ: Prentice Hall, 1996), 335.

the reason for the development of the legal concept of *under color of law* in Richard II's reign in the first place.[95]

Using color as a tool for historical analysis, this essay suggests, provides a means to reexamine familiar events in fresh ways that yield lines of inquiry and understanding about how strategies used by the Elizabethan regime and its opponents functioned. Like the loupe in Johanna Thorpe's window, color trains the analytical eye onto a specific object. With color as a conceptual point of departure, closer scrutiny of the statutes of apparel, that regulated materials of clothing and colors, raises questions about commerce, military, and hierarchies of authority. It also reveals the struggles for social stabilization in an increasingly changed polity. In the 1580s that stabilization became more of a chimera. Apparel proclamations urged the conviction that people should be able to identify a person's occupation at a glance. Color straddled a murky position of visual and rhetorical economies, the apogee being in the Bond of Association, the success of which can be attributed to a number of reasons. Yet color draws attention to the fresh insight that it achieved what it did in part because of its presentation and rhetorical strategies under color of law.

Bibliography

Primary Sources

Allen, William. *A true, sincere and modest defence, of English Catholiques that suffer for their faith both at home and abrode against a false, seditious and slanderous libel intituled; The exectuion [sic]of iustice in England. Wherein is declared, how uniustlie the Protestants doe charge Catholiques with treason ... .* [Rouen : Fr. Parsons' press, 1584]. STC (2nd ed.) / 373. Copy from: Henry E. Huntington Library and Art Gallery.

———. *The Execution of Justice in England by William Cecil and a True, Sincere, and Modest Defence of English Catholics by William Allen.* Edited and introduction by Robert M. Kingdon. Ithaca: Cornell University Press, 1965.

Bracton, Henry of. *Bracton on the Laws and Customs of England.* English translation by the President and Fellows of Harvard College. 1968-1977. http://bracton.law.harvard.edu/

Burghley, William Cecil, Baron. *The execution of iustice in England for maintenaunce of publique and Christian peace, against certeine stirrers of sedition, and adherents to the traytors and enemies of the realme, without any persecution of them for questions of religion, as is falsely reported and published by the fautors and fosterers of their treasons.* [London : Printed by Christopher Barker, 1583 [i.e. 1584]] Short Title Catalogue (2nd ed.) / 4903. Copy from: Henry E. Huntington Library and Art Gallery.

---

95   Plucknett, 421 fn.2.

Calendar of State Papers, Domestic: Edward, Mary and Elizabeth, 1547-80. Edited by Mary Anne Everett Green. London: Longman and Company, 1856, 1865, 1867, and 1869.

Digges, Sir Thomas. "The Daungers that may ensue by the Othe of Association hereafter if it be not qualified by a convenient Act of Parliament." Lansdowne Manuscripts, 98/4.

Journal of the House of Commons. Volume 1, 1547-1629. (1802). URL: http://www.britishhistory.ac.uk/report.aspx?compid=3393&strquery=Journal of the House of Commons

Larkin, Paul L. and James F. Hughes. *Tudor Royal Proclamations.* Volume 1. New Haven: Yale University Press, 1969.

———. *Tudor Royal Proclamations.* Volumes 2 and 3. *The Later Tudors, 1553 – 1603.* Edited by Paul L. Hughes and James F. Larkin. New Haven and London: Yale University Press, 1969.

Parliament Rolls of Medieval England. "Henry VII: November 1487." Edited by Chris Given-Wilson, general editor, Paul Brand, Seymour Phillips, Mark Ormrod, Geoffrey Martin, Anne Curry, Rosemary Horrox. British History Online, http://www.british-history.ac.uk/report.aspx?compid=116565.

Records of London viewers, regarding instances of nuisance and other dispute over buildings, boundaries and ways. From records in the Corporation of London Records Office. Edited by Janet Senderowitz Loengard. Reproduced by kind permission of the London Record Society. URL: http://www.british-history.ac.uk/report.aspx?compid=36057&strquery=ermystede

Smith, Sir Thomas. *De republica Anglorum The maner of gouernement or policie of the realme of England, compiled by the honorable man Thomas Smyth, Doctor of the ciuil lawes, knight, and principall secretarie vnto the two most worthie princes, King Edwarde the sixt, and Queene Elizabeth.* London: Printed by Henrie Midleton for Gregorie Seton, Anno Domini 1583. Short Title Catalogue (2nd ed.) / 22857. Copy from: Henry E. Huntington Library and Art Gallery.

State Papers 12/173/83. "19 October 1584, Corrections to Bond Draft by Sir Francis Walsingham." Ann Arbor: University of Michigan. Microfilm

Statutes of the Realm. Volume 4 (1547-1624). Statutes of Queen Elizabeth. http://heinonline.org.proxy.lib.wayne.edu/HOL/Page?handle=hein.engrep/realm0004&id=431&collection=statore&index=engrep/realm#431.

Stubbes, Phillip. *The anatomie of abuses Containing a description of such notable vices and enormities, as raigne in many countries of the world, but especiallie in this realme of England: together with most fearefull examples of Gods heauie iudgements inflicted vpon the wicked for the same as well in England of late, as in other places else where. Verie godly to be read of all true Christians euery where, but most chiefly, to bee regarded in England. Made dialogue-wise by Philip Stubs, Gent.* Imprinted at London: By Richard

Iohnes, at the sign of the Rose and Crowne next aboue S. Andrewes Church in Holborne, 1595. Short Title Catalogue (2nd ed.) / 23379. http://eebo.chadwyck.com.proxy.lib.wayne.edu/home.

Verstegan, Richard. "Letters and Despatches of Richard Verstegan" (c.1591-1640)." Edited by Anthony G. Petti. *Catholic Record Society* 52. London, 1959.

Secondary Sources

Black, Jeremy. *War in Early Modern World, 1450-1815.* Warfare and History. London: Routledge, 1998.

Cressy, David. "Binding the Nation: the Bonds of Association, 1584 and 1696." *Tudor Rule and Revolution: essays for G. R. Elton from his American friends.* Cambridge: Cambridge University Press, 1982.

Elliott, Charlene. "Purple Pasts: Color Codification in the Ancient World." *Law & Social Inquiry* 33 (2008): 173–194.

Elton, G. R. *The Tudor Constitution*, 2nd edition. Cambridge: Cambridge University Press, 1982.

Dillon, Anne. *The Construction of Martyrdom in the English Catholic Community, 1535 – 1603.* St. Andrews Studies in Reformation History. Aldershot: Ashgate, 2002.

Finlay, Robert. "Weaving the Rainbow: Visions if Color in World History." *Journal of World History* 18 (December 2007): 383-431.

Galtung, Johan."Cultural Violence." *Journal of Peace Research* 27 (August 1990): 291-305.

Haigh, Christopher. "The English Reformation: A Premature Birth, A Difficult Labour and a Sickly Child." *The Historical Journal* 33 (June 1990): 449-459.

Kertzer, David I. "Ritual, Politics, and Power," in *Readings in Ritual* Studies, edited by Ronald L. Grimes. Upper Saddle River, NJ: Prentice Hall, 1996.

Lake, Peter and Steven Pincus. *The Politics of the Public Sphere in Early Modern England*, Politics, Culture and Society in Early Modern Britain. Manchester: Manchester University Press, 2012.

Levin, Carole. "Bond of Association." *Historical Dictionary of Tudor England, 1485-1603.* Edited by Ronald H. Fritze. New York and London: Greenwood Press, 1991.

Lovejoy, Arthur O. *The Great Chain of Being: The Study of the History of an Idea.* Cambridge: Harvard University Press, 1976.

McCoog, Thomas M. "The Flower of Oxford": The Role of Edmund Campion in Early Recusant Polemics. *The Sixteenth Century Journal* 24 (Winter, 1993): 899-913.

New Advent Catholic Encyclopedia, http://www.newadvent.org/cathen/a.htm.

O'Day, Rosemary. *The Longman Companion to the Tudor Age*. London and New York: Longman, 1995.

Pasnau, Robert. "The event of color." *Philosophy Studies* 142 (February 2009): 353 – 369.

Reddy, William M. *The Navigation of Feeling: A Framework for the History of Emotions*. Cambridge: Cambridge University Press, 2001.

Pearson, Terry P. "The Composition and Development of Phillip Stubbes's "Anatomie of Abuses." *The Modern Language Review* 56 (July 1961): 321-332.

Phillips, Kim M. "Masculinities and the Medieval English Sumptuary Laws." *Gender & History* 19 (April 2007): 22-42.

Plucknett, Theodore F. T. *A Concise History of the Common* Law. Fifth Edition. London: Butterworth and Co., 1956.

Robin, Corey. *Fear: The History of a Political Idea*. Oxford: Oxford University Press, 2004.

Schneider, Jane. "Peacocks and Penguins: The Political Economy of European Cloth and Colors," *American Ethnologist* 5 (August 1978): 413-447.

Tillyard, Eustace W. *The Elizabethan World Picture*. New York, Vintage Books, 1959.

Van Der Wee, Herman. "The Western European Woollen Industries, 1500-1750." In *The Cambridge History of Textiles*. Volume I. Cambridge: Cambridge University Press, 2003.

Winter, Steven L. "The Meaning of "Under Color of Law." *Michigan Law Review* 91 (December 1992): 323-418.

Wrightson, Keith. *Earthly Necessities: Economic Lives in Early Modern Britain*. The New Economic History of Britain. New Haven and London: Yale University Press, 2000.

5

From Dun to White: Forts, Power, and the Politics of Restoration in the United Arab Emirates

Victoria Hightower

In the past two centuries, forts, castles, and towers proliferated throughout the cities, towns, and agricultural areas in the land that today is known as The United Arab Emirates (UAE), which became a unified and independent country in 1971. Before that, it was a group of seven, at times antagonistic, emirates: Abu Dhabi, Dubai, Sharjah, Ajman, Um al-Quwain, Ras al-Khaimah, and Fujairah. Not only were the emirates sometimes hostile to one another, but tribes within different areas also fought over the ability to tax goods produced in—or traded among—different cities. In addition to inter-emirate and internal tribal conflicts, the emirates experienced periodic external invasions by the British, Omani, and Wahhabi forces from what is today Saudi Arabia. This history of invasion heightened the necessity for defensive structures.

Today, there are 100 historic forts, castles, and defensive towers in the UAE, a fact that testifies to the instability of the area as well as to the rulers' desires for defensive monuments. This essay draws upon publicly accessible sources, such as newspapers, town plans, sources from the British, and memoirs in order to investigate the evolution of three forts: Qasr al-Hosn (Palace Fort) in Abu Dhabi, al-Jahili in Al Ain, and the Hisn (the Fort) in Sharjah. These forts are both iconic and symbolic of their rulers' authority. They were renovated many times in the years since construction, and often, their renovations were not just structural, but also cosmetic. The forts changed from the dun color of the surrounding sands to a more pristine white in the twentieth century. Since the renovations of the 1990s, their color changed again. Both the Sharjah Hisn and al-Jahili in Al Ain returned to dun, while the Qasr al-Hosn remains white-washed and gleaming. These color changes reflected not only aesthetic choices, but they also made firm statements about the rulers' outlook and the forts' purposes.

Why Build the Forts?

Forts were important structures in the southern Persian Gulf. In addition to their role as defensive structures, they also established territorial boundaries, enhanced authority, or protected vital water sources. Given that much of the emirate land was arid or full desert, water was particularly important. Additionally, forts protected people and gave rulers leverage to co-opt rivals. Rulers governed through consensus; if a ruler was perceived as tyrannical or weak, challengers deposed the ruler or migrated away from his authority.

For rulers along the coast of the lower Gulf, the early nineteenth century was a period of change that altered existing notions of rulership. In the late 1790s, Sharjah's ruling tribe, the Al Qasimi, tried to tax traffic through what they considered their marine territories in the Gulf. The tribe had significant alliances on both the Arab and Persian side of the Gulf and saw the increased traffic as a legitimate target for taxation. The British East India Company considered the action piracy and embarked on wars with the Al Qasimi tribe in 1809 and again in 1819-1820. Their conflict ended in the 1820s with the destruction of the then primary port of the Al Qasimi family, Ras al-Khaima. George Brucks, who conducted a coastal survey in the 1820s, noted that the destruction of Ras al-Khyma by the East India Company Marine was so effective "that it is now difficult to tell what might have been the form of the houses."

Following this bombardment, the British Political Resident, the highest-ranking representative of the East India Company in the Gulf, negotiated a treaty and invited all rulers along the lower Gulf coast to sign it under threat of bombardment. Between 1820 and 1853, the truces became successively stricter and forbade all varieties of maritime violence. This made war virtually impossible for the rulers. Before the truces, armies sailed into battle, rather than risk death, exhaustion, or ambush in the desert. In eliminating the option for maritime transport, these treaties made the British the final arbiter in disputes. They even deputized a representative in Sharjah to remain in the emirate to report on the political situation in the lower Gulf emirates.

With the prospect for maritime expansion eliminated by these treaties, and the power of the al-Qasimi family unquestioned in the north, the al-Nahyan shifted their expansion efforts inland away from British authority. The Buraimi Oasis complex consisted of eight separate oases and their villages. Although a single tribe could dominate the coastal port cities, the proliferation of resources, farms, and water, sustained multiple powerful tribes in Buraimi. The Naim, Al bu Shamis, and Wahhabi tribes vied for control of the Buraimi, Hamasa, and Sa'arah oases and their villages, while the Dawahir tribe controlled the villages and oases around Ain Dhawahir, Hili, Jimi, al-Qattarah, and Mu'atarid. In the 1840s, the Al Nahyan family from Abu Dhabi forged a tribal alliance with the Dhawahir which gave them access to the dates produced at the Dhawahir-controlled oases in return for military aid.

Although forged as a protective alliance after a series of wars in the 1880s against the Dhawahir, the Al Nahyan took control of a portion of the oasis called Ain Dhawahir and renamed it Al Ain. This direct control enabled Al Nahyan and their subjects to purchase date farms, give the Al Nahyan the ability to directly tax agriculture in the oasis, and give their Bedouin allies, which grew over the course of the late nineteenth century, a place to settle during the summers. In addition, it provided proof of Al Nahyan's power during the era when this was questioned because of their growing reliance on British rule.

The expansion of British authority along the coast, together with the rulers' perceived loss of sovereignty, spurred many rulers to assert their power through the building and renovation of forts.

Fort Building and Rulers' Authority

Forts are "the largest of the heritage structures" in existence in the UAE, and much like castles in Europe, served as both a home and defensive structure for politically powerful families.

Forts were aesthetic reminders of a ruler's or his ally's authority, and each of the three forts discussed here was a vital symbol of political authority. Today they serve as a reminder of the ruling family's endurance and power, while also illustrating the past for citizens and tourists alike.

The Qasr al-Hosn is one of the oldest forts in the UAE; it is located in Abu Dhabi, which is the current capital of the UAE and was the headquarters for the Al Nahyan branch of the Bani Yas tribe. This fort had humble beginnings. In the 1760s, a group of the Al Nahyan erected a tower to protect and claim authority over the island's only potable well. Later Al Nahyan rulers incorporated the original tower into the design for the Qasr al-Hosn. The resulting fort became the seat of the Al Nahyan and served as the rulers' permanent residence in the 1790s.

By the twentieth century, a fort was built close to the original tower, with a courtyard and high walls that included two square and two round towers as well as a two-story majlis/meeting area. Its size and structure made it distinctive despite its dun-colored exterior. Until the twentieth century, the Qasr al-Hosn was the only stone building in Abu Dhabi town and was visible both from the sea and land.

Sharjah's fort, the Hisn, was established after the 1819-1820 East India Company bombardment and razing of Ras al-Khaima.

Although the Al Qasimi family controlled Sharjah before the British bombardment, it was not their primary base. The ruling shaikh, Sultan b. Saqr, constructed the Hisn to reassert his power after this defeat. Initially, he built a large defensive tower. Unlike the Abu Dhabi fort, Sharjah's Hisn expanded to include a formal fort around the tower with high walls by the early twentieth century. This added to the grandeur of the structure because, unlike Abu Dhabi, there were many stone buildings in Sharjah constructed from limestone and coral rock. The color of the structure was not discussed, but given the propensity for using gypsum and crushed limestone to plaster buildings, it is entirely possible that the building was very light dun or white.

Located on the edge of the Al Ain oasis, which the Al Nahyan family wrested from the Dhawahir's control in 1887, the al-Jahili Fort is the newest construction of the three discussed here. Initially, the family constructed a simple, dun-colored watchtower to stake their claim to the area and to lookout for attackers coming from the north. Unlike Abu Dhabi's Qasr al-Hosn that was the seat of Al Nahyan power, the al-Jahili fort was an outpost for the family's power and was more a reflection of their ambitions than the reality of their position in the oasis. The family acquired Al Jahili in an effort to expand and control the lucrative trade that moved through the oasis complex. It remained a tower until the middle of the twentieth century.

Each fort discussed here was originally established to mark territory and claim ownership in an area. In the 1760s the Qasr al-Hosn was established around the only well with potable water on the island of Abu Dhabi. The Hisn was established in 1820 to reinforce their claim over Sharjah and to recover from the British attack on the center of their authority, Ras al-Khaima. Al-Jahili in the Buraimi Oasis complex announced the Al Nahyan claim to the oasis. In the next phase of building, new challenges arose for the leaders who each took their forts in very different aesthetic directions.

Figure 5.1 | Qasr al-Hosn Fort, Abu Dhabi, UAE. Note the fort within a fort structure. The smaller fort in the upper left of the larger fort is the original fort. The original tower is at the top corner. The twentieth-century renovations, including the interior villas were removed during the 21st century renovations. Image from Google Earth Pro, 2013 Digital Globe.

From Dun to White

Figure 5.2 | Sharjah Hisn, Sharjah, UAE. The large round tower at the top right is the original tower from 1820. This fort is considerably smaller than the Qasr al-Hosn or the al-Jahili fort. Image from Google Earth, 2015 DigitalGlobe.

Figure 5.3 | Al-Jahili Fort, Al Ain, UAE. The original tower is in the middle of the larger tower at the bottom of the photograph. By the early 20th century, the fort at the top of the photo was built and, when it became a center for the Trucial Oman Scouts, the addition, which juts out towards the bottom left of the structure was added, along with the defensive tiers around the original tower, giving the original tower a "wedding cake" appearance. Image from Google Earth, 2015 DigitalGlobe.

Forts and the Mid-Twentieth Century

The twentieth century marked a significant change for all three of these forts as they were repurposed, renovated, and restored. As with their initial construction, political concerns and pressures were at the forefront of the rulers' minds as they modified the forts. The forts remained important symbols of political power, even as the bases of that power shifted from taxes paid to subjects to the selling of economic concessions. These economic shifts had wide ranging ramifications throughout the emirates, but were particularly difficult for Abu Dhabi's and Sharjah's rulers to rents from landing strips and oil concessions. Consequently, this was a period of transformation for the forts as the rulers sought to reinforce their authority.

From the late nineteenth century, the southern Gulf rulers experienced a series of political and social changes, owing as much to the changing global economy—particularly the economic depressions from the 1870s onward—as to internal rivalries. Rulers' authority was predicated on the number of allied subjects, rather than on the amount of territory controlled. However, successful alliances relied on the rulers' ability to distribute wealth. This relationship was easier during the late nineteenth century when the emirates experienced an economic boom due to rising revenues from the primary commodity produced in the area, pearls. But just as quickly, this commodity declined.

Revenues from pearling began to decrease in 1905, reaching a low by the early 1930s. Compounding the challenges posed by decreasing pearl revenues was the overall depression of the global economy in the first decades of the twentieth century. World War I, the Great Depression, and World War II disrupted global trade, and depending on a single, luxury commodity for income seriously damaged the economic and political power of the ruling shaikhs of Abu Dhabi and Sharjah. The decline of pearling reduced the rulers' ability to tax their subjects and thus decreased their overall revenues. These rulers were unable to distribute wealth to ensure allies' support or to subvert rivals' opposition.

From the 1930s on, oil wealth flowed into Bahrain (1932), Saudi Arabia (1933), and Kuwait (1938), but not into the southern Gulf emirates. Abu Dhabi was the first to discover oil (1958), followed by Dubai in 1966 and Sharjah in 1972. The discovery of oil in Bahrain and the Kingdom of Saudi Arabia stimulated British companies' interests in prospecting in the southern Gulf. The British Royal Navy switched from coal to oil after WWI, and though the British government had oil interests in both Iraq and Iran, they were also aware that the United States was prospecting and drilling for oil in neighboring Saudi Arabia. Securing oil rights in the southern Gulf became important for the British and was beneficial for the rulers of Abu Dhabi and Sharjah.

With these economic concessions, rulers exchanged their absolute sovereignty for money and expertise—in exchange for rent, the rulers gave the concessionaires control of a portion of land without interference. In the case of oil concessions, rulers granted companies the right to explore, exploit, and export oil in the agreed upon area. The companies received almost unlimited control of the exploration area and of the means of extraction. The rulers received a signing fee and portion of the profits, if there were any. At the same time, many rulers also rented territory as airfields or landing strips. Sharjah, for instance, rented land to the Royal Air Force and Imperial Airways as a stopover for their London to Bombay route.

In addition to these concessions and to guarantee the security of these agreements, the British sponsored cooperative institutions such as the Trucial Oman Scouts (TOS) in 1951and the Trucial Oman Council (TOC) in 1952. The former was a militia that worked to reduce smuggling and slave trading, while the latter attempted to institute cooperation between the different rulers to stimulate development. From the 1920s until the 1960s, these plans had the dual effect of reinforcing the rulers' economic power while also exposing internal challenges since these arrangements required that the rulers relinquish yet another small measure of sovereignty. Once again, the forts became centers for the rulers of Abu Dhabi and Sharjah to reinforce their authority and power.

Abu Dhabi spent much of the early twentieth century mired in a succession of crises that emerged from its economic crisis. As the economy declined, tribes defected from their alliances with the Al Nahyan, and different factions within the ruling family vied for power. These disputes disrupted the relationship between the rulers and their subjects. When the crises finally ended in 1928, the ruler of Abu Dhabi, Sheikh Shakhbut b. Sultan (1928-66) tried to restore his authority and repair his relationship with his subjects, but found it very difficult to do so economically. He turned to oil concessions: in a 1939 concession, he earned a 300,000-rupee signing fee and one million rupees annually until oil was discovered. In 1950, he received a 1.5 million rupee signing fee and one million rupees annually until oil was discovered. In spite of these deals, Abu Dhabi continued to lose adherents as significant families migrated from Abu Dhabi territory towards Qatar, Dubai, and Saudi Arabia.

Hoping to shore up his authority, Shakhbut expanded the Qasr al-Hosn using the wealth from the concession agreements. Historians suggest he was miser who stuffed mattresses with rupees rather than put them in a bank. He refused Abu Dhabi merchants the right to import construction materials, despite the ongoing expansion of oil prospecting camps—and later oil drilling camps. He feared oil was another luxury good whose bubble would burst and destroy the economy of his emirate, like pearling. Despite his stingy reputation, Shakhbut expended a significant amount of funds to reinforce his power. He built a bridge connecting Abu Dhabi Island to the mainland, a water pipeline from the Al Ain oasis to Abu Dhabi Island, and he set up a defense force for Abu Dhabi in 1965. In addition, he renovated and expanded the Qasr al-Hosn. Given the incredible poverty in his emirate, this appeared to be a waste of funds, but renovating the fort served his interests insofar as it represented his power and authority.

In his renovation of the Qasr al-Hosn, Shakhbut retained the original structure, building his larger fort around it. The older fort remained in one corner of the newer fort's courtyard and was used for government offices. He maintained the rest of the fort for his family. He also installed air conditioning units in part of the fort in the 1950s.

Sheikh Zayed b. Sultan (1966-2004) became ruler of Abu Dhabi Emirate and upgraded the fort once again. Zayed ascended to power following a coup that overthrew his brother, Shakhbut, and there was speculation as to whether this was engineered by the Al Nahyan family or by the British. The Qasr al-Hosn's renovation signaled a change from his predecessors' policies and asserted Zayed's power and authority. In addition to renovating the interior of the older fort, he built two villas inside the larger fort. He added electricity and insulation, and expanded the air conditioning units to other parts of the fort. It was at this point—sources vary on the date: 1966, 1970, or 1983—that the fort acquired its iconic color. Today's nickname for the Qasr al-Hosn is the White Fort because of the gypsum used on the exterior. Despite the questions about when the fort became white, the shift in color reflected Zayed's desire to incorporate new and different building styles into the fort. It also demonstrates Zayed's need to enhance the visibility of the fort, which served as a reminder of the political change, and the fort was a beacon for merchants and others, distinguishing itself even as more stone buildings were erected in Abu Dhabi.

Zayed cultivated a reputation as a modernizer who sought new and technological solutions to his people's problems. Before Zayed ascended to the leadership of Abu Dhabi, he was the *wali* (governor) of Al Ain from 1946 to 1966. But the area was unstable and the conflicting claims of the Al Nahyan, Wahhabis, and others almost resulted in war in the 1950s. The Buraimi Crisis occurred over the rights to prospect for oil in the area. In 1949, the Wahhabis granted the rights to the Arab American Oil Company (ARAMCO) on the basis that they had an alliance with the Naim and a history of political influence in the oasis complex. The Al Nahyan, the British, and Omani governments saw this as a political challenge and began mobilizing troops. After a series of complex negotiations, the oasis was divided. Three oasis villages went to the Oman—Buraimi, Sa'ara, and Hamasa. Today these three villages are collectively known as Buraimi, Oman. The remaining five oasis villages were given to Abu Dhabi, and named Al Ain. This reinforced Al Nahyan authority within the oasis, but also reflected another loss of sovereignty because they needed to rely on the British to protect their claim during the negotiations.

The question of sovereignty intensified when the TOS commandeered al-Jahili for their use. Zayed's answer to the questions of sovereignty was to begin modernizing life in the oasis. Though his budget was non-existent, he still managed to expand education and healthcare, creating a school in 1958, a dispensary in 1956, and Oasis Hospital in 1960. He also approved the creation of forts around the base of Al Nahyan power, the Al Ain Oasis, including al-Muwayj'i in 1946 and al-Murabba' in 1948; he also substantially expanded al-Jahili.

By 1948, al-Jahili consisted of a tower with an observation platform that stood in the corner of a fort. The fort had four walls and two additional towers for protection. In the late 1950s through the 1960s, the fort transformed from an outpost to the headquarters of the TOS. Between 1957 and 1962, the fort was renovated and expanded dramatically, as the older fort was connected with the tower. The tower acquired its "wedding cake" structure when another wall was added around the original tower. Defenders used one wall for patrolling and the other to thwart invasion. The nearby fort was connected to the tower by a series of walls and new, u-shaped buildings were added for safety as well as housing for soldiers stationed at al-Jahili. These buildings also included administrative spaces.

In addition to these structural changes, the fort was whitewashed with gypsum or lime. This enabled it to stand out across the desert, which was a particularly important feature as the TOS was an integrated militia that included British officers and local soldiers. The British officers, relying on tips, led the soldiers on patrols throughout Al Ain to search for smuggled weapons, goods, and people.

Figure 5.4 | Al-Jahili Fort in 1966. Note the distance between the "wedding cake tower" on the left and older fort structure on the right. Photo by Michael Hamilton-Clark, 1966.

In changing the color from dun to white, the British raised the visibility of al-Jahili and distinguished it from all others in Al Ain. Given that the city had no fewer than five large forts and that the area became a hub for British administration, this was important. Second, the fortification of al-Jahili and the construction of the nearby forts asserted Al Nahyan power in the oasis. This helped to diffuse questions of authority.

In the case of the Qasr al-Hosn and the al-Jahili fort, the color change signified a desire to raise the visibility of the fort for both practical and symbolic reasons. The scale of these projects also served to reinforce the power and authority of the Al Nahyan family at a time when their hold was weak.

In Sharjah, conditions similar to Abu Dhabi prevailed in the early twentieth century. Despite the 1820 British bombardment, Sharjah remained the premier port along the Gulf both economically and politically until 1947, when the British shifted their focus to Dubai.[1] Before 1947, Sharjah hosted the only British official in the emirates and had close contact with other British officials. During the twentieth century, Sharjah's fortunes declined, owing to instability in politics and trade

---

1   James Onley, *The Arabian Frontier of the British Raj: Merchants, Rulers, and the British in the Nineteenth-Century* Gulf, (Oxford: Oxford University Press, 2007), 54; Donald Hawley, *The Trucial States*, (London: George Allen & unwin Ltd., 1970), 328.

and the increasing competition from Dubai, which became a free port in 1902.[2] In the first few decades of the century, the city's port silted and trade declined, ultimately reducing the amount of taxes collected by the ruler.[3] To supplement the loss of revenue, Sharjah's ruler sold concessions. He sold small oil concessions, but his biggest source of income was the rent from the airbase. The strategic location of Sharjah and its favorable winds made it a perfect location for a stopover on the route between Britain and India.

Nonetheless, during the 1950s, Sharjah experienced extreme economic distress. Still, , Shaikh Saqr b. Sultan (1951-1965) spent the vast majority of Sharjah's 200,000 rupee income to reinforce social alliances rather than make improvements in infrastructure.[4] This decision illustrates the importance of these alliances for maintaining power. In 1950, a British official remarked that Sharjah was "moribund" and the "wishful optimism" of the shaikh was unfounded.[5]

As in Abu Dhabi, the combination of the challenges to power and the newfound source of income led to the expansion of the fort as an extension of the ruler's power. In the 1950s and 1960s, Sharjah's Hisn underwent a dramatic transformation. The Qasimi rulers fortified the original tower, constructing walls with additional towers at each corner. By 1954, the fort's color changed once again, transforming from a dun-colored fort to a palace with a spectacular façade of blue and white mosaic. Unfortunately, the white gypsum and lime plaster was not suited to the saline air of the Sharjah. By the 1960s, a travelling Englishman described the structure as crumbling and "painted blue and white like Gorgonzola cheese."[6] The upkeep of this type of façade was simply too extravagant for the shaikhs who suffered from a lack of funds.

The Hisn underwent further change when, in 1969, the ruling Shaikh, Khalid b. Mohammed Al Qasimi (1965-1972), destroyed the fort altogether. It was a symbol of tradition, and he viewed it as a hindrance to Sharjah's modernization. The Hisn divided the two halves of the city's commercial district. and enabled its residents to maintain a clear line-of-sight to the Sharjah Creek and to the interior in order to defend against potential attacks. The fort, a visual reminder of the central place of the ruling family and the extent of their power, obstructed movement about the area.

Khalid saw the fort as a relic of the past that directly contradicted his plans to modernize the city.[7] He wanted the city to follow a more rational grid plan and the Sharjah fort disrupted this entirely. His brother, Dr. Shaikh Sultan b. Mohammad Al Qasimi (1972-present) halted the demolition and began reconstruction of

---

2 H.J. Evans, "Finances of Sharjah," in Penelope Tuson, *Records of the Emirates Primary Documents 1820-1958* Volume 9 1947-1958, (London, Archive Editions, 1990), 649.

3 Evans, "Sharjah," 651; Heard-Bey, *From Trucial States to United Arab Emirates: A Society in Transition* (Dubai: Motivate Publishing, 2004), 299.

4 Evans, "Sharjah," 649.

5 H.J. Evans, "A Note on the Wealth of Dubai" 24 June 1950, in Penelope Tuson, Records of the Emirates Primary Documents 1820-1958 Volume 9 1947-1958, (London, Archive Editions, 1990), 637. And Evans, "Sharjah," 649.

6 Peter Jackson, "Sharjah: 400 years of coastal development," Public Lecture, Sharjah Museum of Islamic Civilization, 2009; P.S. Allfree. *Warlords of Oman*, (A.S. Barnes and Company, South Brunswick and New York, 1969), 19.

7 "Oil and Natural Gas," Helem Chapin Metz, ed. *Persian Gulf States: A Country Study*. Washington: GPO for the Library of Congress, 1993, http://countrystudies.us/persian-gulf-states/85.htm

the fort in the 1970s. This reconstruction restored the iconic tower to its place of prominence and restored the fort to its "proper" color—white.

In each of these situations, the rulers' decisions to change the color of their forts' structures were precipitated by challenges to their power. They needed to appear modern, powerful, and conspicuous stimulated significant renovations to the structures as working buildings. But soon after federation in 1971, the buildings fell out of use and were replaced by more modern structures which the ever-expanding governments required.

Modern Renovations

In the 1990s and early 2000s, rising nostalgia for the past, combined with the decay of many forts and the desire to reinforce emirate-level identities, stimulated a series of renovations to forts throughout the country. The forts were made of mud, and without proper upkeep, they tended to disintegrate into the sand. In efforts to reinforce the history of the area and the power of the rulers, these three forts were renovated, but instead of simply remaining important political structures, they became cultural centers. This opened a new area for rulers to reinforce their authority. Since independence in 1971, the rulers and their families became the protectors of the emirate's heritage and the forts became potent manifestations of this new role.

After federation in 1971, the focus of the country shifted towards modernization, but the federation was incomplete as tensions emerged between emirate-level autonomy and federal government authority. Ideally, each emir was free to rule his emirate as he saw fit as long as he cooperated with the other emirs on issues of national importance. Each ruler held two positions: ruler of their emirate and member on the Supreme Council. For instance, Zayed was both the ruler of Abu Dhabi and the President of the United Arab Emirates.

Modernization plans that started in Al Ain and expanded to Abu Dhabi were extended to the rest of the country after Zayed became President. Abu Dhabi provided the bulk of the national budget because its oil production and reserves dwarfed all other emirates' capabilities. As the preeminent scholar of UAE history, Frauke Heard-Bey explained, "Abu Dhabi's oil wealth was the midwife at the birth of the UAE."[8] It enabled free education from kindergarten through college, state-sponsored health care institutions, and housing programs aimed at moving citizens into stone or concrete-block houses with air conditioning units.[9] Additionally, these modernization campaigns accompanied economic expansion as Emirati families expanded their businesses and the volume of foreign workers increased. The pace of change and the skepticism with which some rulers approached the new system limited the national government's abilities to expand services to all Emirati citizens.

Despite public protests in 1979 in favor of full federalism, the emirates continued to duplicate services.[10] For example, there were multiple militaries until

---

8   Heard-Bey, *Trucial States*, 393.
9   Ibid., 394-395, 405.
10 Ibid., 409.

1996, and roads between emirates were poorly maintained because of disputes about ownership. Six international airports were constructed in the UAE during the 1980s-1990s,[11] although the Dubai and Sharjah international airports were merely fifteen miles apart. These crises represented a larger issue that plagued the individual emirates from the nineteenth century—how does one maintain sovereignty and autonomy given these external needs? The battles over federation raged until the late 1990s, when the primary instigator of emirate-level power, Shaikh Rashid b. Saeed of Dubai, died. The tensions between emirates' autonomy and government authority continue, though less often in terms of blatant resistance to the federal programs. Instead, emirates have focused upon creating a collective identity among their own citizens and to assert their history within the wider national narrative created by the federal government.

These contests over sovereignty represent the growing pains of a new country that was trying to forge a national identity. Culture and history became part of the battleground as each emirate attempted to assert its own place in Emirati history. The pace of change in the UAE between 1971 and the 1990s was meteoric. For instance, the population increased from 220,000 just before federation to 2.4 million by 1996.[12] By 1995, 55,000 people worked in the federal government.[13] Buildings soared from two or six stories to skyscrapers by the end of the 1990s. These changes inspired Sharjah and Abu Dhabi to expand museums and restore their major forts in order to reinforce their citizens' identities and their emirate's place within the larger national narrative.

In Abu Dhabi, the tension between promoting a more unified national identity and a more parochial emirate-level identity was particularly difficult. The government experienced conflicting pressures to share the oil wealth with other emirates' citizens amid its own desire to use its natural resource for its own citizens' benefits. Further, the question of which version of identity to present became important in the 1990s as Abu Dhabi chose to position its history as a national history. This was particularly true in the renovation of the Qasr al-Hosn fort.

The Qasr al-Hosn experienced less degradation than the other two forts because it continued to be used, even after the government offices were transferred to larger, more modern facilities. Although the Qasr al-Hosn ceased to be the center of government after federation, in the 1980s it served as an arts and cultural center, showing films and hosting cultural displays and classical music concerts.[14] In 2007, it became part of the Abu Dhabi Association for Culture and Heritage (ADACH), formerly the Cultural Foundation. ADACH recently renovated the Qasr al-Hosn. It re-opened in 2010 as a cultural center with exhibition halls devoted to travel, preservation, and Emirati, Arab, and Islamic history.

The fort's external appearance changed little, despite extensive interior renovation and environmental conditions that make the white color difficult

---

11 Davidson, 64-67.

12 Heard-Bey, *Trucial States*, 394.

13 Ibid.

14 Samihah Zaman and Nathalie Farah, "Qasr al Hosn: Standing Guard Over a Rich Culture, *Gulf News.com*, August 26, 2011, http://gulfnews.com/news/gulf/uae/general/qasr-al-hosn-standing-guard-overa-rich-culture-1.857177, accessed February 18, 2012.

to maintain. In the 1970s and 1980s, observers described the fort as having a "patchwork" appearance. The proximity to the sea and saline air pitted the white plaster, causing it to flake off. Despite the cost and the difficulty, the Qasr al-Hosn has remained white for several reasons: the color's association with the beginning of independence and with Zayed himself, and the government's desire to maintain the fort's visibility despite the fact that towers were rising around it.

While the government of Abu Dhabi renovated the Qasr al-Hosn to stand as a reminder of the eternal presence of the Al Nahyan family and its power at the helm of the government, the renovations of Al Ain's al-Jahili fort indicate a separate agenda. The Qasr al-Hosn was restored to its 1960s form to reflect the earliest era of oil wealth when Abu Dhabi's rise to global prominence began. The al-Jahili fort represented a more traditional icon, and it reinforces Al Nahyan power and authority within the city of Al Ain.

In Al Ain, the al-Jahili fort also became a public space. The government renovated al-Jahili in the 1980s and again in 2007 to maintain the fort's image as a cultural icon. The current form of the fort bears little resemblance to its former appearance before TOS occupation, and, in fact, has elements that frankly never existed before the renovation. Despite the emphasis on tradition, the fort's renovation included a space for traveling exhibitions and an area suitable for large-scale musical performances, including the WOMAD World Music Festival and the Abu Dhabi Symphony Orchestra.[15] The surrounding area became a public park with fountains and lawns.

Unlike the Qasr al-Hosn, whose renovation completely repurposed the interior, the al-Jahili project emphasized its role as a traditional space. The exterior included mud bricks, and water-based cooling systems were added within the walls to enhance the natural cooling properties of the mud and to avoid the need for unsightly air conditioning ducts that would break the traditional ambiance.[16]

The restoration of al-Jahili demonstrates the need to reinforce a specific view of traditional architecture in the UAE and to invoke a time that never existed for this particular fort. Design elements were borrowed from other forts, and the innovations brought about by Trucial Oman Scouts were abandoned as inauthentic. Despite the fort's white appearance at mid-century, gypsum was deemed environmentally unsuitable as well as "non-traditional."[17] Indeed, photos from the late 1960s show the gypsum flaking off.[18] The current fort is plastered with dun-colored clay.[19]

Furthermore, the renovation changed the form and structure of the fort. Along the exterior the renovation added crenellations along the top of the walls and a new monumental entrance to make the fort look more impressive and imposing to visitors.[20] This new entrance faced Abu Dhabi, reflecting the shift

---

15   "Al Ain Classics Festival," Abu Dhabi: Abu Dhabi Authority for Culture and Heritage, 2009-2010, "Abu Dhabi: Experience the Magic; Culture and Heritage," Abu Dhabi: Abu Dhabi Tourism Authority, n.d., ca 2009-2010.
16   Roswag, Eike. "Rehabilitation of Jahili Fort," Roswag and Jankowski Architekten, 2009, 7, archnet.org/library/downloader/file/3330/file_body/FLS2615.pdf, accessed February 18, 2012, 8.
17   Ibid.
18   Sheehan, 51.
19   Ibid.
20   Ibid., 53.

in purpose for this fort. Additionally, they made the interior of the fort more open, demolishing the administrative office buildings added to the interior by the British. Through this renovation, they re-oriented al-Jahili away from its original purpose—defense, and towards its new focus, reflecting the glory of Abu Dhabi.

Though the architects explain that the decision to return al-Jahili to dun color resulted from the desire to return to materials that were more traditional, it is clear that the plan attempted to complement the fort's desert surroundings, while also maintaining the character of Al Ain itself. Al Ain City is inextricably associated with the desert and the natural world, but it is simultaneously a "garden city" that helps realize Sheikh Zayed's vision of the city as a green zone.[21] Al Ain has many date groves, and the government has established green spaces and public parks. To reinforce this, the fort is constructed on sand, with a park and large lawn around it. Unlike in Abu Dhabi where the Qasr al-Hosn is dwarfed by the skyscrapers around it, in Al Ain, the government established building limits in order to reinforce the scale and imposing nature of the forts in the city. Al-Jahili fort continues to project an imposing presence in Al Ain today because of these regulations, and it continues to be a testament to Al Nahyan power.

As in the Qasr al-Hosn and al-Jahili, the reconstruction of Sharjah's Hisn was an attempt to balance the cultural needs of the population with respect for its iconic past as well as for its practical value. However, unlike the Qasr al-Hosn, whose renovation returned its form to the era of the 1950s-1960s, and the al-Jahili fort that was restored to a form that never existed, the Hisn reverted to its late nineteenth century form—a large fort with high walls and towers in each corner.

This renovation ignored the blue and white period and returned the building to its dun-color, reflecting a specific choice on the part of the Sharjah Museums Department (SMD) and the ruler himself. For the emirates, the designation as old or historic tends to denote the period before federation. The Hisn, established in 1820, is now considered ancient. Though there is substantial archaeological evidence for the long inhabitation of the area, the Hisn does not have the same *cache* that the near past does for popular memory.[22] By restoring the Hisn to the late nineteenth century, SMD emphasized the length of the Al Qasimi family's rule in Sharjah, asserted the primacy of the Hisn in Sharjah's history, and minimized the importance of the mid- twentieth century. As noted above, Sharjah's mid-century experience was one of economic destitution. Therefore, restoring the Hisn to that era would remind Sharjah citizens of the failures of the Al Qasimi family.

The fort now houses a library and museum of Sharjah history. By rebuilding the fort and renovating the adjacent area, and by making it attractive and inviting for individuals to attend festivals with their families, the ruler clearly hopes to create new associations with the building. In February 2012, Sharjah held the third annual Sharjah Light Festival in which many of the heritage landmarks,

---

21   "Al Ain: The Garden City of the Gulf," *AlAinTimesUAE.com,* n.d., http://www.alaintimesuae.com/, accessed, February 18, 2012.

22   The journal *Archaeology in the United Arab Emirates,* ran five volumes from 1977-1989 and can be found on the ADACH website, http://www.adach.ae/en/portal/archeaologyintheuae.journal.aspx, in addition to the beautiful volume edited by Peter Hellyer, Daniel Potts and Hassan al Naboodah, *Archaeology of the United Arab Emirates: Proceedings of the First International Conference on the Archaeology of the UAE,* (Dubai: Trident Press Ltd., 2003).

including the Hisn, were illuminated with spectacular light displays[23] that retold the history of Sharjah both as an independent emirate and as part of the UAE. Natural heritage was interwoven with the faces of the Qasimi sheikhs and Sharjah citizens. One of the presentations started with a view of the universe before moving on to the history of Sharjah itself.[24] This is a blatant assertion of Sharjah's autonomous place in world history, independent of the UAE.

Figure 5.5 | The Sharjah Hisn today after the 1990s renovations. Note the immaculate feeling of the "newer section," the two story entrance versus the more cobbled appearance of the "original" tower. Photo by Alison Kelly, 2012. OR Image from Google Earth, 2015 DigitalGlobe

Conclusion

A constant question in most historical reconstructions is that of authenticity, yet here authenticity is precisely what is being formulated in the preservation and renovation surrounding these forts. All preservation efforts occur in a dialogue with the past, present, and future use of the place as well as with the conflicting dialogues and understanding of the building in the past. The selection of what to preserve is in itself a political act, fraught with rivalries and tensions.[25]

---

23   Lily B. Libo-on, "Festival Lights of Sharjah's Landmarks," *KHaleej Times Online*, February 11, 2012, http://www.khaleejtimes.com/DisplayArticle08.asp?xfile=data/theuae/2012/February/theuae_February272.xml&section=theuae, February 18, 2012.

24   Shibu719, "Sharjah Light Festival 2012," Video. *YouTube.Com*, http://youtu.be/RTqfgaN8tfg, accessed February 18, 2012.

25   Gustavo F. Araoz, "World-Heritage Historic Urban Landscapes: Defining and Protecting Authenticity," *APT Bulletin*, 39(2008): 35-36.

In each of these cases, aesthetic changes in color and form of the forts reflected, and was shaped by, the needs of rulers. The forts symbolize the rulers' power and their practical aspirations. Significant changes to the forts became a means of communication with their subjects. Color was and remains an important feature of this communication.

The decision to whitewash the forts in the mid- twentieth century is not discussed in heritage literature because the histories of these forts are presented as existing in their present form from time immemorial. Yet the shift in color from dun to white was undertaken for practical reasons in the mid- twentieth century, although this color change could reflect the hope that white walls could make the interiors cooler by reflecting the sun's heat. In reality, the gypsum and/or limestone covering had the opposite effect. The forts' walls contained air spaces that permitted the walls to breathe, keeping them cooler in summer and warmer in winter.[26] The aesthetic change signals important shifts in the meaning and purpose of the forts themselves.

Rather than viewing the renovations narrowly as twentieth century innovations aimed at tourist dollars, expanding the period in question reveals that these forts were never simply defensive structures. They were clearly aimed at conveying a ruler's or family's power and authority. The forts' color and structural changes throughout the past two hundred years reveal how changes can reflect and reinforce the fears and desires of the rulers. In the cases presented above, the forts' colors were changed from dun to white as the rulers hoped to highlight something about their ruler. In the case of al-Jahili and the Qasr al-Hosn, simple visibility was the aim, whereas in Sharjah and the mid-twentieth century Hisn renovations, appearing to be modern was the aim. While the use of color is an important indicator of changes in power, the decision to retain or return the fort's original color is also fraught with political meaning. In renovation, these forts were not unilaterally returned to the dun-color of the surrounding desert. Rather, the forts became and remain embroiled in the politics of preservation. These concerns are neither uniform nor isolated from the political needs of the emirs who rule the individual emirates.

In the UAE, the politics of preservation are connected to other serious issues, including the pressures of changing international politics, the phenomenon of a minority rule in which the native-born are not among the demographic majority of the country, and the desire on the part of all emirates to attract tourist money to either replace declining oil revenues or to hedge against a possibility of decline. The renovations of these forts help to uncover the priorities on the part of the government-sponsored heritage organizations, as well as to reveal the attempts by these organizations to influence not only the future, but also the conceptions of the past in the UAE. Renovations reflect the rulers' desire to negate or invoke nostalgia and to remind the inhabitants of the power and glory, and—perhaps more importantly— the long tenure of the rulers and their families in those cities.

---

26   Archie Wells, "The 3000-year-old History of An Arabian Mud Brick Technology," Giles Quarme and Associates, 2003, http://www.quarme.com/pdf/articles_aw/AW%20Mud%20brick%20paper%20to%209th%20Inter.pdf, accessed Feb. 17, 2012, 15-16, also, Mutwalli quoting a builder, 73.

Bibliography

"Abu Dhabi's Tower of Strength with a Long History," *The National,* Dec. 11, 2010, http://www.thenational.ae/news/uae-news/abu-dhabis-tower-of-strength-with-a-long-history, Jan. 26, 2010.

Aitchison, C .U. *Collection of Treaties, Engagements and Sanads Relating to India and Neighbouring Countries.* Calcutta: Govt. of India Central Publications Branch, 1929-1933.

"Al Ain: The Garden City of the Gulf," *AlAinTimesUAE.com,* n.d., http://www.alaintimesuae.com/, accessed, February 18, 2012..

"Al Ain Classics Festival," Abu Dhabi: Abu Dhabi Authority for Culture and Heritage, 2009-2010, "Abu Dhabi: Experience the Magic; Culture and Heritage," Abu Dhabi: Abu Dhabi Tourism Authority, n.d., ca 2009-2010

Allfree. P.S. *Warlords of Oman.* A.S. Barnes and Company, South Brunswick and New York, 1969.

Araoz, Gustavo F. "World-Heritage Historic Urban Landscapes: Defining and Protecting Authenticity." *APT Bulletin,* 39(2008): 35-36.

British Library, London, India Office Records R/15/2/1071

——— R/15/1/120

British Archives, Kew, ADM 127/54

———. ADM 127/52

George Barnes Brucks, "Memoir Descriptive of the Navigation of the Gulf of Persia; with Brief Notices of the Manners, Customs, Religion, Commerce, and Resources of the People Inhabiting its Shores and Islands" in *Survey of the Shores and Islands of the Persian Gulf 1820-1829* prepared for publication by Andrew S. Cook. (London: Archive Editions, 1990)

Carter, Robert. *Sea of Pearls: Seven Thousand Years of the Industry that Shaped the Gulf.* London: Arabian Publishing Ltd, 2012.

Davidson, Christopher. *Abu Dhabi: Oil and Beyond.* New York: Columbia University Press, 2009.

Evans, H.J. "A Note on the Wealth of Dubai" 24 June 1950, 637-641 in Penelope Tuson, *Records of the Emirates PrimaryDocuments 1820-1958* Volume 9 1947-1958. London, Archive Editions, 1990.

———. "Finances of Sharjah," 24 June 1950, 641-649 in Penelope Tuson, *Records of the Emirates PrimaryDocuments 1820-1958* Volume 9 1947-1958, (London, Archive Editions, 1990),

Al –Fahim, Mohammed. *From Rags to Riches: A Story of Abu Dhabi.* London: London Centre of Arab Studies, 1995.

Fox, John W, Nada Mourtada-Sabbah, and Mohammed al-Mutawa. "Heritage Revivalism in Sharjah" in *Globalization and the Gulf* eds. John W. Fox, Nada Mourtada-Sabbah, and Mohammed al-Mutawa. London: Routledge, 2006. 266-287

Hawley, Donald. *The Trucial States.* London: George Allen & Unwin Ltd, 1970.

Heard-Bey, Frauke. *From Trucial States to United Arab Emirates: A Society in Transition.* Dubai: Motivate Publishing, 2004. First published 1982.

———. "The Tribal Society of the UAE and its Traditional Economy," in *The United Arab Emirates: A New Perspective,* 98-116. http://www.uaeinteract.com/uaeint_misc/pdf/perspectives/04.pdf

Hellyer, Peter, Daniel Potts and Hassan al Naboodah. Archaeology of the United Arab Emirates: Proceedings of the First International Conference on the Archaeology of the UAE. Dubai: Trident Press Ltd., 2003.

Hume, Jessica. "A New Urgency to Save the Old," in A Journey through the Sands of Time, The National, CD, December 2, 2009, 223.

Jackson, Peter. "Sharjah: 400 years of coastal development," Public Lecture, Sharjah Museum of Islamic Civilization, 2009.

Libo-on, Lily B. "Festival Lights of Sharjah's Landmarks" Khaleej Times Online, February 11, 2012, http://www.khaleejtimes.com/DisplayArticle08.asp?xfile=data/ theuae/2012/February/theuae_February272.xml&section=theuae, February 18, 2012.

Lorimer, J.G. Gazetteer of the Persian Gulf, Oman and Central Arabia. 6 v. Gerrard's Cross, Archive Editions, 1986, Originally published 1907.

Maitra, Jayanti and Afra al-Hajji. Qasr al Hosn: The History of the Rulers of Abu Dhabi 1793-1966. Abu Dhabi: Centre for Documentation and Research, 2001.

El Mutwalli, Reem Tariq. Qasr al Husn. Abu Dhabi: Abu Dhabi Cultural Foundation, 1997.

"Oil and Natural Gas," Helem Chapin Metz, ed. Persian Gulf States: A Country Study.

Washington: GPO for the Library of Congress, 1993, http://countrystudies.us/persian-gulf-states/85.htm

Onley, James. The Arabian Frontier of the British Raj: Merchants, Rulers, and the British in then Nineteenth-Century Gulf. Oxford: Oxford University Press, 2007.

Persian Gulf Administration Reports 1873-1947. 11 v. Gerrard's Cross: Archive Editions, 1986.

"Project Report: Al Jahili Fort," Barker Langham, 2010, http://www.barkerlangham.co.uk/2010/01/al-jahili-fort/, Accessed February 18, 2012.

Records of the Emirates Primary Documents 1820-1958 12 v. Edited by Penelope Tuson. London, Archive Editions, 1990.

Roswag, Eike. "Rehabilitation of Jahili Fort," Roswag and Jankowski Architekten, 2009, 7, archnet.org/library/downloader/file/3330/file_body/FLS2615.pdf, accessed February 18, 2012.

Sheehan, Peter. "'In the Interests of the General Peace': The Architectural Development of al-Jahili Fort and its part within the Policy of Shaikh Zayed Bin Khalifa in al-'Ain," *Liwa,* 4, no. 7, (2012): 37-57.

Shibu719, "Sharjah Light Festival 2012." Video. 2012. YouTube.Com, http://youtu.be/RTqfgaN8tfg, accessed February 18, 2012.

al-Suweidi, Ali Saqr. Personal interview with author. January 21, 2010 Ghantoot Reserve, Dubai, UAE.

Wells, Archie. "The 3000-year-old History of An Arabian Mud Brick Technology" Giles Quarme and Associates, 2003, http://www.quarme.com/pdf/articles_aw/AW%20Mud% 20brick%20paper%20to%209th%20Inter.pdf, accessed Feb. 17, 2012, 15-16.

"White Fort stands proudly as Time Marches on" July 24, 2010, http://www.thenational.ae/news/white-fort-stands-proudly-as-time-marches-on, Feb. 3, 2012.

Wilkinson, J.C. "Traditional Concepts of Territory in South East Arabia" The Geographical Journal 149 (1983): 301-315.

———. Trucial States 1959-1962, (Muscat: Al Roya Press & Publishing House, 2008), 31.

Zaman, Samihah and Nathalie Farah, "Qasr al Hosn: Standing Guard Over a Rich Culture, Gulf News.com, August 26, 2011, http://gulfnews.com/news/gulf/uae/general/qasr-al-hosn-standing-guard-overa-rich-culture-1.857177, accessed February 18, 2012.

6

The Colors of American Diplomacy

Christopher Jespersen

A giant, yellow octopus envelops the globe, its long tentacles stretching across vast swaths of territory emanating from Japan. Representing that island nation and its people, the octopus conveys the threat of Japanese imperialism and territorial ambitions not just for the region but for the entire world. In addition to its yellow color, the octopus has two black angled slits for eyes and a mouth full of white teeth. The dominant features of the drawing, however, are the bright mustard-colored tentacles and head of the octopus, a giant predator consuming its worldly prey. The danger could not have been more menacing.

Figure 6.1 | Cover Illustration. "The Japanese 'Brain Trust' and How It Plans to Attack." *Simplicissimus*. Vol 39. Issue 44 (1935); Artist: Erich Schilling

The cartoonist, Erich Schilling, was German, and his depiction perfectly reflected the national sense of "gelbe Gefahr"—yellow peril, yellow danger, or yellow threat—that affected much of German national thinking from the onset of the twentieth century to World War I.[1] (Figure 6.1) But Schilling was not the first person to depict this menace. Ariane Knüsel singled out 1895, the Japanese

---
1   John Kuo Wei Tchen and Dylan Yeats, eds., *Yellow Peril! An Archive of Anti-Asian Fear* (London: Verso, 2014),
2. For an excellent compendium of paraphernalia relating to this subject, see *Yellow Peril: Collecting Xenophobia* (New York: American Institute Publication, 2007).

victory in the Sino-Japanese War and its impact on European attitudes, as the time when Japan became the focal point for this German angst. Kaiser Wilhelm II commissioned Hermann Knackfuss to memorialize the issue in a painting rendering the new danger to European interests in Asia since Japan's victory had come as something of a surprise to the West.² (Figure 6.2) Schilling's depiction came decades later, but of the two, he provided the more alarming and memorable imagery.

A decade after Erich Schilling offered such a gripping visual representation for western thinking about Japan, Edgar Snow assessed Japan's military strength and strategic threat to western interests in Asia during World War Two. Snow's article, "Must We Beat Japan First?," sought to counter the Roosevelt administration's focus on Germany. Under a subheading titled "The Yellow Octopus," Snow explained the geographical breadth and extent of Japan's newly won empire: "Japan has scored all her gains to date with but negligible costs in man power, and has captured more equipment than she has expended."³ The depiction Schilling offered in the 1930s was very real in the 1940s.

That a German cartoonist and an American writer or editor would refer to Japan as a yellow octopus was not entirely coincidental. Both Germany and the United States became interested parties in East Asian developments during the 1890s, just as Japan was undergoing enormous political, economic, and social

Figure 6.2 | *Völker Europas, wahrt eure heiligsten Güter* ("Peoples of Europe, guard your dearest goods"), 1895; Artist: Hermann Knackfuss

---

2   Ariane Knüsel, *Framing China: Media Images and Political Debates in Britain, the USA and Switzerland, 1900-1950* (Burlington: Ashgate, 2012), 130.

3   Edgar Snow, "Must We Beat Japan First?," *The Saturday Evening Post*, 215 (October 10, 1942), 91. It is worth noting that Snow does not refer to Japan as a yellow octopus in his article. The subheading was very likely put there by an editor.

changes, and also after the Japanese government began to pursue its regional interests in competition with European countries, including Germany, and the United States.

In March 1947, the popular weekly *Life* magazine ran an excerpt from a book by James Burnham; the title said it all: "The Struggle for the World." Burnham laid out the dire situation the United States faced: namely, the American people had to accept the challenge for world power or cede global control to the Soviet Union. Accompanying the article was a *Life* map, in this case a north-pole projection. (Figure 6.3) While Russia is colored red, the rest of the map is various shades of gray. Mongolia, parts of China, Finland, and Eastern Europe are rendered in pinkish color, and red arrows extend from Russia into India, China, Korea, and from Southeast Asia into

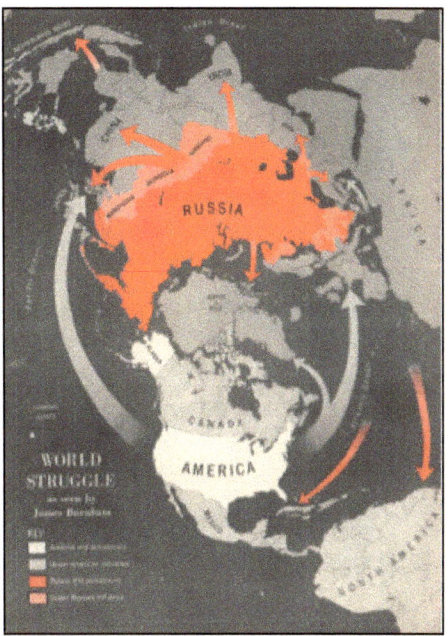

Figure 6.3 | Map entitled "World Struggle as seen by James Burnham"; included in excerpt "The Struggle for the World" by James Burnham published in *Life*. March 31, 1947.

the Dutch East Indies (Indonesia), north to Spitsbergen, and across the Atlantic Ocean to Cuba and South America.[4] Although the Soviet Union was not cast as a large cephalopod grasping the globe in its clutches, the effect was nearly the same as the yellow octopus depicting the Japanese menace: in both instances great and growing dangers were highlighted with vibrant colors straddling the globe.

These two examples used colors to display threats to the United States and Europe as well as their interests in other regions of the world. The vivid depiction in both cases underscored the concerns that these external dangers posed. Colors conveyed the threat, and they did so through an emotional play, especially by tapping into the fears that existing anxieties already engendered. The yellow Japanese, those smaller Asian people and their inscrutable ways, were presented as a rapacious peril bent on extending their hold over the world. And the red Soviets, the communists determined to foster world revolution, were equally serious about constraining American freedoms just a short while after the Japanese had been defeated.[5] The yellow peril, in other words, which raged from the late nineteenth century onward, morphed into the red menace by the mid twentieth century.

Colors have long been used as shorthand for expressing emotions: green with envy, white hot, feeling blue. Discussing a "yellow peril" or a "red menace"

---

4   *Life*, March 31, 1947.

5   Michael L. Krenn makes much the same point about how colors convey imagery, but he focuses on the way colors have described the American empire. See, *The Color of Empire: Race and American Foreign Relations* (Washington: Potomac Books, Inc., 2006), xiii.

connects a perceived threat—either external or internal—with a visually alarming manner of depicting that danger in order to warn Americans of its imminence. The Art Institutes' color therapy blog offers a range of definitions for different colors depending on culture and historical circumstances. Red, for instance, can mean anything from fire, passion, or thrill, to aggression, lust, or revolution. Yellow is associated with sunshine, energy, and warmth, or it can symbolize caution or serve as a warning.[6] Erich Schilling's cartoon, and the essence behind the notion of a yellow peril, obviously intended to warn that Japan and the Japanese people had become a threat much the same as labeling communism a "red menace" gave vibrancy to, and raised alarms about, the subversive and revolutionary nature of the Soviet Union. It is not coincidence that traffic lights worldwide use yellow and red to indicate caution and stop, respectively. Colors express meaning immediately and viscerally.

Rephrasing a question once posed by the European historian Traian Stoianovich ("What is the significance of the color yellow for European history?") and applying it to American history provides the basis for a different question: What has been the significance of colors in American diplomacy or, more directly, have there been colors to American diplomacy and, if so, what have those colors been? As to the latter question, the answer could certainly be red, for the initial concern about Indians and their impact on the frontier throughout colonial times and well into the nineteenth century. It could be black because of the issue of slavery in all its forms and because of its larger impact, but slavery was largely an internal issue, not one that affected the nation's diplomacy to the same immediate degree that other colors did. It could also be yellow because of the growing importance of Asian immigration in the nineteenth century and how that affected relations with Asia. In other words, as much as colors could designate different races, they could also, and most assuredly did, represent threats to America's growing global interests. The use of a specific color to describe a particular threat, in other words, went beyond race, although that was part of it in certain instances. Indeed, for much of American history, and particularly from the 1890s through the 1990s, the colors of the nation's diplomacy were yellow and red, depending on the timeframe and the geographical orientation, and those colors highlighted real or perceived threats, perils, or challenges to the nation.

As many historians have discussed, for much of American history, colors signified the racial classification of different peoples. Europeans were designated white, while Africans were black. Peoples from Asia were considered yellow despite the fact that their actual skin colors vary and are not really yellow at all. With regard to the color yellow and its designation as representing peoples from Asia, Robert Lee stated, "Race is a mode of placing cultural meaning on the body. Yellowface marks the Oriental as indelibly alien."[7]

The history of using colors to depict threats to the United States has been long, especially as colors were designators of race. In his book, *Ideology and American Foreign Policy*, for example, Michael Hunt identified two particular-

---

6   http://www.arttherapyblog.com/online/color-meanings-symbolism/#.UmGnCRZLJG5

7   Robert G. Lee, *Orientals: Asian Americans in Popular Culture* (Philadelphia: Temple University Press, 1999), 2.

ly significant and longstanding threads in the nation's diplomatic history: the hierarchy of race and the perils of revolution. With regard to the former, Hunt noted that from the nation's very beginning, race played a critical role in affecting policy making and in determining the way certain peoples were treated. Race was not defined simply by geographical origins, although that was part of the equation; race was a matter of skin color, and the darker a person's skin, the lower on the hierarchy that person was. Of course, the hierarchy by which all races were evaluated and situated was itself created by whites. The impact of this thinking was clear: "Gripped by ethnocentric impulses of seemingly universal force," Hunt wrote, "Americans used race to build protective walls against the threatening strangeness of other people and to legitimate the boundaries and terms of intergroup contact."[8]

Race, of course, was tied to skin color. From its very beginning, American society was color sensitive: the white European settlers viewed Indians (reds) and Africans (blacks) differently, as they would come to do with Latinos (browns) and Asians (yellow) with the latter's influx in the mid-to-late nineteenth century.[9] And despite their national origins in revolutionary action, white Americans developed decidedly mixed feelings about other revolutions, particularly when revolutions were undertaken elsewhere and by different peoples. Americans approached them with caution or apprehension, particularly after observing how some revolutions were messy, chaotic, and bloody affairs. Especially here, the specter of race intruded. Although poor individual leadership in the form of corruption, despotism, and character shortcomings could be the reason for failed revolutions, another explanation was racial: "the inability of a people to meet the test of revolution and liberty was explained most often in the familiar terms of the hierarchy of race."[10] And the darker the people's skin, the greater the difficulties they faced: "blacks were thought to labor under the heaviest racial burden. Orientals and Latinos did little better. The Filipinos were thought so unworthy of freedom that American troops crushed their revolution, and the Chinese botched their attempt at setting up a republic. Mexicans, like the Cubans before them," Hunt averred in discussing American attitudes, "might aspire to constitutional government, but the traits associated with the black legend made the realization of that goal remote except perhaps under American tutelage."[11] As if that were not enough, all whites were themselves not created equal. Within the Caucasian classification, there were degrees of "whiteness." Among Europeans, for example, Slavs barely made the classification as "whites" and hence failed at revolution.

Hunt's examination into the underpinnings of American diplomacy has two elements, one explicitly tied to, the other less directly but still related to, the issue of race and color. Since the focus here is United States diplomatic relations, the initial answer will begin with a focus on the color yellow, since the fear of the yellow peril led to immigration policies that excluded first, Chinese in 1882, 1894,

---

8   Michael H. Hunt, *Ideology and U.S. Foreign Policy* (New Haven: Yale University Press, 1987), 90.
9   Gary B. Nash, *Red, White and Black: The Peoples of Early North America* (Englewood Cliffs: Prentice Hall, 1992).
10 Hunt, 116.
11 Ibid., 116-7.

and 1904, then Filipinos; Japanese were added with the Root-Takahira agreement in 1908, and all the exclusionary efforts culminated with the Johnson—Reed immigration act of 1924. Concomitant with domestic political pressures to limit Asian immigration were fears of an aggressive China or Japan attaining regional hegemony. Indeed, as soon as the borders were apparently sealed, the problem of the yellow peril took new form and erupted in Asia from the time when Japan defeated China in 1895 over which nation was going to control Korea, to when Japan invaded China in 1931.

In other words, the fear of the yellow peril compelled aggressive military actions beginning in the Philippines in 1898, affected the way the war with Japan was fought in the 1940s, influenced the war in Korea from 1950 to 1953, and, finally, shaped the nature of the war in Vietnam for over two decades. Racially charged language dehumanized the enemy, justified brutal practices (including torture), led to millions of civilian deaths, and caused the unleashing of horrific firepower without regard to the casualties inflicted or the damage done.[12]

As Heinz Gollwitzer pointed out a half century ago, the fear of the yellow peril, the absolute dread of the rise of Asians or an Asian nation, was very real in Europe and the United States and made its way into popular literature on both sides of the Atlantic in the early twentieth century.[13] In Sax Rohmer's *The Insidious Fu Manchu*, for example, the hero, Nayland Smith, explains to his sidekick, Dr. James Petrie, "I have traveled from Burma, not in the interests of the British Government merely, but in the interests of the entire white race, and I honestly believe—though I pray I may be wrong—that its survival depends largely upon the success of my mission."[14]

Across the Atlantic, American author Jack London analyzed the threats faced by whites from the yellow peril:

> There is such a thing as race egotism as well as creature egotism, and a very good thing it is. In the first place, the Western world will not permit the rise of the yellow peril. It is firmly convinced that it will not permit the yellow and the brown to wax strong and menace its peace and comfort. It advances this idea with persistency, and delivers itself of long arguments showing how and why this menace will not be permitted to arise. Today, far more voices are engaged in denying the yellow peril than in prophesying it. The Western world is warned, if not armed, against the possibility of it.

In London's analysis, the contrast with the Japanese was clear, and the Japanese were depraved as well as deprived of goodness: "Religion, as a battle for the right

---

12 John W. Dower, *War Without Mercy: Race & Power in the Pacific War* (New York: Pantheon Books, 1986) provides a comprehensive treatment of World War II. For an overview of U.S. policy toward Asia in the twentieth century, see Michael H. Hunt and Steven I. Levine, *Arc of Empire: America's Wars in Asia from the Philippines to Vietnam* (Chapel Hill: The University of North Carolina Press, 2012).

13 Heinz Gollwitzer, *Die Gelbe Gefahr: Geschichte eines Schlagworts* (Vandenhoeck & Ruprecht, 1962), accessed through Google books: http://books.google.de/books?id=z-ZxdiO1wkYC&printsec=frontcover&hl=de&source=gbs_ge_summary_r&cad=0#v=onepage&q&f=false

14 Sax Rohmer, *The Insidious Fu-Manchu* (New York: Novel Selections, Inc., 1913), 4. For an excellent discussion of this novel, see David Shih, "The Color of Fu-Manchu: Orientalist Method in the Novels of Sax Rohmer," *The Journal of Popular Culture* 42 (2009), 304-317. Sax Rohmer was the pen name of Arthur Sarsfield Ward.

in our sense of right, as a yearning and a strike for spiritual good and purity, is unknown to the Japanese."[15]

The journalist and historian Lothrop Stoddard worried that Western support for Japan during the Russo-Japanese War demonstrated an unsoundness of judgment because of his concern about the yellow peril. He referred to World War I as the "White Civil War" and fretted about white racial solidarity: "Should white men ever really lose their instinct of race-solidarity, they would asphyxiate racially as swiftly and surely as they would asphyxiate physically if the atmospheric oxygen should suddenly be withdrawn."[16]

White Americans were particularly sensitive to race in the early part of the twentieth century. Madison Grant, a lawyer, historian, and physical anthropologist, a graduate of Yale University and Columbia Law School, wrote extensively about racial matters during this time. In *The Conquest of a Continent or the Expansion of Races in America*, he argued, "The world as a whole can be roughly mapped racially according to the most obvious human differentiation—namely, color: white, yellow, red, black, and brown."[17] Grant's purpose was not simply to categorize; his language differentiated, divided, and subjugated certain colors in favor of and by one color, white. The language was exclusionary and divisive. And his approach can be summarized succinctly: the darker the skin color, the greater the threat. By way of argument, Grant thus offered stereotypes. "One of the manifestations of this jealousy" darker skinned people had for whites, or Nordics, as Grant labeled them, "is shown in those numerous cases where members of the colored races, or even dark-skinned members of the Nordic race regard the possession of a blonde woman as an assertion and proof of race equality."[18] Indeed, Grant argued that "Democratic ideals among an homogenous population of Nordic blood, as in England or America, is one thing, but it is quite another for the white man to share his blood with, or intrust his ideals to, brown, yellow, black, or red men."[19]

After citing one author who claimed that mulattoes had a thirty-four-to-one chance of doing better in society when compared to blacks, Grant insisted, "Such a situation naturally puts a premium on white blood in the minds of Negroes, and there puts a prize on bastardy, discouraging any tendency to cultivate pure racial values on the part of the Blacks themselves. The black man who acquires wealth, at once wishes to show visible evidence of his affluence by acquiring a light yellow or 'pink' wife, and the black girl is at a heavy discount matrimonially."[20] The white concern about blacks was a domestic matter. The concern with the yellow peril was framed in language that suggested a wave splashing ashore, wiping out American (white) progress. As such, barriers had to be erected to keep the threat at bay, or at least in the bay—anywhere but on land.

---

15   "The Yellow Peril," in Jack London, ed., *Revolution and Other Essays*, http://www.readbookonline.net/title/298/
16   Lothrop Stoddard, *The Rising Tide of Color Against White World-Supremacy* (New York: Charles Scribner's Sons, 1921), 170.
17   Madison Grant, *The Conquest of a Continent or The Expansion of Races in America* (New York: Scribner's, 1933), 26.
18   Ibid.,15.
19   From the Introduction by Madison Grant to Stoddard's *The Rising Tide of Color*, xxxii. Spelling in original.
20   Ibid., 284.

Whereas much attention had been paid to China as the looming threat to European and American interests in Asia prior to 1895, the Japanese victory changed impressions. On the one hand, this complicated matters, or at least it could have, since the notion of a yellow peril was first applied to China and then transferred to Japan when circumstances changed. On the other hand, it did not matter. As Heinz Gollwitzer explained it, the understanding was that the "gelbe Gefahr" was a threat, from the Chinese or the Japanese (or possibly both together), aimed at or against the white peoples of the West. Initially the fear was of Chinese coolies, or labor, undermining white workers through cheaper wages made possible by their minimal living standards. The next concern focused on Japan's industrial production after the Meiji Restoration was completed. Schilling's cartoon reflected Gollwitzer's third point: namely, that "gelbe Gefahr" could take the form of emancipated "yellow" nations removing the Europeans and Americans from Asia by adopting modern weapons and making use of their numerical superiority. But that was not all: "gelbe Gefahr" posited that the "yellow" nations could achieve world-wide predominance.[21] After the Russo-Japanese War of 1904-1905 ended with Japan's resounding defeat of two Russian navies, Japan appeared poised to threaten European and American interests in Asia, and for those harboring anxieties about its newly developed strength, Japan could be a threat beyond the region.

What was happening in Germany with respect to viewing Asia as a menace—and a yellow one at that—was a more immediate and strident phenomenon in the United States. Indeed, the issue of Asian immigration was significantly more acute in America than it was anywhere in Europe, including Germany. Chinese began arriving on the continental west coast in the late 1840s. Within half a decade California put legal restraints on them. As has been mentioned, in 1882 those restrictions became national as the federal government imposed immigration limits on Chinese, which were later amended to include other peoples from Asia. In 1908 the United States and Japan made what was termed a "gentlemen's agreement" regarding Japanese emigration.[22] In 1924 Congress passed the Johnson-Reed Act barring all immigration from Asia.

That official exclusions on immigration were put into place did not undercut domestic fears of the existing Asians in America; nor did the nation suddenly reconsider its apprehension about Japanese regional interests. On the former, the Supreme Court ruled in 1922 that Takao Ozawa could not become a naturalized citizen despite graduating from a high school in Berkeley, California, attending the University of California, and living in the United States for twenty-eight years. The Court conceded that his skin color might actually be lighter than many persons considered "white" by society, but he was nonetheless a member of the "brown or yellow races" given his birth in Japan and his standing as someone of the Japanese race. As Robert Lee has aptly observed, "The designation of yellow as the racial color of the Oriental is a prime exam-

---

21   Gollwitzer, *Die Gelbe Gefahr*, 20-1.

22   For a detailed introduction into the subject, see Stanford M. Lyman, "The 'Yellow Peril' Mystique: Origins and Vicissitudes of a Racist Discourse," *International Journal of Politics, Culture and Society* 13 (June 2000), 683-747, esp. 695-698.

ple of this social constructedness of race."²³ Nowhere was that truer than in the Supreme Court's ruling.

The domestic political pressures were not the entire story either. American politicians and diplomats refused to accept the Japanese as equals. Joined by London and some of the British dominions, President Woodrow Wilson disallowed a racial equality clause as part of the covenant for the League of Nations even though it had won a majority of the delegates' votes. Also opposing the resolution were Great Britain and Australia.²⁴ A few years later at the Washington Naval Conference, Britain and the United States again joined forces to thwart Japanese desires to build naval tonnage to seventy percent of the British and American fleets on a five-power agreement designed to limit the construction of battleships and cruisers.²⁵ The Anglo-Americans insisted that Japan accept sixty percent, which Japanese officials felt to be yet another insulting and collusive act by the Americans and Europeans.

So the Japanese were from the yellow race, and the growth of Japan as a modern nation represented a threat, one that was colored yellow. Germany's defeat in World War I stripped the nation of its colonial interests in Asia; that largely dissipated the "gelbe Gefahr" phenomenon as far as Germans were concerned, although not entirely as Erich Schilling's cartoon demonstrated. Not so for the United States as its Asian possessions, namely the Philippines, Wake Island, Guam, and Hawaii, remained intact, thus heightening American concerns about Japanese ambitions. America was part of the allied coalition that had defeated Germany. Its territorial interests in Asia, which, like Germany's, dated to the 1890s, remained at the forefront of the nation's developing global ambitions.

Figure 6.4 | "Japan's Aggressor: Admiral Yamamoto." *Time*. 22 December 1941, Vol 38. Issue 25; Artist: Arthur Syzk

The period of the late nineteenth and early twentieth centuries was marked by extraordinary race consciousness in Europe and the United States. Social Darwinism swept intellectual circles as politicians and writers sought to justify their nations' imperial adventures. Colors became short-handed ways to separate regional groups of peoples from the white peoples of northern Europe and much of America, largely by way of justifying the occupation and exploitation of peoples in Africa and Asia. At the same time, as Matthew Frye Jacobson has demonstrat-

---

23 Robert G. Lee, *Orientals: Asian Americans in Popular Culture* (Philadelphia: Temple University Press, 1999), 2.
24 Knüsel, *Framing China*, 160-2.
25 For an excellent summary of Japan's growing discontent during this time period, see Krenn, 63-66.

ed, the notion of true whiteness was contested throughout American history with some previously excluded groups (e.g. the Irish) becoming ultimately absorbed, while others, as Takao Ozawa discovered, remained excluded no matter their actual skin color.[26] The notion of color was thus malleable as the Supreme Court unintentionally acknowledged in the Ozawa case.

The association between the Japanese, the color yellow, and the threat to American interests accelerated during the 1930s and reached its zenith in the United States shortly after the Japanese attack on Pearl Harbor. *Time* magazine depicted this convergence of racial and geo-political forces in its cover portrait of Admiral Yamamoto on December 22, 1941. Sounding very much like the "gelbe Gefahr" phenomenon that affected German political thinking four decades earlier, *Time* remarked on racial divisions by employing colors: "In order to drive the white man from Greater East Asia, Admiral Yamamoto must drive away, or preferably destroy, the white man's bridge to Asia: his fleets."[27] White versus yellow in the battle for Asia was the theme *Time* offered in the hyper-sensitized and jingoistic period after the Japanese attack, and Admiral Yamato, as the cover clearly displayed, was the mastermind of the yellow peril's strike against white interests in the Pacific.

World War Two furthered the notion of a yellow peril in predictable and, in some cases, surprising ways. Dan Gilbert, a prolific author of Christian tracts, pamphlets, and books with such titles as *Crucifying Christ in Our Colleges, The Vanishing Virgin*, and *Evolution: the Root of All Isms*, penned a wartime screed of forty-six pages titled *The Yellow Peril (Japan) and Bible Prophecy*. Gilbert cited Edgar Snow's article in *The Saturday Evening Post* and its reference to Japan as "'*the Yellow Octopus*.'"[28] Gilbert liked the image. He added that Japan was hoping "that the war in Europe will weaken all the white nations, while [Japan] strengthens and extends the grip of the Yellow Octopus in Asia."[29] Kaiser Wilhelm's 1895 vision of an Asian threat had finally come true for Americans, and they identified that peril with the color yellow.

The use of the color yellow to describe the Japanese peaked with World War Two. That connection was clearly racial, but the use of different colors to describe various peoples has another meaning beyond the attachment to race, however significant and longstanding that assignation has been. That colors have been used as part of this shorthanded referencing has been significant, but the very fact that colors were employed—as opposed to strictly geographical location—is also telling. In other words, the colors of American diplomacy have gone beyond relating solely to racial identification, and nowhere has that been clearer than in assigning the color red to Russians.

The color of American diplomacy was yellow focused or yellow obsessed for much of the first half of the twentieth century, but in addition to this grave

---

26 Matthew Frye Jacobson, *Whiteness of a Different Color: European Immigrants and the Alchemy of Race* (Cambridge: Harvard University Press, 1998).

27 *Time*, December 22, 1941, 23.

28 Dan Gilbert, *The Yellow Peril (Japan) and Bible Prophecy* (Grand Rapids: Zondervan Publishing House, 1943), 16. Gilbert had also written a book about how the American communists had tried to change their approach. See Dan Gilbert, *Our Chameleon Comrades: The Reds Turn Yellow!* (San Diego: The Danielle Publishers, 1938).

29 Ibid., 21.

concern, American diplomacy also worried about the color red in the twentieth century. Outside of its connection with American Indians, the color red was affiliated with subversion, infiltration, and betrayal—suggestions of individuals, ideas, and movements that might undermine American society. Moreover, the color red was associated with socialism, secret organizations, of not playing fair or by the rules. There were, in short, potential enemies everywhere, and particularly within the nation's midst, and those enemies were red.[30]

The first red scare in America dates to the 1870s, and with it came the first counter-subversive efforts as well, similar to the counter-revolution that spawned in the wake of Martin Luther's ninety-five theses. Madison Grant lent his racial analysis to this phenomenon as well: "In the Negro section of Harlem a further problem is arising from crosses between Negroes and Jews and Italians. These and other Mulattoes are showing a tendency toward Communism."[31] Blacks, in other words, were in danger of becoming part of the red menace.

Red scares became regular events in American political history during the late nineteenth and early twentieth centuries. The Bolshevik revolution obviously heightened fears. Attorney General Mitchell Palmer's raids in 1919 raised the stakes, and despite the alliance with the Soviet Union during World War Two, the onset of the Cold War immediately after Germany's and Japan's defeats revived fears of the red menace.

That menace was both external and internal. President Harry Truman issued Executive Order 9825, a loyalty order that sought to ferret out communists in the federal government. Not to be outdone, the House Un-American Activities Committee extended its reach beyond the federal government in its zeal to rid the nation of reds, pinks, and other colors in the family. In 1952, Richard Nixon told the *Kansas City Star*, "there's one difference between Reds and Pinks. The Pinks want to socialize America. The Reds want to socialize the world and make Moscow the world capital. Their paths are similar; they have the same bible—the teachings of Karl Marx."[32] Of course Nixon vaulted to national political prominence by attacking the red menace, his most famous case being the conviction of former White House official Alger Hiss on perjury charges in 1951. When Dean Acheson made a statement defending Hiss after his conviction, Nixon impugned the secretary of state for suffering from "color blindness—a form of pink eye toward the Communist threat in the United States."[33]

Others got into the act, none more so than the Reverend Billy Graham. He combined cold war zealotry with Christian virtues, and he praised the likes of Richard Nixon and Senator Joseph McCarthy "who in the face of public denouncement and ridicule, go loyally on in their work of exposing the pinks, the lavenders, and the reds who have sought refuge beneath the wings of the American eagle."[34]

---

30 For an amusing introduction into the topic, see Michael Barson, *"Better Dead Than Red!" A Nostalgic Look at the Golden Years of Russiaphobia, Red-baiting, and Other Commie Madness* (New York: Hyperion, 1992).

31 Ibid., 283.

32 As quoted in Stephen J. Whitfield, *The Culture of the Cold War* (Baltimore: The Johns Hopkins University Press, 1991), 19.

33 As quoted in ibid., 28-9.

34 As quoted in ibid., 45. Here the lavenders referred to homosexual men.

The subversive element at home was matched by the red threat abroad. After World War Two, and especially after the Soviets detonated their own atomic bomb in 1949 and the Chinese Communist Party came to power months later, the stakes could not have been higher. Then the Cold War suddenly heated up in Korea. American and Chinese forces battled for control of the peninsula. The cost in Korean, Chinese, and American lives was enormous.

This external threat necessitated new ways of thinking. In what is usually referred to as the Doolittle Report, the CIA argued in 1954 that the United States had to change the way it fought the Cold War: "As long as it remains national policy, another important requirement is an aggressive covert psychological, political and paramilitary organization more effective, more unique and, if necessary, *more ruthless* than that employed by the enemy." It was not enough to simply fight communism, and it was certainly not permissible to allow rules or restrictions—anything that smacked of niceties—to interfere in the way the war was being fought. "It is now clear," the report continued, "that we are facing an implacable enemy whose avowed objective is world domination by whatever means and at whatever cost. There are no rules in such a game. Hitherto acceptable norms of human conduct do not apply." The red menace was worse than dire; it was cataclysmic.

> If the United States is to survive, long-standing American concepts of 'fair play' must be reconsidered. We must develop effective espionage and counterespionage services and must learn to subvert, sabotage and destroy enemies by more clever, more sophisticated and more effective methods than those used against us. It may become necessary that the American people be made acquainted with, understand and support this fundamentally repugnant philosophy.[35]

In his succinct and insightful novel, *The Quiet American*, Graham Greene captured the nature and color of American diplomacy in the 1950s, particularly as it related to Vietnam, but also as it applied to non-European countries generally. He did so through the character Alden Pyle. An apparently wide-eyed innocent from New England, Pyle is stationed in Vietnam, where he meets the English journalist Thomas Fowler. The two strike up a relationship that revolves around Pyle's nebulous activities on behalf of the United States government, Fowler's reporting on the war between the French and the Viet Minh for his newspaper back in Britain, and Pyle's romantic infatuation with Fowler's Vietnamese mistress, Phuong.

Although Pyle is assigned to the economic mission, he is really an agent of the CIA, and his focus is on creating what he calls a "third force" in Vietnam, or a leader who is neither a communist nor a colonialist. While standing in Pyle's apartment one afternoon, Fowler takes note of the books Pyle has brought with him, focusing specifically on the works of the fictional author York Harding, but who could just as well have been the very real James Burnham. Among the titles were *The Advance of Red China* and *The Rôle of the West*. These were serious books for a serious person on a critical mission fighting the reds in Asia. That

---

35 The first two quotes are from *Report on the Covert Activities of the Central Intelligence Agency*, or the Doolittle Report, J.H. Doolittle, September 30, 1954, p. 2. The third quote is from pp. 2-3. See https://archive.org/stream/CIA-Covert-Activities-Doolittle-Report/doolittle_report#page/n11/mode/2up Accessed February 4, 2012.

these reds had once been part of a yellow peril threatening America through immigration mattered insofar as they were all faceless hordes bent on undermining the American way of life, or at least U.S. interests in Asia. The red communists had supplanted the yellow Japanese.

Pyle's connection to the shadowy figure General Thé takes a very serious turn when his efforts to destabilize the government and have the communists blamed in the process go terribly awry with tragic consequences. After a bomb has exploded in a central square in Saigon, Greene used Fowler, still stunned from the bomb's impact and the devastation it has wrought, to make an insightful observation while getting up from the floor of the bar he is in: "A curious garden-sound filled the café: the regular drip of a fountain, and looking at the bar I saw rows of smashed bottles which let out their contents of multi-coloured stream—the red of porto, the orange of Cointreau, the green of chartreuse, the cloudy yellow of pastis, across the floor of the café."[36] These are the colors of Pyle's indiscriminate destruction, all done in opposition to "The Advance of Red China." Greene set up a mélange of colors, the streaming effects of American diplomacy, as it were, in vibrant rainbow form. The yellow peril had now merged with the red menace, and the United States had responded by creating a multi-colored mess of death and destruction.

Pyle does not see that, of course. Being what Thomas Fowler labels an innocent, Pyle does not understand what he is viewing, not the woman sitting on the ground covering her dead baby, not the man with his legs missing. Instead, Pyle glances at the ground and sees that his shoes have been stained: "He looked at the wet on his shoes and said in a sick voice, 'What's that?' 'Blood,' I said. 'Haven't you ever seen it before?' He said, 'I must get them cleaned before I see the Minister.'"[37]

Greene, of course, would have none of that convenient cleansing for America. Pyle was besmirched, stained by the red blood of civilians; it could not be wiped away. In other words, the color of American diplomacy started out fearful of yellow peril and morphed into deep-seated anxiety about red menace. Whatever the difference in the tones and hues, both colors were founded on fear: anxiety about Japanese aggression, opposition to communism, fear of subversion, and the competition of the Cold War. America had not so much replaced the yellow peril with the red menace as it had merged the two, and the new danger necessitated responding with the same brutality the nation had shown in defeating Japan and ferreting out communists domestically.

Greene was commenting on the early American involvement in Vietnam in the mid 1950s. By the early 1960s, Kenneth Goff was writing in his pamphlet, *Red Tide*, that James Burnham's prediction had come true: "The Red tide is lapping at the shores of America, and slowly but surely we are becoming an island in a Red sea of Communism." *Life* magazine may have provided the map in 1947, but Goff offered the stirring language over a decade later: "The turbulent sea of Communism was now engulfing everything in its path, so that by the 1960's none but a fool would laugh off the coming Red tide." By way of examples, he pointed to Eastern Europe and most of Asia as being under communist domination with

---

36 Graham Greene, *The Quiet American* (New York: Penguin Books, 1977), 160.
37 Ibid., 162.

communist strongholds developing in Latin America and fifth column activists in nearly every country of the globe.[38]

Presidents Kennedy and Johnson were ready to take action. A decade after Alden Pyle set foot in South Vietnam, America's involvement included hundreds of thousands of American troops fighting, yet again, in Asia. And those American soldiers brought with them racially charged assumptions and expectations. In his extraordinary trilogy on the frontier in American history, Richard Slotkin discussed transferring the historical notions of the American frontier to Vietnam, and that transference was suffused with color.

> But beneath that ambiguity the structural principle of both the mythic and the historical versions of the Indian-war scenario is the primary distinction between 'Red' and 'White'—a distinction that overrides the fine discrimination between 'hostiles' and 'friendlies.' When in doubt, it is safer to assume that all Indians are actually or incipiently hostile.[39]

To put it more colloquially, the only good Vietnamese was a dead Vietnamese. Or if a person was Vietnamese and dead, then the person was the enemy. Alden Pyle's one bomb detonated in the square became millions of bombs dropped from the sky or shells lofted by artillery.

That colors then served as signifiers of race and revolutionary movements, or in some instances both, but in any case, that colors served to highlight the nature of perceived or even manufactured threats to American interests helped shape the response to these threats. Employing colors as shorthand stimulated fear, aroused public anger, and fostered aggressive policies as ways of responding. For most of the twentieth century, American diplomacy reacted viscerally to the colors yellow and red.

The collapse of the Berlin Wall in 1989 and the realization that the United States had prevailed in the Cold War should have ushered in a new era with regard to color and American diplomacy, and in an interesting respect, it did. Gone were the references to yellow and red enemies. Instead, what arose in the aftermath of the September 11, 2001, attacks was not the idea that Al Qaeda could be described as yellow, red, or some other color; instead, the notion arose of the United States itself being the colors red, white, and blue, obviously in line with the national flag. A popular bumper sticker declared: "These Colors Don't Run."

Colored fabrics, of course, do run when washed in water of a certain temperature, but the wordplay that the three colors that constitute the American flag would not run in the laundry or from threats to national interests might seem a bit silly, but it was a genuine and rather easy expression of national sentiment in response to 9/11. A year later, Gigi Brienza archly noted in the *Christian Science Monitor* that while Americans were proud to display these bumper stickers, about the steadfast (and colorfast) colors of their flag, they seemed completely uninter-

---

38   Kenneth Goff, *Red Tide* (Englewood, CO: Soldiers of the Cross, 1962), 1.

39   Richard Slotkin, *Gunfighter Nation: The Myth of the Frontier in Twentieth-Century America* (Norman: University of Oklahoma Press, 1998), 547.

ested in determining which countries provided their gasoline. She contrasted this lack of curiosity with the growing concern about the type of coffee Americans drank.[40] A decade after 9/11, the author of The Francis Blog offered a witty exegesis of the phrase "These Colors Don't Run" and included a parody that he found particularly apt.[41]

Figure 6.5 | "These Colors Don't Run" Parody. *The Francis Blog*, 14, July 2011. Artist Unknown

The British heavy metal band Iron Maiden took up the theme—thus cementing another century of the Anglo-American special relationship, no doubt—in its 2006 album *A Matter of Life and Death* with the song titled "These Colours Don't Run." The lyrics include the refrain, "Far away from the land of your birth, We fly the flag in some foreign earth, We sailed away like our fathers before, These colours don't run from cold, bloody war."[42]

Interestingly enough, whereas American diplomacy has largely dropped references to threats as colors, they are still found in German popular culture. Stephen Leeb and Gregory Dorsey published *Die Gelbe Gefahr* with the subtitle about how China's avarice for raw materials is threatening Germany's way of life.[43] And *Der Spiegel* has run a cover story about China being a yellow threat focusing on Chinese efforts at technology espionage.[44]

President George W. Bush was not interested in subtleties, humor, music, or espionage when he spoke before both houses of Congress on September 20, 2001, in the immediate aftermath of the shocking 9/11 attacks. He emphasized a simple dichotomy: "Every nation, in every region, now has a decision to make. Either you are with us, or you are with the terrorists." On the motivation for the attacks, he continued: "They hate our freedoms—our freedom of religion, our freedom of speech, our freedom to vote and assemble and disagree with each other."[45] It did not matter that Osama bin Laden had never spoken about the first amendment or the Bill of Rights. It made for moving oratory at a time when the nation was still staggering from the audacity and success of the attacks. And it also laid down a line of demarcation. Recently, Michael Hunt and Steven Levine have traced the pattern of American diplomatic and military actions in Asia from the Philippines

---

40 Gigi Brienza, "Want to 'buy American' at gas pump?" *The Christian Science Monitor*, December 20, 2002: http://www.csmonitor.com/2002/1220/p13s01-coop.html

41 http://andyfrancis.blogspot.com/2011/07/these-colors-dont-run.html

42 Bruce Dickinson, Stephen Percy Harris, and Adrian Frederick Smith, "These Colours Don't Run," A Matter of Life and Death (EMI: 2006). The song has been set to a montage of World War II movies in this Youtube video: https://www.youtube.com/watch?v=TEPAirsQy-Q

43 Gregory Dorsey and Stephen Leeb, *Die gelbe Gefahr: Wie Chinas Gier nach Rohstoffen unseren Lebensstil gefährdet* (FinanzBuch Verlag, 2012).

44 "Die gelben Spione: Wie China deutsche Technologie ausspäht," *Der Spiegel* 35 August 27, 2007.

45 http://georgewbush-whitehouse.archives.gov/news/releases/2001/09/20010920-8.html.

to Japan, Korea, and Vietnam, and have noted how the legacy of brutality has been transferred to Southwest Asia, in particular Iraq and Afghanistan.[46]

Testifying before the Senate in December 2001 about the review of threats to America and American interests he received in the morning, Attorney John Ashcroft remarked, "If ever there were proof of the existence of evil in the world, it is in the pages of these reports. They are a chilling daily chronicle of hatred of Americans by fanatics who seek to extinguish freedom, enslave women, corrupt education, and to kill Americans wherever and whenever they can."[47] The threat was as all-encompassing as anything the yellow Japanese or red Communists presented in previous decades.

Bush used 9/11 to support his scheme to invade Iraq, despite the lack of any connection between Saddam Hussein and Osama bin Laden. No matter. Bush and members of his administration set up the binary opposition: us versus them, a notion that dates to colonial times when the white European settlers came to North America and found the land inhabited by people of different customs and of different skin color. The difference was that for over a century the United States had been going abroad in search of the same opposition. It was not really true, then, that America's colors did not run; they ran straight into an unnecessary and completely fabricated war in Iraq.

The color of American diplomacy has thus changed over the years; at the same time certain colors have remained remarkably consistent in their use. Initially red (Indians) gave way to yellow (Asians) and then returned to red (subversives). For the most part, these colors have resulted from fear, specifically white fear of others. Despite the increasingly mixed and vastly more heterogeneous nature of American society, this fear has not dissipated as much as it has been transferred. In other words, the impact of color has been ever present, even into the twenty-first century. When George Bush called for action in the wake of 9/11, the president brought to the fore the true colors of American diplomacy: black and white, us and them, a Manichean vision of the world where everyone else is a threat no matter where they reside. It is a sad legacy, one borne of the insistence that American interests span the globe. As long as that remains the case, the colors of American diplomacy will not change.

Bibliography

Barson, Michael. *Better Dead Than Red!" A Nostalgic Look at the Golden Years of Russiaphobia, Red-baiting, and Other Commie Madness.* New York: Hyperion, 1992.

Brienza, Gigi. "Want to 'buy American' at gas pump?." *The Christian Science Monitor*, December 20, 2002: http://www.csmonitor.com/2002/1220/p13s01-coop.html

---

[46] Hunt and Levine, *Arc of Empire*, 274-5.

[47] Ashcroft testifying at the Department of Justice Oversight: "Preserving Our Freedoms While Defending Against Terrorism," Hearings before the Committee on the Judiciary, U.S. Senate, 107th Congress, 1st session, December 6, 2001, p. 310, accessed at http://www.gpo.gov/fdsys/pkg/CHRG-107shrg81998/pdf/CHRG-107shrg81998.pdf.

Bush, George W. Address to a Joint Session of Congress and the American People. September 20, 2001. Retrieved from http://georgewbush-whitehouse.archives.gov/news/releases/2001/09/20010920-8.html

"Color Meanings & Symbolism." Retrieved from http://www.arttherapyblog.com/online/color-meanings-symbolism/#.UmGnCRZLJG5

Dickinson Bruce, Stephen Percy Harris, and Adrian Frederick Smith, "These Colours Don't Run." *A Matter of Life and Death*. EMI: 2006.

Doolittle, J.H., William B. Franke, and William D. Pawley. *Report on the Covert Activities of the Central Intelligence Agency*. September 30, 1954, https://archive.org/stream/CIA-Covert-Activities-Doolittle-Report/doolittle_report#page/n11/mode/2up (Accessed February 4, 2012.)

Dorsey, Gregory, and Stephen Leeb. *Die gelbe Gefahr: Wie Chinas Gier nach Rohstoffen unseren Lebensstil gefährdet.* FinanzBuch Verlag: 2012.

Dower, John W. *War Without Mercy: Race & Power in the Pacific War*. New York: Pantheon Books, 1986.

"Die gelben Spione: Wie China deutsche Technologie ausspäht." *Der Spiegel* 35 August 27, 2007.

Gilbert, Dan. *Our Chameleon Comrades: The Reds Turn Yellow!*. San Diego: The Danielle Publishers, 1938.

_____. *The Yellow Peril (Japan) and Bible Prophecy*. Grand Rapids: Zondervan Publishing House, 1943.

Goff, Kenneth. *Red Tide*. Englewood, CO: Soldiers of the Cross, 1962.

Gollwitzer, Heinz. *Die Gelbe Gefahr: Geschichte eines Schlagworts*. Vandenhoeck & Ruprecht, 1962, accessed through Google books: http://books.google.de/books?id=z-ZxdiO1wkYC&printsec=frontcover&hl=de&source=gbs_ge_summary_r&cad=0#v=onepage&q&f=false

Grant, Madison. *The Conquest of a Continent or The Expansion of Races in America*. New York: Scribner's, 1933.

Greene, Graham. *The Quiet American*. New York: Penguin Books, 1977.

"Preserving Our Freedoms While Defending Against Terrorism," Hearings before the Committee on the Judiciary, U.S. Senate, 107th Congress, 1st session, December 6, 2001. http://www.gpo.gov/fdsys/pkg/CHRG-107shrg81998/pdf/CHRG-107shrg81998.pdf

Hunt, Michael H. *Ideology and U.S. Foreign Policy*. New Haven: Yale University Press, 1987.

Hunt, Michael H., and Steven I. Levine. *Arc of Empire: America's Wars in Asia from the Philippines to Vietnam*. Chapel Hill: The University of North Carolina Press, 2012.

Jacobson, Matthew Frye. *Whiteness of a Different Color: European Immigrants and the Alchemy of Race*. Cambridge: Harvard University Press, 1998.

Knüsel, Ariane. *Framing China: Media Images and Political Debates in Britain, the USA and Switzerland, 1900-1950*. Burlington: Ashgate, 2012.

Krenn, Michael L. *The Color of Empire: Race and American Foreign Relations*. Washington: Potomac Books, Inc., 2006.

Lee, Robert G. *Orientals: Asian Americans in Popular Culture*. Philadelphia: Temple University Press, 1999.

Life, March 31, 1947.

London, Jack. "The Yellow Peril." In *Revolution and Other Essays*, edited by Jack London. Retrieved from http://www.readbookonline.net/title/298/

Lyman, Stanford M. "The 'Yellow Peril' Mystique: Origins and Vicissitudes of a Racist Discourse." *International Journal of Politics, Culture and Society* 13 (June 2000).

Nash, Gary B. *Red, White and Black: The Peoples of Early North America*. Englewood Cliffs: Prentice Hall, 1992.

Rohmer, Sax. *The Insidious Fu-Manchu*. New York: Novel Selections, Inc., 1913.

Shih, David. "The Color of Fu-Manchu: Orientalist Method in the Novels of Sax Rohmer," *The Journal of Popular Culture* 42 (2009), 304-317.

Slotkin, Richard. *Gunfighter Nation: The Myth of the Frontier in Twentieth-Century America*. Norman: University of Oklahoma Press, 1998.

Snow, Edgar. "Must We Beat Japan First?" *The Saturday Evening Post*, 215 (October 10, 1942).

Stoddard, Lothrop. *The Rising Tide of Color Against White World-Supremacy*. New York: Charles Scribner's Sons, 1921.

Tchen, John Kuo Wei, and Dylan Yeats, eds. *Yellow Peril! An Archive of Anti-Asian Fear*. London: Verso, 2014.

Time, December 22, 1941.

"These Colors Don't Run." The Francis Blog. Retrieved from http://andyfrancis.blogspot.com/2011/07/these-colors-dont-run.html

Whitfield, Stephen J. *The Culture of the Cold War*. Baltimore: The Johns Hopkins University Press, 1991.

Yellow Peril: Collecting Xenophobia. New York: American Institute Publication, 2007.

Part II

Color and Representation in Art and Literature

7

Metachromatics: The Historical Division Between Color and Line/Form as Analytic

Robert Machado

[The role of color] is to tell us what agitates the heart, while drawing shows us what passes in the mind...Color is a mobile, vague, intangible element, while form...is precise, limited, palpable, and constant...Drawing is [thus] the masculine side of art, color the feminine.[1]

Color is enslaved by the line that becomes writing.[2]

Since as early as Book Six of Aristotle's *Poetics*, which regards color as a superfluous and potentially insidious element of imaging, systems of representation have theorized color use and methods for its interpretation by differentiating a hermeneutics of color from one of line and form.[3] Despite historical shifts in modes of representation and valuation, this notion of chromatics as a discourse separate and opposite from line and form has remained durable across the arts, both fine and applied, visual and verbal. Its relations thus constitute a range of symbolic and socioeconomic antagonisms, accommodations, and displaced desires, all within a broad scope of cultural productions, which are both generative and symptomatic.

Through this classical binarization of elements, aesthetic traditions have identified and reinscribed in line and form the authority and privilege that accompany the control of boundaries, definition, and narrative. Within this binary, and according to this logic, color typically has been consigned to a deferential position, adding and circulating "intangibles" such as vitality and allure within

---

1 Charles Blanc, *The Grammar of Painting and Engraving*, trans. Kate Newell Doggett (New York: Hurd and Houghton, 1874), 146.

2 Yves Klein, "The Evolution of Art towards the Immaterial," in *Colour*, ed. David Batchelor (Cambridge, MA: MIT Press, [1954] 2008), 119.

3 For example, as Aristotle explains, "...the first essential, the life and soul, so to speak, of Tragedy is Plot... Compare the parallel in painting, where the most beautiful colors laid on without order will not give one the same pleasure as a simple black-and-white sketch of a portrait." Aristotle, *Poetics*, trans. Ingram Bywater (Digireads.com Publishing, [350 BCE] 2005), 29.

media (including sculpture, etching, drawing, painting, prints, photography, cinema, and verbal description) whose ontologies line and form most frequently have been used to essentialize. This dualistic structure of relations, which offers a pretense of rhetorical balance, stability, and harmony to contrasted and ranked terms, has invited similarly articulated social relationships and cultural values to be reinforced or contested by aesthetic analogy.

Charles Blanc's influential nineteenth-century aesthetic primer (above), designed to equip art's practitioners and audiences with a "grammar" for production and "appreciation," provides a salient example from the history of art and visuality of the susceptibilities of this model to ideology. Yves Klein's martialization of the model's terms nearly a century later suggests, in stark relief, broader implications, and the transmedial dynamics of this enduring formalism and its contentious meta-relations. It is, for example, in part how social critics such as Nisard were able to link "over-attention" to color with privileging imagination over reason (a symptom of decadence);[4] why Adorno regarded color as escapist spectacle or "mere" folk expression;[5] why Le Corbusier and Ozenfant experienced color as destabilizing volume;[6] and why color throughout history has been the site of so many "chromophobic" displacements, described by David Batchelor,[7] as well as utopian idealizations.

The historical effectiveness with which this binary has been used to enlist normalized relations from disparate fields to reinscribe power relations, essentialist constructions of identity and experience, and the epistemological presumptions of binarism itself within critical methodology suggests the value of investigating its structural dynamics—and its ruptures—within and between modes of representation more broadly.

This chapter will seek to provide a framework through which to identify and recuperate such dynamics and sites of exchange. To accomplish this goal, it will adapt a variety of recent strategies within visual culture studies, philosophies of color, inter-art analysis, transmedial narratology, and a strain of "activist" new formalism that, in making a continuum with new historicism,[8] has called for renewed attention to "the processes and structures of mediation through which particular discourses and whole classes of discourses…come to represent the real…[at] the eclipse or exclusion of other contenders for that title."[9] As a working definition, "metachromatics" names this approach, which investigates a historical "aboutness" of color co- constituted through its opposition to line/form (hereafter color–line/form).

---

4   Désiré Nisard, *Études de moeurs et de critique sur les poëtes Latins de la décadence* (Paris: Gosselin, 1834).

5   Theodor W. Adorno, *Aesthetic Theory*, trans. Robert Hullot-Kentor (New York: Continuum International, [1970] 1997); *Minima Moralia: Reflections from Damaged Life*, trans. E. F. N. Jephcott (London; New York: Verso, 1978).

6   C.E. Jeanneret (Le Corbusier) and Amédée Ozenfant, "Purism," in *Modern Artists on Art: Ten Unabridged Essays*, ed. and trans. Robert L. Herbert (Englewood Cliff, NJ: Pretentice-Hall, [1920] 1965), 70–72.

7   David Batchelor, *Chromophobia* (London: Reaktion, 2000).

8   Historicism here recognizes a process, following Armstrong and others, which allows for the articulation of "different diachronicities and synchronicities." Carol Armstrong, "All-Time Favorites," *Art Forum* (Summer, 2011): 88.

9   Marjorie Levinson, "What is New Formalism?" *PMLA* 122, no. 2 (2007): 561.

Method

Generally speaking, methodologies for investigating relations between verbal and visual artifacts often involve comparisons of objects which bear related subject matter, or that appear to tell similar stories. In this case, we can consider specific cinematic adaptations of novels and paintings, pictorial versions of poems, and poetic/ekphrastic versions of pictures.[10] Broader interart comparisons also have provided significant historical and generic insight into the mutual reinforcement or antagonism of "sister arts," understood by scholars such as Mitchell as a struggle for dominance between images and words,[11] or by Gaudreault and Philippe as a historiographical process by which new media come into being.[12]

Other foundational approaches, however, have sought to problematize the nature of media itself by locating common structural ground between them. Studies such as Frank's idea of "spatial form" in modern literature;[13] Steiner's likening of painting to literature;[14] Mitchell's theory of the transmedial mobile image;[15] and more recently, postclassical narratology's transmediation of description and the relocation of narrativity from artifact to "cognitive frame,"[16] invite audiences to "view" verbal texts spatially, to "read" pictorial elements as grammatically articulated verbal signs,[17] or to follow disembodied images across artifacts that they inhabit as "triggers" of the mind.[18] These approaches contest the notion of

---

10   "Ekphrasis" here refers to its narrower usage within twentieth-century analyses of verbal representation and painting employed by scholars such as Dubois, Heffernan, and Hollander. As Webb explains, however, ekphrasis within classical rhetoric and for most of history has been used to refer to any vivid description of visual impressions. Page DuBois, *History, Rhetorical Description and the Epic from Homer to Spenser* (Totowa, NJ: Biblio Distribution Services, 1982); James A. W. Heffernan, *Museum of Words: The Poetics of Ekphrasis from Homer to Ashbery* (Chicago: University of Chicago Press, 1993); John Hollander, *The Gazer's Spirit: Poems Speaking to Silent Works of Art* (Chicago: University of Chicago Press, 1995); Ruth Webb, "Ekphrasis Ancient and Modern: The Invention of a Genre," *Word & Image* 15, no. 1 (1999): 5–33.

11   W. J. T. Mitchell, *Iconology: Image, Text, Ideology* (Chicago: University of Chicago Press, 1986).

12   André Gaudreault and Marion Philippe, "A Medium is Always Born Twice," *Early Popular Visual Culture* 3, no. 1 (2005): 3–15. Refer also to Hagstrum's landmark study on literary pictorialism. Jean H. Hagstrum, *The Sister Arts: The Tradition of Literary Pictorialism and English Poetry from Dryden to Gray* (Chicago: University of Chicago Press, 1958).

13   Frank's essay most often is cited as beginning this discussion within literature. Joseph Frank, "Spatial Form in Modern Literature," in *The Idea of Spatial Form* (New Brunswick: Rutgers University Press, [1945] 1991).

14   Wendy Steiner, *The Colors of Rhetoric: Problems in the Relation Between Modern Literature and Painting* (Chicago: University of Chicago Press, 1982).

15   W. J. T. Mitchell, *What Do Pictures Want?: The Lives and Loves of Images* (Chicago: University of Chicago Press, 2005).

16   Werner Wolf, "Narratology and Media(lity): The Transmedial Expansion of a Literary Discipline and Possible Consequences," in *Current Trends in Narratology*, ed. Greta Olson (Berlin; New York: De Gruyter, 2011), 145–80; Ansgar Nünning, "Towards a Typology, Poetics and History of Description in Fiction," in *Description in Literature and Other Media*, eds. Werner Wolf and Walter Bernhart (Amsterdam: Rodopi, 2007), 91–125.

17   For an early narratological demonstration of this approach, see: Mieke Bal, *Narratology: Introduction to the Theory of Narrative*, 2nd edition (Toronto: University of Toronto Press, 1997).

18   Transmediality here refers to the essential media independence of narrative and its discursive formations. Werner Wolf, "Pictorial Narrativity," in *Routledge Encyclopedia of Narrative Theory*, eds. David Herman, Manfred Jahn, and Marie-Laure Ryan (London; New York: Routledge, 2005), 431. For more on contemporary methods within transmedial studies, see for example Ryan; and Wolf and Bernhart. For an earlier iteration of the concept of transmediality within the context of structuralism, see for example Barthes. Marie-Laure Ryan, "On the Theoretical Foundations of Transmedial Narratology," in *Narratology Beyond Literary Criticism: Mediality, Disciplinarity*, eds. Jan Christoph Meister, Tom Kindt, and Wilhelm Schernus (Berlin; New York: Walter de Gruyter, 2005), 1–23; Werner Wolf and Walter Bernhart, *Description*; Roland Barthes, *Image, Music, Text*, trans. Stephen Heath (New York: Hill and Wang, 1977).

essential medial difference now commonly traced to Lessing's eighteenth century revisionist aesthetics.[19]

My interest here is not to privilege any one of these approaches, to diminish or reassert material differences between media, or to reclaim objects for any particular discipline; rather, it is to suggest a mechanism that might be deployed as an application within any number of approaches and fields that investigate the production, distribution, reception, and use of representation—broadly construed—and the discourses that maintain or disrupt them.

Mary Louise Pratt's post-colonial concept of the "contact zone" serves as a useful model for consideration within this context.[20] Pratt is especially interested in colonial frontiers: specifically, the co-constitution of colonizing and colonized subjects through their various forms of contact—their interactions, mutual understandings, practices, etc.—which, in her study, can be located within modes of European travel writing. For Pratt, the process of subject formation within these transactional spaces is determined not by a separateness of colonizer and colonized, nor by unidirectional flows of power, but by their articulations—the ways in which subjects absorb, repel, and use each other.

Without suggesting a moral or formal equality of terms between, for example, pictorial uses of color and actual colonized subjects, the investigation of color across disciplines benefits from recognition of a similar historical "zone" of contact between color and iterations of line and form—one that continues to influence determinations of identity, intelligibility, socio-cultural associations and value, theoretical engagement as well as normative reading/reception patterns, and even spheres of labor (both metaphorical and literal). This flux of absorption, resistance, and mutual reinforcement—and possibilities for the (re)configuration of identities and relations of power in light of this dynamic—are central to the purposes of this investigation.

A diagram of this zone of contact and of binary relations whose alignments the discourse of color – line/form historically has been used to mediate, offers here a schematic that might add clarification, facilitate elaboration, and encourage conceptual permutation within the study of color (Figure 7.1). Neither comprehensive nor fixed in its terms, it provides a system through which to chart and to compare sets of concepts and relations to power, whose mediation by color – line/form can be understood ultimately as "eventful" and "narratable" (an argument discussed more below).[21]

---

19 Gotthold Ephraim Lessing, *Laocoön: An Essay on the Limits of Painting and Poetry*, trans. Edward Allen McCormick (Baltimore: Johns Hopkins University Press, [1766] 1984).

20 Mary Louise Pratt, *Imperial Eyes: Travel Writing and Transculturation* (Hoboken: Taylor & Francis, 2007).

21 As an additional way to flesh out the arbitrariness of this "oppositional" relation and the ontologies that its dynamics help to articulate through the production of associated contraries and implications, see Greimas and his "semiotic square," which provides a constructive framework through which to consider the processes involved in the conceptualization of possibility. A. J. Greimas, *On Meaning: Selected Writings in Semiotic Theory* (Minneapolis: University of Minnesota Press, 1987).

Color	Systems of harmony, discord, & the meta-narratives governing tellability	Line/Form
perceptual color	micro-/event/storia	color word
explicit description		narrative
static & non-event (spatial)		acion & event (temporal)
contemplative		
cinematic "attractions"		cinematic narrative
painting/tinting		photography/drawing
muteness (untellability)		speech (tellability)
pre/extra-lingual		lingual
Lyotardian sublime		
ornament		instrument
immateriality		materiality
metaphysics		science
(innate) artistry		acquired techne
art		intellect
non-normativities		normativities
feminine sphere		masculine sphere
subjectivity		objectivity
primitive		evolved

Figure 7.1 | Metachromatics, and the orientation of concepts according to the mediation of color – line/form. Examples here will be discussed below and throughout.

As a way to begin to discuss this strategy and its promise for addressing problems within color studies broadly across media, this chapter will allow the details and workings of theory to emerge from contexts of possible application. In keeping with one of the critical goals of *The Use of Color in History, Politics, and Art*, instead of undertaking an enhanced treatment of any one area of interest, this approach will seek to advance color as a critical lens by foregrounding ways in which color and line and form, "twin abstractions" assembled by humans, according to Baudelaire,[22] often are put to work in the service of other abstractions and the ideologies that give rise to them. Of particular interest will be the relation of the discourse of color – line/form to an often over-looked area of historiography (1839–1935) in which conspicuously colored "black-and-white" photography and cinema existed as a popular iteration of composite representation.[23] "Verbal

---

22 Charles Baudelaire, "The Life and Work of Eugène Delacroix," in *The Painter of Modern Life and Other Essays*, trans. and ed. Jonathan Mayne (London: Phaidon Press, [1863] 1964), 51.

23 This periodization, founded on the cultural prevalence of this photo-painterly composite, does not ignore monochrome photography's rich conceptual "pre-history," its technological development prior to the announcement of photography by Louis Daguerre in 1839, aesthetic differences between technological iterations, black-and-white photography's continuing cultural presence, or earlier developments of viable (but commercially-limited) "natural" color films, such as Autochrome (photography) and Kinemacolor (cinema) established by 1908. These dates instead intend to add further dimensionality to influential historical accounts of photography, such as Mirzoeff's broader periodization of the Age of Photography (1839–1982), by reflecting a period marked by the realization of two emergent types of indexicality within dominant culture: the presumed objective line/form of monochromatic photography (1839), and the commercial realization of "objective" color cinema through the first feature-length three-strip Technicolor film, *Becky Sharp* (1935). While the realization of three-strip Technicolor feature films did not of course signal the decline of black-and-white cinema, which retained a significant cultural presence until well

coloration," identified historically as an aspect of description set in subordinate opposition to the "line" of plot and narrative—or as little more than "icing on the narrative cake"[24]—also will be suggested as a provocative area for analogous reconsideration within contexts such as comparative media studies, the pragmatics of visualization and aesthetic response, and the constitution of narrativity as a category of experience.[25]

Disegno-colore: Origin Story Points to the Rule

Discussions of the historical division in aesthetics between color and line/form most often begin with accounts of the debate between Venetian and Florentine approaches to painting within the history of Renaissance art. Instances of vibrant and self-referential color within figurative settings are said to have been favored by the so-called colorists of Venice, while Florentines insisted on the primacy of drawing and the tighter restriction of color to mimetic supplementation.[26] According to Ball, this competition for the prioritization of *colore* or *disegno* within academies of art generally lasted until the beginning of the seventeenth century. By this time, as Ball recounts, "Vasari and the scholars of Italian academies largely secured the superiority of *disegno* over *colore*...and a muted palette [once spread to France] became the predominant style of European art."[27]

Paintings often discussed as representative of this aesthetic divergence during the sixteenth century—such as those by Titian and Michelangelo—do not, however, exactly support such clear delineation. As Ball's study suggests, sometimes Michelangelo's use of color, for example, can appear just as bright and self-reflexive as color deployed by Titian. Their mutual attention to drawing and to perspective also challenges claims of their partisanship based on strictly differing approaches to line/form. For Ball, such similarities lend support to the view that the history of this factionalization derives from additional sources, namely, from a problem-

---

after WWII, it did, however, popularize a technological achievement that allowed for the appearance of the enhanced mimetic integration of photo-cinematic color and line/form, and thus claims for the fulfillment of a telos that posited an evolution of still and moving photography toward "total" realism. For more on Mirzoeff's periodization, see: Nicholas Mirzoeff, *An Introduction to Visual Culture* (London; New York: Routledge, 1999), 65.

24 Michael Riffaterre, "On the Diegetic Functions of the Descriptive," *Style* 20, no. 3 (1986): 281.

25 Here and throughout, references to "pragmatics" follow its definition by Archer and Grundy as the study of meaning in context, where context is understood as always both presumptive and emergent. Dawn Archer and Peter Grundy, eds., *The Pragmatics Reader* (New York: Routledge, 2011), 9. Pragmatics, traditionally a branch of linguistics, here suggests a broader or transmedial approach to objects of study based on this heuristic notion of context. For more on this interactive approach to context, see, for example, Alessandro Duranti and Charles Goodwin, *Rethinking Context: Language as an Interactive Phenomenon* (Cambridge, England: Cambridge University Press, 1992).

26 The Venetian faction, led by Titian (c. 1488/1490–1576) and "successors" such as Tintoretto (1518–1594) and Veronese (1528–1588), were inspired by, among other things, colorful Byzantine art brought west from Constantinople following the crusades of the thirteenth and fourteenth centuries. They also were influenced by the introduction of oil painting techniques to Venice by the 1470s through figures such as Giovanni Bellini (1430–1516). Philip Ball, *Bright Earth: Art and the Invention of Color* (Chicago: University of Chicago Press, 2003), 123–124. Venetians were said to prefer applications of bright hues that aroused self-reflexive "detraction" from linear form. Represented by painters such as Leonardo da Vinci (1452–1519), Raphael (1483–1520), and Michelangelo (1475–1564), the Florentine school, seeking divergence from the flat planes and schematic color codes of medieval artistic orthodoxy, arguably insisted instead on expressions of beauty through the linearity of mathematically- determined *disegno* focused on proportion.

27 Philip Ball, *Bright Earth*, 129. Within the late seventeenth century in French academies, the two sides were represented by the chromatically "sober" Poussinistes (Nicolas Poussin, 1594–1665) and the more florid Rubenistes (Peter Paul Rubens, 1577–1640).

atic historiography. He argues that conceptions of the rivalry in painting between Venice and Florence, construed according to practices that uniformly favored either color or line/form, reflect to an appreciable extent a "nineteenth century fiction," which originates with Vasari.[28]

With his *Lives of the Artists*, Vasari promoted the view that the brightened colors of Titian merely compensated for, or distracted from, poor draftsmanship. For Vasari, instances of chromatic conspicuousness within paintings by Titian and others entailed a weak grasp of line/form (among other deficiencies) and the questionable loosening of its authority. Vasari's recourse to this binary, despite, perhaps, contradictory visual evidence, followed historical precedent. As a Florentine advocating for Florence within an aesthetic-municipal rivalry, Vasari invoked a then familiar bias against color(ation) and its legacy of associations, such as the authority of design over color within academic art theory based on a distinction between "immutable qualities attributed to the mind and the deceptive, transient, changeable body."[29] In doing so, he was able to reinforce the institutional values of the academy and those that it empowered. His treatment of color as a secondary practice (for which, not incidentally, training was limited) also allowed him to identify with a position of power far more symbolically extensive than pictorial aesthetics.

Ball's critical rereading of this now frequently retold story of origins, just briefly introduced here, highlights the rhetorical utility of this politicized construct and its ability to frame and to institutionalize allegiances in reduced and oppositional terms.[30] Without discounting genuine differences represented by, in this case, the aesthetic schools of Venice and Florence and their respective painters, this history underscores color – line/form as a discursive mechanism able to help found and to perpetuate the very notion of opposing "schools," even despite, if Ball is right, empirical observation that might suggest otherwise. It emphasizes the degree to which perception involves the mediation of values and frameworks for interpretation. It also typifies a process by which aesthetic systems are able to constitute and naturalize values and frameworks diachronically as well as within contemporaneous fields.

Historical arguments describing the perceptual impossibility of even separating line/form from color make this point even more provocative. As the early twentieth-century English art critic Clive Bell explained, "The distinction…is an unreal one; you cannot conceive of a colourless line or a colourless space; neither can you conceive a formless relation of colours"[31]—an observation on which Josef Albers would later elaborate through experiments on the influence of shape, size, and number on chromatic identity and interaction.[32] This paradox of common

---

28 Giorgio Vasari, *Lives of the Artists*, trans. George Bull (Harmondsworth: Penguin, [1568] 1965).

29 Joanna Woodall, *Portraiture: Facing the Subject* (Manchester, England; New York: Manchester University Press, distributed in the US by St. Martin's Press, 1997), 4.

30 For a detailed history of the concepts underpinning the division between design and color within sixteenth- and seventeenth-century Italian art and theory, see: Maurice George Poirier, *Studies on the Concepts of "Disegno," "Invenzione," and "Colore" in Sixteenth- and Seventeenth-Century Italian Art and Theory* (New York: New York University, 1976).

31 Clive Bell, "The Aesthetic Hypothesis," in *Twentieth Century Theories of Art*, ed. James Matheson Thompson (Montreal: McGill-Queen's University Press, [1914] 1990), 82.

32 Josef Albers, *Interaction of Color* (New Haven: Yale University Press, [1920] 2006).

visual experience is just one among many involved in the perception of color, its cognition, and related determinations of cultural value and meaning.

It reminds us, for example, that monochromatic visual arrays, as in "black-and-white" photography and engraving, are able to constitute "achromatic" pictures that might be considered acceptable representations of the world, or even, demonstrative of "a high state of intellectual and aesthetic cultivation."[33] It also points to several areas of chromatic interest that have occupied the sciences and humanities for millennia. These include questions of where color resides; how it is identified, measured, and represented using languages and systems of harmony and organization; and what it might mean, for whom, and according to which processes of production, reception, and transmission. Factoring into these contexts as well is the history of the discursive application of color – line/form and its uses in representing, rationalizing, and naturalizing other dichotomous notions of inherent difference and relation.

Roger Fry for example, like others before him whose aesthetics responded to the rhetorical effectiveness of this discourse, demonstrated the utility of the binarization of color – line/form within a formalist schema that also reinscribed problematic ideological positions.[34] According to his hierarchy of "emotional elements of design," which implicated earlier aesthetic and philosophical suspicions of color as mere *qualia*,[35] color represented "the only element [among line, mass, space, light] not of critical or universal importance to life." While Fry's idealization here might at worst seem to exemplify a dated or specious formulation within a circumscribed area of aesthetic history, his familiar assertion of color's superfluity and line's authority points to wider political significance. In fact, it exemplifies a broader tradition in aesthetics in which existing social hierarchies and relations of power have been able to appropriate additional cultural influence through favorable codification.

Charles Blanc provides another useful example from this tradition. According to this influential nineteenth-century critic, color was "the peculiar characteristic [only] of the lower forms of nature." Channeling neoclassical notions of the great chain of being, Blanc explained "the higher we rise in the scale of being… drawing becomes the medium of expression, more and more dominant." For Blanc, when painting attends to "higher" forms, it can occasionally even "dispense with color" altogether.[36] Slippery terms of value such as "high" and "low," and color as a marker of opprobrium within conceptions of divinity, morality, reason, or even representability itself, lend themselves to other traditions that regard (subjects of) color as base. Nineteenth-century photographic portraiture, for example, and manuals for tinting—which most often assumed the white skin of sitters and provided only rare instruction for photographing or chromatically treating com-

---

33 Ogden Rood, *Modern Chromatics* (New York: Van Nostrand Reinhold, [1879] 1973), 305.

34 Roger Fry, "An Essay in Aesthetics" [1909], in *Colour*, ed. David Batchelor, 54.

35 Gage explains this philosophical debate as one over the determination of color as either an unreliable attribute of visual phenomena (ancient skeptics or Locke) or perceptual information that mediates our knowledge of the world (Berkeley or Goethe). John Gage, *Color and Meaning: Art, Science, and Symbolism* (Berkeley and Los Angeles: University of California Press, 1999), 36.

36 Charles Blanc, *The Grammar*, 4–5.

plexions of color—underscore the vulnerability of aesthetic theory and practice to the politics of identity.

A pattern of similar examples, from across the arts and artistic periods, reflects the prevalence of color's association with "low" or ignoble constructions/subjects and its subordination to line/form and those identified with it. With this in mind, we can consider other cultural extensions of *disegno e colore* beyond its seventeenth-century "resolution" within Italian academies, especially those whose ubiquity might raise the stakes.

The Chromophobic/Chromophilic Dilemma

Colour is less important than form, but casts over it a peculiar charm. If form is wrongly seen or falsely represented, we feel as though "the foundations were shaken"; if the colour is bad, we are simply disgusted.[37]

The history of what Bachelor has called "chromophobia"—loosely defined as the fear of, or prejudice against, color and its threats of "corruption"—is extensive.[38] Bachelor's book of the same title offers a variety of examples from across the arts, cinema, literature, and philosophy since Plato, which speaks to this "condition's" range of influence. For Bachelor, *disegno-colore* plays a critical role in the manifestation of chromophobia and its transmission. Through it, color has come to stand in for, or to be indicative of many motifs, including, the inessential, the subjective, the fleeting, the vulgar, the emotional, the infantile, the primitive, the feminine, the queer, etc.

Especially relevant to my focus here is that the political response to chromophobia, through "chromophilia" (its opposite), rarely gets beyond an affirmation of chromophobic terms, which suggests a chromatic and political bind. In fact, as Batchelor explains, rather than establishing its own terms of value, chromophilia tends to embrace and to concentrate the terms of chromophobia: through it "color remains other; in fact, it often remains more other than before."[39] The implications of this pejorative othering, however, have been left relatively unexplored. The tendency for color to be enlisted as a stand-in for alterity—an "other" *shaped,* muted, and marginalized by centered notions of line/form and its values—suggests a key hegemonic function of the discourse of color – line/form.[40] Through this, chromophilia risks "absolutization" as other which, as Rancière and others have discussed, can "lead to, or at least feed into, political forms of othering that threaten to achieve the opposite of what they

---

37 Ogden Rood, *Modern Chromatics*, 306.

38 David Batchelor, *Chromophobia*, 102.

39 Ibid., 71.

40 Hegemony here is meant in the sense defined by Raymond Williams. He explains that hegemony is "not only the articulate upper level of 'ideology,' nor are its forms of control only those seen as 'manipulation' or 'indoctrination.' It is a whole body of practices and expectations, over the whole of living: our senses and assignments of energy, our shaping perceptions of ourselves in the world. It is a lived system of meanings and values—constitutive and constituting—which as they are experienced as practices appear as reciprocally confirming." Raymond Williams, *Marxism and Literature* (Oxford: Oxford University Press, 1977), 110.

have been designed to do."⁴¹ "Chromatic" associations such as inessentiality, infantilism, and emotionality, for example, are familiar terms of gender-based marginalization found throughout history. The presence of the authority of line/form even within celebrations of color that embrace such qualities suggests its claim on normativity (and reach of power) through determinations of difference that can limit power.

Within eighteenth-century treatises on character, for example, color was understood as more appropriate to the representation of women than the line and form of design prioritized for men because femininity presumed a lack of "interiority" afforded to the "dualistic" male subjectivity.⁴² In keeping with such assumptions, even an empowered or so-called chromophilic "feminine" subjectivity, expressed through fashion, style, etc., seems vulnerable to these and other dominant chromophobic associations. Color in this sense can other, or "out," as a stain or restrictive mark, and thus jeopardize access to institutions of power.

This chromophobic/philic dilemma suggests real-world limitations that can be compounded by its naturalization.⁴³ The consensus of powerful black or "achromatic" navy suits, for example, which might be said to dominate Wall Street, "Western" courtrooms, stages of political debate, etc., hints at a nexus of authority that (a)chromatic coding can reinforce and perpetuate.⁴⁴ As Baudrillard argued, for example, whatever "registers zero on the color scale (such as white, black, gray)" is "correspondingly paradigmatic of dignity, repression, and moral standing" according to the "traditional" treatment of color, which is perceived as a "threat to inwardness."⁴⁵ In addition, sartorial preference among the "serious" for dark or achromatic colors has pointed for many to the ink (and perhaps line/form) of literary/literate culture since the printing press, or to other references to modernity.⁴⁶ However, it also suggests a pathway of association through which color can stand in for and conflate illiteracy, frivolity, lawlessness, politi-

---

41 Thomas Claviez, "Done and Over with—Finally? Otherness, Metonymy, and the Ethics of Comparison," *PMLA* 128, no. 3 (May, 2013): 608.

42 Joanna Woodall, *Portraiture*, 11.

43 Here I follow Eagleton in understanding naturalization as a process that renders the beliefs of a particular ideology "natural and self-evident," and that identifies them with "the common sense of a society" such that it becomes difficult to imagine how they might ever be different. It is the process by which an ideology is able to offer itself as an "Of course!" or "That goes without saying." Terry Eagleton, *Ideology: An Introduction* (London; New York: Verso, 2007) 58–59.

44 So-called achromatic colors, distinguished by their "desaturation" (or lack of dominant hue, the dominant wavelength in a color), typically include black, white, gray, and brown. Navy in this case, however, is understood as bearing a perceptual nearness to black (and thus to achromaticity) based on its low degree of "brightness": the amount of light reflected by a color. Hue, saturation, and brightness (value, lightness) are measures of color frequently used to categorize the "three-dimensionality" of color space. Color perception, however, more broadly is an intersection of physics, psychology, linguistics (i.e., color lexa, color naming, color naming systems), philosophy, aesthetics, and cultural experience.

45 Jean Baudrillard, *The System of Objects*, trans. James Benedict (London: Verso, [1968] 2005), 31.

46 Woodall, for example, explains the notion of black-and-white as an especially modern aesthetic in part due to its heritage, which involves reference to the utilitarianism of an urban work environment, and a sober disciplined lifestyle. Black-and-white as an aesthetic discourse also refers back to its widespread use within seventeenth-century Dutch Burgher portraiture, in which black-and-white bore connotations of virility. For Woodall, bourgeois identity gains a heritage of community and spiritual uprightness in part through this use of black. Joanna Woodall, *Portraiture*, 5. For more on the history of the color black, see: Michel Pastoureau, *Black: The History of a Color* (Princeton, NJ: Princeton University Press, 2009).

cal marginality, femininity, etc. and other qualities based on heteronormative or related assumptions.

A recent photograph of an advertisement from the New York City subway, featuring a domestic couple "of color," provides a specific example of this dilemma for consideration (Figure 7.2). In many ways, it might be understood as an allegory or cautionary tale of the chromophobic/philic dilemma in action. It also suggests the continuing relevance of color – line/form to constructions of identity and power, as well as the acceptability of its premises, within everyday public spaces. Preserving the slight obscurity of text within this photograph, which includes a male bystander sitting in front of it, is meant to incorporate a reminder of the situational contingency involved in the production of meaning (in this case, "humorous" comparisons made by subway passengers between the man in the advertisement and the man beneath it helped to reinforce its misogyny).

Figure 7.2 | Advertisement for the AT&T GoPhone. Digital photograph by author from the New York City subway (2012).

The advertisement reads: "You compromised on your Saturday afternoon./ Don't compromise on your wireless plan./ $50 Unlimited Talk." Although the advertisement's direct address communicates the nature of this compromise only implicitly, it appears to solicit identification with a heteronormative male subject's chromophobic and domestic suffering (his pink shirt, slack and effete, in this case looks *picked out for* him—and part of the imposition conveyed by his return glance rather than indicating any chromatic complicity). An expressive reading of this collaboration of word and image might be summarized in this way:

You
    like the male in this picture: trapped, reduced, and weakened by feminization and domestication (represented here, in part, by a suffocating profusion of color)

compromised
    a fool's bargain that showcases your emasculation

on your Saturday afternoon.
    Saturday afternoon suggests natural activities outdoors, perhaps with "the guys," not time indoors with your domestic partner, feigning subtle and chromatic discriminations for which you are not naturally equipped as a male. Moreover, "Saturday" afternoon is the only day/time of the week that is really "yours," with Sunday anticipating the work of Monday, and Friday bearing its residue.

Don't
    be similarly trapped, reduced, feminized, unnatural, and illogical like this man, and

compromise on your wireless plan.
    a compromise, on evidence, that your female partner likely would make.

$50 Unlimited Talk.
    "Fifty" and "unlimited" in their respective lack of decimalization and qualification are decisive and without nuance. Half of $100, $50 also suggests a welcome return to (masculine) logic and fairness. Together these signs offer a propitious contract much different from your previous compromise. They also provide an oasis in which to experience autonomy (talking on the phone) without temporal restriction. With "$50 Unlimited Talk," the GoPhone takes a stand against female domination and its irrational preoccupations: conditions from what your partner "naturally" suffers, and makes you suffer through, when unchecked.

    While an alternative argument could be made that signs of domesticity (in the form of nascent home renovation) and consumerism surround the male in the image, and that color perhaps plays little role in the meaning of the ad, a closer look suggests the ways in which the discourse of color – line/form provides a ready structure for the above reading and its problematic assumptions. The female's association with color in the image, and the thrall of this relation, as we know, draws on a long history of chromatic gendering tied to misogynist essentializing. In addition, the very crux of the "pregnant moment," captured here by photography, appears to turn on its representation of the chromophobic/philic dilemma.[47]

    The female in this picture faces colored fabric and is photographed mid-speech. This orientation reinforces a sense of her chromophilic "communication" (visual and verbal) with the colored material itself. The male in this scenario, similarly registering a gendered predilection, looks at us ("men") and not the chromatic choices on display (or her). His refusal to respond to her apparent gesture of rhetorical enthusiasm (Isn't it good?) resists both her—and color's—dominance

---

47 A "pregnant moment" refers to a depicted moment from which a viewer/reader infers a before-and-after. Lessing, for example, sees this moment as one that invokes the imagination of the viewer. Gotthold Ephraim Lessing, *Laocoön* ([1766] 1984). The concept of the pregnant moment often is associated with a mode of pictorial narrativity activated within single pictures understood to depict a scene of action. For more on this form of narrativity, see, for example, Julia Thomas, *Victorian Narrative Painting* (London: Tate, 2000).

over space and "his" afternoon. It also allows for an interpretation that his response is not required, which reinforces the misogynistic illogic of the compromise.

Although the female might shift her attention from the colorful fabric to his dismissive glance (a possibility that adds narrative/dramatic suspense), naturalized assumptions about her female and chromophilic "nature" make her continued "distraction" more likely. The fixity and apparent endlessness of her (over) attention to a colored textile, compounded through photography's temporal suspension, reinforces this notion. It also allows for, or even promotes, analogical extensions that might reinscribe other typological assumptions, such as she/he/domesticity/"nature" never changes. His similarly unwavering return glance seeks comparable pity for what amounts to this (misogynistic take on) inescapable "reality."

On a variety of levels, color within this picture can be understood as overwhelming a sense of masculine order. For example, colors organized along the walls of the room and protruding into the foreground dominate the image with an uncertain and "alternative" chromatic systemization of space. Ambiguities in the nature of the arrangement of colors within this system may speak to general challenges often involved in chromatic discrimination and vocabulary. However, irregularities within and between color sections along the walls also suggest an order founded only on pretense.

Criteria frequently used to categorize color, such as hue, brightness, and saturation, appear to shift in priority and without justification within this "order." As a result, this "system," aligned with "feminine" proclivity seems unable to make up its mind. Its feminized chromatic grammar "lines" the space to suggest an incomprehensible or capricious (seizure of) authority, which arguably plays on stereotypes of black or African American femininity as "domineering." It also encroaches on viewers to warn of the more general creep of feminization and to suggest the necessity of its regulation: the feminization of your Saturday and of wireless phone plans typifies greater threats to power and order.

These chromophobic assumptions, as with the hierarchies of Fry, Blanc, or even those of later "progressive" aesthetics such as the constructivism of Rodchenko, which upheld "line" as "the path of advancement" and "the first and last thing…in painting and any construction…or organism,"[48] might seem ambiguous, circumscribed, or harmless enough. They bear meaningfully, however, on constructions of identity and on the structuring of relations between people. Within the advertisement, it is she who selects the tint of drapery for whatever perhaps dismissible reason (aesthetic criteria can appear vague); but his shirt of the same tint also then appears to fall within her sphere of influence. The subtext is that female authority over "trivial" aesthetics can quickly advance to more significant areas of life. This threat of "unnatural" domination and loss of self, an everyman's take on domestication, warns of what happens when women/"others"/chromophilics/colors usurp heteronormative masculine authority. The solution proposed by the ad is to publically underscore male authority over important decisions (such as financial matters) and to sanction the brazen address of only

---

[48] Aleksandr Rodchenko, "Extract from notes for a lecture given at Inkhuk (Institute of Artistic Culture)," in *Rodchenko*, ed. David Elliott (Oxford: Museum of Modern Art, [1921] 1979), 128.

a particular masculinist consumer. Unconditioned public sexism, like the blunt terms of the contract, is part of this masculinist relief and return to "order."

These implicit narratives, which color – line/form helps to organize here within the context of everyday social space and ephemera, suggest the continuing relevance of this discourse to identity, distributions of power, and the processes of naturalization. Such stories also raise questions about the influence of color – line/form within other possible domains or zones of contact. Iterations of classical narrative theory, for example, which draw on metaphor to construe plot as "line" and description as (mere) added "color," hint at the politics of metanarratives perhaps embedded within dominant theories of telling. As we will see, this thread leads to problems in the conceptualization of narrativity itself, not only within theories of verbal representation, but within visual fields such as cinema, and its origins within nineteenth-century photography.

Narrativity and The (Added) Color Problem in Early Cinema

> From 1895–1930 (in particular 1908–1921) it is estimated that 85% of all film is non-black-and-white.[49]

> [After watching archived colored nitrate prints for over five years] I could find no recipe, no hidden theory, no codes that applied to all the films I saw. This was very disturbing because we're always looking for logic, for codes, but I simply couldn't find any.[50]

> Non-photographic color in silent cinema was seldom mentioned in contemporary film reviews, and when color was mentioned, it was seldom discussed beyond general descriptions like "pretty," "true," "effective," and other generalizations.[51]

Responding to questions regarding the readability of color in cinema during its first decades, scholars within the last fifteen years have grown increasingly attentive to the problematics of color within cinematic expression, especially as it pertains to narrative. Faced with objects of study and methodologies that have been newly destabilized by missing and perhaps irrecoverable chromatic effects lost in the transitory aniline dyes of early colored films, the possible infidelity (or omission) of color in test prints long held to be reliable "copies" of film "originals," and challenges to aesthetic restoration such as the obsoleteness of early nitrate

---

49 Giovanna Fossati, moderator, "Moderated Discussion Session 1," in *Disorderly Order: Colours in Silent Film*, eds. Daan Hertogs and Nico De Klerk (Amsterdam: Stichting Nederlands Filmmuseum, 1996), 12. As Misek explains, this "80 to 90 percent" estimate originates from Blair. It is considered accurate for films produced during the 1910s and 1920s; the number might be slightly lower for films produced between the 1890s–1900s. Richard Misek, *Chromatic Cinema: A History of Screen Color* (Chichester, UK; Malden, MA: Wiley-Blackwell, 2010), 18; G. A. Blair, "The Tinting of Motion Picture Film," *Transactions of the Society of Motion Picture Engineers* 10 (1920): 45.

50 Peter Delpeut, contributor, "Moderated Discussion Session 1," in *Disorderly Order*, eds. Daan Hertogs and Nico De Klerk, 23.

51 Eirik Frisvold Hanssen, *Early Discourses on Colour and Cinema: Origins, Functions, Meanings* (Stockholm: Almqvist & Wiksell International, 2006), 13.

film stock and the greater light intensity of early projection apparatuses, film scholars have begun to work through many of the reconfigurations that the color problem poses.[52]

As the above excerpts taken together suggest, the decoding of color in early cinema is a challenge for a variety of reasons. Usai continues:

> Much as we know that a certain color once existed in a silent film, we must also acknowledge that it is now impossible to experience its actual rendering on the screen. As time goes by, the entity slowly mutates into an imaginary object, a creation of the mind. We collect the few surviving fragments, the apparatus, the chemical formulas, the memoirs of the technicians who designed the systems, the opinions of those who saw them at work.[53]

Likely in part to avoid what Usai fears might be the "empty exercise" or "false consciousness" of extracting meaning from corrupt or unstable prints, not to mention that often different cuts and chromatic treatments of the same film exist, Uricchio's earlier study of Griffith's *The Lonedale Operator* (1911), posits a heuristic whereby the instability of early color may be circumvented "by focusing on the discourse *about* color"; that is, on "evidence regarding its reception and promotion."[54]

However, as Hanssen explains above, accounts of color's meaning—and the meanings of individual colors—within early cinema thus far have been relatively difficult to locate.[55] This is true not only of cinema before its institutional expansion during the "nickelodeon boom" in the US (1905–1909),[56] but even, as Patalas

---

52 For example, as Fossati, assistant researcher at the Nederlands Filmmuseum archives in 1995, explains, "it's sometimes impossible to transfer very light pink tinting to acetate stock without unacceptably distorting the color in toned areas; the colors on a safety print are different from those on the nitrate prints; pink colors, for example, disappear, or tinting on the nitrate looks like toning in the acetate. And of course the colors have changed on the nitrate too." Colors fade, black-and-white images through solarization become "colored," etc. Giovanna Fossati, "Moderated Discussion," 14–15. For more on recent treatments of color in early cinema, see: Joshua Yumibe, *Moving Color: Early Film, Mass Culture, Modernism* (New Brunswick: Rutgers University Press, 2012); Richard Koszarski, ed., special topic issue: "Color Film," *Film History* 12, no. 4 (2000): 339–463; Richard Koszarski, ed., "Special Topic Issue: Early Colour," *Film History* 20, nos. 1–2 (2009): 1–183; Wendy E. Everett, ed., *Questions of Colour in Cinema: From Paintbrush to Pixel* (Oxford: Peter Lang, 2007); Angela Dalle Vacche and Brian Pierce, eds., *Color: The Film Reader* (New York: Routledge, 2006); Eirik Frisvold Hanssen, *Early Discourses*; L. McKernan, ed., special topic issue: "Color," *Living Pictures: The Journal of the Popular and Projected Image Before 1914* 2, no. 2. (2003); Paolo Cherchi Usai, *Silent Cinema: An Introduction* (London: British Film Institute, 2000); Leonardo Quaresima, *The Tenth Muse: DOMITOR Conference, VII International Film Studies Conference: Proceedings* (Udine: Dipartimento di storia e tutela dei beni culturali, Università degli studi di Udine, 2001); Luciano Berriatúa, ed., *All the Colours of the World: Colours in Early Mass Media: 1900–1930* (Reggio Emilia, Italy: Diabasis, 1998); Jacques Aumont, *La couleur en cinéma* (Paris: Cinémathèque française, 1995); Richard Misek, *Chromatic Cinema*; and Tom Gunning, "Colorful Metaphors: The Attraction of Color in Early Silent Cinema," in *Il Colore nel Cinema*, eds. Monica Dall'Asta and Guglielmo Pescatore (Bologna: Editrice CLUEB, 1995), 249–55. The valuable contributions of Misek, and Gunning, in particular, will be addressed below.

53 Paolo Cherchi Usai, *Silent Cinema*, 40.

54 William Uricchio, "Color and Dramatic Articulation in *The Lonedale Operator*," in *Il Colore*, eds. Monica Dall'Asta and Guglielmo Pescatore, 268–72.

55 Eirik Frisvold Hanssen, *Early Discourses*, 13. Such comments can be accessed within any number of early publications on cinema, such as *Variety* or *Moving Picture World* after 1906.

56 References to film periodization here and below follow Brewster's three-phase model. According to Brewster, the first phase, often referred to within other models as "early cinema," is the variety-theater/fairground period (until 1906–7). This phase is stylistically dominated by "cinematic attractions" (discussed more below). Phase two (until about 1912) and three (which continues to the present) involve more elaborate film narrative. Ben Brewster,

has noted, during applied color's[57] "final decade" [in the 1920s] during which it is still "rare to find any reflections on tinting and toning." According to Patalas, even "in the reviews of the twenties color is rarely mentioned at all."[58]

Gunning offers a point of departure that helps to address this bind.[59] His intervention also perhaps suggests an area for clarification and elaboration within the context of metachromatics.

Color as Attraction

> As we watch a film, the continuous act of recognition in which we are involved is like a strip of memory unrolling beneath the image of the film itself, to form the invisible underlayer of an implicit double exposure.[60]

Color within films produced during cinema's first decades, irrespective of coloration process (for the most part), stands in stark relief from the line/form of the black-and-white media to which it was added. As Gunning explains, color "appears as something superadded to the more dominant form of reproduction, an extra-sensual intensity which draws its significance at least in part from its difference to black and white."[61] He contextualizes this observation with other additions of color to black-and-white print media that he locates within popular culture during the last half of the nineteenth century in the US (in comics, pulps, etc.). From these intertexts, he shows that such color mostly "announced sensational content" and "endow[ed]…surplus to…use value" rather than adding in any restrictive metaphorical sense to narrative content.[62] Color serves as a loose sign, in part of defiance, which "existed in opposition to black and white" (an opposition exemplified for Gunning in later films such as *The Wizard of Oz* [1939]).[63] For Gunning, these conditions then absorb color into a broader typology within cinema referred to as the "pure attraction," which in many respects also reflects distinctions borne by historical designations of "description."

Briefly summarized, within the cinematic "attraction," display or "showing" takes precedence over diegetic "telling," temporal progression, and "narrative absorption."[64] According to this idea, "the desire to display may *interact* with the

---

"Periodization of Early Cinema," in *American Cinema's Transitional Era: Audiences, Institutions, Practices*, ed. Charlie Keil (Berkeley: University of California Press, 2004), 66–75.

57 Before the institutional dominance of "natural color" processes in cinema, color typically was added to cinema through hand application (freehand or through stencils), the bathing methods of tinting and toning, or combinations of all three. For more on these processes, see: Paolo Cherchi Usai, *Silent Cinema*, 21–43.

58 Enno Patalas, contributor, "Moderated Discussion Session 1," in *Disorderly Order*, eds. Daan Hertogs and Nico De Klerk, 21.

59 Tom Gunning, "Colorful Metaphors."

60 Maya Deren, "Cinematography: The Creative Use of Reality," *Daedalus* 89, no. 1 (January 1, 1960): 153–54.

61 Tom Gunning, "Colorful Metaphors," 250.

62 Ibid., 252.

63 Ibid., 253.

64 Tom Gunning, "The Cinema of Attraction: Early Film, Its Spectator, and the Avant-Garde," *Wide Angle* 8, nos. 3–4 (1986): 1–14. Revised in *Early Cinema: Space Frame Narrative*, ed. Thomas Elsaesser (London: British Film Institute, 1990), 56–62. Citations refer to the BFI edition. The concept of the cinematic "attraction," adapted and developed in large part by Tom Gunning and André Gaudreault from Sergei Eisenstein, applies to the predominant

desire to tell a story" but the two remain ontologically separate (Gunning distinguishes, for example, the famous close-up of the outlaw firing a pistol at the camera in *The Great Train Robbery* as essentially non-narrative material within this film).[65] As "pure presence," "pure curiosity," and "pure instance,"[66] a strict construction of Gunning's attraction appears to oppose the implicit "impurity" of narrative; it is an opposition that recalls, within the context of narrative/description theory, the "need to define 'the other' of narrative" and "to assign the representation of objects to a distinct mode of writing."[67] Attention to color given this formulation suggests a problematic alignment that we might articulate this way:

---
color/formlessness/sensuality/purity/non-narrative showing

vs.

black-and-white/line and form/non-sensuality/impurity/narrative telling

---

Gunning certainly recognizes that color, within early cinema and its larger cultural contexts, "communicates" to audiences. He also allows that in one sense the cinematic attraction does in fact "speak," but is mostly limited to "here it is, look at it!"[68] This apparent conceptual dissonance, which seems to diminish from the attraction—and thus color—the politically powerful qualities of legibility, story, voice, etc., through a celebration of the purity and sensuality of display, recalls by now a fraught division.

This model of the attraction, reinforced by contemporary revisions and extensions, has been said to "liberate the analysis of film from the hegemony of narratology...[and] enable us to focus...on *the event* of appearing as itself as a legitimate aesthetic category."[69] As is evident within other chromatic contexts, however, this articulation invokes problematic terms familiar to the chromophobic/philic dilemma. Røssaak's position against (classical) "narratology" and thus narrative (as if monolithic) also moves us closer to a central difficulty that is in part traceable to notions derived from classical narrative theory.

---

address of early cinema, or "kine-attractography" (1890–1910) (Gaudreault's formulation), before the rise of longer story films c. 1906–1907. It refers generally to a film segment that seems to prioritize visuality for the audience. From cinema's inception through about 1903, "attractions" consisting of loosely-integrated combinations of single-shot films, slides, stage acts, etc., which foregrounded the appeal of discursive variety, were frequently presented by exhibitors and lecturers. For more on these cinematic programs, see: Charles Musser, *The Emergence of Cinema: The American Screen to 1907* (New York: Scribner, 1990). For more on "kine-attractography," see: André Gaudreault, *Film and Attraction: From Kinematography to Cinema* (Urbana: University of Illinois Press, 2011). For more on the attraction in cinema, refer to: Sergei Eisenstein, "The Montage of Attractions," in *The Film Factory*, eds. Richard Taylor and Ian Christie (Cambridge, MA: Harvard University Press, [1923] 1988), 87–88; Sergei Eisenstein, "The Montage of Film Attractions," in *Selected Works, vol. 1, Writings, 1922-34*, ed. and trans. Richard Taylor (London: British Film Institute, [1924] 1996), 39–58; Tom Gunning, "An Aesthetic of Astonishment: Early Film and the (In)credulous Spectator," *Art and Text* 34 (1989): 31–45; and Wanda Strauven, ed., *The Cinema of Attractions Reloaded* (Amsterdam: Amsterdam University Press, 2006).

65 Emphasis mine. Tom Gunning, "'Now You See It, Now You Don't': The Temporality of the Cinema of Attractions," in *The Silent Cinema Reader*, ed. Lee Grieveson (London; New York: Routledge, [1993] 2004), 43.

66 Ibid., 48.

67 Ruth Ronen, "Description, Narrative and Representation," *Narrative* 5, no. 3 (October, 1997): 283–84.

68 Tom Gunning, "Now You See It," 44.

69 Emphasis mine. Eivind Røssaak, "Figures of Sensation: Between Still and Moving Images," in *The Cinema of Attractions Reloaded*, ed. Wanda Strauven, 322.

Classical narrative theory generally reduces narrative to a series of causally- and logically-related events able to be organized into a plot.[70] According to this theory, the dynamics and distribution of these events, and their states, also generally must follow the pattern of equilibrium, disequilibrium, and equilibrium restored. This determination of narrative, essentialized by a restrictive conceptualization of "event," obtains even within many recent postclassical revisions.[71]

Elements said to be "outside" of the events of narrative, such as description construed as material inassimilable by plot, are generally considered gaps or pauses that "interrupt the *line* of fabula."[72] (Fabula can be understood as the essential constituents of narrative reassembled by readers/audiences from the sjuzet: those constituents assembled by the text in any order.)

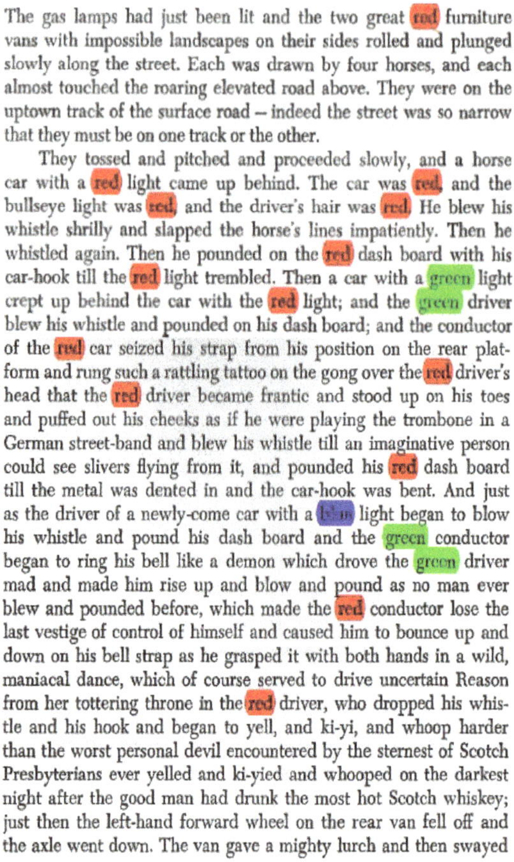

The gas lamps had just been lit and the two great red furniture vans with impossible landscapes on their sides rolled and plunged slowly along the street. Each was drawn by four horses, and each almost touched the roaring elevated road above. They were on the uptown track of the surface road — indeed the street was so narrow that they must be on one track or the other.

They tossed and pitched and proceeded slowly, and a horse car with a red light came up behind. The car was red, and the bullseye light was red, and the driver's hair was red. He blew his whistle shrilly and slapped the horse's lines impatiently. Then he whistled again. Then he pounded on the red dash board with his car-hook till the red light trembled. Then a car with a green light crept up behind the car with the red light; and the green driver blew his whistle and pounded on his dash board; and the conductor of the red car seized his strap from his position on the rear platform and rung such a rattling tattoo on the gong over the red driver's head that the red driver became frantic and stood up on his toes and puffed out his cheeks as if he were playing the trombone in a German street-band and blew his whistle till an imaginative person could see slivers flying from it, and pounded his red dash board till the metal was dented in and the car-hook was bent. And just as the driver of a newly-come car with a green light began to blow his whistle and pound his dash board and the green conductor began to ring his bell like a demon which drove the green driver mad and made him rise up and blow and pound as no man ever blew and pounded before, which made the red conductor lose the last vestige of control of himself and caused him to bounce up and down on his bell strap as he grasped it with both hands in a wild, maniacal dance, which of course served to drive uncertain Reason from her tottering throne in the red driver, who dropped his whistle and his hook and began to yell, and ki-yi, and whoop harder than the worst personal devil encountered by the sternest of Scotch Presbyterians ever yelled and ki-yied and whooped on the darkest night after the good man had drunk the most hot Scotch whiskey; just then the left-hand forward wheel on the rear van fell off and the axle went down. The van gave a mighty lurch and then swayed

Figure 7.3 | Anonymous [Stephen Crane], "Travels in New York / The Broken-Down Van," 1892. In Stallman and Hagemann, *The New York City Sketches*, 3–4. Coloration mine.

Elements extraneous to this "line," while often considered important to the conveyance of plot or aspects of its motivation, by this understanding are suppressed

---

70 Gerald Prince, *A Grammar of Stories: An Introduction* (The Hague: Mouton, 1973), 183. Classical narrative approaches generally are understood as following the work of French Structuralists such as (early) Barthes, Tzvetan Todorov, Bremond, Greimas, and Genette. Roland Barthes, "Introduction to the Structural Analysis of Narratives" [1966], in *Image, Music, Text*, 79–124; Tzvetan Todorov, "La grammaire du récit," *Languages* 12 (1968): 94–102; Claude Bremond, *Logique du récit* (Paris: Seuil, 1973); A. J. Greimas, *Structural Semantics: An Attempt at a Method*, trans. Danielle McDowell, Ronald Schleifer, and Alan Velie (Lincoln: University of Nebraska, [1966] 1983); Gérard Genette, "Frontiers of Narrative," in *Figures of Literary Discourse*, ed. Marie-Rose Logan and trans. Alan Sheridan (New York: Columbia University Press, [1966] 1982), 127–46.

71 The term "postclassical narratology" derives from Herman and refers generally to the shift from text-based Structuralist theories of narrative to greater considerations of reading contexts and their socio-cultural influence. Postclassical approaches also integrate thematic emphases, such as feminist, queer, ethnic, postcolonial approaches to narrative. David Herman, *Narratologies: New Perspectives on Narrative Analysis* (Columbus: Ohio State University Press, 1999). For an introduction to "phase two" of the postclassical approach, see: Jan Alber and Monika Fludernik, eds., *Postclassical Narratology: Approaches and Analyses* (Columbus: Ohio State University Press, 2010).

72 Emphasis mine. Mieke Bal, *Narratology*, 37.

or marginalized as adjunctive, "supportive,"[73] or "relief-giving":[74] an ontological function also historically attributed to color. It recalls, for example, a general notion of color as "pure mood" relieving "intellect";[75] or, specific to photo-cinematic composites, Talbot's explanation of "a common practice to *relieve* the monotonous black-and-white by the introduction of colouring effects."[76]

As Lukács warned (with chromatic flourish), when description, construed as supplement, relief, etc., becomes autonomous from the line/form of plot, "the peripheral begins to bloom everywhere."[77] Within the context of metachromatics, this chromatically-charged warning, and narrative "line" posed in opposition to supplemental description, again raises red flags.

As we can see, for example, within a section of text from Stephen Crane's city sketch "Travels in New York" (Figure 7.3)—part of the realist genre of "local color literature"—color's marginalization according to the schema of classical narrative theory cannot effectively account for the experiential "event" of the explicit eruption and interaction of color within the "achromatic" or tacitly-colored spaces of diegesis and discourse, nor the "narrativity" that might accompany its processing. Chromatic addition, in this case, through a profusion of color words, or what H. G. Wells called "chromatic splashes" in Crane's writing,[78] not only serves to modify or qualify proximal existents (characters and setting) through which actions of plot might be motivated.[79] As a separate register that oscillates between embodied descriptor and self-referencing material, color on some level resists incorporation and determination by the line/form of existents and plot, and asserts itself as "facture" and within constellations of meaning awaiting narrativization. Such color, as Melville explains within the context of the visual arts, but which can be applied more broadly, "is not only contained [within painting]," but can "assign frames" [of meaning, experience, etc.] even while "conceal[ing] itself within this assignment."[80]

The explicit "application" of color to an achromatic (or tacitly-colored) and resistant "ground" also promotes the invocation of coloration as a separate discourse, and the narratives, or "micro-events," and "micro-storie" associated with its labor (to be discussed below).[81] Tacit coloration, on the other hand, might

---

73 Paul Hopper, "Aspect and Foregrounding in Discourse," *Syntax and Semantics* 12 (1979): 216.

74 Werner Wolf, "Description as a Transmedial Mode of Representing: General features and Possibilities of Realization in Painting, Fiction and Music," in *Description in Literature*, eds. Werner Wolf and Walter Bernhart, 56.

75 Walter Benjamin, "A Child's View of Colour," trans. Rodney Livingstone, in *Walter Benjamin: Selected Writings, vol. 1: 1913–1926*, ed. Marcus Bullock and Michael W. Jennings (Cambridge, MA: Belknap Press, [1914–15] 1996), 51.

76 Emphasis mine. Frederick Arthur Ambrose Talbot, *Moving Pictures* (New York: Arno Press, [1912] 1970), 299.

77 Georg Lukács, "Narrate or Describe?" in *Writer and Critic and Other Essays*, ed. and trans. Arthur Kahn (London: Merlin, [1936] 1970),131.

78 H. G. Wells, "Stephen Crane, from an English Standpoint," *North American Monthly Review* 171 (August, 1900): 237.

79 For Chatman and Prince, events and existents are the fundamental elements of a story. Seymour Chatman, *Story and Discourse: Narrative Structure in Fiction and Film* (Ithaca, Cornell University Press, 1978); Gerald Prince, *A Dictionary of Narratology* (Lincoln: University of Nebraska Press, 1987).

80 Stephen Melville, "Color Has Not Yet Been Named: Objectivity in Deconstruction," in *Deconstruction and the Visual Arts: Art, Media, Architecture*, eds. Peter Brunette and David Wills (Cambridge; New York: Cambridge University Press, 1997), 45.

81 As Ankersmit explains, "micro-storie" (plural, from the Italian, "storia") consist of apparently insignificant historical events, which, however, might exemplify "essential tensions, frictions, or conflicts of a period." Frank

be understood as denoting only the implied presence of color within iterations of line/form whose constitutions may entail or suggest it. For example, just as photo-cinematic media may tacitly signify the brown of a tree that it represents in black-and-white, so may "tree" tacitly implicate browness within an utterance. The relation of these frames of meaning to concepts of narrative and description, and their inflection of the discourse of color –line/form, is of central concern to metachromatic investigation.[82]

To return to Crane's "Travels in New York," for example, on a diegetic level we can experience a hardly motivated play of color words as colored lights "staged" on a darkened city street. In addition to the possible association of this play with pictorial impressionism[83] (a comparison, however, inadequate or aesthetically parodied, especially given the story's mischievous inclusion of an "unclassified boy" whose finger-"paint" in black automotive grease defaces an "impossible landscape"),[84] verbal color here also likely invoked other contemporary chromatic entertainments. These included popular serpentine and umbrella dances, such as *Serpentine Dance—Annabelle* (1897) and *Farfale* [sic] (1907) (Figures 7.4 and 7.5), as well as experiments in "naturally" colored (moving) photography based on emergent theories of "additive mixing."

According to this phenomenon, popularized by James Clerk Maxwell in the mid-1850s, the mixing of red, green, and blue light (additive primaries) produced the "effect" of white light on human vision and thus the illusion of natural color.[85] Crane's use of colored lights consisting only of additive primaries that "mix" throughout a single sentence that runs (cinematographically) nearly a page long suggests perhaps an early sensational experiment in photo-cinematic synaesthesia within this pseudo-"travelogue"—a popular genre of early cinema noted for its frequent also use of color. The interlacing of references to sound and color within "Travels" also allows for the invocation of contemporary synaesthetic treatises linking harmony and discord in music to chromatic arrangement, such as Lady Archibald Campbell's *Rainbow-Music*,[86] or technologies such as Alexander Wallace Rimington's *Clavier à Lumières* (or color organ) (1893).

Ankersmit, "Micro-storie," in *Routledge Encyclopedia*, eds. David Herman, Manfred Jahn, and Marie-Laure Ryan, 308. Typically, micro-storie are considered minor, aberrant events. Here, however, the concept of micro-storia can be adapted to encompass the aberrance of explicit and self-reflexive chromatic appearance, the relative historical insignificance of color labor(ers), and color's broader subordination to line/form.

82   Although a more expansive theoretical treatment of the narrativity of description (forthcoming) is not possible here, this topic is critical to metachromatics and its relation to narrative theory.

83   Gaskill provides perhaps a more apt comparison of Crane's use of "flat" colors to those popularized by Art Nouveau and the covers of *Harper's Magazine* (1889–92). Nicholas Gaskill, "Red Cars with Red Lights and Red Drivers: Color, Crane, and Qualia," *American Literature* 81, no. 4 (December, 2009): 719–45. See also Halliburton, who considers the influence on Crane of the concept of primary colors as articulated by Goethe; and Hough, who also discusses Goethe's influence. David Halliburton, *The Color of the Sky: A Study of Stephen Crane* (Cambridge, England: Cambridge University Press, 1989), 113; Robert L. Hough, "Crane and Goethe: A Forgotten Relationship," *Nineteenth-Century Fiction* 17 (September, 1962): 135–48.

84   Stephen Crane, (unsigned), "Travels in New York/The Broken-Down Van," *New York Tribune* (July 10, 1892), in *The New York City Sketches of Stephen Crane*, eds. R.W. Stallman and E. R. Hagemann (New York: New York University Press, 1962), 3–4.

85   The concept of additive mixing allowed for developments in early "naturally" colored photography, as well as early "naturally" colored moving pictures.

86   Archibald Campbell, *Rainbow-Music; or, The Philosophy of Harmony in Colour-Grouping* (London: Bernard Quaritch, 1886).

Figure 7.4 | Video stills from Thomas Edison, *Serpentine Dance—Annabelle* (c. 1897; New York: Anthology Film Archives, 2005), DVD. Hand coloration, anonymous.

Figure 7.5 | Video still from Società Italiana Cines, *Farfale ("Butterflys")* [sic] (1907; Los Angeles: Flicker Alley, 2007), DVD. Hand coloration, anonymous.

Moreover, the verbal "switching" of emphasis from events constituted by the "line" of plot, to perceptual "events" of chromatic interaction, also reflected a popular mode of generic alternation familiar from other types of composite entertainment during this period derived from conventions of variety and vaudeville—a mode realized within early cinematic programs and their individual "attractions" as well.[87] The "flat" application of "primary" or so-called psychologically-unique color words (red, green, and blue) in Crane's sketch,[88] which at times "escape" from their roles as (mere) modifiers, also can be contextualized with historically-contemporary avant-garde experiments in poetry—such as Rimbaud's chromatic alphabet by which vowels irrespective of word were said to bear color—as well as with other aesthetic-scientific ideas about color dynamics filtering throughout culture during this period.[89]

In addition to psychological studies of "the color sense in literature,"[90] individual colors such as "red" and "yellow,"[91] and color's interaction with theosophical "thought-forms,"[92] the phenomenal effects of color become a widespread topic of interest during this era. During this period, experiences attributed to color that suggested shifts in its relation to line/form included: Irradiation: the spreading of color to surrounding spaces (discussed by Helmholtz by 1867 [English trans. 1881] and Sutter in 1880);[93] simultaneous contrast: the invocation of complementary colors in the eye (Goethe 1810 [English trans. 1840] through Chevreul 1839 [English trans. 1854]);[94] luster: the visual dissonance or "flickering effect"[95] of color within neo-impressionist paintings (c. 1886–1891); and the "fringing" of early cinematic color processes in which conspicuous halos of red and green momentarily disrupt mimetic illusionism—an "escape" of color from line/form that recalled chromatic slips within earlier hand-painted artifacts (Figures 7.6 and 7.7). Crane's figurative light show here invites further consideration of these shifts within the context of literary expression and perhaps an experience of early "multimedia" by readers.

---

87 See Allen for more on the relation between vaudeville and film from 1895–1915. Robert C. Allen, *Vaudeville and Film: 1895–1915* (New York: Arno Press, 1980).

88 Primary colors are those not able to be derived from the mixing of other colors. Although green can be produced by subtractively mixing yellow and blue, it tends to be considered psychologically "unique" and thus often "primary."

89 Arthur Rimbaud, *A Season in Hell*, trans. Delmore Schwartz (Norfolk, CT: New Directions, [1873] 1940). Rimbaud's chromatic experimentation can be understood within a broader context of interest in color experience within poetry during this period. See, for example, Cronin, for his study of color within nineteenth-century poetry. Richard Cronin, *Colour and Experience in Nineteenth-Century Poetry* (Houndmills, Basingstoke, Hampshire: Macmillan Press, 1988).

90 Havelock Ellis, *The Colour-Sense in Literature* (London: The Ulysses Book Shop, [1896] 1931).

91 Havelock Ellis, "The Psychology of Red," *Popular Science Monthly* 57 (September, 1900): 517–26; Havelock Ellis, "The Psychology of Yellow," *Popular Science Monthly* 68 (May, 1906): 456–63.

92 Annie Besant, *Thought-Forms* (Wheaton, IL: Theosophical Publishing House, [1901] 1971).

93 Hermann von Helmholtz, "On the Relation of Optics to Painting," in *Popular Lectures on Scientific Subjects*, trans. Edmund Atkinson (New York: Appleton, 1881), 73–138; David Sutter, "The Phenomena of Vision," *L'art* 6, no. 1 (February–March, 1880).

94 Johann Wolfgang von Goethe, *Theory of Colours*, trans. Charles Lock Eastlake (Cambridge, MA: MIT Press, [1810] 1970); Michel Eugène Chevreul, *The Principles of Harmony and Contrast of Colors and Their Applications to the Arts*, trans. Charles Martel (New York: Reinhold, [1839] 1967).

95 Ogden Rood, *Modern Chromatics*.

Figure 7.6 | *Left:* Video still from Thomas Edison and Edwin Porter, *The Great Train Robbery* (1903; New York: Kino International, 2002), DVD. Hand coloration, anonymous.

Figure 7.7 | *Right:* Video still from *Rive del Nilo* (1911). Kinemacolor. Courtesy of Cineteca del Comune di Bologna, Archivo cinematografico Ansaldo, National Film and Television Archive, and Europafilmtreasures.eu.

Despite color's capacity to suggest narratives and metanarratives organized by line/form and its own aspects of mediality,[96] theories of color also have espoused its ability to transcend such signification altogether. The artist Yves Klein once remarked that even the most mimetic uses of color within representational painting "wink" at or mock the dictates of narrative,[97] a defiance that Kristeva would later articulate within the study of Giotto's painting as part of the "triple register" of color,[98] and what Barthes more generally would term as escape from the "obvious meaning" of composition's perceived intentions.[99]

A similar notion of a sublime escape from narrative within early cinematic attractions, despite perhaps the appeal of its sense of liberation, reinforces the question of further theoretical excavation. Although for Gunning "pure" display or "appearance" to some extent restricts narrativity to "Here it is: look at it!" appearance always happens through *things* and the narratives that they constitute (however prototypical). Even within "prototypical" attractions, for example, such as a single-shot serpentine dance (Figure 7.4), or a strong man flexing before the camera,[100] content is narrativized according to context and the "situation" of its

---

96   For a recent study of such narratives and metanarratives, see, for example, Andrea Feeser, Maureen Daly Goggin, and Beth Fowkes Tobin, eds., *The Materiality of Color: The Production, Circulation, and Application of Dyes and Pigments, 1400–1800* (Burlington: Ashgate, 2012).

97   Yves Klein, "Evolution of Art," in *Colour*, ed. David Batchelor, 121.

98   Julia Kristeva, "Giotto's Joy," in *Desire in Language*, trans. Thomas Gora, Alice Jardine, and Leon S. Roudiez (New York: Columbia University Press, [1972] 1980), 210–36. For Kristeva, color is constituted by an index of value (of a referent), instinctual pressure (cathexis), and a (larger) symbolic order of which it is part. For more on deconstruction and color, see, for example, Derrida and Melville. Jacques Derrida, *The Truth in Painting* (Chicago: University of Chicago Press, 1987); Stephen Melville, "Color Has Not Yet Been Named," in *Deconstruction*, eds. Peter Brunette and David Wills.

99   Roland Barthes, "The Third Meaning," in *Image, Music, Text*, 54.

100   Take, for example, Eugen Sandow (in the 1894 Edison film) as he passes through a routine that displays certain parts of his covered and uncovered body from front to back, top to bottom, flexed and released. His gestures and actions interact with cultural expectations for a Prussian + strong + man + "on display"—a performance of normativity that likely invokes and reinforces masculinist, exoticist, and even nationalist narratives (among others). Imagining challenges to such invocations, initiated through "unexpected" costuming, gesture, dance, etc. that violate typological expectation (one can imagine many alternatives), helps to foreground the "constructedness" of identity, whose

processing.[101] Within cinema studies, Aumont et al. point to this idea in the explanation that even the simplest display of an object on film inescapably "carries a whole array of values that it [the object] represents and narrates."[102] According to this more postclassical and "tacit" sense of narrative, "every figuration and representation in film calls forth narration or an embryonic form of it" (through figure-to-ground relations, socio-historical contextualization, generic intertexts, etc.).[103] Narrative situation in this sense consists of the interactions between framed signs (with framing determined in part by notions of frame, and what is deemed inside/outside of it), embodied viewers/readers situated within historical and social contexts, the pragmatics of goal-driven reading processes and competencies (conscious or not) linked to those contexts, and individual "backstories" that this narrative situation and its elements trigger for processing (which Maya Deren shows vividly through metaphor, above).

This conception of narrativity might productively factor more directly into our understanding of "attractions," especially in light of the many narratives that (added) color in cinema might be said to call forth. These include those "mute" narratives that seem only to reaffirm normativity as a set of "non-stories" to be taken for granted. In this case, we can consider, for example, stories and assumptions underpinning contexts of labor, which (silently) accompanied experiences of "merely" colorful additions.

The Labor of Color

Røssaak's evocation of an alternative concept of eventhood within cinematic aesthetics reinforces the need for the re-articulation of "event."[104] Instead of, however, perhaps reifying what we might experience as "the event" of color's "appearance," we can involve in its conceptualization the range of cultural practices involved in color's application and use. Rather than idealizing,[105] we can pursue, for example, a metachromatic historicization of the idealization of color and its labor.

---

narratives, to some extent, Sandow performs.

101 For a useful summary of this more pragmatics-centered approach to narrativity, see: Jacob L. Mey, "Pragmatics," in *Routledge Encyclopedia*, eds. David Herman, Manfred Jahn, and Marie-Laure Ryan, 493–98.

102 Jacques Aumont et al., *Aesthetics of Film*, trans. Richard Neupert (Austin: University of Texas Press, 1992), 69.

103 Musser also clarifies, within the context of attractions, that many early-cinema surprises and displays are in fact functions of narrative or imbricated with narrative. Charles Musser, "Rethinking Early Cinema: Cinema of Attractions and Narrativity," *The Yale Journal of Criticism* 7, no. 2 (1994): 203–32.

104 For more on aesthetics within the context of early cinema, see: Joshua Yumibe, "Silent Cinema Colour Aesthetics," in *Questions of Colour in Cinema: From Paintbrush to Pixel*, ed. Wendy E. Everett (Bern; Oxford: Peter Lang, 2007), 41–56.

105 The de-contextualization, de-storification, and purification of appearance itself also comprise a narrative whose genealogy might be traced in a variety of ways. It recalls, for example, Heidegger's notion of a "present-at-hand," Barthes's "message without a code," the aspirations of any number of avant-gardes, and Pater's assertion of art as always "striving to be independent of the mere intelligence, to become a matter of pure perception, to get rid of the responsibilities to its subject or material." Martin Heidegger, *Being and Time* (Albany: State University of New York Press, [1927] 2010); Roland Barthes, "Rhetoric of the Image," in *Image, Music, Text*, 32–52; Walter Pater, *The Renaissance: Studies in Art and Poetry* (London: Macmillan, 1888), 143. It also may be considered part of the longer history of the desire for enargeia and the so-called natural sign. For more on this history, see: Murray Krieger, *Ekphrasis: The Illusion of the Natural Sign* (Baltimore: Johns Hopkins, 1992).

Figure 7.8 | *Pathé coloring lab, Paris* (1912). Reproduced from Talbot, *Moving Pictures*, 289.

As Fossati explains, during cinema's first decades, "hand-painting and later stenciling was almost exclusively a women's [sic] job."[106] In fact, color within one of the earliest Kinetoscope films, Thomas Edison's *Annabelle* (1894), was applied by the wife of an Edison employee (Edmund Kuhn) in the Edison lab in Llewellyn Park, New Jersey.[107] "Ms. Kuhn" [as records describe her] also likely was responsible for the coloration of some of the earliest projected films, such the "umbrella" and "serpentine" dances shown during the New York debut of Vitascope at Koster & Bial's Music Hall, on April 23, 1896.[108] By the turn of the twentieth century, the normalization of this gendered practice was institutionalized by cinema through the hands of "color girls" who frequently labored in workshops and factories considered by many to be "sweatshops."[109] This industry expanded the profitability of cinematic color, as well as other forms of screen media, such as lantern slides. The legacy of this physical touch of color applied by women within cinema, however, also can be considered within much later forms of cinematic productions that featured so-called natural color (i.e, productions in which color was not "added"). For example, the majority of color decisions from 1934 to 1949 even within Technicolor productions, the first "real color" cinema to gain wide market exposure, were supervised (made) by Natalie Kalmus, wife

---

106   Giovanna Fossati, "When Cinema was Coloured," in *All the Colours of the World*, ed. Luciano Berriatúa, 122.

107   Ibid., 123.

108   Charles Musser, *The Emergence of Cinema*, 116–17. These and similar dance spectacles were popular within Kinetoscope parlors and later as projections. They were offered by all major production companies in the 1890s following the popularity of Loïe Fuller's illuminated dance performances in France.

109   Most notable among these was the workshop headed by Elisabeth Thuiller in Paris—now commonly recognized by a picture regularly cited (Figure 7.8). According to her technical guidance and decisions about color, 220 females applied color to films such as Georges Méliès's *Cendrillion* (1899) and *Jeanne d'Arc* (1900), and films by Pathé. See also commentary on the factory conditions and pay structure of female colorists in "The Wages of Girls who Color Slides," *Moving Picture World* 4, no. 25 (June, 1909): 830–31.

of Technicolor founder Herbert T. Kalmus.[110] This tradition of gendered labor, which informs the contextualization of color within cinema during at least its first half-century, adds new resonance to Gunning's observation that color within early cinema "existed in opposition to black and white."[111]

Richard Misek argues that the combination of color and black-and-whiteness within cinema, on the other hand, represented a new medium.[112] He notes that until the late-1920s within cinema, there existed a "visual mismatch between the outlines of objects and their colors" and that "no such cultural construct" had existed before.[113] In this, however, he overlooks the much longer tradition of color – line/form and the history of divided labor that it reinforced. Moreover, for Misek this differential comprised a relation of "cooperative interaction"[114] rather than "opposition," which elides historical inequities involved in "cooperation" both symbolically and in terms of actual labor.

Figure 7.9 | *Left:* Video still from Louis Lumière, *Card Party* (1895; Los Angeles: Flicker Alley, 2007), DVD. Hand coloration, anonymous.

Figure 7.10 | *Right:* [*Three unidentified women in mourning dress reading a letter*] (c. 1865). Tintype. 3 x 2 3/8 in. Hand coloration, anonymous. Courtesy of the International Center of Photography, *America and the Tintype (September 19, 2008–January 14, 2009)*. Gift of Steven Kasher, 2007.

As the earlier comments on dominant labor practices suggest, broader traditions of labor—among other aspects of culture—should be considered within this or any notion of media specificity. In fact, the very history of photo-indexical monochromality, from which the black-and-white of cinema derives, stems in part from conceptions of the so-called "pencil of nature" and the mediation of its line/form by male operators. A painted version of Lumière's *Card Party* (1895) (Figure 7.9) provides a typical example of the cine-painterly "mismatch" cited by

---

110 As Misek explains, between 1930s–50s, Natalie Kalmus as color consultant for Technicolor productions was responsible for making its color decisions. Richard Misek, *Chromatic Cinema*, 36. For insight into theories of color that informed these decisions, see: N. Kalmus, "Color Consciousness," *Journal of the Society of Motion Picture Engineers* 35, no. 2 (1935): 139–47.

111 Tom Gunning, "Colorful Metaphors," 253.

112 Richard Misek, *Chromatic Cinema*, 15.

113 Ibid., 18.

114 Ibid., 24.

Misek as specific to cinema. Its longer history, however, is immediately recalled when juxtaposed with forms of painted photography that prefigured moving pictures throughout the nineteenth century (Figures 7.9 and 7.10).[115]

The concept of the cultural series by Gaudreault and Philippe,[116] and Gaudreault's observation that early cinema is not in fact "cinema" as we know it but its own genre linked to moving photography ("kine-attractography" [1890–1910]),[117] invite us to trace this "mismatch" of color in cinema, and its relations of gender and labor, more directly to this forbearer in nineteenth-century photography. As Abel reminds us, before 1907, cinema or "moving pictures" often was considered an extension or derivative form of still photography, just as it had been at the 1900 Universal Exposition in Paris.[118] It also was likened to other forms of optical entertainment, including images within optical view boxes from as early as the eighteenth century—in which colors were made to suddenly change as an attraction—and magic lantern projections, whose colorists, including women, also were among the first to be employed to color films.[119]

This history can be examined further by recalling that the very year of Daguerre's announcement of photography in 1839 also featured its first successful hand coloration (in the form of painted daguerreotypes).[120] In fact, without this added color, the monochromatic line/form of early photography for many was said to lack the "feminine side" of art (recall Blanc's primer) required for successful or faithful representation. Added color within early photo-indexical media—static or moving—thus can be understood as bearing meaningful associations with gender, which should be considered within theories of its meaning (or apparent "lack" of meaning). The stakes of this recognition, in fact, become higher as we acknowledge early attempts in photo-cinematography to establish media difference according to masculinist notions of difference, and male claims on empirical reality itself.

Color Girls and Early Photography

Promoted in its earliest stages as the unmediated "light writing" of the "pencil of nature,"[121] the line/form of photography quickly replaced mediated graphic and sculptural representation,[122] dominant since Antiquity, as the preeminent tech-

---

115   This is not to suggest, however, that the effects of this mismatch within still and moving photography are identical. The ontological difference in temporality between the two media might allow, for example, for a greater sense of color's agency through its sudden appearance and disappearance, movement, transgression or observance of boundaries of line/form, etc.

116   The concept of the cultural series can be understood (briefly) as a medial and generic situation that explains the relation between forms of representation. André Gaudreault and Marion Philippe, "A Medium Is Always Born Twice."

117   André Gaudreault, *Film and Attraction*.

118   Richard Abel, *French Film Theory and Criticism: 1907–1939* (Princeton, NJ: Princeton University Press, 1988), xv.

119   Giovanna Fossati, "When Cinema was Coloured," in *All the Colours*, ed. Luciano Berriatúa, 122.

120   Heinz K. Henisch and Bridget Ann Henisch, *The Painted Photograph, 1839–1914: Origins, Techniques, Aspirations* (University Park, PA: Pennsylvania State University Press, 1996), 21.

121   See, for example, William Henry Fox Talbot, *The Pencil of Nature* (New York, Da Capo Press, [1844–6] 1968); and M. A. Root, *The Camera and the Pencil; or, The Heliographic Art* (New York, Appleton, 1864)

122   Trevor Fawcett, "Graphic Versus Photographic in the Nineteenth-Century Reproduction," *Art History* 9, no. 2 (June, 1986): 185–212.

nology of realism.¹²³ This invention of an apparently unmediated technology for picturing reality—indexed in "black-and-white" and animated by cinematography toward the end of the century—enhanced previous conceptual divisions between color and line/form and their associations. As an emergent scientific tool, which reproduced reality in monochromatic arrays and was largely handled by men, early photography soon became identified with the masculinized authority and primacy of line/form in its theoretical and institutional situation.¹²⁴ Reacting to the proliferation of this unmediated ("infallible") imaging—and its emboldened discursive alignment with rationality, masculinity, and patriarchy as a newly-mechanized iteration of empirical truth¹²⁵—theorists of color (detractors and advocates) began to underscore color's oppositional value and its orientation as a distinctly different semiotic register and practice.

Color within photography, as within painting during this era, offered itself as a symbolic material, which could provide a mediated counterforce to the indifference of the camera, its neutralized (male) "operators," and the often apparent lifelessness of its machine-made products. In keeping with the history of painting, this touch was able to render the "inner spirit" of subjects by "embodying the insight of the artist."¹²⁶ These attributes also resonated with a broader experience of industrialization, which, for many, these alienating images were prone to invoke.¹²⁷ As discussed above, enthusiasm for this mechanized transcription of reality was accompanied by frequent expressions of anxiety. Monochrome images ominously appeared to reflect death, or the impassive discourse of science, which deprived the body or nature of spirit and essence. We hear something similar in Gorky's now often-quoted reaction to early cinema, which for him carried "a warning, fraught with a vague but sinister meaning that makes your heart grow faint."¹²⁸

According to Kracauer, the so-called reality effect of added color within cinema responded to this warning. In his estimation, in fact, "*any* color suggests dimensions of total reality ungiven in black-and-white representations" (emphasis mine). He continued, "The addition of color…enlivens images which, victimized and silent, all too easily assumed a ghost-like character. Tinting was a ghost-laying

---

123 It is important to note, however, that not everyone accepted this notion of technological evolution. As Needham argued, "the camera's work, perfect and truthful as it is, can [n]ever supplant the nerve line of free-hand drawing." C. A. Needham, "Picturesque Photography," *The Photographic Times and American Photographer Journal* 14, no. 158 (New Series 38) (February, 1884): 83. Also involved in the negotiation of realism, graphic art, and emergent photo-cinematic indexicality in the nineteenth century is the legacy of resemblance to prototype as a way to constitute "unmediated" realism. As Woodall explains, for example, within sixteenth-century portraiture, the identity of a sitter was produced through a process of emulation that presumed reference to prototype as a guarantor of realism. Joanna Woodall, *Portraiture*, 3.

124 For more generally on the processes through which media emerge, see: André Gaudreault and Marion Philippe, "A Medium is Always Born Twice."

125 Debate over photography's indexical truth value still is prominent within contemporary theory. See, for example, James Elkins, ed., *Photography Theory* (New York; London: Routledge, 2007).

126 Joanna Woodall, *Portraiture*, 6.

127 Newhall underscores the historical concern over missing color, which can be found frequently within commentary on early photography. Beaumont Newhall, *The Daguerreotype in America*, 3rd revised edition (New York: Dover, 1961), 96.

128 Quoted in Jay Leyda, *Kino: A History of the Russian and Soviet Film* (London: Allen & Unwin, 1960), 408.

device."[129] Similarly, early inventors of added-color processes within photography, such as Johann Baptist Isenring, regarded the application of paint to daguerreotypes as a corrective to this condition:

> an additional invention [that] contributed significantly to the solution of that difficult problem, namely whether and how the (through necessity) cold, dead, and stiff photographic imprint can, through the intervention of free-hand art, and by its help, be somehow transformed into a beautiful artistic entity.[130]

Within early photography, and later cinema, classic binary relations between color and line/form reinforced dominant labor practices according to gender and traditions of domestic work. In fact, the tasking of (generally unattributed) coloration to women within nineteenth-century popular photography to some extent began with the wives of the first photographers and their skill in the painting of miniatures. As a result, hand-applied color within photography (and later cinema) not only could frequently assume color's familiar symbolic feminization across a classic divide, its facture could inhere a feminine "touch." This sign could insinuate feminine gesture, authorization, sensuality, mercurialness, morality, domesticity, forms of art and craft, nostalgia for pre-industrial industry labor practices, "life," etc.[131]—an essentialization that recalled assumptions from an earlier tradition within eighteenth-century portraiture by which female painters were assumed capable of rendering the masculinity of sitters as "virtuous."[132]

Within photography and cinema, the separate register of this touch was especially apparent in the "mismatch" of dye or paint—most often vibrant and flat—applied over photo- cinematic media. Mid-nineteenth-century photographic painting manuals,[133] as well as late-nineteenth-century trade periodicals and critical commentary on cinema, often refer to or imply the "feminine" tactility of color within these media, or added color's indirect channeling of feminine "energies." However, the females responsible for the actual additions of color mostly remained anonymous.

A listing from *The Photographic Times and American Photographer* (1884) exemplifies these mostly lost female voices and the contexts of their labor (Figure 7.11). It also problematizes the notion of "cooperative interaction" referenced by

---

129 Scholarly consensus has now distanced itself from any binding notions of the chromatic consistency of "reality effects" across early cinema, acknowledging the wide-ranging functional contingencies of tint and tone now reflected in the archives. Earlier scholarship, however, such as Kracauer's, found the signification of color within cinema less problematic, arguing that "shades of red helped to amplify a conflagration or the outbreak of elemental passions, while blue tints were considered a natural for nocturnal scenes involving the secret activities of criminals and lovers." For Kracauer, hues "established audience moods in keeping with the subject and action." This generalization, however, does not hold across films. Siegfried Kracauer, *Theory of Film* (Oxford: Oxford University Press, 1960), 136.

130 Quoted in Heinz K. Henisch and Bridget Ann Henisch, *The Painted Photograph*, 22.

131 For more on the politics of this "touch," see: Robert Machado, "The Politics of Applied Color in Early Photography," *Nineteenth-Century Art Worldwide* 9, no. 1 (2010).

132 Joanna Woodall, *Portraiture*, 148.

133 See, Snelling, for example, for guidelines on gender-specific color codes in tinting. Henry Hunt Snelling, *The History and Practice of the Art of Photography; or, The Production of Pictures, Through the Agency of Light. Containing All the Instructions Necessary for the Complete Practice of the Daguerrean and Photogenic Art, both on Metallic Plates and on Paper*, 4th edition (New York: G. P. Putnam, [1849] 1853), 137–38.

As Dry Plate Photographer.—Situation wanted by a first-class dry plate photographer, also proficient in any branch. Will give instructions to any photographer to manufacture his own plates. Address Barkman, photographer, box 80, Newton, N. J.

As Colorist.—A young lady, first-class colorist and spotter, also competent to attend reception room, would like a position, city or country. Best city references. Address A. V. B., care of D. Garber, 74 Broadway, New York City.

As Operator.—A first-class operator is desirous of an engagement. Formerly with Rockwood, 17 Union Square, and late with Anderson, 785 Broadway. Thoroughly practical. New York City preferred. J. T. Decker, 91 Water Street, or box 868, Newburgh, N. Y.

As Operator.—A first-class operator and dry plate manipulator desires a position. Address John Carbutt, 628 Chestnut Street, Philadelphia, Pa.

As Retoucher.—Situation wanted by a lady who has had experience as a teacher at Cooper Institute. Address Box C., Times Office.

A position in reception room of some good gallery, by a young lady. Can do reouching, printing and toning. Salary moderate at first. Address M. E. P., Box 355, Otsego, Mich.

As Retoucher and Reception-room Lady. Reasonable wages first year. Address Ada E. Starbird, care Mrs. E. N. Lockwood, Ripon, Wis.

Figure 7.11 | "Employment Offered and Wanted," 1884. In Taylor, ed., *The Photographic Times and American Photographer Journal,* 108.

Misek. As this "Employment Offered and Wanted" column demonstrates, women seeking positions as colorists or retouchers announce themselves diminutively by gender and through low salary requirements that they euphemize as "reasonable." Entries by males seeking positions as photographic operators, however, vary significantly in tone. Their gender also is "announced," but only implicitly through omission, which reinforces a sense of masculinist authority.

The entry that cites teaching experience at the Cooper Institute, where the coloration of photographic media often was taught to women, reinforces the extent to which the tradition of (re)touching, and likely its signification, assumed qualities of gender.[134] As Martha Louise Rayne's *What Can a Woman Do,* a guide to female employment, explains, "it is common circumstance to find the wife or sister of a male photographer employed in the office."[135] But women, educated or not, requesting photographic positions, still voiced their willingness to attend to (domestic) reception room duties. Even Martha Ewing, business partner of George Harris and co-owner of the famous Washington photography firm Harris & Ewing, Inc. (1905–1945), also served as "his photo colorist and receptionist" until she sold her stake in the business.[136] Nomenclature within the last item of the listing "Employment Offered," which requests the services of a "Lady Retoucher," underscores a divide that existed across the spectrum of employment.

This listing, which suggests divisions of labor, does not, of course, indicate that photography was beyond the reach of women, especially toward the end of the nineteenth century.[137] In addition to professional roles within popular photog-

134 See, for example, "The Cooper Union," The Nation (June 5, 1866).

135 Martha Louise Rayne, *What Can a Woman Do; or, Her Position in the Business and Literary World* (Petersburgh, NY: Eagle, 1893), 128.

136 Kathleen Collins, *Washingtoniana Photographs: Collections in the Prints and Photographs Division of the Library of Congress* (Washington: The Library of Congress, 1989), 102.

137 As Gover explains, "photography, a male bastion before 1880, emerged as a career option and avocation for women. By 1900, more than 3500 women worked as professional photographers." Jane C. Gover, *The Positive Image: Women Photographers in Turn of the Century America* (Albany: State University of New York Press, 1987), 17. These women, however, notes Rosenblum, until just recently had been "scanted in the histories of the general histories of the

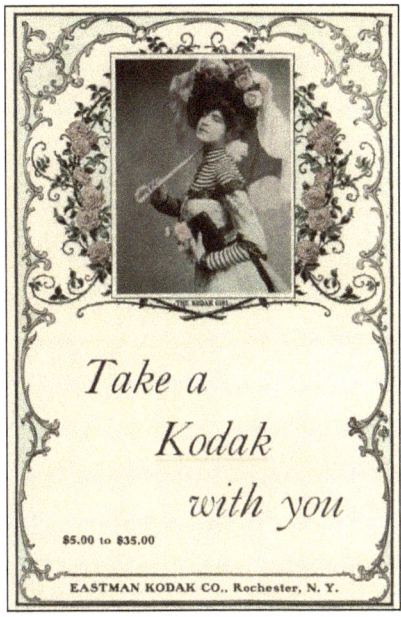

Figure 7.12 | *Left:* Kodak, "Take a Kodak with You," 1901. Photograph is color tinted. From Emergence of Advertising in America - Database # K0018, *Ellis Collection of Kodakiana*, a project of the Digital Scriptorium and John W. Hartman Center for Sales, Advertising & Marketing History. Rare Book, Manuscript, and Special Collections Library, Duke University.

Figure 7.13 | *Right:* Detail by author.

raphy held by figures such as Frances Benjamin Johnston (1864–1952), amateur photography offered women creative outlets that were considered by many to be especially appropriate for domestic spheres. Advice to these women, given by women, appeared in journals such as *The Photo-American Series*. Women also were targeted as "Kodak girls" holding flowers (performing femininity) and cameras, in magazines such as *Harper's* (Figures 7.12 and 7.13).

Articles such as "Amateur Photography through Women's Eyes" (1894) by Elizabeth Flint Wade, and the column "Our Women Friends" (1892–1897), edited by Adelaide Skeel, provide additional access to these often overlooked voices.[138] As Gover explains, Skeel's column featured a monthly section for questions and letters to the editor that generally reflected "the world of women and photography...and their struggle to master the new art form."[139] But earlier advice from Skeel, within essays such as "Blues" (Figure 7.14), suggests a

Figure 7.14 | Adelaide Skeel, "Blues," 1888. In Canfield, ed., *Photography and Photographic Times: The American Annual of Photography*, 48, 50.

---

medium." Naomi Rosenblum, *A History of Women Photographers*, 3rd edition (New York: Abbeville Press, 2010), 7. Histories of photography still generally scant "paraphotographic" labor(ers) and their contribution to composite forms of nineteenth-century photography.

138   Elizabeth Flint Wade, "Amateur Photography through Women's Eyes," *The Photo-American Series* 15 (June, 1884): 235; Adelaide Skeel, ed., "Our Women Friends," *The Photo-American Series* (1892–97).

139   Jane C. Gover, *The Positive Image*, 67. See Gover, as well, for more on networks of women communicating through various photographic journals.

specific chromatic context germane to this new art form (and to metachromatics) that merits special attention.[140]

Skeel's playfully transgressive advice—likely addressed to women—to allow themselves to make and to distribute cyanotype prints of everyday life indicates a bold and perhaps feminist intervention. Her argument that these photographers should "pay no heed" to dominant proscriptions and authorities (most-often male) and to allow such things as "blue cows, blue trees, and blue faces" to distinguish their work from that of "real photographers" suggests an alternative and perhaps gendered tradition of photography in need of further investigation. Alternative/"minor" feminized channels of exhibition and commerce such as the "Bazaars" mentioned by Skeel also suggest valuable research to be done.

The unauthorized blue register of these "unreal photographers," much like the anonymous chromatic touches of "lady colorists," "lady retouchers," and the "events" of narrativity into which they can be drawn, deserve recognition. Skeel's cyanotypes, however, like the rest of her photographs, and the bulk of female vernacular photography during the nineteenth century, have not been institutionally archived.[141] This omission exists despite the opinion that the most notable person in the history of cyanotype, male or female, is Anna Atkins (1799-1871), commonly recognized as the first female photographer, suggesting perhaps a relatively overlooked chromatic tradition.[142]

Negative reactions to monochromatic colored photography, such as Henry Peter Emerson's, "No one but a real vandal would print a landscape in red, or in cyanotype" (1890, a year after "Blues"),[143] recall now-familiar debates over impressionist and post-impressionist painting and color science during this era, in which images by Skeel and other women (such as Johnston, who also often worked in blue) might be situated. Such intersections promote the consideration of these and other "low forms" of popular "blues" and "reds," and the "amateurs" who made them, within discussions of emergent modernism across media and popular culture, including verbal imagery. These also should be factored into the broader tradition of color as a term of alterity to (black-and-white) line/form.

MetaConclusion

As we have seen, the discursive workings of color – line/form bear significantly on representation, its interpretation and uses, and the stories that shape and are shaped by its processes. The ideological contexts and zones of "contact"

---

140 Adelaide Skeel, "Blues," in *Photography and Photographic Times: The American Annual of Photography*, ed. C. W. Canfield (New York: Scovill Manufacturing Company, 1888), 48, 50.

141 *The Photographic Album Collection*, assembled by collector Barbara Levine at the International Center of Photography, New York, is beginning to redress this deficiency. This collection of vernacular photograph albums, dating from 1887–1938, is considered by ICP to be "the most comprehensive collection of photograph albums in the country." Barbara Levine, collector and assembler, *Photographic Album Collection* (International Center of Photography, New York, 2012).

142 Atkins was among the first to put cyanotype into practice. See Anna Atkins, *Photographs of British Algae: Cyanotype Impressions* (London: 1843–53). See also Ware for a history of the medium. Mike Ware, *Cyanotype: The History, Science and Art of Photographic Printing in Prussian Blue* (London: Science Museum, 1999).

143 Peter Henry Emerson, *Naturalistic Photography for Students of the Art*, 2nd revised edition (London: Sampson Low, Marston, Searle & Rivington, 1890), 196.

into which this binary so frequently has been drawn also suggest these workings' continued relevance to aesthetics as the very terrain of politics in the sense described by Rancière.[144] A (meta-)picture by Johnston, which suggests this terrain again here, concludes this chapter (Figure 7.15). Its female subjects, line/form, and Prussian blue, await metachromatic attention.

Figure 7.15 | Frances Benjamin Johnston, *[Female students posing with exercise equipment in a gymnasium, Western High School, Washington, D.C.]*, c. 1899. Cyanotype. Courtesy of Library of Congress: *Frances Benjamin Johnston Collection*.

Bibliography

Abel, Richard. *French Film Theory and Criticism: 1907–1939*. Princeton, NJ: Princeton University Press, 1988.

Adorno, Theodor W. *Aesthetic Theory*. Translated by Robert Hullot-Kentor. New York: Continuum International, [1970] 1997.

———. *Minima Moralia: Reflections from Damaged Life*. Translated by E. F. N. Jephcott. London; New York: Verso, 1978.

Alber, Jan, and Monika Fludernik, eds. *Postclassical Narratology: Approaches and Analyses*.

Theory and Interpretation of Narrative. Columbus: Ohio State University Press, 2010. Albers, Josef. *Interaction of Color*. New Haven: Yale University Press, [1920] 2006.

---

144 Jacques Rancière, *The Politics of Aesthetics* (London: Continuum, 2009).

Allen, Robert C. *Vaudeville and Film: 1895–1915*. New York: Arno Press, 1980.

Ankersmit, Frank. "Micro-storie." In Herman et al. 2005, 308–309.

Archer, Dawn, and Peter Grundy, eds. *The Pragmatics Reader*. New York: Routledge, 2011. Aristotle. *Poetics*. Translated by Ingram Bywater. Digireads. com Publishing, [350 BCE] 2005. Armstrong, Carol. "All-Time Favorites." *Art Forum* (Summer, 2011): 87–90.

Atkins, Anna. *Photographs of British Algae: Cyanotype Impressions*. London, 1843–53. Aumont, Jacques. *La couleur en cinéma*. Paris: Cinémathèque française, 1995.

Aumont, Jacques, Alain Bergala, Michel Marie, and Marc Vernet. *Aesthetics of Film*. Translated by Richard Neupert. Austin: University of Texas Press, 1992.

Bal, Mieke. *Narratology: Introduction to the Theory of Narrative*. 2nd ed. Toronto: University of Toronto Press, 1997.

Ball, Philip. *Bright Earth: Art and the Invention of Color*. Chicago: University of Chicago Press, 2003.

Barthes, Roland. *Image, Music, Text*. Translated by Stephen Heath. New York: Hill and Wang, 1977.

———. "Introduction to the Structural Analysis of Narratives." In Barthes, *Image*, [1966] 1977, 79–124.

———. "Rhetoric of the Image." In Barthes, *Image*, [1964] 1977, 32–51.

———. "The Third Meaning." In Barthes, *Image*, [1970] 1977, 52–68.

Batchelor, David. *Chromophobia*. Focus on Contemporary Issues. London: Reaktion, 2000.

———, ed. *Colour*. Documents of Contemporary Art. Cambridge, MA: MIT Press, 2008. Baudelaire, Charles. "The Life and Work of Eugène Delacroix." In *The Painter of Modern Life and Other Essays*. Translated and edited by Jonathan Mayne, 41–68. London: Phaidon Press, [1863] 1964.

Baudrillard, Jean. *The System of Objects*. Translated by James Benedict. London: Verso, [1968] 2005.

Bell, Clive. "The Aesthetic Hypothesis." In *Twentieth Century Theories of Art*, edited by James Matheson Thompson, 79–93. Montreal: McGill-Queen's University Press, [1914] 1990.

Benjamin, Walter. "A Child's View of Colour." Translated by Rodney Livingstone. In *Walter Benjamin: Selected Writings. Volume 1: 1913–1926*, edited by Marcus Bullock and Michael W. Jennings, 50–51. Cambridge, MA: Belknap Press, [1914–15] 1996.

Berriatúa, Luciano, ed. *All the Colours of the World: Colours in Early Mass Media: 1900–1930*. Reggio Emilia, Italy: Diabasis, 1998.

Besant, Annie. *Thought-Forms*. Wheaton, IL: Theosophical Publishing House, [1901] 1971. Blair, G. A. "The Tinting of Motion Picture Film." *Transactions of the Society of Motion Picture Engineers* 10 (1920): 45.

Blanc, Charles. *The Grammar of Painting and Engraving*. Translated by Kate Newell Doggett. New York: Hurd and Houghton, 1874. Bremond, Claude. *Logique du récit*. Paris: Seuil, 1973. Brewster, Ben. "Periodization of Early Cinema." In Keil, *American*, 66–75.

Campbell, Archibald. *Rainbow-Music; or, The Philosophy of Harmony in Colour-Grouping*. London: Bernard Quaritch, 1886.

Chatman, Seymour. *Story and Discourse: Narrative Structure in Fiction and Film*. Ithaca, Cornell University Press, 1978.

Chevreul, Michel Eugène. *The Principles of Harmony and Contrast of Colors and Their Applications to the Arts*. Translated by Charles Martel. New York: Reinhold, [1839] 1967.

Claviez, Thomas. "Done and Over With—Finally? Otherness, Metonymy, and the Ethics of Comparison." *PMLA* 128, no. 3 (May 2013): 608–14.

Collins, Kathleen. *Washingtoniana Photographs: Collections in the Prints and Photographs Division of the Library of Congress*. Washington: The Library of Congress, 1989.

"Cooper Union, The." *The Nation* (June 5, 1866).

Crane, Stephen (unsigned). "Travels in New York / The Broken-Down Van." *New York Tribune* (July 10, 1892). In *The New York City Sketches of Stephen Crane*, edited by R. W. Stallman and E. R. Hagemann, 3–14. New York: New York University Press, 1966.

Cronin, Richard. *Colour and Experience in Nineteenth-Century Poetry*. Houndmills, Basingstoke, Hampshire: Macmillan Press, 1988.

Dall'Asta, Monica and Guglielmo Pescatore, eds. *Il Colore nel Cinema*. Bologna: Editrice CLUEB, 1995.

Dalle Vacche, Angela, and Brian Pierce, eds. *Color: The Film Reader*. In focus-Routledge Film Readers. New York: Routledge, 2006.

Delpeut, Peter, contributor. "Moderated Discussion Session 1." In Hertogs et al., *Disorderly*, 11–25.

Deren, Maya. "Cinematography: The Creative Use of Reality." *Daedalus* 89, no. 1 (January 1, 1960): 150–67.

Derrida, Jacques. *The Truth in Painting*. Chicago: University of Chicago Press, 1987.

DuBois, Page. *History, Rhetorical Description and the Epic from Homer to Spenser*. Totowa, NJ: Biblio Distribution Services, 1982.

Duranti, Alessandro, and Charles Goodwin. *Rethinking Context: Language as an Interactive Phenomenon*. Cambridge, England: Cambridge University Press, 1992. Eagleton, Terry. *Ideology: An Introduction.* London; New York: Verso, 2007.

Edison, Thomas A. *Annabelle, [no. 1] / Annabelle Butterfly Dance / [Annabelle Butterfly Dance, no. 1].* 35 mm, black and white, some prints featuring hand coloration, 50 ft. Produced by W. K. L. Dickson, camera by William Heise. 1894.

———. *Great Train Robbery, The.* 35 mm, black and white with hand coloration, 11 min. Directed by Edwin Porter. 1903. In *The Movies Begin: A Treasury of Early Cinema, 1894–1913.* Volume 1. Film Preservation Associates and The British Film Institute. Produced for video by David Shepard. New York: Kino International, 2002.

———. *Sandow / Eugen Sandow / Sandow, no. 1.* 35 mm, black and white, 50 ft. Produced by W. K. L. Dickson, camera by William Heise. 1894.

———. *Serpentine Dance—Annabelle / Serpentine Dance / [Annabelle Serpentine Dance, no. 4].* 35 mm, black and white with hand coloration, 50 ft. Produced by James White, camera by William Heise. 1897. In *Unseen Cinema 7, Viva la Dance: The Beginnings of Ciné-Dance.* Curated by Bruce Posner, produced for DVD by David Shepard, administered by Robert A. Haller and Winfried Günther, and distributed by Image Entertainment. New York: Anthology Film Archives, 2005.

Eisenstein, Sergei. "The Montage of Attractions." In *The Film Factory,* edited by Richard Taylor and Ian Christie, 87–88. Cambridge, MA: Harvard University Press, [1923] 1988.

———. "The Montage of Film Attractions." In *Selected Works. Volume I. Writings, 1922–34,* edited and translated by Richard Taylor, 39–58. London: British Film Institute, [1924] 1996.

Elkins, James, ed. *Photography Theory.* New York; London: Routledge, 2007.

Ellis, Havelock. *Colour-Sense in Literature, The.* London: The Ulysses Book Shop, [1896] 1931.

———. "Psychology of Red, The." *Popular Science Monthly* 57 (September, 1900): 517–26.

———. "Psychology of Yellow, The." *Popular Science Monthly* 68 (May, 1906): 456–63. Emerson, Peter Henry. *Naturalistic Photography for Students of the Art.* 2nd revised ed. London: Sampson Low, Marston, Searle & Rivington, 1890.

"Employment Offered and Wanted." *The Photographic Times and American Photographer Journal* 14, no. 158 (New Series 38) (February, 1884): 108. Edited by J. Traill Taylor.

Everett, Wendy E., ed. *Questions of Colour in Cinema: From Paintbrush to Pixel.* Oxford: Peter Lang, 2007.

Fawcett, Trevor. "Graphic versus Photographic in the Nineteenth-Century Reproduction." *Art History* 9, no. 2 (June, 1986): 185–212.

Feeser, Andrea, Maureen Daly Goggin, and Beth Fowkes Tobin, eds. *The Materiality of Color: The Production, Circulation, and Application of Dyes and Pigments, 1400–1800*. Burlington: Ashgate, 2012.

Fossati, Giovanna, moderator. "Moderated Discussion Session 1." In Hertogs et al., *Disorderly*, 11–25.

———. "When Cinema Was Coloured." In Berriatúa, *All the Colours*, 121–32.

Frank, Joseph. "Spatial Form in Modern Literature." In *The Idea of Spatial Form*. New Brunswick: Rutgers University Press, [1945] 1991.

Fry, Roger. "An Essay in Aesthetics." In Batchelor, *Colour*, 2008, 54–55.

Gage, John. *Color and Meaning: Art, Science, and Symbolism*. Berkeley and Los Angeles: University of California Press, 1999.

Gaskill, Nicholas. "Red Cars with Red Lights and Red Drivers: Color, Crane, and Qualia." *American Literature* 81, no. 4 (December, 2009): 719–45.

Gaudreault, André. *Film and Attraction: From Kinematography to Cinema*. Urbana: University of Illinois Press, 2011.

Gaudreault, André, and Marion Philippe. "A Medium is Always Born Twice." *Early Popular Visual Culture* 3, no. 1 (2005): 3–15.

Genette, Gérard. "Frontiers of Narrative." In *Figures of Literary Discourse*, edited by Marie-Rose Logan, and translated by Alan Sheridan, 127–46. European Perspectives. New York: Columbia University Press, [1966] 1982.

Goethe, Johann Wolfgang von. *Theory of Colours*. Translated by Charles Lock Eastlake. Cambridge, MA: MIT Press, [1810] 1970.

Gover, C. Jane. *The Positive Image: Women Photographers in Turn of the Century America*. SUNY Series in the New Cultural History. Albany: State University of New York Press, 1987.

Greimas, A. J. *On Meaning: Selected Writings in Semiotic Theory*. Theory and History of Literature 38. Minneapolis: University of Minnesota Press, 1987.

———. *Structural Semantics: An Attempt at a Method*. Translated by Danielle McDowell, Ronald Schleifer, and Alan Velie. Lincoln: University of Nebraska, [1966] 1983.

Gunning, Tom. "Aesthetic of Astonishment, An: Early Film and the (In)credulous Spectator." *Art and Text* 34 (1989): 31–45.

———. "Cinema of Attraction, The: Early Film, its Spectator, and the Avant-Garde." *Wide Angle* 8, nos. 3–4 (1986): 1–14. Revised in *Early Cinema: Space Frame Narrative*, edited by Thomas Elsaesser, 56–62. London: British Film Institute, 1990. Citations refer to the BFI edition.

———. "Colorful Metaphors: The Attraction of Color in Early Silent Cinema." In Dall'Asta et al., *Il Colore*, 249–55.

———. "'Now You See It, Now You Don't': The Temporality of the Cinema of Attractions." In *The Silent Cinema Reader*, edited by Lee Grieveson, 41–50. London; New York: Routledge, [1993] 2004.

Hagstrum, Jean H. *The Sister Arts: The Tradition of Literary Pictorialism and English Poetry from Dryden to Gray.* Chicago: University of Chicago Press, 1958.

Halliburton, David. *The Color of the Sky: A Study of Stephen Crane.* Cambridge Studies in American Literature and Culture. Cambridge, England: Cambridge University Press, 1989.

Hanssen, Eirik Frisvold. *Early Discourses on Colour and Cinema: Origins, Functions, Meanings.* Stockholm Cinema Studies 2. Stockholm: Almqvist & Wiksell International, 2006.

Heffernan, James A. W. *Museum of Words: The Poetics of Ekphrasis from Homer to Ashbery.* Chicago: University of Chicago Press, 1993.

Heidegger, Martin. *Being and Time.* SUNY Series in Contemporary Continental Philosophy. Albany: State University of New York Press, [1927] 2010.

Helmholtz, Hermann von. "On the Relation of Optics to Painting." In *Popular Lectures on Scientific Subjects*, translated by Edmund Atkinson, 73–138. New York: Appleton, 1881.

Henisch, Heinz K. and Bridget Ann Henisch. *The Painted Photograph, 1839–1914: Origins, Techniques, Aspirations.* University Park, PA: Pennsylvania State University Press, 1996.

Herman, David. *Narratologies: New Perspectives on Narrative Analysis.* Theory and Interpretation of Narrative Series. Columbus: Ohio State University Press, 1999.

Herman, David, Manfred Jahn, and Marie-Laure Ryan, eds. *Routledge Encyclopedia of Narrative Theory.* London; New York: Routledge, 2005.

Hertogs, Daan, and Nico De Klerk, eds. *Disorderly Order: Colours in Silent Film.* Amsterdam: Stichting Nederlands Filmmuseum, 1996.

Hollander, John. *The Gazer's Spirit: Poems Speaking to Silent Works of Art.* Chicago: University of Chicago Press, 1995.

Hopper, Paul. "Aspect and Foregrounding in Discourse." *Syntax and Semantics* 12 (1979): 213–41.

Hough, Robert L. "Crane and Goethe: A Forgotten Relationship." *Nineteenth-Century Fiction* 17 (September, 1962): 135–48.

Jeanneret, C. E. (Le Corbusier), and Amédée Ozenfant. "Purism." In *Modern Artists on Art: Ten Unabridged Essays*, edited and translated by Robert L. Herbert, 70–72. Englewood Cliffs, NJ: Prentice-Hall, [1920] 1965.

Johnston, Frances Benjamin. *[Female students posing with exercise equipment in a Gymnasium, Western High School, Washington, D.C.].* [c. 1899]. Cyanotype. Courtesy of Library of Congress: *Frances Benjamin Johnston Collection.*

Kalmus, N. "Color Consciousness." *Journal of the Society of Motion Picture Engineers* 35, no. 2 (1935): 139–47.

Keil, Charlie. *American Cinema's Transitional Era: Audiences, Institutions, Practices.* Berkeley: University of California Press, 2004.

Klein, Yves. "The Evolution of Art towards the Immaterial." In Batchelor, *Colour*, 2008, 120–22.

Kodak. "Take a Kodak with You." In *Emergence of Advertising in America* - Database # K0018, *Ellis Collection of Kodakiana*, a project of the Digital Scriptorium and John W. Hartman Center for Sales, Advertising & Marketing History. Rare Book, Manuscript, and Special Collections Library, Duke University, 1901.

Koszarski, Richard, ed. Special topic issue: "Color Film." *Film History* 12, no. 4 (2000): 339–463.

———, ed. Special topic issue: "Early Colour." *Film History* 20, nos. 1–2 (2009): 1–183. Kracauer, Siegfried. *Theory of Film.* Oxford: Oxford University Press, 1960.

Krieger, Murray *Ekphrasis: The Illusion of the Natural Sign.* Baltimore: Johns Hopkins, 1992.

Kristeva, Julia. "Giotto's Joy." In *Desire in Language*, translated by Thomas Gora, Alice Jardine, and Leon S. Roudiez, 210–36. New York: Columbia University Press, [1972] 1980.

Lange, Eric and Serge Bromberg, eds. *Discovering Cinema.* DVD. Los Angeles: Flicker Alley, 2007.

Lessing, Gotthold Ephraim. *Laocoön: An Essay on the Limits of Painting and Poetry.* Translated by Edward Allen McCormick. Baltimore: Johns Hopkins University Press, [1766] 1984.

Levine, Barbara, collector and assembler. *Photographic Album Collection.* International Center of Photography, New York, 2012.

Levinson, Marjorie. "What is New Formalism?" *PMLA* 122, no. 2 (2007): 558–569.

Leyda, Jay. *Kino: A History of the Russian and Soviet Film.* London: Allen & Unwin, 1960. Lukács, Georg. "Narrate or Describe?" In *Writer and Critic and Other Essays*, edited and translated by Arthur Kahn, 110–48. London: Merlin, [1936] 1970.

Lumière, Louis. *Card Party.* 35 mm, black and white with hand coloration, 50 ft. 1895. In Lange and Bromberg, *Discovering Cinema.*

Machado, Robert. "The Politics of Applied Color in Early Photography." *Nineteenth-Century Art Worldwide* 9, no. 1 (2010).

McKernan, L., ed. Special topic issue: "Color." *Living Pictures. The Journal of the Popular and Projected Image before 1914* 2, no. 2 (2003).

Melville, Stephen. "Color Has Not Yet Been Named: Objectivity in Deconstruction." *Deconstruction and the Visual Arts: Art, Media, Architecture*, edited by Peter Brunette and David Wills, 33–48. Cambridge; New York: Cambridge University Press, 1994.

Mey, Jacob L. "Pragmatics." In Herman et al., *Routledge Encyclopedia*, 462–67.

Mirzoeff, Nicholas. *An Introduction to Visual Culture.* London; New York: Routledge, 1999. Misek, Richard. *Chromatic Cinema: A History of Screen Color.* Chichester, UK; Malden, MA: Wiley-Blackwell, 2010.

Mitchell, W. J. T. *Iconology: Image, Text, Ideology.* Chicago: University of Chicago Press, 1986.

———. *What Do Pictures Want?: The Lives and Loves of Images.* Chicago: University of Chicago Press, 2005.

Musser, Charles. *The Emergence of Cinema: The American Screen to 1907.* History of the American Cinema. New York: Scribner, 1990.

———. "Rethinking Early Cinema: Cinema of Attractions and Narrativity." *The Yale Journal of Criticism* 7, no. 2 (1994): 203–32.

Needham, C. A. "Picturesque Photography." *The Photographic Times and American Photographer Journal* 14, no. 158 (New Series 38) (February, 1884): 82–83.

Newhall, Beaumont. *The Daguerreotype in America.* 3rd revised ed. New York: Dover, 1961. Nisard, Désiré. *Études de moeurs et de critique sur les poëtes Latins de la décadence.* Paris: Gosselin, 1834.

Nünning, Ansgar. "Towards a Typology, Poetics and History of Description in Fiction." In Wolf and Bernhart, *Description*, 91–125.

Pastoureau, Michel. *Black: The History of a Color.* Princeton, NJ: Princeton University Press, 2009.

Patalas, Enno, contributor. "Moderated Discussion Session 1." In Hertogs et al., *Disorderly*, 11–25.

Pater, Walter. *The Renaissance: Studies in Art and Poetry.* London: Macmillan, 1888.

Pathé coloring lab, Paris. In Talbot, *Moving Pictures*, 289.

Poirier, Maurice George. *Studies on the Concepts of "Disegno," "Invenzione," and "Colore" in Sixteenth- and Seventeenth-Century Italian Art and Theory.* PhD Diss. New York University, New York, 1976.

Pratt, Mary Louise. *Imperial Eyes: Travel Writing and Transculturation.* Hoboken: Taylor & Francis, 2007.

Prince, Gerald. *Dictionary of Narratology, A*. Lincoln: University of Nebraska Press, 1987.

———. *Grammar of Stories, A: An Introduction*. The Hague: Mouton, 1973.

Quaresima, Leonardo. *The Tenth Muse: DOMITOR Conference, VII International Film Studies Conference: Proceedings*. Udine: Dipartimento di storia e tutela dei beni culturali, Università degli studi di Udine, 2001.

Rancière, Jacques. *The Politics of Aesthetics*. London: Continuum, 2009.

Rayne, Martha Louise. *What Can a Woman Do; or, Her Position in the Business and Literary World*. Petersburgh, NY: Eagle, 1893.

Riffaterre, Michael. "On the Diegetic Functions of the Descriptive." *Style* 20, no. 3 (1986): 281–94.

Rimbaud, Arthur. *A Season in Hell*. Translated by Delmore Schwartz. Norfolk, CT: New Directions, [1873] 1940.

Rive del Nilo. Kinemacolor. 1911. Courtesy of Cineteca del Comune di Bologna, Archivo cinematografico Ansaldo, National Film and Television Archive, and Europafilmtreasures.eu.

Rodchenko, Aleksandr. "Extract from Notes for a Lecture Given at Inkhuk (Institute of Artistic Culture)." In *Rodchenko*, edited by David Elliott. Oxford: Museum of Modern Art, [1921] 1979.

Ronen, Ruth. "Description, Narrative and Representation." *Narrative* 5, no. 3 (October, 1997): 274–86.

Rood, Ogden. *Modern Chromatics*. New York: Van Nostrand Reinhold, [1879] 1973.

Root, M. A. *The Camera and the Pencil; or, The Heliographic Art*. New York: Appleton, 1864.

Rosenblum, Naomi. *A History of Women Photographers*. 3rd ed. New York: Abbeville Press, 2010.

Røssaak, Eivind. "Figures of Sensation: Between Still and Moving Images." In Strauven, *The Cinema*, 321–36.

Ryan, Marie-Laure. "On the Theoretical Foundations of Transmedial Narratology." In *Narratology Beyond Literary Criticism: Mediality, Disciplinarity*, edited by Jan Christoph Meister, Tom Kindt, and Wilhelm Schernus, 1–23. Narratologia: Contributions to Narrative Theory 6. Berlin; New York: Walter de Gruyter, 2005.

Skeel, Adelaide. "Blues." In *Photography and Photographic Times: The American Annual of Photography*, edited by C. W. Canfield, 48–50. New York: Scovill Manufacturing Company, 1888.

———, ed. "Our Women Friends." *The Photo-American Series*, 1892–97.

Snelling, Henry Hunt. *The History and Practice of the Art of Photography; or, The Production of Pictures, Through the Agency of Light. Containing All the Instructions Necessary for the Complete Practice of the Daguerrean and Photogenic Art, both on Metallic Plates and on Paper*. 4th ed. New York: G. P. Putnam, [1849] 1953.

Società Italiana Cines. *Farfale* ("*Butterflys*" [*sic*]). 35 mm, black and white with hand coloration, 50 ft. 1907. In Lange and Bromberg, *Discovering Cinema*.

Steiner, Wendy. *The Colors of Rhetoric: Problems in the Relation between Modern Literature and Painting*. Chicago: University of Chicago Press, 1982.

Strauven, Wanda, ed. *The Cinema of Attractions Reloaded*. Film Culture in Transition. Amsterdam: Amsterdam University Press, 2006.

Sutter, David. "The Phenomena of Vision." *L'art* 6, no. 1 (February–March 1880).

Talbot, Frederick Arthur Ambrose. *Moving Pictures*. The Literature of Cinema. New York: Arno Press, [1912] 1970.

Talbot, William Henry Fox. *The Pencil of Nature*. Reprinted by Da Capo Press New York, [1844–6] 1968.

Thomas, Julia. *Victorian Narrative Painting*. London: Tate, 2000.

[Three unidentified women in mourning dress reading a letter]. [c. 1865]. Tintype. 3 x 2 3/8 in. Hand coloration, anonymous. From the International Center of Photography, America and the Tintype (September 19, 2008–January 14, 2009). Gift of Steven Kasher, 2007.

Todorov, Tzvetan. "La grammaire du récit." *Languages* 12 (1968): 94–102.

Uricchio, William. "Color and Dramatic Articulation in *The Lonedale Operator*." In Dall'Asta et al., *Il Colore*, 268–72.

Usai, Paolo Cherchi. *Silent Cinema: An Introduction*. London: British Film Institute, 2000. Vasari, Giorgio. *Lives of the Artists*. Translated by George Bull. Harmondsworth: Penguin, [1568] 1965.

Wade, Elizabeth Flint. "Amateur Photography through Women's Eyes." *The Photo-American Series* 15 (June, 1884): 235.

"Wages of Girls Who Color Slides, The." *Moving Picture World* 4, no. 25 (June, 1909): 830–31. Ware, Mike. *Cyanotype: The History, Science and Art of Photographic Printing in Prussian Blue*. London: Science Museum, 1999.

Webb, Ruth. "Ekphrasis Ancient and Modern: The Invention of a Genre." *Word & Image* 15, no. 1 (1999): 5–33.

Wells, H. G. "Stephen Crane, from an English Standpoint." *North American Monthly Review* 171 (August, 1900): 233–42.

Williams, Raymond. *Marxism and Literature*. Oxford: Oxford University Press, 1977.

Wolf, Werner. "Description as a Transmedial Mode of Representing: General Features and Possibilities of Realization in Painting, Fiction and Music." In Wolf and Bernhart, *Description*, 1–90.

———. "Narratology and Media(lity): The Transmedial Expansion of a Literary Discipline and Possible Consequences." In *Current Trends in Narratology*, edited by Greta Olson, 145–80. Narratologia: Contributions to Narrative Theory 27. Berlin; New York: De Gruyter, 2011.

———. "Pictorial Narrativity." In Herman et al., *Routledge Encyclopedia*, 431–35.

Wolf, Werner, and Walter Bernhart, eds. *Description in Literature and Other Media*. Studies in Intermediality. Amsterdam: Rodopi, 2007.

Woodall, Joanna. *Portraiture: Facing the Subject*. Critical Introductions to Art. Manchester, England; New York: Manchester University Press, distributed in the US by St. Martin's Press, 1997.

Yumibe, Joshua. *Moving Color: Early film, Mass Culture, Modernism*. New Brunswick: Rutgers University Press, 2012.

———. "Silent Cinema Colour Aesthetics." In Everett, *Questions of Colour*, 41–56.

8

Jean-Léon Gérôme and the Color of Flesh

Pamela J. Sachant

ars adeo latet arte sua
So does his art conceal his art.[1]

The French academic painter Jean-Léon Gérôme (1824-1904) is well known for his Orientalist subjects, many of which featured languorous and voluptuous women in exotic and mysterious locales. He is equally known for his scenes of classical antiquity in which figures and settings are depicted in exquisite detail. Gérôme rendered these fantastically idealized paintings with such historical and visual accuracy that the line between the imaginary and the real can be difficult to discern, giving viewers during his lifetime a means to suspend Victorian sensibilities and more fully enter into the sybaritic experience he offered to them.

Gérôme's ability to depict the color of flesh through illusion was often noted by critics as key to the success of his paintings of nude women. It is ironic, therefore, that his equally masterful representations of women in painted (polychrome) sculpture were decried by some as too realistic.

This study explores the role and significance of women's flesh tones in two works by Gérôme that exist in both sculpted and painted form, *Pygmalion and Galatea* and *The Ball Player*, within the cultural context of critical and popular responses to his life-like work. While highly representational images were both expected and prized in the official art world of nineteenth-century France, there were largely unspoken but culturally understood norms and boundaries within which illusionism was to function. Specifically in the realm of polychrome sculpture, responses ranged from that of art historian and critic Charles Blanc, who argued that white marble raised sculpture above the vagaries of the real, to poet Jules Laforgue, who claimed that color united with form transcended the merely decorative.[2] Gérôme's work was both the epitome of the aesthetic ideals of the

---
1   Ovid, "Pygmalion," *Metamorphoses*, trans. Frank Justus Miller (New York: G. P. Putnam's Sons, 1926), vol. II, 82.
2   Charles Blanc was of tremendous influence in both his teachings and writings. He was named first editor of

time and a transgression of social standards that equated the illusionism he sought with lesser or debased art forms. Gérôme's use of color is key to understanding the expectations and limitations the artist worked within and consciously flaunted.

In and around 1890, Gérôme painted at least four versions of *Pygmalion and Galatea* (Figure 1).[3] Each painting captures the moment when Galatea comes to life, awakened from her stony sleep by Pygmalion's kiss. Each is set in Pygmalion's studio, surrounded by his tools and equipment and in the midst of other sculptures, paintings, and studio props. The number and subjects of the background sculptures and paintings vary, but, of greater significance, the moment from Ovid's narrative that is depicted in all of the works is essentially the same: the coming to life of the ivory virgin. In addition, the viewer's orientation to the sculptor and his creation is different in each painting; the viewer circles around the central duo, creating a distinctive viewing point in each. In the version under discussion here, painted in 1890, Galatea is seen from behind as she leans down and to her right in order to kiss Pygmalion; in other versions she faces the viewer or presents her left side, with Pygmalion to the left of the composition.

In 1891 Gérôme began a marble version of *Pygmalion and Galatea* (Figure 2), with the sculpted figures based upon those in his paintings.[4] At the time of its exhibition in the Salon of 1892, the life-size marble sculpture was polychromed. The only indication today of the original colors is some green in the folds of Pygmalion's drapery, brown on the sculpting stand, and "slight flesh colouring" on Galatea.[5] The existing hues do indicate, however, that Gérôme followed a similar color scheme in both sculpture and painting. Although there are some differences between the figures in the two, for example, the placement of both Pygmalion and Galatea's arms around her torso, the angle at which she leans to her right, and the fall of Pygmalion's drapery, the overall compositions relate to one another closely.[6] This correspondence between his two- and three-dimensional work and the polychroming of his sculptures can be seen in other of Gérôme's later works including the second pair under discussion here, the sculpture of *The Ball Player* (Figure 3) and the painting *Self-Portrait Painting 'The Ball Player'* (Figure 4).

As he had with *Pygmalion and Galatea*, Gérôme created a full-size preparatory plaster in advance of the life-size tinted marble, which was exhibited at the Salon of 1902. Unlike *Pygmalion and Galatea* and more in keeping with his normal working practices, however, *The Ball Player* exists in several sizes ranging from

---

the *Gazette des Beaux-Arts* in 1859, and published *Grammaire des arts du dessin architecture, sculpture, peinture*, an examination of nineteenth-century color theories in relation to aesthetics that would impact Post-Impressionist artists such as Georges Seurat, in 1867. Jules Laforgue was a champion of the Impressionists.

3   Gerald Ackerman stated that Gérôme "painted a series of pictures of the group... [a]t least three of the pictures are finished paintings, as far as I can see from old photographs." *The Life and Work of Jean-Léon Gérôme* (New York: Harper and Row, 1968), 268.

4   In a letter written to Fanny Field Hering in the winter of 1890-1891, Gérôme stated, "Among my pictures are a large *View of Cairo*, the *Pygmalion and Galatea* (which I intend shortly to put into *marble*), and some lions." Fanny Field Hering, *Gérôme, his life and works* (New York, 1892), 286.

5   Ackerman, *The Life and Work of Jean-Léon Gérôme*, 140.

6   In the paintings Pygmalion stands upon a box, absent in the sculpture, necessitating a reduction in the height of the sculpting stand upon which Galatea is placed and alterations to the pair's relative proportions.

7.5 to 65 inches, and in different media, including ivory, bronze, and marble.[7] The figure holds two balls in her extended right hand with a third in the left hand clasped at the small of her back. As she twists her body to look over her left shoulder at a trio of theatrical masks surrounding her entwined feet, she is preparing to drop a ball into the gaping mouth of a second mask. *Self-Portrait Painting 'The Ball Player'* was begun circa 1902 as well, but was found unfinished in Gérôme's studio at the time of his death two years later, just before his eightieth birthday. It depicts the artist, palette in hand, applying paint to the sculpture. Light comes in the room from the window visible at the left, bathing the anterior of the figure and reflecting off the varnished surfaces of some of the paintings grouped on the wall to the right.

Originating in the ancient world, the practice of polychroming sculpture was a subject of much discussion in the nineteenth century.[8] Proponents of the practice looked to classical Greece and the work of sculptors such as Phidias and Praxiteles, largely known through writings and Roman reproductions, for both legitimacy of and inspiration for their own efforts. Those who objected cited the example of Michelangelo and other Renaissance masters who abandoned the practice of polychroming sculpture, which had continued through the Middle Ages. The debate largely centered on the suitability of color, with its appeal to the senses, in the service of an art form believed best suited to intellectual appreciation. In the middle of the century, the dual strains of realism and aestheticism were united in the work of Charles Cordier, for example, through his use of *polychromie naturelle*, the joining of differently colored marbles in one work. Cordier combined various types of stone found in the French colony of Algeria to create genre portraits of the inhabitants of that region, calling them a "study of race, widening the circle of beauty."[9] Of equal interest, and also possessing ties to the art of the ancient world was *polychromie artificielle*, the combination of marble with other materials ranging from gems to metals. Although both types of polychrome were practiced throughout the 1800s, the potential of *polychromie artificielle* was boldly explored mid-century as well in a work by Pierre-Charles Simart exhibited at the 1855 Universal Exhibition in Paris. Positive critical response to Simart's *Athena*, which—at a height of nearly ten feet and composed of colored and natural ivory, silver, and gilded bronze—was an obvious reference to Phidias's Parthenon Athena, encouraged the continuing exploration and practice of both *polychromie naturelle* and *polychromie artificielle*.

A key element in critical commentary on the polychrome sculpture by both Cordier and Simart was the blending of the scientific and the artistic. When Cordier first exhibited his portraits in the 1848 Salon, he used the sitters' names; when they were again shown, at the 1851 Great Exhibition in London, they were

---

7   Édouard Papet, "'Father Polychrome': The Sculpture of Jean-Léon Gérôme," in *The Spectacular Art of Jean-Léon Gérôme*, ed. Laurence des Cars et al. (Skira: Milan and New York: 2010), 322-325.

8   For a detailed history and analysis, see Andreas Blühm, "In Living Colour: A Short History of Colour and Sculpture in the Nineteenth Century," in *The Colour of Sculpture*, ed. Andreas Blühm (Amsterdam: Van Gogh Museum, 1996), 11-60.

9   Antoinette Le Normand Romain and Jean-Luc Olivié, "La polychromie," in *La Sculpture Française au XIXe Siècle* (Paris: Editions de la Réunion des Musées nationaux, 1986), 149, quoting from Cordier's *Memoires*.

anonymously identified by race. Additional busts were commissioned for the Muséum national d'histoire naturelle, further indicating the fluid distinction between such work as belonging to the realm of science or art, and the greater acceptance of Cordier's work when linked to interest in ethnographic studies of the day.[10] Categorization of Simart's work was questioned as well, with claims that it was, rather than a work of high art, simply a speculative reconstruction, lacking in the truth or power of the original.[11]

In 1864, Charles Blanc commented on modern polychromy in an article devoted to sculpture that was part of a series entitled "Grammaire des Arts du Dessin: Architecture, Sculpture, Peinture" in the *Gazette des Beaux-Arts*.[12] In the last section of the article, Blanc describes the appropriateness of the use of gold and ivory in ancient sculpture of deities, stating that the beauty of the materials prompted the best efforts of those who worked with them. The use of the same materials in contemporary sculpture, on the other hand, was to be condemned as the modern works lack "the noble meaning and the severe dignity" of the great art of antiquity.[13] In the preceding edition of the journal, in a review of Baron Marochetti's *The Queen of Peace*, Blanc stated that it was an example of that rare work when the use of various media was successful: "There is thus, perhaps, an exception to be made, in the use of polychromy, for figures of small dimensions which are intended as a decoration in a private space."[14] Marochetti's work, meant to represent and please an individual taste, was on the level of the sumptuous, ornamented idol of the ancient world. Like the idol, Blanc asserted, it was based on the refined and majestic images of deities, but lacked the universal, moral quality of monumental art.

Regardless of the disapproval of some critics, the practice of polychroming sculpture had become so prevalent in fin-de-siècle France that, in the *Gazette des Beaux-Arts* review of the Salon of 1892, a ten-page section in Edmond Pottier's lengthy article on the sculpture exhibition was devoted to the subject.[15] Pottier first provides a historical overview of the technique, describing its practice among the ancients, especially the Greeks and Romans, and its revival in the Middle Ages. He refers to archeological findings attesting to the brilliant coloration of Greek and Roman works, arguably offensive to modern eyes and sensibilities accustomed to seeing them in their present bleached state. That distaste, he states, along with the tradition of not tinting stone (a practice followed since the Renaissance), may predispose the modern viewer to consider the new trend in polychrome as an aberration in art.

Pottier then applauds the small group of sculptors trying "to break free from the imperious yoke of habit" and return to the ancient practice. Referring

---

10   Blühm, "In Living Colour," 35-36.

11   Ibid., 22, referring to Charles-Ernest Beulé, "La statuaire d'or et d'ivoire: le minerve de M. Simart," *Review des Deux Mondes* (1856).

12   Charles Blanc, "Livre Deuxième: Sculpture, V. La Sculpture a deux manières de représenter les objets: le bas-reliefs et la ronde-basse," *Gazette des Beaux-Arts* 17 (1864): 59-79. This and other articles were included in his 1867 book, *Grammaire des arts du dessin architecture, sculpture, peinture*.

13   Ibid., 79.

14   Blanc, *Gazette des Beaux-Arts* 16 (1864): 567.

15   Edmond Pottier, "La Polychrome," in "Les Salons de 1892: II, La Sculpture," *Gazette des Beaux-Arts* 8 (1892): 5-44.

to the first polychrome Gérôme exhibited, *Tanagra*, which appeared in the Salon of 1890, Pottier describes the artist as both a "forerunner" in the use of polychromy and the group's leader. That work, Pottier states, "marks a date in a new era of contemporary sculpture" that will be looked upon with respect by artists of the twentieth century.[16] June Hargrove speculates that in referencing the painted figurines that were discovered in 1873 at the town of Tanagra, Gérôme may have sought the legitimacy provided by the ancient Greek practice of polychrome.[17] Doing so, he would bridge the gap seen by Blanc and other critics between the monumental and the decorative, which was in part based upon the pure white of ancient Greek marbles that had lost their original paint over time. Again referring to the 1890 work, *Tanagra*, Pottier states that Gérôme is original in that he is inspired by but does not copy the polychroming of the ancients, instead adapting their techniques to modern tastes and giving his works a delicacy of hue and "life that one does not forget."[18]

In critiquing Gérôme's offering to the Salon of 1892, *Pygmalion and Galatea*, Pottier attests triumphantly, "It is not possible to more ingeniously demonstrate that highly subtle polychromy is capable of giving the illusion of life."[19] Pottier holds up the work as a model of what is pleasing and appropriate in painted sculpture. But even Gérôme is not excluded from his criticism, for Pottier asserts that a chryselephantine work by the sculptor also in the 1892 Salon, *Bellona*, is "strange and audacious," and regrets that he could not have come up with a more simple and elegant solution for the composition.[20]

Pottier's contrasting responses to Gérôme's two works in the 1892 Salon, *Pygmalion and Galatea* with its use of tints to enliven marble, and *Bellona* with its combination of bronze, painted plaster, and glass, must be put in the context of discussions at the time on the appropriate use of materials in polychrome works. These discussions had their origins in the Renaissance *paragone* or comparison of painting, with its ability to represent the colors and forms of nature in illusionistic space, and to sculpture, with its ability to represent forms naturalistically in three-dimensional space. According to Blanc, the role of the artist, as it had been in the classical world, was to seek the ideal; in the case of sculpture, the ideal was found through the use of white marble, which was removed from the temporal and impermanent.[21] With the addition of color, the artist had abandoned the moral duty of art. Eugène Guillaume agreed that the artist should pursue ideal forms in sculpture, but stated that color was suitable if the subject was noble. He argued, however, that "[w]hen simple reality is incorporated, the work becomes insipid, even morbid."[22]

---

16   Ibid., 29.

17   June Hargrove, "Painter-sculptors and Polychromy in the Evolution of Modernism," in *The Colour of Sculpture*, 111-112.

18   Pottier, "La Polychrome," 30.

19   Ibid.

20   Pottier, "La Polychrome," 32.

21   Wolfgang Drost, "Colour, Sculpture, Mimesis: A 19th-Century Debate," in *The Colour of Sculpture*, 64, citing Blanc, *La sculpture*, (Paris, n.d.), 166, 170.

22   Drost, "Colour, Sculpture, Mimesis," 68, quoting Guillaume's review of the 1879 Salon.

Jules Laforgue, on the other hand, argued that polychrome "was successful and appropriate when colour was not merely applied to the form, but when both were conceived together."[23] Laforgue, who supported the work of Cordier as well as the Impressionist painters, represented a shift in thinking from questioning the applicability of color in relation to any sculpture to considering the appropriate use of materials within an individual work. This shift parallels changes in thinking about the use of color in painting that had been taking place over the course of the nineteenth century. The work of chemist Michel Eugène Chevreul on the optical qualities of color and mixtures of color led to his theory of simultaneous contrast. His explanations of the mutual influence of color and development of a 72-part color wheel to illustrate the visible spectrum of color and the relationship of one to another had tremendous influence on artists from the time of the publication of his findings in 1839.[24]

In addition to changes in the understanding of color sparked by Chevreul's findings, there were, as well, industrial innovations that transformed the way artists used paint: the invention of new pigments and the metal paint tube. These new pigments, with greater intensity and opacity, altered artists' working practices. The Impressionists used color as both a means of expression and an aid in defining form in their painting. While this was an area of contention in Impressionist work, their direct application of paint and palette based on the juxtaposition of color exerted changes in critical and popular reception of all artists' work, including sculpture.[25]

Although polychrome sculpture had gained wide acceptance by the turn of the century, or at least no longer served as the point of contention it had in much of the nineteenth century, Gérôme's use of color again received mixed reviews when he exhibited *The Ball Player* in the 1902 Salon. Henry Marcel compared entries by Denys Puech and Gérôme. Puech, according to Marcel, resolves the problem of polychrome, "in the manner of the ancient Greeks, by a combination of totally arbitrary tones ...without any worry of literally reproducing nature."[26] Gérôme instead imitates nature with the application of his color, in an attempt to give a sense of life to his figure. Marcel goes on to describe the effect produced in the artists' differing approaches to color:

> The marquetry of M. Puech, with his openly subjective transposition, creates an attractively decorative effect with the brilliance of the materials and the richness of the colors. M. Gérôme's callipygian woman gives, with its dimples, its folds of skin at the waist, its crude tonality and insipid skin, at the most, the itching illusion of a dissolute display.[27]

---

23 Blühm, "In Living Colour," 41, citing Laforgue's review of an 1886 exhibition of polychrome sculpture at the National Gallery in Berlin.

24 Michel Eugène Chevreul, *De la loi du contraste simultané des couleurs et de l'assortiment des objets colorés* (Paris: Pitois-Levrault, 1839).

25 Anthea Callen, *Art of Impressionism: Painting Technique and the Making of Modernism* (New Haven: Yale University Press, 2001).

26 Henry Marcel, "Les Salons de 1902, La Sculpture," *Gazette des Beaux Arts* 28 (1902): 133.

27 Ibid.

Marcel was shocked by and disapproved of Gérôme's attempt: his sculpture was too lifelike, resulting in an overstepping of the boundaries of taste and suitability in art. Puech's use of color, as in the work of the Impressionist and Post-Impressionist painters, emphasized color as a means, a tool, in the representation of the object. The "subjective transposition" in the work of Puech forefronts the materials and colors he used. In separating the work from its mimetic properties, Marcel emphasizes its role as a work of art, not a reproduction of nature.

Gérôme's work, on the other hand, with its "itching illusion of dissolute display" reflected a debasement of sculpture from the monumental to the merely illustrative. The work of art is moved from the realm of aesthetic contemplation to the level of anatomical study or, worse, erotic spectacle. This is not the case in Puech's work, according to Marcel, as color is not used so as to mimic nature, but for "an attractively decorative effect." Thus, Marcel is not so much objecting to the materials used by each artist, but to the effect produced in Gérôme's work.

* * *

Why is it that *Pygmalion and Galatea* gives the "illusion of life," as claimed by Pottier, while, according to Marcel, *The Ball Player* is a mere "copy of life?" Paradoxically, these responses do not correspond to the visual characteristics of the two sculptures: the figure of Galatea is only partially tinted, for we know that she is not yet fully alive, while the figure of *The Ball Player* is fully colored in an illusionistic manner. Thus, intellectual cognition does not follow from visual perception. In fact the visual confirmation of Galatea's status as an inanimate object liberates the viewer to visually engage with the work in a manner and to the degree that is necessary to allow it to transcend its status as object and become real. In other words, the initial perception of the form as object frees the viewer to absorb its sight without threat of confrontation, determine that it is a culturally relevant female form, and authenticate it as a reflection of reality.

The nineteenth-century viewer was aided in this endeavor, as was its maker, by an educational system that provided a strong foundation in classical literature, including Ovid's story of Pygmalion and Galatea. In the first century Roman poet's tale, the sculptor, disillusioned by the imperfections of living women, created an ideal with which he falls in love. Growing desperate, he appealed to Venus for a wife in the image of his sculpted figure, and upon kissing it:

> The ivory grew soft to this touch and, its hardness vanishing, gave and yielded beneath his fingers... The maiden felt the kisses, blushed and, lifting her timid eyes up to the light, she saw the sky and her lover at the same time.[28]

Features of Ovid's tale are especially significant in relation to Pottier's critique of the sculpture: parallels in the story and the critic's words clearly indicate his familiarity with the myth. Indeed, Pottier's words actually echo Ovid's as each describes the kisses and caresses exchanged by the sculptor and his creation as she comes to life:

---

28 Ovid, *Metamorphoses*, 84-85.

Standing on its base, the statue leans over with an irresistible and sudden élan toward her lover and, taking him by the head, she kisses him full on the mouth...Galatea's legs are still frozen in the cold nudity of white marble, while the upper part of her body is already rosy with the rush of blood which begins to circulate within her.[29]

Further, Pottier's acceptance of the basic premise of Gérôme's work indicates the assimilation of Ovid's story into the fabric of nineteenth-century French art and cultural beliefs. This was in turn based upon interpretations of the tale that had developed in the preceding century.

When the subject of Pygmalion and Galatea was taken up by the sculptor Étienne-Maurice Falconet in 1763, his friend Denis Diderot's only criticism of the work, *Pygmalion aux pieds de sa statue qui s'anime*, was that "he propose[d] more physical contact between the artist and his creation."[30] Ovid's story was much adapted in eighteenth-century France in literary and visual arts. As J. L. Carr describes, while both ancient and modern versions of the tale center on the theme of the animation of matter, in the eighteenth century the focus was upon states of being and the process of the transformation. Carr states that the function of sculptures that appear in the background of pastoral scenes by early eighteenth-century painters such as Antoine Watteau, background references to the Pygmalion theme, can be "summed up as forming a link between the human and divine...the proof that magic is at work in art...The statue legend, therefore, illustrates the point of contact between art and magic."[31]

By the second half of the eighteenth century, as suggested by Diderot's objection to Pygmalion's simply looking in adoration at Galatea in Falconet's work, the divine power of animation was conflated with the human capacity to arouse, as the process of transformation from inanimate object to sentient being was seen in terms of awakening the senses, and the artist as possessing the power to both create and animate. From that standpoint, then, it was not a far removal to one in which the portrayal of Pygmalion becomes, as Carr concludes in his discussion of the literary and visual manifestations of the tale of transformation in the eighteenth century, "a reflection of the author's own personality and a mouthpiece for his ideas; the statue then represents a projection of the author's aesthetic ideal or his erotic desire."[32]

This continues into the nineteenth century, as seen in works by artists such as Gérôme, with some additional cultural and artistic influences. Charles Bernheimer has conducted a study of the prostitute in nineteenth-century French novels and paintings in which he argues that she both signified availability to the male viewer and became the location of his desire, "not only because of her prominence as a social phenomena but, more important, because of her function

---

29 Pottier, "La Polychrome," 30.

30 J. L. Carr, "Pygmalion and the 'Philosophes': The Animated Statue in Eighteenth-Century France," *Journal of the Warburg and Courtauld Institutes* 23 (1960): 247.

31 Ibid., 244.

32 Ibid., 255.

in stimulating artistic strategies to control and dispel fantasmatic threat to male mastery."[33] In his work Bernheimer compares images of female prostitutes to writings on them and then, employing Freudian theories on the origins of and mechanisms unconsciously employed to cope with male anxiety, analyzes the psychological functions of such works. Male sexual anxiety stems from the unconscious memory of the sight of the castrated other/woman; anxiety is stimulated whenever a male sees or is threatened with seeing another such site of mutilation (a nude woman). Coping mechanisms take several forms. The first that occurs in narcissistic formation, according to Freud, is autoeroticism, deriving sexual pleasure from the self, often by touch. Another means of coping is scopophilia, deriving sexual pleasure from looking. The one looking, the voyeur, tries to escape anxiety by obsessively reenacting the original trauma, imagined perception of female castration, from a situation of mastery and control. The voyeur's fear of the sight of the original trauma is safely displaced as disdain, which is then projected onto the woman viewed and, finally, assigned as evidence of her own debasement. The reassurance of touching one's own body merges with the desire to view another; gazing at and/or touching oneself while at the same time as gazing at another is doubly reassuring for the gazer.[34] A third means of coping is to control the terror through the construction of a safe object of desire. Slightly different from the strategy of the voyeur, distancing of the self from a debased other, here the male viewer assigns his own desire to the desired other.

The story of Pygmalion and Galatea is, as well, essentially a myth of male empowerment, of the construction of the feminine as an aesthetic fiction. The sculptor, disgusted with the imperfections of human females, decides to carve a figure more beautiful and pure than any living woman. Thus, the sculptor triumphs over the horror of the castrated other with his creation of a narcissistic substitute. He molds the form of her body into the shape he desires, strokes the sculpture awakening passion in himself, and, in so doing, brings his creation to life. As Leonard Barkan describes, "Pygmalion revolts here not only against women but against the whole rule of nature"; he turns from nature to art and empowers himself as the creator of living forms.[35] In the eighteenth century, according to Carr, literary and artistic interpretations of the tale emphasized this link between human and divine, the connection between art and magic, and the power of both the creative artist and artistic creation. This continues into the nineteenth century with the culturally-determined sign of the female nude now signifying sexual availability (i.e., she is a prostitute), as well as the significations of aesthetic ideal and erotic desire assigned to the female form in the eighteenth century.[36]

The construction of woman as an aesthetic form enables the man to have power over her (and project his desire onto her) because he has disguised his

---

33   Charles Bernheimer, *Figures of Ill Repute: Representing Prostitution in Nineteenth-Century France* (Cambridge and London: Harvard University Press, 1989), 2.

34   Sigmund Freud, "Instincts and Their Vicissitudes," *The Standard Edition of the Complete Psychological Works of Sigmund Freud* (London: Hogarth: 1957), vol. XIV, 130.

35   Leonard Barkan, *The Gods Made Flesh: Metamorphosis and the Pursuit of Paganism* (New Haven and London: Yale University Press, 1986), 76.

36   Bernheimer discusses this at length in *Figures of Ill Repute*, Ch. 6, "Degas's Brothels: Voyeurism and Ideology."

original fear of her mutilated body. However, if confronted with the real, the fantasy can no longer be supported, and the man is again subject to (castration) anxiety. Breaking down of the fantasy can occur, for example, when the evidence of the woman's corporeal body overpowers the aesthetic fiction that had been created as a substitution for it. One way this is achieved in art occurs when the artist abandons the cultural ideal of the female form, forcing the viewer into awareness of the body's structure and the workings of the body. The viewer then establishes identification with the body as a like structure, which is irreconcilable with the ideal of the female form.

Most of Gérôme's oeuvre comprises works devoted to the themes of the Orient and the classical world. The construction of the Orient in such works, as Edward Said describes, is through the articulation of Western experience of a foreign culture that has been both colonized and demonized over the centuries.[37] The construction of the reality of such scenes is through "a plethora of authenticating details" inserted into them which, "supposedly there to denote the real directly, are actually there simply to signify its presence in the work as a whole…They are signifiers of the category of the real, there to give credibility to the "realness" of the work as a whole, to authenticate the total visual field as a simple, artless reflection."[38]

Thus, rather than an interest in the depiction of what could be seen, Gérôme, in both his Orientalist and Classical works, represented exotic realities of his own creation, which only appeared to be reflections of reality. The differences in the critical responses to Gérôme's sculptures of *Pygmalion and Galatea* and *The Ball Player* reside in his success in reflecting back to the viewer the illusion of reality expected in both art as a whole and in this genre. The viewer is a participant in the myth of the artist's power to give life to his art; the fervency of Pottier's position that the "illusion of life" was evident in Gérôme's *Pygmalion and Galatea* was a manifestation of the acceptance of that fantasy. *The Ball Player,* on the other hand, deviates from cultural expectations of the ideal female form and devolves into, as the critic Marcel states dismissively, a "mere copy of life." The differences between the two sculptures, although perhaps slight to the contemporary viewer, indicate the imperative of the adherence to a norm that informed a culturally and psychologically driven standardization of the female form.

Nearly a mirror image of Galatea, the excuse for the extreme twisting of the figure's torso and awkward rigidity of the legs in *The Ball Player* is in the exercise of a game of Gérôme's invention, which provided him with the excuse to display a female nude in a complicated pose under the legitimizing rubric of a classical theme. But, whereas Galatea was in the midst of coming alive with the awakening touch of the sculptor, this figure refers to no power other than her own. She is an autonomous being whose actions are self-referential. Furthermore, the fact that her flesh is modeled after a human prototype is clear to the viewer: with the folds of flesh at the small of her back and her tinted nipples, she is too nearly a corporeal being for the viewer to adopt a comfortable aesthetic distance. Such representation explains Gerald Ackerman's discomfort in discussing the work: "Even now,

---

37   Edward Said, *Orientalism* (New York: Pantheon Books, 1978).
38   Linda Nochlin, "The Imaginary Orient," *Art in America* 71 (May 1983): 122-123.

we must overcome some personal embarrassment to observe the work closely, and to see how sensitive and full of observation it is, especially in the marvelous back, or the handsome legs."³⁹ As Marcel claimed, "this dissolute display" is of a naked woman, not an idealized female nude. Thus, it is Gérôme's violation of the cultural norms of representation, unexpectedly transforming the casual observation of the flâneur into the charged and invasive gaze of the voyeur, that sparks the critic's indignant protest.

Gérôme began paintings of himself at work on his sculptures in 1886, at the age of sixty-two. Susan Waller refers to Gérôme's late group of self-portraits, which includes the works under discussion here, as evidence of an "anxiety of lateness" fostered by "his advancing age and by the decline of institutional structures and values on which he had built his career."⁴⁰ In creating these paintings, the artist was attempting to stabilize his professional reputation and artistic legacy. Waller sees in these works a displacement of the erotic gaze, and a separation of the erotic gaze from the aesthetic gaze, as the artist aligns himself with the traditions of high art, not the vulgarities of contemporary representations.

In addition, however, these are painted documentaries of the artist in the act of creation. The multiple views of the same scene in which he shifts the orientation of the sculptures depicted signal Gérôme's need to reassure himself of their existence, that is, the proof of his potency as a creative male force. This, too, is the role of *Self-Portrait Painting 'The Ball Player'* within the artist's oeuvre. Begun at the age of seventy-eight, in the last years of the artist's life, Gérôme depicts himself in the act of bringing his work to life, as if endowing himself with the power to continue to do so. In his role of Pygmalion, the artist closes the gap between art and life with his addition of color. Far from imposing an intellectual distance by adhering to aesthetic standards of an idealized beauty, Gérôme prompts a visceral response through his particularities of folding flesh and muscular movement in a woman who sinuously twists her body, the warm tones of which proclaim vibrant life. And, as the figure comes alive under the hand of the artist, he too is renewed.

Bibliography

Ackerman, Gerald M. "Gérôme's Sculpture: The Problems of Realist Sculpture." *Arts Magazine* 60 (February 1986): 82-89.

———. *The Life and Work of Jean-Léon Gérôme*. New York: Harper and Row, 1986.

Albert, Maurice. "Le Salon des Champs-Elysées, II, La Sculpture." *Gazette des Beaux-Arts* 4 (1890): 59-68.

Bapst, Germain. "La Sculpture Chryséléphantine." *La Revue de famille* II (1892): 334-343.

---

39 Ackerman, *The Life and Work of Jean-Léon Gérôme*, 152.

40 Susan Waller, "Fin de Partie: A Group of Self-Portraits by Gérôme," *Nineteenth-Century Art Worldwide* 9 (Spring 2010), http://www.19thc-artworldwide.org/index.php/spring10/group-of-self-portraits-by-gerome.

Barkan, Leonard. *The Gods Made Flesh: Metamorphosis and the Pursuit of Paganism*. New Haven and London: Yale University Press, 1986.

Bernheimer, Charles. *Figures of Ill Repute: Representing Prostitution in Ninteenth-Century France*. Cambridge and London: Harvard University Press, 1989.

Bersani, Leo. *The Freudian Body: Psychoanalysis and Art*. New York: Columbia University Press, 1986.

Blanc, Charles. "La Reine de la Paix, par M. le Baron Marochetti." *Gazette des Beaux-Arts* 16 (1864): 566-567.

———. "Grammaire des Arts de Dessin: Architecture, Sculpture, Peinture. Sculpture." *Gazette des Beaux-Arts* 17 (1864): 59-79.

Blühm, Andreas. "In Living Colour: A Short History of Colour and Sculpture in the Nineteenth Century." In *The Colour of Sculpture 1840–1910*, edited by Andreas Blühm, 11–60. Amsterdam: Van Gogh Museum, 1996.

Callen, Anthea. *Art of Impressionism: Painting Technique and the Making of Modernism*, New Haven: Yale University Press, 2001.

Carr, J. L. "Pygmalion and the 'Philosophes': The Animated Statue in Eighteenth-Century France." *Journal of the Warburg and Courtauld Institutes* 23 (1960): 239-255.

Chevreul, Michel Eugène. *De la loi du contraste simultané des couleurs et de l'assortiment des objets colorés*. Paris: Pitois-Levrault, 1839.

Doyle, Allan. "Groping the Antique: Michelangelo and the Erotics of Tradition." In *Reconsidering Gérôme*, edited by Scott Allan and Mary Morton. Los Angeles: J. Paul Getty Museum, 2010.

Drost, Wolfgang. "Colour, Sculpture, Mimesis: A 19th-Century Debate." In *The Colour of Sculpture 1840–1910*, edited by Andreas Blühm, 61-72. Amsterdam: Van Gogh Museum, 1996.

Freedberg, David. *The Power of Images: Studies in the History and Theory of Response*. Chicago and London: The University of Chicago Press, 1989.

Freud, Sigmund. "Instincts and Their Vicissitudes." *The Standard Edition of the Complete Psychological Works of Sigmund Freud*. London: Hogarth: 1957.

Gérôme, J.-L. "Notes et Fragments." *Les Arts* 1904: 22-31. (Following introductory remarks by Frédéric Masson, "J.-L. Gérome, Notes et fragments inédites": 8-21.)

Hargrove, June. "Painter-sculptors and Polychromy in the Evolution of Modernism." In *The Colour of Sculpture 1840–1910*, edited by Andreas Blühm, 83-102. Amsterdam: Van Gogh Museum, 1996.

Hering, Fanny Field. "Gérôme." *The Century Magazine* 37 (February 1889): 482-499.

———. *Gérôme, His Life and Works*. New York, 1892.

Le Normand Romain, Antoinette and Jean-Luc Olivié. "La Polychromie." in *La Sculpture Française au XIXe Siècle*. Introduction by Anne Pingeot. Paris: Editions de la Réunion des musées nationaux, 1986.

MacKenzie, John M. *Orientalism: History, theory and the arts*. Manchester and New York: Manchester University Press, 1995.

Marcel, Henry. "Les Salons de 1902, La Sculpture." *Gazette des Beaux-Arts* 28 (1902): 123-141.

Masson, Frédéric. "J.-L. Gérôme, peintre de l'orient." *Figaro Illustré* 29 (July 1901): 1-24.

Nochlin, Linda. "The Imaginary Orient." *Art in America* 71 (May 1983): 118-131, 187-191.

———. "Imaginary Orients." Public Lecture. Metropolitan Museum of Art, New York, 16 May 1996.

Ovid. *Metamorphoses*. Translated by Frank Justus Miller. New York: G. P. Putnam's Sons, 1926.

Panzanelli, Roberta, Elke D. Schmidt, and Kenneth D. S. Lapatin. *The Color of Life: Polychromy in Sculpture from Antiquity to the Present*. Los Angeles: J. Paul Getty Museum, 2008.

Papet, Édouard. " 'Father Polychrome': The Sculpture of Jean-Léon Gérôme." In *The Spectacular Art of Jean-Léon Gérôme*, edited by Laurence des Cars, Dominique de Font-Réaulx, and Édouard Papet, 291-329. Milan & New York: Skira, 2010.

Paris. *Jean-Léon Gérôme, 1824-1904: sculpteur et peintre de "l'art officiel"*. Galerie Tanagra, 1974.

Pottier, Edmond. "Les Salons de 1892, II, La Sculpture." *Gazette des Beaux-Arts* 8 (1892): 5-44.

Said, Edward W. *Orientalism*. New York: Pantheon Books, 1978.

———. *Culture and Imperialism*. New York: Alfred A. Knopf, 1993.

Sanyal, Sunanda K. "Allegorizing Representation: Gérôme's Final Phase," *Athanor* 15 (1997): 38-45.

Schneider, Mechthild. "Pygmalion Mythos des schöpferischen Künstlers: Zur Aktualität eines Themas in der französischen Kunst von Falconet bis Rodin." *Pantheon* 45 (1987): 111-123.

Timbal, Charles. "Gérôme: Etude Biographique." *Gazette des Beaux-Arts* 14 (1876): 218-231, 334-346.

Vesoul. *Jean-Léon Gérôme, 1824-1904: peintre, sculpteur et graveur, ses oeuvres conservées dans les collections françaises publiques et privées.* Ville de Vesoul, 1981.

Waller, Susan. "Fin de Partie: A Group of Self-Portraits by Gérôme," Nineteenth-Century Art Worldwide Vol. 9, No. 1 (Spring 2010), available on-line at http://www.19thc- artworldwide.org/index.php/spring10/group-of-self-portraits-by-gerome.

9

"Whiteness" and Identity in Jean Rhys's *Wide Sargasso Sea* and Michelle Cliff's *Abeng*

April Conley Kilinski

Jean Rhys's 1966 novel *Wide Sargasso Sea,* set during the 1830s and '40s in the British West Indies, begins immediately after the abolition of slavery in the British Empire. This novel interrogates the construction of whiteness in colonial fiction by telling the story of Bertha in her own voice and childhood identity as Antoinette Cosway. Antoinette's family, who once owned slaves, is destitute at the beginning of the novel as a result of the father's death and the change in slavery laws. In order to restore the family's status, her mother marries an Englishman, who arranges for Antoinette to marry Rochester Mason when she comes of age. Mason's fixed ideas about race and gender transform Antoinette into Bertha Mason, the mad woman in the attic of *Jane Eyre.* Rhys herself was born in Dominica, and spent her childhood there. The daughter of a white Creole mother and Welsh doctor, Rhys moved to England at the age of sixteen and spent much of her restless and unsettled adult life on the continent. Antoinette has, therefore, often been seen as an autobiographical character who mirrors Rhys's own feelings of fragmented identity.

Michelle Cliff's 1984 narrative *Abeng*, on the other hand, is set in the period immediately before Jamaican independence (1952-1958) from the British; it tells the story of Clare Savage, a light-skinned mullato girl who struggles to find her place in color conscious, colonial Jamaica. Like her protagonist, Michelle Cliff was born in 1946 in Kingston, Jamaica. Three years later, the light-skinned Cliffs immigrated to New York where they were encouraged to pass as whites. However, they never completely acclimated to life in New York, and the family returned to Jamaica in 1956. On their return, Cliff, like Clare Savage, was sent to St. Andrews private girls' school where she received a colonial education. In similar fashion to her protagonist, Cliff's family returned to New York in 1960, and, like Clare, Cliff was educated in the United States and in Britain, receiving degrees in European and Renaissance history (Cliff tells Clare's story from 1960 onward in a sequel, *No Telephone to Heaven*). As with Clare in *Abeng,* Cliff began her own writing through journals, which she started keeping after reading Anne Frank's diary.[1]

Both narratives are coming of age stories for the protagonists, Antoinette and Clare, respectively. In both texts, the girls are visibly "white," but the authors privilege questions of identity and home for these characters since they are neither "native" (black, insider) nor colonizer (white, outsider) in Jamaica. Straddling the lines of these culturally constructed notions of race, Antoinette and Clare are intermediate characters who, not surprisingly, experience, in Patrick Hogan's words, an "'alienating hybridity,' the estrangement from both traditions, the paralyzing conviction that one has no identity, no real cultural home, and that no synthesis is possible."[2] And, despite the fact that both novels engage with politically significant moments in Jamaica's history, Rhys's character experiences her estrangement from white and black identity as a kind of personal tragedy. Cliff, on the other hand, reworks Clare's hybridity for her empowerment through an understanding of history.

I argue that in the same way that *Wide Sargasso Sea* intertextually engages the colonial novel *Jane Eyre* to give a voice to Bertha, Cliff's novel intertextually engages *Wide Sargasso Sea* to show how complicity with colonial attitudes about race, and particularly whiteness, impede empowered identity. While Cliff's novel posits a hope for resistance through an understanding of history, both narratives demonstrate that corporeal markers of race hinder fully integrated insider status in colonial/postcolonial countries damaged by hierarchical constructions of race.

Colonial "Whiteness" and Creoles: *Wide Sargasso Sea*

As mentioned above, Rhys's novel interrogates the construction of whiteness in colonial fiction by telling Bertha's story in her own voice. Rhys further challenges constructions of whiteness in the colonial era when she rewrites Bronte's characterization of Bertha (Antoinette) as dark and insane—both of which are implications of racial impurity. Antoinette is a white Creole (one who is of European descent, but who was born outside of Europe), who also happens to be the daughter of slave holders. In her excellent analysis of Rhys's text, Belinda Edmondson notes that the white Creole "occupies an ambiguous space in West Indian society. On the one hand she is the descendant of the colonizer" and her color accords her "power and privilege if she chooses...Still, the white creole is in many ways culturally 'black,' or Afro-Caribbean: the Afrocentric dynamic permeates all classes and races of Anglophone Caribbean society regardless of its particular configurations within those groups. The creole is, in this sense, representative of both colonizer and colonized."[3] This position as insider and outsider characterizes Antoinette.

When her family loses its economic position after slavery ends and the father dies, the racial status of Antoinette's Creole family is called into question. As a

---

[1] Cora Agatucci, "Michelle Cliff," in *Contemporary African American Novelists: A Bio-Bibliographical Critical Sourcebook*. Ed. Emanuel S. Nelson (Westport, CT: Greenwood Press, 1999), 94-101.

[2] Patrick Hogan, *Colonialism and Cultural Identity: Crises of Tradition in the Anglophone Literatures of India, Africa, and the Caribbean* (New York: State University of New York Press, 2000), 17.

[3] Belinda Edmondson, "Race, Privilege, and the Politics of (Re)Writing History: An Analysis of the Novels of Michelle Cliff," *Callaloo* 16, no. 1 (1993): 180.

number of critics note, their status as white in the British Empire is tenuous from the opening lines of the novel: "They say when trouble comes close ranks, and so the white people did. But we were not in their ranks."[4] Significantly, though the primary reason for their shift in racial status is an economic one, Antoinette, her mother, and brother are also left out of the "circle of whiteness" because "[t]he Jamaican ladies had never approved of my mother, 'because she pretty like pretty self' Christophine said."[5] Annette's vanity and her status as sexualized female—she is Cosway's second, much younger wife—positions her outside of Victorian ideals of "proper" femininity. Thus, Annette's exclusion from whiteness hinges on her condition as outsider (she is from Martinique), her economic fall, and her flawed gender performance. These three factors also determine Antoinette's "whiteness." However, despite her loss of status, Antoinette never fully relinquishes a position of privilege relative to the black women in her narrative. Moreover, "Antoinette rarely shows herself concerned about the public dimensions of the oppression that she and other women suffer in the present historical moment of the West Indies. She prefers to see the oppression that she and her mother suffer in purely private terms."[6] Her lack of historical awareness makes her unable to contextualize her oppression or to effectively resist it.

Annette distances herself from Antoinette, leaving Antoinette vulnerable to the taunts of a local child who calls her "white cockroach."[7] Christophine (the Cosway's black servant) sympathizes with her isolation, and, though she "[says] nothing," Tia arrives "with her mother Maillotte, Christophine's friend."[8] Antoinette's friendship with Tia becomes central to her narrative about herself, since she finds a camaraderie with Tia that she has not known before: "soon Tia was my friend and I met her nearly every morning at the turn of the road to the river… We boiled green bananas in an old iron pot and ate them with our fingers…Late or early we parted at the turn of the road. My mother never asked me where I had been or what I had done."[9] Several features of Antoinette and Tia's friendship are relevant. First, their interaction occurs away from the Cosway plantation—the place aligned with colonization and isolation. As such, they provide Antoinette a connection to a *place* outside of the one associated with her white privilege. Second, Antoinette and Tia develop a deep intimacy when they swim, eat, and even sleep together, thereby also giving her connection to a *person* outside of her white privilege. Finally, Annette does not question Antoinette's relationship with Tia until racial questions fracture it. Cliff will echo and rework all of these features in Clare and Zoe's relationship in *Abeng*.

While Antoinette does find a sense of belonging through her friendship with Tia, their camaraderie is short lived, since race soon presents itself into their relationship. When Tia fails to concede that Antoinette has lived up to her end of

---

4   Jean Rhys, Wide Sargasso Sea (New York: W.W. Norton Co., Inc.), 17.
5   Ibid., 17
6   Carmen Wickramagamage, "An/other Side to Antoinette/Bertha: Reading 'Race' into *Wide Sargasso Sea, "Journal of Commonwealth Literature* 35, no. 1 (200): 39.
7   Rhys, *Wide Sargasso Sea,* 23.
8   Ibid., 23.
9   Ibid., 23.

a childish bet for Antoinette's pennies, Antoinette calls Tia a "cheating nigger."[10] When her power (in the form of her money) is threatened, Antoinette reverts to racism. More importantly, however, is Tia's response when she reminds Antoinette of her low economic status: "Plenty of white people in Jamaica. Real white people, they got gold money. They didn't look at us, nobody see them come near us. Old time white people nothing but white nigger now, and black nigger better than white nigger."[11] Thus, Tia reflects the social attitude that class constructs race, and a fall from economic grace positions one as a "nigger." As Vivian Nun Halloran rightly asserts, "For Tia, Antoinette is a 'nigger' because her family cannot properly perform its whiteness through the display of wealth typical of other members of the ruling white planter class in Jamaica."[12] After this accusation, Tia steals Antoinette's clean dress and replaces it with an old, dirty one, thereby outwardly completing Antoinette's transition from "white" to "black." Interestingly, when Antoinette comes back to her house, she finds white visitors (whom Christophine identifies as the "new whites") who laugh at her for the way she looks. When her mother also scolds her for her shabby appearance and laments that she does not have a clean dress to change into, Antoinette believes that "what Tia said is true."[13] Her capitulation to her "outsider" status with regard to other whites causes Antoinette to feel "Not myself any longer."[14] Thus, her shift in economic status and resulting "racial" status also bring about Antoinette's first psychological collapse in the novel.

While Antoinette accepts her changed economic and concomitant racial status, her mother refuses to do so, choosing instead to sell her last piece of jewelry to make new clothes for herself and for Antoinette. By presenting herself with the appropriate accoutrement of high economic standing, Annette finds her new husband, Mr. Mason, a wealthy Englishman. Mr. Mason's wealth and Englishness restore Antoinette's family's status as "white" in their community. As Maria Olaussen puts it, when Mr. Mason marries Annette, "he 'rescues' Antoinette from growing up worthless, from being a 'white nigger.' This he does by reestablishing the black-white dichotomy, reintroducing the connection of white with wealth and domination, and the connection to England."[15] The community of former slaves signifies their acceptance of this change by targeting Antoinette's house in their riot. Significantly, Tia joins the crowd that attacks Antoinette's family. While she and her family are leaving the house, Antoinette says,

> Then, not so far off, I saw Tia and her mother and I ran to her, for she was all that was left of my life as it had been. We had eaten the same food, slept side by side, bathed in the same river. As I ran, I thought, I will live with Tia

---

10   Ibid., 24.

11   Ibid., 24.

12   Vivian Nun Halloran, "Race, Creole, and National Identities in Rhys's *Wide Sargasso Sea* and Phillips's *Cambridge*," *Small Axe: A Caribbean Journal of Criticism* 21 (2006): 91.

13   Rhys, *Wide Sargasso Sea*, 26.

14   Ibid., 28.

15   Maria Olaussen, "Jean Rhys's Construction of Blackness as Escape from White Femininity in 'Wide Sargasso Sea," *ARIEL: A Review of International English Literature* 24, no. 2 (1993): 70.

and I will be like her... When I was close I saw the jagged stone in her hand but I did not see her throw it. I did not feel it either, only something wet, running down my face. I looked at her and I saw her face crumple up as she began to cry. We stared at each other, blood on my face, tears in hers. It was as if I saw myself. Like in a looking-glass.[16]

Tia's second rejection as a result of Antoinette's whiteness and alignment with English oppressors through Mr. Mason, along with her displacement from her home solidify Antoinette's "alienating hybridity"[17] in the rest of the novel. Elizabeth Dalton's discussion of Antoinette's wound from a psychoanalytic perspective associates it with menstruation and its "unconscious link with castration" as well as "another severance—that from the mother."[18] As such, her separation—from the place and person of her connection to something outside of white privilege—results from the corporeal whiteness of her body. This wound also severs Antoinette from her "mother land," represented by a connection to the Jamaican landscape through her friendship with Tia, and from an "insider" identity that aligns her with Tia's blackness. At this moment, she assumes a white, female identity that opens up the space of negotiation with Bronte's narrative when Mr. Mason arranges her marriage to the character Bronte's audience knows as Rochester, though he remains unnamed in Rhys's narrative.

The fact that Mr. Mason arranges for Antoinette to marry an Englishman suggests that she maintains her "white" status into her adult life by virtue of her connection to Mr. Mason. However, her "whiteness" remains tenuous despite the marriage. When Rochester takes over the narrative in the second part of the novel, we learn that Antoinette fails to meet his expectations for a "proper" English wife. Her first failing lies in her love of the land. When Rochester and Antoinette go to Granbois, Rochester feels alienated and disoriented, while Antoinette claims the land as her own. She even tells him: "I love it more than anywhere in the world. As if it were a person. More than a person."[19] Moreover, she dismisses England as something unreal, a dream.

Antoinette not only loves the land, she also cares for, and to some extent, understands the people. She defends Christophine against Rochester's stereotypical assertions about Christophine's laziness, and she explains many of Amélie's mannerisms. Most damagingly, Antoinette is intimate with Christophine, often hugging her and sharing secrets with her in patois. Rochester confronts Antoinette about her relationship with Christophine saying, "'*I* wouldn't hug and kiss them,' [black people, especially Christophine] I'd say, 'I couldn't.'"[20] Antoinette's response is to laugh at him. Rochester soon begins to resent his lack of control over Antoinette's feelings as well as his dependency upon her because of her knowledge of the place and its people. His resentment, exacerbated by his feeling of being

---

16 Rhys, *WSS*, 45.
17 Hogan, *Colonialism*, 17.
18 Elizabeth Dalton, "Sex and Race in *Wide Sargasso Sea*." *Partisan Review* 67 no. 3 (2000): 433.
19 Rhys, *WSS*, 89.
20 Rhys, *WSS*, 89.

forced into his marriage, causes him to position Antoinette as outside his English identity when he notes that she has "Long, sad, dark alien eyes. Creole of pure English descent she may be, but they are not English or European either."[21]

However, he regains a sense of power after visiting Daniel, who claims in a letter to Rochester that he is Antoinette's half-brother by her father. Daniel tells Rochester that Antoinette's mother was crazy and that her father has many illegitimate children. When Rochester returns to their home after visiting Daniel, he confronts Antoinette with Daniel's claims. The power Daniel's information accords him causes Rochester to feel "calm, it was the first time I had felt calm or self-possessed for many a long day."[22] Having control of Antoinette empowers Rochester to further alienate Antoinette by questioning her racial purity. Lee Erwin contends that Daniel represents a contamination of Antoinette's racial purity not because of her father's sexual exploits with women of color, "but [because] the moral categorization fundamental to the nineteenth-century English novel here speaks through Rochester tacitly to assign blame to the planters' wives as guardians of sexual morality."[23] Put simply, women are the keepers of racial purity through their "correct" appropriation of Victorian notions of female sexuality. Since Daniel and others like him exist, the fault must be with the women who failed in their role.

Daniel's information confirms Rochester's earlier doubts about Antoinette since, like her mother before her, Antoinette fails to display proper "white" femininity because she enjoys sex. Rochester says of her, "Very soon she was as eager for what's called loving as I was—more lost and drowned afterwards."[24] Dyer's writing on whiteness is instructive here since, as he notes, "their [white women's] very whiteness, their refinement, makes of sexuality a disturbance of their racial purity."[25] Having firmly positioned Antoinette as outside his English whiteness, Rochester seeks to replace her identity by calling her Bertha. The act of re-naming not only furthers removal from whiteness by recalling the way that slaves were often renamed by their masters, but it also elides her previous identity.

Antoinette's lack of identification and connection to Rochester's white Englishness contributes to her descent into madness at the end of the novel. By taking away her identity in Granbois when he takes away her "whiteness," Rochester repeats Antoinette's earlier alienation from Coulibri when Tia rejects her. Being denied a racial insider position from both groups leaves Antoinette with no sense of self or place. She tells Rochester that Amélie was singing "a song about a white cockroach. That's me. That's what they call all of us who were here before their own people in Africa sold them to the slave traders. And I've heard English women call us white niggers. So between you I often wonder who I am and where is my country and where do I belong and why was I ever born at all."[26] Rochester

---

21   Ibid., 67.

22   Ibid, 127.

23   Lee Erwin, "'Like Looking in a Looking-Glass': History and Narrative in *Wide Sargasso Sea.*" *Novel: A Forum on Fiction* 22 no. 2 (1989): 148.

24   Ibid, 92.

25   Dyer, *White* (New York: Routledge, 1977), 60.

26   Ibid., 102.

furthers her alienation when he has sex with Amélie next door to Antoinette's room so that she can hear them. Thus, he behaves as the English slave owners before him (including Antoinette's father), thereby fully performing his white, English, male identity, while denying her a white, English, female identity. Rochester's affair and his refusal to accept her, precipitates Antoinette's madness. Rhys rewrites the reason for her madness at the conclusion of *Jane Eyre* when Bertha sets fire to Thornfield Hall. She is not insane because of her "blackness;" rather, she is insane because Rochester's authority over "whiteness" as an English male denies her access to that identity.

Homi K. Bhabha's concept of hybridity and its relation to mimicry, which works against fixed ideas about race, informs this reading of the text. In *Wide Sargasso Sea,* Antoinette becomes what Bhabha calls the "*reference* of discrimination" produced through Rochester's "strategy of disavowal."[27] When Rochester rejects Antoinette, he does so because she references for him racial impurity. His "disavowal" of her causes a "process of splitting as the condition of [her] subjection... where the trace of what is disavowed is not repressed but repeated as something *different*—a mutation, a hybrid." Antoinette's identity splits as a result of Rochester's rejection, but her "blackness" is not repressed; it is repeated as something different—Rochester's sense of Antoinette as not English or European, but white nonetheless. Therefore, while Rochester denies Antoinette's white Englishness, her hybridity "is the name for the strategic reversal of the process of domination through disavowal (that is, the production of [a] discriminatory identit[y] that [secures] the 'pure' and original identity of authority."[28] Bhabha bases his theory on "Macaulay's Minute," in which Lord Macaulay recommends an education for Colonized (especially Indian) people that reproduces English education, especially through literature. Macaulay argued that this education should come from "a class of persons Indian in blood and color, but English in tastes, opinions, in morals, and in intellect."[29] Because of the hybridity inherent in Macaulay's recommendation, Bhabha argues that the "mimicry reveals the limitation in the authority of colonial discourse, almost as though colonial authority inevitably embodies the seeds of its own destruction ... [the disruption comes] from the fact that ... mimicry is also potentially mockery"[30] By engaging with Bronte's *Jane Eyre,* Rhys shows that Antoinette's hybrid identity destabilizes "pure," white, English, female identity while also "mocking" the very idea of racial purity. Bertha must be locked away in Bronte's narrative so that her hybridity does not threaten Rochester's power, which is premised on the notion of racial purity.

Significantly, Rhys represents the fire at the end of the novel through Antoinette's dream that figures as a kind of attempt to reclaim Tia and identification with Jamaica. She dreams about her childhood home at Coulibri and recalls that, in the dream, "Tia was there. She beckoned me and when I hesitated, she laughed. I heard her say, You frightened? And I heard the man's voice, Ber-

---

27 Homi K. Bhabha, *The Location of Culture* (New York: Routledge, 1994), 159.
28 Ibid., 159.
29 Quoted in Ashcroft, Griffiths, and Tiffin, *Post-Colonial Studies: The Key Concepts* (London: Routledge, 2000), 140.
30 Ibid., 140-141.

tha! Bertha! All this I saw and heard in a fraction of a second. And the sky so red. Someone screamed and I thought, *Why did I scream?* I called 'Tia!' and jumped."[31] While she seeks to reclaim her self through identification with her black childhood friend and the land in Jamaica, she ultimately fails, since, as Erwin contends, "any attempt to realize the fantasy of a merging of 'Antoinette' with 'Tia,' or blackness, can only annihilate that which wishes to occupy the other place."[32] Since her story figures in the colonial novel of *Jane Eyre*, she must ultimately be removed from Bronte's narrative for the "real" white woman, Jane, whose position as heiress (upper class) and display of femininity (chaste and demure) exemplify Victorian notions of white femininity. The mutually constructed performance of both race and gender are crucial for the project of Empire.

"Census Whites": *Abeng*

Michelle Cliff's novel *Abeng* tells the story of Clare Savage, who, like Antoinette, is from a wealthy, light-skinned family in Jamaica. Like Antoinette's family, Clare's also owned slaves; unlike Antoinette, Clare is of mixed race, but her father (and his family) ascribe to the race/class hierarchy established during colonization and do everything to avail themselves of their racial privilege, believing "that a degree of European ancestry [gives] them superiority over the black masses."[33] The legacy of a social structure dictated by race was formulated on British colonial policies and attitudes about race, and thus was deeply entrenched in everyday life in Jamaica. As Richard Dyer asserts, "social groups must be visibly recognizable and representable, since this is a major currency of communication of power. Being visible as white is a passport to privilege."[34]

The main form of exclusion within the British Empire was based on race. As Sean Hawkins and Philip D. Morgan note, this was due to the fact that "by the middle of the nineteenth century pseudo-scientific thinking was fully developed and the emergence of Social Darwinian ideas refined belief in white domination as well as the subordination of blacks."[35] This "scientific racism" was, in turn, influenced by the relationship between class and color in the context of the British Empire. By employing these theories of scientific racism, the British sought to place "social ranking and social disability on a biological and 'scientific' footing."[36] As a result, many of those in the regions of contact began to internalize these ideas, particularly those people considered to be "coloured," or having a mixed-race background, such as Clare's family in *Abeng*. The attempt on the part of mixed-race people to differentiate themselves from those considered black

---

31 Rhys, *WSS*, 123.

32 Erwin, "'Like Looking in a Looking-Glass': History and Narrative in *Wide Sargasso Sea*," 155.

33 J.R. Ward, "The British West Indies in the Age of Abolition, 1748-1815," in *Oxford History of the British Empire Volume II*, ed. P.J. Marshall (Oxford: Oxford University Press, 1998), 438.

34 Richard Dyer, *White* (New York: Routledge, 1997), 44.

35 Hawkins and Morgan, "Blacks and the British Empire: An Introduction," in *Black Experience and the British Empire*, ed. Philip D. Morgan and Sean Hawkins (Oxford: Oxford University Press, 2004), 14.

36 Anne McClintock, *Imperial Leather: Race, Gender, and Sexuality in the Colonial Contest* (New York: Routledge, 1995), 49.

stemmed directly from the desire to escape the full brunt of British racism.[37] In Jamaica there operated a "tripartite social structure inherited, in its essential features, from the slavery era"[38] that consisted of black, brown, and white, with blacks on the bottom, coloreds in the middle, and whites on top. This system also relied upon a close association between race and class. As Johnson notes, in most British Caribbean societies, light-skinned members of this group [planter class] in Jamaica often aspired to whiteness, forming the "census whites" who were white by self-definition in the census but were widely known to be of mixed ancestry.[39] Thus, "White as a skin colour is also a category that is internally variable and unclear at the edges...not being really of one hue means that whiteness may also be seen as multiplicitous and expressively dynamic. It also...makes it amenable to being, within bounds, a matter of ascription—white people are who white people say are white."[40] Those who are more closely aligned as *visibly* as well as *socially* (via class status) "white," are more likely to benefit from its privilege, an important consideration for this discussion of *Abeng*.

In her autobiographical essay, "If I Could Write This in Fire, I Would Write This in Fire," Cliff asserts that she looks back on her life as someone who grew up in similar (and in many places almost identical) circumstances to her protagonist, Clare, and wonders "when the background changed places with the foreground, [and tries to] locate the vanishing point: where the lines of perspective converge and disappear. Lines of color and class. Lines of history and social context. Lines of denial and rejection. When did *we* (the light-skinned Jamaicans) take over for *them* as oppressors?"[41] This question is what she explores throughout the autobiographical narrative as she tells Clare's story as a rewriting of the constructions of "whiteness" among mixed-race people in Jamaica. Cliff employs a third-person narrator to tell not only Clare Savage's story but also the untold history of the Jamaican people. Cliff also exposes the pretense inherent in fixed notions of race, which have become entrenched in Jamaica's social fabric to the advantage of an elite few. Thus, as Françoise Lionnet contends, "Cliff is...an *auto-ethnographer*, because her narratives belong in a new genre of contemporary autobiographical texts by writers whose interest and focus are not so much the retrieval of a repressed dimension of the *private* self but the rewriting of their ethnic history, the recreation of a *collective* identity through the performance of language."[42] By reworking many features of Rhys's narrative with an attention to history, Cliff creates the possibility of resistance rather than complicity for Clare and others who share her history.

Abeng opens with the following lines: "The island rose and sank. Twice. During the periods in which history was recorded by indentations on rock and

---

37 Hawkins and Morgan, "Blacks and the British Empire: An Introduction,"17.

38 Howard Johnson, "The Black Experience in the British Caribbean in the Twentieth Century," in *Black Experience and the British Empire*, ed. Philip D. Morgan and Sean Hawkins (Oxford University Press, 2004), 317.

39 Ibid., 318.

40 Dyer, *White*, 48.

41 Michelle Cliff, *The Land of the Look Behind: Prose and Poetry* (Ithaca, NY: Firebrand Books, 1985), 62.

42 Francoise Lionnet, "Of Mangoes and Maroons: Language, History, and the Multi-Cultural Subject of Michelle Cliff's Abeng," *De/Colonizing the Subject: The Politics of Gender in Women's Autobiography*, ed. Sidonie Smith and Julia Watson (Minneapolis, MN: University of Minnesota Press, 1992), 321-345.

shell. This is a book about the time which followed that time. As the island became a place where people lived. Indians. Africans. Europeans."[43] These opening lines establish the fact that this book is concerned with history. Unlike Antoinette's first person, account of her own story in *Wide Sargasso Sea*, Clare's story in *Abeng* is told in a third person narrative that includes the history of Jamaica. Moreover, the history recorded in this book serves as a revisionist history of the colonial version taught to Clare at school and by her father. The narrator's interruptions throughout the novel seek to fill in the gaps of that colonial history by telling the stories of those (such as Indians, Africans, and women) who were left out of colonial accounts.

Significantly, Clare's narrative spans the years from 1956-1958, when Jamaica began the process of independence. These dates coincide with Clare's own growth of political consciousness, which occurs through her friendship with Zoe and her brief encounter with Winifred Stevens at the end of the novel. Much of Clare's political awakening happens as a result of her own crisis of identity wherein she struggles with her position as the white-looking daughter of mixed-race parents. When the novel opens, however, Clare's sense of identity is rooted in her father's ideals and racism. Significantly, Kitty (Clare's mother) sanctions Boy's (her father's) misrepresentation of his past to Clare because Clare looks like Boy. As a light-skinned, white-looking child, Clare belongs to Boy. In direct contrast to the stories Boy and her colonial teachers tell Clare, Cliff's narrator regularly interjects the untold history of Jamaica into the otherwise essentially linear plot. These interjections imply that knowledge of this history has the potential to make Clare a revolutionary, should she choose to understand her history and embrace a politically "black" identity rather than the "white" one that her father advocates. This structure also prioritizes history in a way that Rhys's narrative does not.

Though both of Clare's parents are also racially mixed, her father, Boy Savage, is light-skinned and what is called *buckra* in Jamaica, a condition which guarantees him a high class position. As a member of the upper class, Boy considers himself white, drawing on and emulating the values of his white ancestors. In fact, "His first name was James, and his middle name, Arthur; in the family and among the friends he kept from school he was called 'Boy,' sometimes 'Boy-Boy,' an imitation of England, like so many aspects of their lives."[44] Boy's great-grandfather, who was white, owned a plantation as well as slaves, and Boy and his family go to great lengths to preserve this part of history for themselves. Cliff's narrator explains that "The definition of what a Savage was like was fixed by color, class, and religion, and over the years a carefully contrived mythology was constructed, which they used to protect their identities. When they were poor, and not all of them white, the mythology persisted. They swore by it. It added depth to their conversation, and kept them interested in each other. Only in each other."[45] Boy takes great pains to pass on his English-identified values to Clare. He does this by sharing with her his religious beliefs, which are influenced by his own colonial ed-

---

43   Cliff, *Abeng*, 3.
44   Ibid., 22.
45   Ibid., 29.

ucation, by taking her to visit the plantation house that his ancestors used to own, and by sending her to an elitist school, where she will receive a colonial education.

At the age of ten, "Boy won a scholarship to a Jesuit boarding school in Brownstown, in the center of the island,"[46] where he received a colonial education as well as a "respect [for] elitism."[47] After being drafted into the cause of the Royal Army during World War I, Boy learned about Calvinism and became convinced that he was one of the Elect, a status he believes "he had been born to."[48] Boy assures Clare that she, too, is part of the Elect since "She was a true Savage… Her fate was sealed."[49] Boy's appreciation for elitism and his desire to emulate white values and behaviors is also reflected in his choice of the church his family attends. At John Knox church, "a Scottish school teacher played Presbyterian hymns at a harpsichord, which…had never adjusted to the climate…It seemed that English people must sing softer—or not at all—and that the climate of that place—damp and dreary—surpassed the clear light and deep warmth of Jamaica. They had always thought of their climate as a gift; the harpsichord told them different."[50] Thus, the church and its ministers reinforce the colonial idea in their congregation that English culture is superior to that of the Jamaicans. It is not surprising, then, that Boy chooses John Knox for his church, since it affirms for him his class position as part of the white elite.

Not only does Boy use Clare's religious training to try to convince his daughter that she is white, he also takes her to visit the plantation house that his great-grandfather once owned and tells her "about her distinguished [white] ancestor."[51] When they go inside the house, Boy describes for Clare how the house used to be decorated with imported furnishings from "England and Ireland mostly. Staffordshire. Wedgwood. Waterford. Royal Doulton,"[52] furthering the constructed mythology of prosperity and whiteness that his family has been telling each other for generations. However, when Boy and Clare walk outside the house, they find "the foundation stones of some of the outbuildings, and faint gullies marking out the earth where others had been. These buildings out back, only a few yards from the great house, had once contained molasses and rum and slaves—the points of conjunction of the system known as the Triangle Trade."[53] Thus, by valorizing and aligning themselves with their white ancestor, Boy and his family become complicit in the violence done to slaves and even to some of their own, unclaimed ancestors. By taking Clare to visit this house and by assuring her that she is "white because [she is] a Savage,"[54] Boy invites Clare to share in that complicity.[55] Like Antoinette's, Clare's status as white depends on her father's

---

46 Ibid., 42.
47 Ibid., 45.
48 Ibid., 44.
49 Ibid., 45.
50 Ibid., 6.
51 Ibid., 24.
52 Ibid., 25.
53 Ibid., 25.
54 Ibid., 73.
55 Ironically, the untold history of violence against slaves that the Judge and others like him enacted reveals that

status and economic standing. And, just as Antoinette shares in the privilege of whiteness made possible by oppressing black people, so too does Clare's status as "census white" invite complicity and denial of self.

Boy's ideas regarding race and class, as well as his version of history, are corroborated for Clare by her colonial education at St. Catherine's School for Girls, where she is taught that "Jamaica had been a slave society. The white and creole mistresses hastened to say that England was the first country to free its slaves,"[56] thereby rescuing the reputation of the British slave owners. Moreover, like her father and his family, Clare's teachers mention very little about Jamaican history. Thus, Clare's sense of her own history is warped and only half complete.

As a result of her father's teaching and of the colonial education she receives, Clare in many ways perceives herself as white since she identifies with white characters in her readings, such as Pip from *Great Expectations*. She also believes that she will have to leave Jamaica since "England. America. These were the places island people went to get ahead."[57] In a reversal of Antoinette's desire to call the West Indies home, Clare believes that she is obligated to go to the colonial "mother" country rather than imagining that she can and should find her purpose and sense of identity and belonging in her own country among her own people. However, despite Boy's best attempts to indoctrinate Clare into believing that she is white, she knows "that her mother [is] not." As a result, she experiences her first crisis of identity when faced with the reality that she is not, in fact, white but, rather, mixed.

Here too, Homi K. Bhabha's concept of hybridity and its relation to mimicry, which works against fixed ideas about race, proves useful.[58] With regard to the concept of mimicry, Bhabha says that "what emerges between mimesis [an exact reproduction] and mimicry is a *writing*, a mode of representation, that marginalizes the monumentality of history, quite simply mocks its power to be a model, that power which supposedly makes it imitable."[59] In choosing to write a work informed by the marginalized histories of colonial texts, Cliff refuses to properly align her text with the texts of the white education her character receives, thereby evidencing an important slippage in the mimicry that Clare's parents encourage in her. Therefore, *Abeng* can be understood to employ what Bhabha terms "the metonymic strategy" which "produces the signifier of colonial *mimicry* [in *Abeng*, education and complicity in hierarchical structures of racial identity] as the affect of hybridity—at once a mode of appropriation [here education as a tool for writing] and of resistance [the use of that tool to decry the received colonial education]."[60] As this "discrimination [here the colonized characters in *Abeng*]

---

instead of "civilizing" a "heathen" nation, the whites who colonized the country and built up their economy through the bodies of slaves were, in fact, the real savages. Clare, on the other hand, means light or clear, suggesting that her clarity of insight can save her from her savage history.

56   Ibid., 30.
57   Ibid., 36.
58   For a full discussion of Bhabha's concept of hybridity, see "Signs Taken for Wonders," and for mimicry, see "Of Mimicry and Man" both in *The Location of Culture* (New York: Routledge University Press, 1994).
59   Bhabha, "Of Mimicry and Man," 125.
60   Bhabha "Signs Taken for Wonders," 172.

turns into the assertion of the hybrid, the insignia of authority [in this context, the power and privilege accorded in proportion with 'whiteness'] becomes a mask, a mockery."[61] Understood in these terms, it becomes clear that Cliff seeks to expose the performativity of race by embracing hybridity in Clare, thereby undermining the power vested in supposedly fixed categories of domination.

Clare exists in the in-between space of Boy's white-identified position and Kitty's Jamaican-identified position, and these separate parental identifications serve as an extension of the metropole/colony dichotomy that existed under British colonization. Like Boy, Kitty forms much of her identity and how she relates to her country through her religious beliefs. Kitty's choice of church reflects her belief that "God and Jesus were but representations of Nature, which it only made sense was female, and the ruler of all."[62] Her respect for nature is demonstrated in her knowledge about the medicinal qualities of many plants that are indigenous to Jamaica. Unfortunately, Kitty does not articulate her beliefs to Clare the way that Boy does, nor does she teach her daughter what she knows about the land and its plants. Kitty withholds this valuable information from Clare along with her affection. Like Annette with Antoinette, Kitty withdraws from Clare because of racial coding. In fact, the narrator tells us that Clare

> Had been handed over to Boy the day she was born…Maybe Kitty never questioned this decision of hers to keep darkness locked inside. Perhaps she assumed that a light-skinned child was by common law, or traditional practice, the child of the whitest parent. This parent would pass this light-skinned daughter on to a white husband, so she would have lighter and lighter babies…Better to have this daughter accept her destiny and not give her any false notion of alliance which she would not be able to honor. Let her passage into that otherworld be as painless as possible. Maybe Kitty thought that Clare would only want this thing, to pass into whiteness, looking as she did, speaking well because of her lessons at St. Catherine's, reading English books and English descriptions of history. Perhaps she thought it would be best for her.[63]

Like the rest of her family, Kitty capitulates to the class and race system in Jamaica that accords more privilege to those with lighter skin. The narrator points out that "The Freemans did not question this structure or the fact that the white people brought money and seemed able to buy themselves any place on the island that suited them. The Freemans fit themselves into the structure and said that yes they were red people, and that was nothing to be ashamed of. At the same time preserving their redness."[64] While they do not aspire to whiteness the way that the Savages do, Kitty and her family do not question the class/racial hierarchy

---

61   Ibid., 172.
62   Ibid., 53.
63   Ibid., 128-129.
64   Ibid., 54.

established through colonization, nor do they attempt to alter it, since they seek to maintain their own relatively privileged position as "red." Since Kitty's perception of race is fixed like Boy's, she seeks to spare her fair-skinned child from the oppression attendant to her conception of blackness by giving Clare what she believes to be the most advantageous position—the position of whiteness, which of necessity denies Clare the history not acknowledged by the colonizers.

Although Boy's and Kitty's beliefs ensure that their daughter will learn history only from her white teachers at St. Catherine's, Clare could have had an opportunity to learn something of her unrecorded history from Kitty's mother, Miss Mattie, whom Clare visits in the summer. Like Kitty, Miss Mattie also refuses to share her religious beliefs and traditions with Clare because she and her friends also subscribe to Kitty's and Boy's beliefs that Clare should embrace only her "whiteness" since she has "good" hair which falls "to her shoulders without any extraordinary means" and since she "inherited her father's green eyes—which all agreed were her 'finest feature.' Visibly she was the family's crowning achievement, combining the best of both sides, and favoring one rather than the other."[65] Mattie and others, like Kitty, assume that Clare belongs in a privileged position of whiteness and that she would not want anything else. The narrator suggests that the class/race hierarchy which exists in Jamaica—and this capitulation to white privilege as a position to be aspired to by those who can—results from an ignorance of native history.

The narrator, who introduces Jamaican history, seeks to rectify this problem by frankly discussing the conditions of slavery, the fact that women were raped by their owners, and the reason why slavery was abolished—because of "the Victorian mania for cleanliness" which made "the trade in palm oil…more profitable than the trade in men and women." Slavery did not end because of any kind of compassion on the part of the English, as Clare has been led to believe by her teachers, but that "of all the slave societies in the New World, Jamaica was considered among the most brutal."[66] Evidence of this brutality occurs on the night before emancipation when Judge (Boy's white ancestor) and others burn their slaves, since "at that moment these people were his property, and they were therefore his to burn."[67]

However, it is through another history of oppression that Clare first begins to question her father's version of her identity, which casts her as white, when she encounters *The Diary of Anne Frank*. Because of her identification with Anne and her conviction that what happened to Anne and other Jewish people was not justified, Clare also begins to question her own privileged position as white. During a discussion with her father about the Holocaust, she wonders "how she could be white with a colored mother, brown legs, and ashy knees."[68] Like Antoinette, Clare finds herself a kind of outsider to her "whiteness." However, with her attention to history and an understanding of oppression born from racism, Cliff

---

65   Ibid., 61.
66   Ibid., 18.
67   Ibid., 40.
68   Ibid., 73.

reworks Antoinette's narrative of loss by according this moment an important role in Clare's ever-developing political consciousness.

Another incident much more closely connected to Clare's life prompts similar questions when Doreen, who has a "deep-brown body," has an epileptic fit at school and none of the teachers come forward to help her except Miss Maxwell, who is the "dark physical education teacher."[69] When Clare asks her mother about why the other teachers did not help Doreen, Kitty responds by saying, "you know how Englishwomen are—they think that they are ladies; they are afraid of the least little sign of sickness or anything like that." Clare understands "lady" to mean someone who "dress [es] and [speaks] well…[,] [who] speaks 'properly.'"[70] In this way, Clare comes to understand that race often determines who "wins" throughout history, which, in turn, causes her to question her own racial status, even as she learns that race is often connected to "proper" gendered behavior as well, since being a "lady" coincides with being white. The latter discovery also causes her to question her gender position.

Miss Mattie seeks to ensure Clare's "proper" gender behavior when she arranges for Zoe to be her playmate. That way Clare will not bother Joshua, since she "was getting too old to be running around with boys."[71] She also believes that Clare is "not a girl who should be spending too much of her time on chores,"[72] which indicates a capitulation on her part to the class status Clare achieves as a result of her color. Since Zoe's mother, Ruth, lives on Miss Mattie's land, she has no choice but to comply with Miss Mattie's request that her daughter spend time with Clare.

Through her friendship with Zoe, Clare seeks to step outside of the complicated boundaries of her racial position: "[they] were well aware that there were differences between them, of course…But in their friendship the differences could become more and more of a background, which only rarely they stumbled on and had to confront. They had childhood—they had make-believe. They had a landscape which was wild and real and filled with places in which their imaginations could move."[73] Thus Cliff asserts that connection to the land is the starting place for moving beyond the boundaries of colonial identity: "this landscape…does not simply contain an unwritten history but also contains the potential to heal that history."[74] This connection to the land and the intimacy that the girls develop as a result mirrors Antoinette's friendship with Tia. However, while Clare and Zoe find female solidarity with each other, they are also aware of the lack of control they are afforded in their own lives by virtue of their sex.

Clare's idea to steal Miss Mattie's gun and to kill Cudjoe the pig is thus an attempt to assert some kind of control. The hunting excursion could have been an important step for Clare in asserting her independence and agency by claiming her own power since she wants "to do something so dem will know we is smad-

---

69   Ibid., 96.
70   Ibid., 98-99.
71   Ibid., 91.
72   Ibid., 92.
73   Ibid., 95.
74   Belinda Edmondson, "Race, Privilege, and the Politics of (Re)Writing History: An Analysis of the Novels of Michelle Cliff," *Callaloo* 16, no. 1 (1993): 188.

dy."[75] However, Zoe's indictment of Clare's actions when the trip fails reveals that Clare has been selfish in her desires and has not considered the implications for Zoe who does not share her privileged position. Zoe tells her:

> Wunna know, wunna is truly town gal. Wunna a go back to Kingston soon now. Wunna no realize me have to stay here. Wunna no know what people dem would say if two gal dem shoot Massa Cudjoe. Dem would talk and me would have fe tek on all de contention. Dem will say dat me t'ink me is buckra boy, going pon de hill a hunt fe one pig. Or dat me let buckra gal lead me into wickedness. Or dey will say me t'ink me is Guinea warrior, not gal pickney. But wunna never reckon with dat, Wunna jus' go ahead with wunna sint'ing. Country people dem don't forget no-t'ing."[76]

Clare is chastened by Zoe's speech, and though she denies being "buckra," she loses her enthusiasm for the hunt and feels "silly. Stupid"[77] in light of Zoe's rebuke.

While this might have been a turning point in Clare's relationship with Zoe and with her own identification as white, gender identity issues intervene when a man violates their privacy and objectifies their naked bodies when the girls go swimming after making up. Thus, Clare resorts to two incongruous sources of power: the stolen gun and her education. She drops her patois and speaks like a buckra. As MacDonald-Smythe contends, "Clare's method of self-empowerment is also shaped by the patriarchal and imperialist inclinations encouraged by her father. Faced with what she presumes to be a challenge to her subjectivity and sexuality, Clare defends her selfhood with brute force, with the power to wield a rifle, the assumption of the authority of the white man. She acts like the buckra."[78] Clare shoots the gun, despite Zoe's objection, and ultimately kills Mattie's bull. Like Antoinette, who reverts to racial invectives when her power is threatened by Tia, Clare's assertion of white identity immediately after she and Zoe fight also effectively ends her friendship with Zoe. And, like Antoinette's break with Tia, this event removes Clare from her potential place of belonging (she is sent away to live with a family friend) when she is aligned with whiteness rather than with Zoe.

After Clare shoots the bull, Miss Mattie condemns her because she believes that the evil which caused Clare to steal the gun and then shoot her grandmother's prized bull stems from the sense of privilege she has since she is *buckra* like her father. While Boy and Kitty lament Clare's irresponsibility which costs them money to repay Mattie for the bull, the fact that they send Clare to stay with Beatrice Phillips for the rest of the summer suggests that her biggest failing to their mind was her refusal to comply with proper gender expectations, which for Kitty are also tied up in race. She tells Clare that Mrs. Phillips can teach her how to be a "lady" (read white), which Kitty sees as imperative to a proper performance of whiteness. This discussion recalls her telling Clare

---

75 Rhys, *Wide Sargasso Sea*, 118.
76 Ibid., 118.
77 Ibid., 119.
78 Antonia McDonald-Smythe, *Making Homes in the West Indies: Constructions of Subjectivity in the Writings of Michelle Cliff and Jamaica Kincaid* (New York: Garland, 2001).

about why the white teachers at her school failed to help the dark girl who had the epileptic seizure. So, for Kitty (and for Boy), race, class, and gender are all intimately connected in a certain code of conduct that would properly define limits for all three.

Beatrice, the woman they send Clare to live with, epitomizes white bigotry—most clearly in the way that she beats her servants. She provides Clare with an objective look at the ignorance and nastiness of racism that Clare has been unable to see in her father because she loves and admires him. Beatrice cares for her dogs more than for people, she has nasty habits like killing ticks with her fingers, and she shows her cultural ignorance when she claims that a coloratura singer is by definition colored.[79] She tells Clare not to protest because she is not so pure herself. Despite Beatrice's show of fidelity by letting Clare live with her and sleep in the same room with her, Beatrice still wants to make it clear that she is in control. She thus offers the kind of training that should teach Clare that she is better than those who are considered coloured but not quite good enough, or, to use Bhabha's words, that she is "white but not quite."[80]

While Clare is staying with Beatrice, she meets Beatrice's sister, Mrs. Stevens, who, according to Beatrice, is insane. Beatrice explains her condition as having to do with her sister's unwillingness to occupy a proper gender role—she read books, wanted to leave Jamaica, and declared that she did not want to get married. When she was forced to marry, her husband left her because he "couldn't endure a woman who wouldn't be a woman."[81] Beatrice tells Clare that Mrs. Stevens went mad and stopped washing.

Even though Beatrice forbids her to speak to Mrs. Stevens, Clare does talk to her and learns that Winifred was not sent to the convent because she refused to marry, but because she was pregnant with a black man's child. Mrs. Stevens tells Clare that her pregnancy and unsanctioned relationship with a black man is what has "crossed her up"[82] and that Clare should take care not to let them—white people—do the same thing to her. Winifred Stevens also admits that she "knew better. I know that God meant that coons and buckra people were not meant to mix their blood. It's not right. Only sadness comes from mixture." She claims that she stopped washing because "all the water in the world cannot wash away what I did,"[83] but she also says that she named her child and that she thinks about her every day. She even seems to see something of her child in Clare when she tries to touch her.

Here again we see the idea that blackness and contact with blackness is what causes madness, but it seems from what Winifred says and how the others, like her sister, treat her, that this is really a case in which high valuation of whiteness and inclination toward white racist values is actually what drives Winifred insane.

---

79   Cliff, *Abeng*, 157.
80   Bhabha, *Location of Culture*, 128.
81   Cliff, *Abeng*, 159.
82   Ibid., 162.
83   Ibid., 164.

Rather than the blackness of her lover or of her child, what really works against her sanity are the social constraints that say she was wrong to love or even to get close to a black person. Thus, "her refusal to wash" may illustrate her sense of shame, but it may "also indica[te] that she rejects the Victorian 'mania for cleanliness.' In refusing to wash [that is], she identifies with blackness; in essence[,] she becomes the black woman she needed to be in order to love the man of her choice."[84] Winifred, then, becomes the direct counterpoint to the "lady" that Clare is supposed to become by learning from Beatrice how to be "white." Because of Winifred's position as metaphorically black, Clare is able to admit to Winifred that she herself is mixed, even though she has not been able to do that with Beatrice. To Winifred she confesses that her mother is red, rather than relying on her father's whiteness for her racial identity as she has done with Beatrice.

More importantly, as a consequence of shared disclosures, Winifred tells Clare that her own life did not turn out as it should have because she misunderstood her history. She then tells Clare how things really came about in Jamaica: "They brought people here in chains and then expected to prosper. They killed off all the Indians and all the snakes and believed they were doing good…They are all gone now—the ones who did these things—gone to their reward. But the afterbirth is lodged in the woman's body and will not be expelled. All the waste of birth. Foul-smelling and past its use."[85] In her reading of these lines in the text, M. M. Adjarian says,

> Colonialism gave rise to the multicolored children of Jamaica and more specifically to the circumstances that brought about Mrs. Steven's doomed affair. Rather than being expelled along with the infants, however, the British imperial placenta that nourished these children from within their mother's bodies remains implanted within the maternal womb. If an air of decay, corruption, and death seems to exist in Jamaica, then, it is because the historical memories of the colonizers and the colonizers' crimes against the colonized, though buried deep, are strong across centuries.[86]

Significantly, it is Winifred (who has stepped outside of her racial, class, and gender system) who knows the history of slavery and oppression that brought the Jamaica that they know into existence and who teaches Clare. Winifred therefore acts as Clare's "true benefactor" since she "represents the black and white races, the outcast and the English gentlewoman. Clare is supposed to become a genteel Englishwoman under the guidance of Mrs. Philips, but she receives her real education from the mad woman and thus is transformed from girl to womanist."[87] Clare starts her period that night of re-education right after she has a very important dream about Zoe. Clare's menstruation coincides with her growing

---

84 Kathleen J. Renk, *Caribbean Shadows and Victorian Ghosts* (Charlottesville, VA: University of Virginia Press, 1999), 108.
85 Cliff, *Abeng*, 165.
86 M.M.Adjarian, *Allegories of Desire: Body, Nation, and Empire in Modern Caribbean Literature by Women* (Westport, CT: Praeger Publishers, 2004), 20.
87 Kathleen J. Renk, *Caribbean Shadows and Victorian Ghosts*, 107.

political consciousness, a consciousness which signals that there is hope in her generation—in children who know they are mixed and embrace that truth rather than try to reject it.

That night Clare has a dream in which she sees herself throwing a rock at Zoe and then saying she is sorry and making a compress for the bloody wound. This bears a strong similarity to what happens in the scene in *Wide Sargasso Sea* with two very important exceptions. First, the white child (Clare) throws the rock at the black child (Zoe) rather than vice versa. Second, Clare apologizes and tries to make amends. As Edmondson notes, "If we consider this scene within the context of its literary history, Cliff is rewriting an historical relation of black and white West Indian women not only to link their cultural identities but to acknowledge the white woman's relation to power."[88] Clare's dream act is symbolic displacement of what Winifred has told her about her white ancestors that day—they also metaphorically threw rocks at the black people on the island. She wakes up from tending to Zoe's wound to find that she has started her period, and the narrator describes it "as the blood lining of her womb…breaking away,"[89] which points to Winifred's comment about the afterbirth in the body: something is being expelled here, and it happens for the first time after she tries to reconcile with Zoe in her dream. Clare's body thereby becomes a metaphor for her own political awakening as she subconsciously, and then physically, tries to rectify something that is wrong and then expel it through her menstrual flow. Moreover, by re-writing the scene from *Wide Sargasso Sea*, Cliff seeks to repair the psychological and physical "castration" that Antoinette feels when Tia throws the rock at her.

Furthermore, as M. M. Adjarian points out, "when Clare begins her first menstrual cycle, she cleanses her body in a nearby stream, mingling her blood with island waters. In this quasi-ritual act of mingling fluids, woman and land become one."[90] The idea that Clare's body is now connected to Jamaica and its reconciliation is further clarified in the next passage of the novel: "Clare pictured the flesh of her insides expanding and contracting, then settling…All had happened as Zoe said it would…Something had happened to her—was happening to her."[91] This image of her insides expanding and contracting and then settling echoes the opening lines of the book: "The island rose and sank. Twice. During periods in which history was recorded by indentions on rock and shell."[92] At this point Clare is becoming more aware of her history and her place in her country, and this knowledge is connected to her own body and the body of the land whose fate is now intimately connected to hers. While Antoinette's "castration," (and its concomitant connection to menstruation) as a *personal* tragedy affords her no control over her body and removal from the land, Clare's menstruation provides connection to the land, and, aided by historical understanding, connects her body to *collective* resistance when she chooses a politically "black" identity.

---

88   Belinda Edmondson, "Race, Privilege, and the Politics of (Re)Writing History: An Analysis of the Novels of Michelle Cliff," 183.
89   Cliff, *Abeng*, 166.
90   M.M.Adjarian, *Allegories of Desire: Body, Nation, and Empire in Modern Caribbean Literature by Women*, 50.
91   Cliff, *Abeng*, 166.
92   Ibid., 3.

Antoinette imagines her reunion with Tia and Jamaica through a dream, and Cliff also reclaims a politically "black" identity for Clare in her dream. The last lines of the book refer to this all-important dream about Zoe: "She was not ready to understand her dream. She had no idea that everyone we dream about we are."[93] Though Clare cannot yet fully understand her dream or her history and her connection to Jamaica, she subconsciously understands that her alignment with whiteness alienates her from her homeland and its people, even if they are part of who she is. Since Clare's story is not bound by another narrative, as Antoinette's is through its connection to *Jane Eyre,* Clare does not have to be removed as a result of failed gender and racial performance. Rather, Clare can choose her identity since Cliff's narrative has demonstrated that while race and gender inform and mutually construct each other, these categories are not "fixed" categories. Clare's political awakening gets fully realized in the sequel novel, *No Telephone to Heaven.*

While Cliff succeeds in reversing many of the desires for "whiteness" and privilege found in Rhys's novel, the impulse to align with "blackness" and to reconnect to Jamaica remains unfulfilled in the novels discussed here. Moreover, just as Antoinette's attempt at reconnection ends in her death through flames, so too does Clare's at the end of *No Telephone to Heaven.* While it should be noted that Clare's death occurs as the result of her alignment with "black" rebels who fight against racist representations of Jamaicans in film, their party is attacked because someone in their group betrays them. Therefore, though Clare resists her racial position as white, as well as the history of oppression it represents, her reclamation of an alienated identity and homeland are still somehow figured as illusive and imaginary spaces where bodily connection can come only through death and transformation of the body into something other than itself. Moreover, Clare's betrayal by a fellow black revolutionary cautions readers against assuming that aligning with a resistant "black" identity can erase the history that makes the friendships between the two pairs of girls so fleeting in each novel. Ultimately, Tia and Zoe's dark bodies stand as the corporeal reminders that Antoinette and Clare cannot belong to, or be at home in, a land where their "white" bodies represent the oppressor, while their positions as insiders also construct them as oppressed by the very racial hierarchies of color that grant them their oppressor status.

Bibliography

Adjarian, M. M. *Allegories of Desire: Body, Nation, and Empire in Modern Caribbean Literature by Women.* Westport, CT: Praeger Publishers, 2004.

Agatucci, Cora. "Michelle Cliff." In *Contemporary African American Novelists: A Bio-Bibliographical Critical Sourcebook,* edited by Emanuel S. Nelson, 94-101. Westport, CT: Greenwood Press, 1999.

Ashcroft, Griffiths, and Tiffin. *Post-Colonial Studies: The Key Concepts.* London: Routledge, 2000.

---

93 Ibid., 166.

Bhabha, Homi K. *The Location of Culture.* New York: Routledge, 1994.

Bickford-Smith, Vivian. "The Betrayal of Creole Elites, 1880-1920." In *Black Experience and the British Empire,* edited by Philip D. Morgan and Sean Hawkins, 194-227. Oxford: Oxford University Press, 2004.

Butler, Judith. *Gender Trouble: Feminism and the Subversion of Identity.* New York: Routledge, 1989.

Cliff, Michelle. *Abeng.* New York: Plume, 1984.

———. *The Land of the Look Behind: Prose and Poetry.* Ithaca, NY: Firebrand Books, 1985.

Dalton, Elizabeth. "Sex and Race in *Wide Sargasso Sea.*" *Partisan Review* 67 no. 3 (2000): 431-442.

Dyer, Richard. *White.* New York: Routledge, 1997.

Edmondson, Belinda. "Race, Privilege, and the Politics of (Re)Writing History: An Analysis of the Novels of Michelle Cliff." *Callaloo* 16, no. 1 (1993): 180-191.

Erwin, Lee. "'Like Looking in a Looking-Glass': History and Narrative in *Wide Sargasso Sea.*" *Novel: A Forum on Fiction* 22 no. 2 (1989): 143-158.

Halloran, Vivian Nun. "Race, Creole, and National Identities in Rhys's *Wide Sargasso Sea* and Phillips's *Cambridge.*" *Small Axe. A Caribbean Journal of Criticism* 21 (2006): 87-104.

Hawkins, Sean and Philip D. Morgan. "Blacks and the British Empire: An Introduction." In *Black Experience and the British Empire,* edited by Philip D. Morgan and Sean Hawkins, 1-34. Oxford: Oxford University Press, 2004.

Hogan, Patrick Colm. *Colonialism and Cultural Identity: Crises of Tradition in the Anglophone Literatures of India, Africa, and the Caribbean.* New York: State University of New York Press, 2000.

Johnson, Howard. "The Black Experience in the British Caribbean in the Twentieth Century." In *Black Experience and the British Empire,* edited by Philip D. Morgan and Sean Hawkins, 317-346. Oxford: Oxford University Press, 2004.

Lionnet, Francoise. "Of Mangoes and Maroons: Language, History, and the Multi-Cultural Subject of Michelle Cliff's Abeng." In *De/Colonizing the Subject: The Politics of Gender in Women's Autobiography,* edited by Sidonie Smith and Julia Watson, 321-345. Minneapolis, MN: University of Minnesota Press, 1992.

McClintock, Anne. *Imperial Leather: Race, Gender, and Sexuality in the Colonial Contest.* New York: Routledge, 1995.

McDonald-Smythe, Antonia. *Making Homes in the West/Indies: Constructions of Subjectivity in the Writings of Michelle Cliff and Jamaica Kincaid.* New York: Garland, 2001.

Olaussen, Maria. "Jean Rhys's Construction of Blackness as Escape from White Femininity in 'Wide Sargasso Sea." *ARIEL: A Review of International English Literature* 24, no. 2 (1993): 65-82.

Renk, Kathleen J. *Caribbean Shadows and Victorian Ghosts.* Charlottesville, VA: University of Virginia Press, 1999.

Rhys, Jean. *Wide Sargasso Sea.* New York: W. W. Norton Co., Inc., 1982.

Ward, J. R. "The British West Indies in the Age of Abolition, 1748-1815." In *Oxford History of the British Empire Volume II.* Edited by P.J. Marshall, 415-439. Oxford: Oxford University Press, 1998.

Wickramagamage, Carmen. "An/other Side to Antoinette/Bertha: Reading 'Race' into *Wide Sargasso Sea.*"*Journal of Commonwealth Literature* 35, no. 1 (2000): 27-42.

Wyndham, Francis. "Introduction." In *Wide Sargasso Sea, Norton Paperback,* 5. New York: W.W. Norton & Co., Inc., 1982.

Part III
Color in Contemporary Discourse and Debates

10

Pink is the New Green: Raising Little Shoppers from Birth

Amy Hagenrater-Gooding

> Commercialism distorts our culture by turning every event into a reason to consume. Anthropologists say that holidays reflect a culture's values. In America, every holiday is a sales event.[1]

Every Saturday morning, my children and I go grocery shopping. If I am lucky, I can maneuver past the toiletries and head straight to the grocery section, but if I encounter too much traffic in the aisle or need to take a detour, it is inevitable: we are going to end up in a sea of pink. Two entire rows in our Walmart Super Center are bedecked in various shades of delectable pink. If I were a wise parent, I would keep walking, but of course I go down the aisle, allowing my daughter to take it all in. Barbie, Lalaloopsy, Pillow Pets, Strawberry Shortcake: all of it calls to her and I succumb; I let her get the $5 pink princess doll whose head will come off after she tries to yank on the doll's rubberized body one too many times in an effort to get her plasticine dress off.

Early on, girls are drawn to pink, a color most associated with the feminine, and often encouraged by their mothers, who recognize not only their own childhood but also their own femininity, which is also targeted by marketers. Advertisers aim for a "cradle to grave" kind of loyalty which often becomes cross-generational, with the mother inherently encouraging gender roles and "the pink think" that she grew up with herself. Gender prescribed messages "turn girls and boys into objects, who are judged by how well they meet the stereotypes."[2] One's girlishness (and, conversely, one's boyishness) is often a marker of acceptance or rejection based on one's peer group. Advertisers exploit the insecurities inherent in one's desire to fit in with others, so much so that the "pink it and shrink it" mantra of marketers persists well into adulthood. By making a product pink and making

---

1 Rajmohan Joshi, *Encyclopedia of Journalism and Mass Communications* (New Delhi: Gyan, 2006), 232.
2 Diane Levin, "Too Young To Be A Consumer: The Toll of Consumer Culture on the Rights of Childhood," *CCFC*, May 1, 2009, http://www.commercialfreechildhood.org/resource/too-young-be-consumer-toll-consumer-culture-rights-childhood.

it smaller, manufacturers target women.³ And it works. In fact, pink might be more aptly correlated to green, the color signifying monetary earning potential, and advertisers have taken notice. From birth, girls are conditioned through the sea of pink in big-box retail stores that merchandise in shades from bubble-gum pink to Barbie doll fuchsia, among other products marked for girls.

It was not always this way. As Peggy Orenstein notes in *Cinderella Ate My Daughter*, "Children weren't color-coded at all until the early twentieth century." Typically, children wore white since clothes were laundered through boiling. Further, "when nursery colors were introduced, pink was actually considered the more masculine hue, a pastel version of red, which was associated with strength. Blue, with its intimations of the Virgin Mary, constancy, and faithfulness, symbolized femininity."⁴ A desire for increased sales caused a shift to marketing pink to girls. Advertisers refer to this as "the pink factor." This trend explains why virtually any toy may be available in pink. From baseball gloves and lacrosse sticks to Lego toys and Tonka trucks, pink means money. Lynn Peril, in *Pink Think: Becoming a Woman in Many Uneasy Lessons,* attributes the shift to Brooks Brothers shirts in 1948, a staple for men.⁵ Even Elvis, a masculine hot-blooded icon, wore pink, yet this color in the Brooks Brothers shirt caught on for female coeds. The company designed a fuller shirt for female customers. Peril notes Mamie Eisenhower's love of the shade of pale pink that soon became known as "First Lady Pink" in 1953. While fashion trends came and went, the marker of pink as a feminine signifier remained.

Many people will be aware of the Disney princesses as individual entities (Snow White, Cinderella, Sleeping Beauty, etc.), but it was not until Disney marketed the nine princesses as a collection under the new leadership of Andy Mooney at Disney Consumer Products that Disney's revenue shot up. Orenstein observes, "There are now more than 25,000 Disney Princess items" often exploiting the attraction of girly-girl pink.⁶ In the twenty-first century, toys for girls have moved beyond Barbie to Pinkalicious and Fancy Nancy, who extol the joy of pink in feather boas, high heels, and lipstick, all of which are excessive female markers. The female heroines of children's books do not measure 36-24-36, nor do they have hourglass figures as Barbie does (scaled to real life 36-18-33); they are cherubic, candy-colored and spunky, yet they are somewhat subdued with a love of ruffles, lipstick, dresses, and pearls all cast in a pink hue. The marketing is unmistakable. While Barbie may be passé in some circles, these new figures do more of what it means to be a girl: dress up, have teas, and above all else, look pretty in pink. Initially it might seem that these dolls are a departure from the curvy figure and docile nature represented by Barbie, but they are repeating the same stereotypes. Fancy Nancy is a character who, like many little girls, loves dress up. But what gets marketed is the production of the spectacle of the girly-girl performance. She wears sparkly ruby slippers, boas, and strands of necklaces

---

3   Amy Swanson, "Marketing to Women: Why the 'Pink It and Shrink It' Strategy Doesn't Always Work." *Quality Logo Products,* June 2, 2012, http://www.qualitylogoproducts.com/blog/marketing-to-women-pink-it-shrink-it/.
4   Peggy Orenstein, *Cinderella Ate My Daughter* (New York: HarperCollins, 2011), Kindle Edition.
5   Lynn Peril, *Pink Think: Becoming a Woman in Many Uneasy Lessons* (New York: W.W. Norton, 2002), Kindle Edition.
6   Orenstein, *Cinderella Ate My Daughter.*

that manifest what it means to be a girl. Girls are encouraged to indulge in "fancy" behavior themselves. Although the character uses a strong vocabulary (Ecstatic! Parasol! Gorgeous!), and the accompanying books encourage reading, it is the underlying persistent focus of pink, of girly culture, that makes the color itself the ideal. Pinkalicious is another culprit. The character from the self-titled series *Pinkalicious* suffers "pinkitis;" in other words, she loves too much pink. She eats too many pink cupcakes and turns pink. (One cannot help but think the cautionary tale should stop here.) The doctor suggests a cure of green, the vegetables that Pinkalicous deplores. While the title book is assumed to be about nutrition, it does not present healthful eating as enjoyable eating like the pink cupcakes that Pinkalicious cannot resist. It should be noted further that books in the series continue various plot lines, enabling the title character to get closer to her love of pink (pink lemonade in *Pinkalicious and the Pink Drink*). In the overarching plot, the books extol "pink" as prized above all others. In *Pinkalicious: Tickled Pink*, young readers are told: "I was in the library, looking for a good book. I poked around the shelves until I found something with a bright pink cover and shiny gold letters."[7] Value is determined by one's proximity to girly-ness, to pink. Although these books encourage a love for reading, they do so at a cost. [8] The wholesale branding of girls as pink lovers and pink consumers starts young and transitions steadily into adolescence. Orenstein says, "Pink, it seems, is the new gold."[9]

While this indoctrination persists, pink moves from a marker of girlhood and innocence into one of implicit sexuality, and young women buy in. By the time a woman is an independent adult able to make her own purchases, she brings a good deal of money into the marketplace. Lisa Johnson and Andrea Learned in *Don't Think Pink* note that "While women's combined earnings are estimated at around $1 trillion annually, her spending power overall is estimated at over $2 trillion each year."[10] Women spend their money on products that perpetuate the consumerist identity they have known since childhood: they buy pink products, which contributes to a sexualized identity. The "Pink" line released in 2004 by Victoria's Secret appeals to teens and college-aged women; it features sexy, yet comfortable underwear, loungewear, bags, and perfume. Most items in the Victoria's Secret Pink line are comparatively simple and tame, but displaying "Pink" across one's bottom or chest seems more than a simple declarative statement: it is a branding of a color associated with selling sex. It is this paradox—marketing a line of comfortable clothing by a company that trades in burgeoning sexuality—that is problematic. For young girls, this makes for a confusing transition from

---

7   Victoria Kann, *Pinkalicious: Tickled Pink* (New York: Harper Collins, 2010), 4.

8   The character of Pinky Dinky Doo is, perhaps, a better example of how pink can be used but not overtly be the focus. Created by Jim Jinkins, the series features seven-year-old Pinky who "Thinks Big" to solve various conundrums that crop up in each episode. She and her brother, Tyler, often go to the "Story Box" where she will weave a made-up story that will somehow correlate to the problem at hand. Not only does the series encourage imagination, but Pinky often introduces a new vocabulary word heralded by trumpet by her pet, Mr. Guinea Pig. The "pink" in this series is little more than an alliterative name. The emphasis isn't pink or being prettified, but rather learning about plot, structure, imagination and vocabulary.

9   Peggy Orenstein, "What's Wrong With Cinderella?" *New York Times*, December 24, 2006, http://www.nytimes.com/2006/12/24/magazine/24princess.t.html?pagewanted=all.

10 Lisa Johnson and Andrea Learned, *Don't Think Pink* (New York: AMACON, 2004), 9.

childhood to adolescence, one that is not easy to reconcile with one's developing sexuality. As Andrea Levy writes in *Female Chauvinist Pigs*,

> The tricky thing is that adolescents don't automatically know what to do to make themselves feel sexy or secure or confident. They sometimes have 'confused bodies' and they frequently have confused heads. Adolescent girls in particular—who are blitzed with cultural pressure to be hot, to *seem* sexy—have a very difficult time learning to recognize their own sexual desire, which would seem a critical component of feeling sexy.[11]

In other words, the self-exploration of sexuality is much different and more difficult than the performance or mimetic behavior of sexiness that is encouraged by pink advertising and ideology. By constantly repeating a signifier—PINK—on a fashion trend, the ubiquity of the signified almost becomes devoid of meaning, representing the stereotyped.

Again, it is not just pink that is a concern, but it is all that pink entails that is problematic. Victoria's Secret markets a universal ideal of beauty by selling sexiness. The Victoria's Secret website crashed after a fashion show featuring the Victoria's Secret Angels drew too many viewers to see the endless parade of scantily clad supermodels in their lacy under-things. The consumption of the female body is what pink culture perpetuates. Nancy Friday claims, "Beauty is the currency of the land. It buys everything. It matters not that the beauty is our own sex."[12] A woman copes with this consumption by constantly trying to replicate and pinkify herself as a consumer of thongs, perfumes, push-up bras, and lotions. As Simone De Beauvoir writes in *The Second Sex*, "Woman…is even required by society to make herself an erotic object. The purpose of the fashions to which she is enslaved is not to reveal her as an independent individual, but rather to cut her off from her transcendence in order to offer her as prey to male desires."[13] Not only is it the whole of her body that becomes a commodity, but her parts are also rendered and sold individually, especially her "pink" parts.

What is most disconcerting is that young women buy into a male enterprise celebrating soft-core pornography under the guise of female empowerment. Levy discusses Joe Francis and his entrepreneurial venture *Girls Gone Wild* (first released in 1998) as a vehicle by which girls believe they are celebrating and championing their sexuality when they are essentially being duped. Girls, often on spring break or in college towns out for a good time, are asked to show their pink: their breasts and genitals, and they are asked to engage in sexy acts with their girlfriends (never men). Francis has earned an estimated $100 million on the *Girls Gone Wild* franchise alone.[14] The women, on the other hand, often get only hats or shirts that advertise the franchise. More troubling is the probability that the young women – often inebriated – may not consider the ramifications of their

---

11   Andrea Levy, *Female Chauvinist Pigs* (New York: Free Press, 2005), 12.
12   Nancy Friday, *The Power of Beauty* (New York: HarperCollins, 1996), 226.
13   Simone De Beauvoir, *The Second Sex* (New York: Vintage, 1949), 529.
14   Levy, *Female Chauvinist Pigs*, 12.

actions, particularly if they are influenced by the behavior of celebrities. Paris Hilton's sex tape with Rick Solomon that was leaked just prior to her reality show debut *The Simple Life*,[15] and her blatant display of her genitalia on the red carpet of P. Diddy's birthday party in 2004 come to mind. From Britney Spears to Miley Cyrus, young women parade themselves in various states of undress wittingly or unwittingly exposing themselves on film. Instead of ruining a career, such behavior often boosts a female celebrity's image. Sexuality and sexiness aren't examined, but they are commercialized through one stock image or standardized act: "...it's about endlessly reiterating one particular—and particularly commercial—shorthand for sexiness."[16] While the women who engage in this enterprise, including celebrities, appear confident in exposing their bodies, there is also great commodification in exploiting women's insecurity with their pinkedness.

Pink, as a trope, has been associated with not just sexuality, but with the sexual. When Steven Tyler released "Pink" with Aerosmith in 1997, he wasn't paying homage to the palette merging of red and white.[17] The double entendre in the song is apparent: "Pink it's my new obsession/...Pink on the lips of your lover cause/Pink it's the love you discover/Pink as the bing on your cherry/...Pink it's the color of passion/...Pink when I turn out the light." While musicians might herald women's "pink" in song, the beauty industry has exploited women's insecurities where their "pinkness" is concerned. The newest advertising campaign for the Summer's Eve line of feminine hygiene products is the "Hail to the V." In the latest TV ad, viewers hear the sound of an arrogant British woman proclaim, "It's the cradle of life. It's the center of civilization. Men have fought for it, battled for it, died for it. One might say it's the most powerful thing on earth." The visuals show Egyptian culture, Asian battles, and knights jousting, all conveying a sense of historic and continued importance. Viewers might not know what is being discussed, but they know it is of value—until the scene abruptly changes to a supermarket where a woman contemplates the purchase of a bottle of vaginal wash. The voice changes to that of an American woman saying, "So c'mon ladies. Show it a little love." The implication is that a woman's pink body parts need specific commercial products. While the ad is controversial on its own, the idea of marketing to women with the underlying assumption that they are not clean enough brings forth myriad issues. De Beauvoir writes:

> It is true enough that at the moment of puberty boys also feel their bodies as an embarrassment, but being proud of their manhood from an early age, they proudly project toward manhood the moment of their development...The little girl, on the contrary, in order to change into a grown-up person, must be confined within the limits imposed upon her by her femininity. The boy sees with wonder in his growing hairiness vague promises of things to come: the girl stands abashed before the "brutal and prescribed drama" that decides her destiny. Just as the penis derives its privileged evaluation from the social

---

15 Ibid.,28.
16 Ibid., 30.
17 Aerosmith, *Nine Lives* (Sony, 1997), CD.

context, so it is the social context that makes menstruation a curse. The one symbolizes manhood, the other femininity; and it is because femininity signifies alterity and inferiority that its manifestation is met with shame.[18]

The "wounded, shameful and culpable" self that emerges for young women at the experience of their first menses is perpetuated by marketers who prey on the suggestion that the vagina is unclean, impure, and in need of special ointments or salves to make it acceptable. Not only do advertisers suggest that a woman's genitalia needs more than soap and water, but also that its outer appearance is troubling. Vajazzling, a process whereby a woman waxes her genitalia and then adorns herself with Swarovski crystals, is presented as an aesthetic indulgence and is openly advertised on beauty salon billboards and discussed by celebrities who tout its importance to one's self-esteem. Jennifer Love Hewitt, appearing on *The George Lopez Show* on January 12, 2010, proclaimed the importance of vajazzling after a difficult break-up. "It looks like a little disco ball down there," she tittered. Although Lopez made light of her comment, Love Hewitt rationalized: "But for the ladies…I was feeling awful, I had been through a horrible break-up and I was like, uh, this is just awful and I need something to make me feel better." But self-esteem cannot be gained through prettifying one's genitalia, although this is what business and the entertainment industry would have us believe. As if this practice were not enough, vaginal rejuvenation has become de rigueur in some circles. Such surgery tightens the muscles of the vaginal wall for women who have given birth. Popularized by Dr. David Matlock, a California gynecologist who has appeared on television shows such as *The View* and *Dr. 90210*, procedures like "The Mommy Makeover" and "Designer Laser Vaginoplasty" are requested by more than just the Hollywood sub-set:

> The American Society of Plastic Surgeons began tracking vaginal rejuvenation in 2005 and recorded 793 procedures that year. That figure is widely regarded as low, because many doctors who perform these operations are gynecologists, whose primary professional association, the American College of Obstetricians and Gynecologists, does not keep such statistics.[19]

Elective genitoplasty, or the desire to have a "designer vagina," caters to the idea that there is a perfect look for one's genitalia. "It's one more thing we can feel insecure about," Laura Bermen, a Chicago-based therapist notes.[20] And, as if that were not enough, "My New Pink Button" is advertised online as a "simple to use genital cosmetic colorant that restores the pink back to woman's genitals".[21] Developed by Karan Mari and retailing for $29.95, the temporary dye comes in shades ranging from "Bettie" and "Ginger" to "Marilyn" and "Audry," depending on the level of intensity one might seek and the level of one's genital color loss. The product prom-

---

18 De Beauvoir, *The Second Sex*, 315.
19 Sandra Boodman, "Cosmetic Surgeries New Frontier," *Washington Post*, March 03, 2007, accessed June 2, 2012, http://www.wordsworkcom.com/files/WashingtonPost_030607.pdf.
20 Ibid.
21 "My New Pink Button," *My New Pink Button*, Last modified 2013, http://www.mynewpinkbutton.com/.

ises to restore that "youthful pink color back to your labia." Equating pink with youthfulness is not new, but now many women obsess or worry about the color of their vaginas. As guest poster Marley P. noted on the Feminist Fatale website:

> The beauty industry runs on selling women an innate insecurity and notion that self-worth is implicitly tied to what we look like and simultaneously co-opts feminist ideals of empowerment as a way to sell a product. We are not being sold empowerment; in fact, we are being duped into believing that empowerment and liberated sexuality can be bought.[22]

Yet, women buy in.

Some women might find themselves scoffing that anyone would be duped into purchasing such contrived notions of femininity or identifying with societal or Hollywood versions of what makes an ideal woman. It is important to note, however, that it is not just about buying a product that is the concern, but also buying into an idea, which often leads back to a product, that can be troubling. No representation of this "pink" idea was better sold to women than in the HBO hit *Sex and the City*. The series, based on the work by Candace Bushnell, ran from 1998-2004 and had female viewers championing the relationships and intricacies of the four women represented in the series: Carrie (played by Sarah Jessica Parker) represented the introspective, fashionable diva; Miranda (Cynthia Nixon) was the ambitious lawyer who eventually represented the maternal constituent; Charlotte (Kristen Davis) was the wealthy, innocent hopeful holding out for love and perfection; and finally Samantha (Kim Cattrall) embodied the fiercely independent and widely sexual free-wheeling woman. The four women often stood as a whole, and each character was integral to the show. In much the way the Madonna-Whore complex divides aspects of the feminine, this television series perpetuates and portrays aspects of all women caricaturized and exaggerated into individual characters.[23] Women all over the country would play games and partake in quizzes asking: "Are you a Samantha?" or "Are you a Charlotte?" To further identify with the TV characters, many women would try to dress the part, adopting fashion trends seen in the series. In Amy Sohn's shiny fuchsia-pink, crocodile-textured coffee table book *Sex and the City: Kiss and Tell* (a book Pinkalicious might approve of), a large section is devoted to the other character of the show: the fashion. Sohn writes, "Items that appear in episodes (a flower on the label, Ray-Ban aviator sunglasses, a nameplate necklace) zoom into popular culture faster than a midtown taxi."[24] The designer for the show, Patricia Fields, often created the iconic pieces, and it is these costly, objects that sometimes made the show look like one long advertisement functioning as a tribute to product placement. In many ways, the items, the products themselves, were centerpieces of the storyline. Perhaps no

---

22 Marley P, "Is empowerment found in a "pink disco ball" vagina?" *Feminist Fatale*, Last modified May 23, 2010, http://www.feministfatale.com/tag/waxing/.

23 This tactic can also be seen on ABC's *Desperate Housewives*. The characters of Bree, Gabby, Susan, and Lynette directly correspond to Charlotte, Carrie, Samantha, and Miranda in part. The means by which women are neatly divided assists in their compartmentalization and makes them easier targets to market to.

24 Amy Sohn, *Sex and the City: Kiss and Tell* (New York: Pocket, 2002), 67.

one item is more significant than the shoes: Manolo Blahniks. In *A Woman's Right to Shoes,* Carrie attends a baby shower at the apartment of her friends Kyra and Chuck. Guests are asked to remove their shoes before entering but when Carrie prepares to leave, she finds that her $485 shoes are gone. Determining that she has spent well over that amount in wedding gifts, baby shower presents, and birthday presents for Chuck and Kyra, she registers (through an invitation sent to them indicating a marriage to herself) at Manolo Blahnik for the same shoes that were lost at their apartment. In response to Carrie's one-upmanship, Kyra sends Carrie the shoes. Shoes figure prominently throughout the series. In *Ring a Ding Ding,* Carrie comes to grips with the realization that she has spent $40,000 on shoes and, as a result, doesn't have any money to pay the bank to buy back her apartment. The pivotal joke in this episode is uttered by Carrie: "I will literally be the old woman who lived in her shoes." Bankrupting oneself for designer shoes is funny in a television series, but when women bankrupt themselves seeking identity in things and products, the matter becomes serious. In the first film that further perpetuates the *Sex and the City* empire, shoes play, again, a central role.[25] In the film, Carrie and Mr. Big purchase a penthouse apartment and plan to get married. When he decides he cannot go through with the ceremony, Carrie is left homeless and jilted. When she returns to the penthouse to collect the blue Manolos she left in the closet, she encounters Big. Viewers see Big apologize and propose, not using a ring, but rather one of her diamond-encrusted shoes. Another pivotal piece in the program that sparked a shopping trend was the name necklace. In the last episode, *An American in Paris, Part Deux,* Carrie finds her missing nameplate necklace in the lining of her purse, a poignant reminder not to lose herself to a man. Even the Cosmopolitans consumed by the female characters were part of the merchandising of the "pink" attitude embodied by the series. As such, the series did much to perpetuate a consumer culture by, for, and targeted to, women.

In many ways marketers have determined an ideal way to capitalize on pink marketing. While some consumers might reject the implicit girly-ness and overtly feminine cues by the marketing of pink, by turning pink into a symbol of "girrrll" power and rescripting it, pink can be many things to many different consumers. It is a signifier full of consumer possibility. Although some children's books embrace pink as mentioned before, others take on pink as something to overcome. In *The Paper Bag Princess,* Elizabeth is a beautiful princess with fine clothes, but when the dragon burns her castle and her clothes, she focuses more on saving her Prince Ronald than bemoaning her paper bag dress appearance. When she overcomes myriad obstacles to save Ronald, she is told by the prince, "You smell like ashes, your hair is all tangled and you are wearing a dirty old paper bag. Come back when you are dressed like a real princess."[26] She glibly retorts: "Ronald, your clothes are really pretty and your hair is very neat. You look like a real prince, but you are a bum." The last illustration shows golden hues (not pink) with Elizabeth clicking her heels as she goes off into the sunset, on her own. Another children's book that uses this perspective is *Not All Princesses Dress in Pink.* The princesses in this story

---

25 *Sex and the City,* Directed by Michael Patrick King (HBO Films and New Line Cinema, 2008), DVD.
26 Robert Munsch, *The Paper Bag Princess* (Toronto: Annick, 1996), 21-23.

always retain their sparkly crown (which acts as a sort of refrain in the narrative), but they are a departure from the aforementioned Disney princesses. We read: "Some princesses, when they choose, never pick out fancy shoes, but soccer cleats for outdoor sports with shin guards and some baggy shorts" or "Some princesses roll around, wrestling on the muddy ground, then get right up to skip and dance in tattered, stained, and muddy pants."[27] Just as the merchandise mentioned above might appeal to mothers who seek nostalgia and aim to return to those pink ideas they grew up with, this kind of product appeals to mothers seeking to rebel from traditional stereotypes. Women are duped by the anti-pink rhetoric just as much as they are by promotions that sell pink products. From the pink camouflage and pink NFL jerseys encouraging rough and tumble sports play, women are still sold the pink. The recent line of Legos sold to girls, "LadyFigs" are curvier but by utilizing pink on a creative toy traditionally marketed to boys, marketers can persuade consumers to feel that they are usurping marketing strategies and rebelling against the Princess model, all the while continuing to buy in.

This reversal continues in adolescence through music. "Bubble-gum" pop is not exclusively the domain of the feminine, but many of its signature female icons utilize the pink attraction by attempting to "own" it or by protesting the pink movement. Alecia Beth Moore, also known as Pink, embraces her namesake but seeks to overturn and reverse disturbing consumerist trends. In her 2006 song "Stupid Girls," Pink takes on celebrities by ridiculing plastic surgery, excessive tanning, unnecessary purging to maintain a skinny body type, and other hyper-sexualized feminine behavior. Pink's lyrics function as an observation of girl culture: "What happened to the dreams of a girl president/She's dancing in the video next to 50 Cent."[28] She continues to assert her reversal on this trend: "I'm so glad that I'll never fit in/That will never be me/Outcasts and girls with ambition/That's what I wanna see."[29] In the video for her song, viewers see a young pig-tailed girl bombarded by media images. On each side of her is a good and bad figure (represented by "angel" Pink and "devil" Pink) illustrating the conflict besetting young girls. This is further mirrored by objects that are on the table on each end. To the left are dolls, pink objects of play, and beautification toys. To the right are books, a football, and a microscope. When the video begins, the young girl clutches a Barbie, but as the video progresses and the young girl sees images of girls distorting themselves for the "pink" ideal, she chooses to put down the doll, abandon the pink things to the one side of the table, and elects to pick up a football instead. Another song that plays on this reversal is No Doubt's 1995 song "Just a Girl." Gwen Stefani intones: "Take this pink ribbon off my eye/I'm exposed and it's no big surprise/Don't you think I know exactly where I stand?/The world is forcing me to hold your hand."[30] Stefani continues to proclaim that she is a "typical prototype" and that she is "all pretty and petite," lamenting that she does not have any rights. She proclaims "I've had it up to here." The popular song func-

---

27 Heidi Stemple and Jane Yolen, *Not all Princesses Dress in Pink* (New York: Simon & Schuster, 2010), 10-12.
28 Pink, *I'm Not Dead* (2006, LaFace), CD.
29 Ibid.
30 No Doubt, *Tragic Kingdom* (1995, Interscope), CD.

tions as an anthem celebrating what it is to be a girl, but it also condemns scripts that prescribe how a girl should behave. In the video, Stefani is sequestered in the women's room while the male members of the group jam away in the men's room. As the video progresses, other women enter to fix their hair and lipstick. Meanwhile, those who enter the men's room continue to celebrate and perform. The men are there to see while the women are to be seen. It is not until the men invade the women's space that the women perform themselves, minus the trappings of appearance and the vestiges of pink subterfuge. Other female icons perpetuate feminine ideology and pink think by overturning traditional scripts (Madonna and Lady Gaga are two examples),[31] but what is most important is not how many participate, but the idea that girl power is an extension of pink consumerism. Music, toys, and fashion have markets catering to consumerism, but women's health is also marketed through pink culture.

Much has been made of the "girl power" movement and the heralding of women's health issues. Breast cancer awareness exploits the profit of pink by saturating the marketplace with pink ribbons and pink products (hair dryers, candy bars, clothing, etc.) with only a marginal portion going to any verifiable scientific research. Initially commercialized in 1992 by Evelyn Lauder (Estee was her mother-in-law) and former *Self* magazine editor-in-chief Alexandria Penney, pink has become almost synonymous with breast cancer research.[32] While the intentions of marketing the pink ribbon may have been altruistic and good, in many ways this particular "pink think" consumerism has taken on a life of its own. The Breast Cancer Awareness group (BCA) labels such overt and exploitive use of pink in securing funding for breast cancer awareness as "pinkwashing," claiming that some companies offer little more than lip service in their campaign against breast cancer. Estee Lauder, for example, refuses to sign the Compact for Safe Cosmetics, an acknowledgement that no ingredients that could cause breast cancer are knowingly used in the manufacture of cosmetics. In 2008, the BCA rallied against Yoplait's pink yogurt lids. In a campaign called "Think Before You Pink," the BCA charged Yoplait and General Mills with using growth hormones, specifically rGBH, or products derivative of such, in their production. Barbara Brenner, BCA's executive director, has taken on many big companies that appear to support breast cancer awareness while advertently or inadvertently contributing to causes of cancer. The BCA effectively contributed to Yoplait's removal of rGBH in its yogurt. As Brenner points out: "If shopping could cure cancer, cancer would have been cured long ago."[33] Gayle Sulik's book *Pink Ribbon Blues* further expounds on these views.

---

31   Douglas Kellner observes in his article "Madonna, Fashion and Identity" (1994) that "Madonna reverses relations of power and domination and provides strong affirmative images of women. But one could argue that Madonna merely transposes relations of domination, reversing the roles of men and women, rather than dissolving relations of domination" (199). The same could be said of Lady Gaga who utilizes her male alter ego, Jo Calderone, to reverse her traditional female gender and "perform" pink and male ideologies in turn.

32   There is some dispute about the origin of the pink ribbon. The BCA claims that Charlotte Haley initiated the peach ribbon after seeing her sister, daughter, and grandmother fall victim to breast cancer. Haley made cards with peach ribbon to raise funding for breast cancer research with each card touting: "The National Cancer Institute's annual budget is $1.8 billion, only 5 percent goes for cancer prevention. Help us wake up our legislators and America by wearing this ribbon." Penney wanted to place ads for the ribbon in *Self* magazine.

33   Zoe Kesselring, "Are Pink Products Causing Cancer?" *KMBC*, Last modified May 5, 2010, http://www.kmbc.com/news/health/breast-cancer-awareness/Are-pink-products-causing- cancer/-/22136508/1608272/-/944niy/-/index.html

She argues that the pink think has tinted attitudes about the realities of breast cancer. We would much rather focus on a bumper sticker that advertises "Save the Ta-Tas" than the fact that women are spending more on treatment and are enduring more invasive tactics to fight breast cancer than they were fifty years ago, but the risk of fatality remains the same. Slogans sell; statistics do not. Brenner says that the marketing of pink ribbons creates what she labels a "she-ro" kind of culture. Sulik explains that "the she-ro is a feminine hero with the attitude, style and verve to kick cancer's butt while wearing 6-inch heels and pink lipstick."[34] The problem is that this is reductive, assuming that all women don this either/or kind of thinking. Not all women experience the fight against breast cancer with happy optimism. Sociologist Arlie Hochschild explores these "feeling rules," or the way we are expected to feel or not feel in a certain situation. Sulik writes:

> In pink ribbon culture, feeling rules govern how best to fight the war on breast cancer. Optimism translates to a brand of social support that almost demands commodification of the illness and a model of survivorship focused on acquiescence to mainstream ideals.[35]

Women exhibit, or should, according to the implicit marketing of the pink ribbons, a wholesale feeling of "I am woman, hear me roar" in eking out a corner to battle breast cancer. The ribbons offer, intrinsically, prescriptive rather than descriptive emotions, casting a generalized blanket over every woman's experience or emotion. Further, marking October—or Pinktober—as breast cancer awareness month, and utilizing pink ribbon iconography and pink-think in events like Susan G. Komen's "Race for the Cure" allow women and men to participate in and market their allegiance and support for an illness without questioning the effectiveness of such campaigns or the results from such charitable efforts. As Sulik notes, "Members of the breast cancer audience can see themselves as altruistic, conscientious, and socially aware whenever they buy or display pink."[36] In many ways, the color pink has been branded and consumers buy in, forming a part of their consumerist identity as linked to *the* cause.[37] To retaliate, the National Breast Cancer Coalition (NBCC) created the "Not Just Ribbons" campaign to shift the focus from simple awareness to policy issues, and to examine the correlation between breast cancer and the environment in order to create a meaningful patient bill of rights.[38] The advertising and campaigning can be reductive: woman=breast=pink does nothing to solve the problem—or to address the men who battle breast cancer. Pink marketing produces breast cancer support while perpetuating a consumerist trend ubiquitous in shopping malls and parking lots across the country.

---

34   Gayle Sulik, *Pink Ribbon Blues* (Oxford: UP, 2010), 366-67.

35   Ibid.,17.

36   Ibid.,129.

37   Contrast this with Lance Armstrong's LIVESTRONG support for cancer. Consumers buy in to the yellow bracelets in much the same way, but the symbolism and trope of the LIVESTRONG campaign is much more masculine and aggressive as opposed to the cutesy pink feminine ribbons supporting breast cancer awareness.

38   Sulik, *Pink Ribbon Blues*, 366-67.

On a much more benign level, pink is also exploited in terms of physical fitness and the body images many women carry into adulthood. Certainly there are famous weight loss systems (SlimFast, NutriSystem, Jenny Craig) that cater to the woman who wants to lose weight, but by incorporating color into the marketing strategy, the weight loss industry targets women overtly. The P.I.N.K. Method is a fitness routine/program that purports to focus on women because of their unique nutritional needs. Developed by Cynthia Pasquella, a clinical nutritionalist, the P.I.N.K. Method came about through Pasquella's own struggle with weight and health. The program gained a following after her appearance on television shows that target a female viewership, including *Dr. Phil* and *The Doctors*. The program focuses on the basics of weight loss: exercise and low-fat, low-calorie foods, but it personalizes the plan and targets it to women with "pink" smoothies for breakfast. The pink functions as little more than a symbol on the box of the accompanying DVDs, with pink used as an acronym: power, intensity, nutrition, and "kardio." Pasquella speaks on the website about how her program gives women more than fitness, but also self-confidence. Women who purportedly met with success during the program point to their wrists and take turns reading the mantra printed on the P.I.N.K. method bracelet: "I think. I live. I am. Pink." The website also forecasts a halcyon time when they might be able to focus on men and offer a BLUE Method. This begs the question: are men and women's fitness needs so different that they warrant a singularized approach, or is this just a marketing ploy for profits based on exploiting women's insecurities? Another program that seems to do the same is the Pink Patch. In the website of the same name, readers are told: "A smashing success in the UK—now available in the U.S.! The Pink Patch has helped thousands of women lose weight and finally get the bodies they've always dreamed of having".[39] Much like a nicotine patch, the Pink Patch adheres to one's upper arm or abdomen and promises to "help you get skinny" by using "all-natural herb ingredients." Targeted to young women and "created by women for women," the Pink Patch further insists that it will help users manage their weight, boost their self-esteem, and gain confidence. Pink can, ultimately, solve any body issue, or so marketers would have consumers believe. The most recent controversy concerns Pom Wonderful pomegranate juice. Ads are cast in rich magentas and warm pinks. The visuals are simplistic, but the claims in the advertisements are not. Pom's advertising copy might run "Heart therapy," "Survival Kit," or "Cheat death." Because the company utilized a heart in place of the "O" in Pom and claimed that drinking the juice could contribute to a healthier heart (among other such claims), the Federal Trade Commission in 2010 issued a complaint against the company for maintaining false claims. In May of 2012, the company was ordered to refrain from making such errant claims on its product. Piggybacking on the use of pink to market to one's health and wellness, especially with breast cancer concerns, *The Pink Ribbon Diet: A Revolutionary Plan to Lower Your Breast Cancer Risk* sells preventative medicine, not just fixative cures. Mary Flynn, working for the Susan G. Komen for the Cure Foundation, extols the virtue of a Mediterranean diet based on plant-based olive-oil (PBOO), as opposed to the

---

39   "The P.I.N.K. Method: Lose Weight Fast," *P.I.N.K. Method*, 2011, https://www.pinkmethod.com.

National Cancer Institute's recommendation of a low-fat diet. The book provides recipes and foods to help "lower your risk," as the title claims. While eating a healthful diet is important, the consumer connection among health, wellness, pink, and women's consumer culture is unmistakable. One study noted how much revenue is generated: "Based on the findings of Marketdata's 11th edition of the U.S. Weight Loss & Diet Control Market study, the worth of the weight-loss industry was estimated at $61 billion in 2010."[40] The money the weight-loss industry makes is staggering, but by cultivating a "pink" culture that targets women even more than usual, the commodification of women's bodies is increased exponentially. Moreover, the homes where many women spend their time are pinkified.

Although we are fourteen years into the twenty-first century, the observation by Betty Friedan about women's domestic sphere in 1963 still rings eerily true: "The feminine mystique says that the highest value and the only commitment for women is the fulfillment of their own femininity," and often this occurs through the presentation of the home.[41] Although women have moved out of the home and into the workplace, marketers continue to target women when it comes to household products, sometimes excessively with the marker of pink. Many companies connect the feminine sphere of the home with fundraising for breast cancer awareness. KitchenAid gives a portion of its profits from the sale of a line of mixers and other kitchen products to the Susan G. Komen Breast Cancer Foundation. A percentage of Dyson's pink vacuum profits are donated to The Breast Cancer Research Foundation. Swiffer's limited-edition collection of pink products also raises donations for the cause. The Apollo 135 piece tool kit also comes in pink, allowing women to fix up the home in style AND contribute to breast cancer awareness. One can buy a "Pink is Perfect" household sponge. Women can also buy pink bottled Downy to do their charitable duty and keep their laundry soft. Friedan observed that "a new stove or softer toilet paper do not make a woman a better wife or mother, even if she thinks that's what she needs to be."[42] Women are savvy consumers and know they are targets of consumer marketing, but when they respond to pink marketing ploys, they participate in "pink think," why not buy the pink product if one NEEDS it AND it contributes to a good cause? By perpetuating that altruistic desire and products women ultimately buy, women are participating in "pink think" and buying in to pink marketing ploys.

Since much about the domestic sphere has changed, marketers who typically direct products like beer and cigarettes to men have found a way to market to women: through pink. Camel released Camel No. 9, a cigarette marketed to women with unmistakable packaging: a black and pink box. As a *New York Times* columnist notes, even the nomenclature is reminiscent of Chanel No. 5 or Love Potion No. 9, but the senior marketing director of R.J. Reynolds, Brian Stebbins, asserts that it is more associative of the notion of being sophisticated or dressed to the nines.[43] At any rate, the company targets women in an effort

---

40 Tracey Sandilands, "The Financial Side of the Weight Loss Industry," *Houston Chronicle*, 2012, http://small-business.chron.com/financial-side-weight-loss-industry-38200.html.

41 Betty Friedan, *The Feminine Mystique* (New York: W.W. Norton, 1963), 43.

42 Ibid., 229.

43 Stuart Elliot, "A New Camel Brand Is Dressed to the Nines," *New York Times*, February 15, 2012, http://www.

to snag a market share dominated by other companies. By offering giveaways, advertising in magazines like *Cosmopolitan* and *Glamour*, and utilizing the pink, the consumer industry encourages women to purchase products used by both sexes but now particularly targeted to women. Alcohol ads, unlike cigarette ads, are primarily directed to men. Shazz Lewis, the Maryland based producer of Chick beer, aims to target the 25% of female beer drinkers in the U.S.[44] While the beer does have fewer calories than other lagers, what sells is the packaging: "Colored with hot pink and black, the six-pack box features an image of a purse and each bottle has a little black dress on the label."[45] Much like the Camel No. 9 cigarette pack, the Chick beer utilizes similar color interplay. Playing on sophistication, humor, and the classic enticement of pink, marketers continue to try to ensnare women.

Although pink can be used to market products, as we have seen, it can also be used to market political ideas. CODEPINK is a grassroots group established in 2002 touting a distinctly anti-war message. The group takes its name from a parody of George W. Bush's codes for levels of alerts for homeland security. From the group's website: "While Bush's color-coded alerts were based on fear and used to justify violence, the CODEPINK alert is a feisty call for women and men to "'wage peace.'" The group has protested violence and war, supported international and national women's issues, and has urged political leaders to take action. What they also do on their website is merchandise. Women can buy shirts in various shades of pink with clever slogans ("The truth will set you free, but first it will piss you off"—Gloria Steinem). Bumper stickers, books, nail polish, and posters are also sold on the site. Whether or not one subscribes to the political leanings of the group, it is evident that the clever double entendre of the pink marketing (poking fun at Bush's security levels and calling on feminine support) is effective.

Pink can function as a color that represents femininity, sexuality, sophistication, girly-ness, and—for the masculine counterparts—the "other" gender. The "othering" of the color pink can function as a means of political, judicial, and legal control. Arizona Sheriff Joe Arpaio uses pink underwear to demean inmates. Inmates are often clad in pink, or housed in cells with pink walls. In this instance, pink is a signifier of control, calling on the feminization implicit in the color, but utilized as a means of oppression and belittlement as the innately feminine color is donned by the masculine. Arpaio, recognizing the effect of the psychological subversion, markets his "Go Joe" pink boxers for $15.00 and his pink handcuffs for the same price at pinkunderwear.com. Proceeds from these sales fund prison projects or local causes. Arpaio relies on the symbolic female association with the color pink to subjugate the masculine inmates, implying that they are weak, effeminate, or girly. In a culture that perpetuates division between the sexes, enforcing pink on the men can function as a powerful means of control. Also, the utilization of pink in noting gay causes is

---

nytimes.com/2007/02/15/business/media/15adco.html.
44   Megan Gibson, "New 'Chick' Beer is a Lady-Catered Brew in a Girly, Pink Package," *Time*, September 11, 2011, http://newsfeed.time.com/2011/09/07/new-chick-beer-is-a-lady-catered-brew-in-a-girly-pink-package/
45   Ibid.

reminiscent of other reversals of pink. Pink as a political tool and means of subjugation was used in Nazi Germany. The downward-pointing pink triangle indicated prisoners who were labeled homosexual. In the 1970s, however, the gay community reversed the punitive significance by reclaiming the pink triangle as a signifier of gay rights and gay pride. Pink can be a source of empowerment or control, sometimes concurrently.

In 1949, Simone De Beauvoir wrote the oft-repeated maxim: "One is not born, but rather becomes, a woman."[46] She continued to observe, "No biological, psychological, or economic fate determines the figure that the human female presents in society; it is civilization as a whole that produces this creature... Only the intervention of someone else can establish an individual as an Other."[47] How does one become a woman? How does one embrace that biological designation? Often this comes through gendered construction, here outlined through the codification of the color pink. Pink designates women and girls, segregating them from the masculine sphere.[48] The use of pink as a color-coded signifier links women to contrived femininity and manipulates that link for financial gain. . As Friedan writes, "Like a primitive culture which sacrificed little girls to its tribal gods, we sacrifice our girls to the feminine mystique, grooming them ever more efficiently through the sexual sell to become consumers of the things to whose profitable sale our nation is dedicated."[49] From birth, girls are exploited by the cultural assumptions symbolized by pink. Colors function as signs, directing the viewer to meaning. The color pink is one such sign, imbued with context and fraught with baggage; consumers recognize the salient points of such a symbol. What this color-coding says about us is that we are a marketable culture. We expect to be marketed to and advertisers know what works. But by buying in, we are putting our sexuality, our femininity, our independence, and even our health into the coffers of Madison Avenue.

Bibliography

Aerosmith. *Nine Lives*. Sony, 1997. CD.

"An American Girl in Paris: Part Deux." *Sex and the City*. HBO, 2004. TV.

Boodman, Sandra. "Cosmetic Surgeries New Frontier." *Washington Post.* March 03, 2007. Accessed June 2, 2012. http://www.wordsworkcom.com/files/WashingtonPost_030607.pdf

CODEPINK. "About Us." codepink4peace.org. Accessed March 2, 2007. http://codepinkalert.org/article.php?list=type&type=3.

---

46 De Beauvoir, *The Second Sex*, 267.
47 De Beauvoir, *The Second Sex*, 267.
48 The marking of men and masculinity is a subject worthy of examination as well. Not only is the corollary blue a countered marketing tool, but issues such as aggressiveness, violence, and dominance are often enforced, not so much by one signal color, but by the absence of the other, the color pink.
49 Friedan, *The Feminine Mystique*, 231.

De Beauvoir, Simone. *The Second Sex*. New York: Vintage, 1949.

Elliot, Stuart. "A New Camel Brand Is Dressed to the Nines." *New York Times*. February 15, 2012. http://www.nytimes.com/2007/02/15/business/media/15adco.html

Flynn, Mary, and Nancy Verde Barr. *The Pink Ribbon Diet*. Cambridge: Da Capo, 2010.

Friday, Nancy. *The Power of Beauty*. New York: Harper Collins, 1996.

Friedan, Betty. *The Feminine Mystique*. New York: W.W. Norton, 1963.

Gibson, Megan. "New 'Chick' Beer is a Lady-Catered Brew in a Girly, Pink Package." *Time*. September 11, 2011. http://newsfeed.time.com/2011/09/07/new-chick-beer-is-a-lady-catered-brew-in-a-girly-pink-package/

Johnson, Lisa, and Andrea Learned. *Don't Think Pink*. New York: AMACON, 2004.

Joshi, Rajmohan. *Encyclopedia of Journalism and Mass Communications*. New Delhi: Gyan, 2006.

Kann, Victoria. *Pinkalicious: Tickled Pink*. New York: HarperCollins, 2010.

Kellner, Douglas. "Madonna, Fashion, and Identity." In *Women in Culture, edited by* Lucinda Joy Peach, 187-200. Oxford: Blackwell, 1994.

Kesselring, Zoe. KMBC, "Are Pink Products Causing Cancer?" *KMBC*. Last modified May 13, 2010. http://www.kmbc.com/health/breast-cancer-awareness/Are-pink-products-causing-cancer/1608272

Levin, Diane. "Too Young To Be A Consumer: The Toll of Consumer Culture on the Rights of Childhood." *CCFC*. May 1, 2009. http://www.commercialfreechildhood.org/resource/too-young-be-consumer-toll-consumer-culture-rights-childhood

Levy, Andrea. *Female Chauvinist Pigs*. New York: Free Press, 2005.

Marley, P. "Is empowerment found in a "pink disco ball" vagina?" *Feminist Fatale*. Last modified May 23, 2010. http://www.feministfatale.com/tag/waxing/.

Munsch, Robert. *The Paper Bag Princess*. Toronto: Annick, 1996.

"My New Pink Button." *My New Pink Button*. Last modified 2014. http://www.mynewpinkbutton.com/

No Doubt. *Tragic Kingdom*. Interscope, 1995. CD.

Orenstein, Peggy. *Cinderella Ate My Daughter*. New York: Harper Collins, 2011.

Orenstein, Peggy. "What's Wrong With Cinderella?" *New York Times*. December 24, 2006. http://www.nytimes.com/2006/12/24/magazine/24princess.t.html?pagewanted=all

Peril, Lynn. *Pink Think: Becoming a Woman in Many Uneasy Lessons.* New York: W.W. Norton, 2002.

"The P.I.N.K. Method: Lose Weight Fast." *P.I.N.K. Method.* 2011. https://www.pinkmethod.com.

Pink. *I'm Not Dead.* LaFace, 2006. CD.

"Ring a Ding Ding." *Sex and the City.* HBO, 2002. TV.

Sandilands, Tracey. "The Financial Side of the Weight Loss Industry." *Houston Chronicle.* 2012. http://smallbusiness.chron.com/financial-side-weight-loss-industry-38200.html

Sex and the City. Directed by Michael Patrick King. HBO Films and New Line Cinema, 2008. DVD.

Sohn, Amy. *Sex and the City: Kiss and Tell.* New York: Pocket, 2002.

Swanson, Amy. "Marketing to Women: Why the 'Pink It and Shrink It' Strategy Doesn't Always Work." *Quality Logo Products.* June 2, 2012. http://www.qualitylogoproducts.com/blog/marketing-to-women-pink-it-shrink-it/

Stemple, Heidi and Jane Yolen. *Not all Princesses Dress in Pink.* New York: Simon & Schuster, 2010.

Sulik, Gayle. *Pink Ribbon Blues.* Oxford: UP, 2010.

11

Understanding Color, Race, and Identity through the (Body) Politics of Barack Obama

Celnisha L. Dangerfield

The United States and its "founding fathers" are often associated with the ideals of bravery, dogged determination, and freedom—that is, freedom from tyranny and religious persecution. The stories of the earliest settlers excelling, in spite of the challenges that they met in the "new world," became the "mythos"[1] that undergirded the story of a nation.[2] Still, despite the fact that there were a number of positive themes that one could identify, there were some deeds and indiscretions along the way that left a blot—an indelible stain—on the history of a great nation. For while the country's founding fathers believed in "life, liberty and the pursuit of happiness," it would become clear that those ideals were only attainable by some—particularly white, Anglo-Saxon, Protestant men who were also landowners. Thus, any discussion of the founding and subsequent growth of the United States would be incomplete without inspecting the roles of skin color, race, ethnicity, socio-economic status, and gender in the shaping of the country's foundation. Indeed, it is only upon close inspection of the foundation of the United States (with all of its cracks, fissures, and glaring imperfections) that one begins to see—and more clearly understand—this country's present-day social ills.

While the interlocking oppressors of race, color, class, and gender have all had an influence on power differentials in the United States, skin color and race have a particularly complicated place in the story that is American history. The complete history of the United States cannot be recounted without sharing the role of people of color in the country's growth and advancement. While the founding fathers had great plans for this nation, it was the survival skills of the land's native tenants—or the red man—that helped the original colonists—or the white man—survive during those harsh, early years. Unfortunately, the Native Americans would be paid back in chicanery as their land was taken and their way

---

[1] Mythos refers to the enduring narratives that shape the landscape of a culture.
[2] See Robert Wuthnow, *American Mythos: Why Our Best Efforts to Be a Better Nation Fall Short* (Princeton, NJ: Princeton University Press, 2006).

of life completely altered. The backs of African slaves—or the black man—were used to build the economic infrastructure of this country (through farming and the production of cash crops), resulting in a very rich populous in which people of color were relegated to the outer sanctum of "proper" society. One might also recall that Asian workers—or the yellow man—were used to build this nation's earliest railroad system. Today, Hispanic (immigrant) workers—or the brown man—do much of the low-paying, menial labor in this country. Even in this very brief history lesson, it is easy to see that the country's rise to power is directly related to the oppression and subjugation of people of color. Indeed, along the way to becoming a great nation, blood was shed and lives were changed, forever altering the legacy of an entire nation, family units, and scores upon scores of named "nobodies."

It is impossible to deny that race and skin color continue to be a part of the equation when discussing the issues of poverty and unemployment (or under-employment),[3] educational inequality,[4] disparate incarceration rates,[5] and many of the other social ills of our time. Yet, remarkable strides have been made toward creating a place where people of color (red, brown, yellow, or black) are more likely to be treated as equals. Particularly in the last fifty years with the remarkable accomplishments of the Civil Rights Movement and its mandate for change, the laws of this land have been used to argue for greater equality in areas such as voting rights and educational opportunities. However, despite some progress, there are areas that have not seen advancement--and in some cases, the situation appears more dismal. For instance, a Pew Research Center Race Study reveals that the "economic gulf between blacks and whites that was present half a century ago remains."[6] Many Blacks are just a few generations from slavery, or at the very least, from their sharecropping ancestors, and there remains the existence of some very apparent social issues that cannot be separated from skin color.

Still, many would argue that nothing has illuminated the progress of US race relations more than the election of Barack Obama to the position of President of the United States of America.[7] On November 4, 2008—for the first time in the nation's history—a non-White person was elected to hold the highest office in the land. In a country where blacks were once considered three-fifths of a person and counted as such in the legislative process,[8] the "evolved"[9] electoral process of the United States of America helped create a once inconceivable reality, one in

---

[3] The unemployment rate for African Americans hit its highest rate in 27 years (16.7%) in August 2011, despite the fact that unemployment fell to 8% during that same month for White Americans (Censky 2011).

[4] See the NAACP's African Americans and Education Fact Sheet for more information on education inequality.

[5] Glenn Loury, *Race, Incarceration, and American Values*. (Cambridge, MA: MIT Preess, 2008).

[6] Pew Research Center, "King's Dream Remains an Elusive Goal; Many Americans See Racial Disparities," August 22, 2013, http://www.pewsocialtrends.org/files/2013/08/final_full_report_racial_disparities.pdf.

[7] Adam Nagourney. *Obama Elected President as Racial Barrier Falls*. November 4, 2008. http://www.nytimes.com/2008/11/05/us/politics/05elect.html.

[8] This statement refers to the Three-fifths compromise. This was an agreement reached to give slave-holding Southern states the right to count their slaves as three-fifths of a person for the purpose of taxation and representation.

[9] The term "evolved" is used to highlight the reality that women and Blacks were not originally among the voting populous, a privilege traditionally given to White men that owned land. Even after Black people were given the right to vote, they were still disenfranchised through strategies such as poll taxes, reading tests, and other forms of intimidation.

which a person of color could assume the role of "Commander-in-Chief" of the most powerful country in the world. In the time immediately after Obama was elected into office, some argued vehemently that racism was no longer an issue. Those operating under this belief cited Obama's win as "the" indicator that skin color was no longer being used to determine a person's ability to ascend to the highest heights. However, while President Obama is a beacon of hope that change is indeed possible, conversations around his election and presidency might more accurately signal that the old cliché rings true: "The more things change, the more they remain the same."

This book explores the way color is considered across an array of disciplines. This chapter contributes to that broader discussion by exploring the social construction of meaning and identity as it specifically relates to skin color and the perception of race in the United States. The Black male body will take center stage as President Barack Obama is presented as a rhetorical text around which a historical frame of reference will be constructed. The present-day reality of how color is both (de)constructed and experienced, as well as the debates and discussions surrounding the election of Barack Obama to the Presidency will all be used to shed light on some of the racial carry-overs from days gone by. Of particular significance to the critique will be the synthesis of communication literature on "meaning," body politics and Black masculinity, constructivism, and identity negotiation. Taken together, one will be left to consider the sustained influence of skin color on the understanding of race in the twenty-first century. Moreover, the reader will be asked to grapple with questions of whether this country's racial progress is as significant as once thought.

The "Colorful" History of Race in the US

Before delving into a discussion of the theoretical underpinnings for this work, one must first look at the historical significance of color—specifically in the United States—and its impact on a nation's understanding of race. One's racial identification and his/her color are not necessarily synonymous; however, the concept of grouping people by skin color (or whether one is lighter or darker on the color continuum) has been the argument supporting racial delineations for centuries. Race is a rather fluid construct, and this truth makes in-group and out-group identification extremely challenging. It is the fluidity of the concept of race across space and time, the generalizations made across large groups of people, and the construct's ability to survive despite indefinite delineations that are reasons why race and color are worthy of deeper exploration. In *Sorting Things Out: Classification and its Consequences*,[10] communication scholars Bowker and Star discuss the reality that humans have an innate desire to divide everything into categories, with groupings ranging from diseases to people. Though this is helpful in many ways, the human need for classification has created a "monster" that refuses to be tamed. Race is such a villain, for it is a strange concept whose very meaning

---

10   Geoffrey C. Bowker and Susan L. Star, *Sorting things out: Classification and its consequences* (Cambridge, MA: MIT Press, 1999).

varies in different parts of the world. In places such as Brazil and Mexico[11] for example, one's skin color is not the chief marker to identify racial classification.[12] Yet in the United States and in many European nations, race has most often been used to define the categorization of people based on observed phenotypic markers (i.e. skin color, hair texture, size of one's nose and lips). Of the phenotypic markers noted, the most pronounced, non-social/biological element that has been a constant in the connotative explanation of race would be the color of one's skin. Still, skin color cannot be (and has not been) the sole determinant of a person's racial identification in the United States.

One's ancestry has carried just as much influence as the color of one's skin—if not more. That is because ancestry was used to classify a person as Black even if every physical trait indicated that they were indeed White, especially during American slavery, Reconstruction, and even into much of the twentieth century. Known as the "one-drop rule," the belief was that if a person were biracial and appeared to be racially White, that person still would not be considered White because of the presence of even one drop of "Black blood." This led to attempts (with untold successes) by Blacks with light skin and European features to move away to places other than where they were born. The relocation served as a way to "erase" ancestry by putting a person in a place where no one knew of the Black family member of record. This allowed the person in question to "pass" for White based solely on phenotypic features, void of any immediate record of their ancestral lineage. The mere fact that this was even possible underscores the preposterous notion of race as a biological construct. As noted earlier, ideas about color and race are enduring; that truth is reinforced because the practice of deciding a person's race by ancestry is still in place in the United States today. Lassiter notes, "There is a tendency for children of mixed races (if one parent is white) to be classified as white. However, when one parent is African American, the children are classified as African American or Black, regardless of skin color." [13]

So while the concept of race was originally presented as a geographical model, it morphed into a biological/physical construct with a hierarchical system of rank.[14] Especially with the demographic shift underway in the United States, it is no longer acceptable to view race so simply,[15] especially after considering that research from the Human Genome Project declares that 99.9 % of all DNA is

---

11 According to NTC's Dictionary of Mexican Cultural Code Words (DeMente 1996), the term criollos (translated "people of color") was used to differentiate Mexican-born Spaniards from those born in Europe. This delineation of Mexican-born whites from European-born whites was of critical importance because only those born in Spain were initially allowed to hold any political power. This example is offered because it clearly demonstrates that the categorization "of color" in Mexico once centered around birth place more than ancestry, and the categorization had direct influence on one's socio-economic status. All of these aspects taken together merely affirm the social construction of racial groups—sometimes even outside of the United States.

12 See Evelyn Glenn, *Shades of difference: Why skin color matters* (Palo Alto, CA: Stanford University Press, 2009) and Martin Marger, *Race and ethnic relations: American and global perspectives* (Belmont, CA: Wadsworth 2011).

13 Sybil Lassiter, *Cultures of color in America: A guide to family, religion, and health* (Westport, CT: Greenwood, 1998), xii.

14 Stephen Gould, "The geometer of race." *Discover* (1994): 65-69. Kevin Cokley, "To be or not to be Black: Problematics of racial identity," in *The quest for community and identity: Critical essays in Africana social philosophy*, Robert E. Birt (Lanham, MD: Rowman & Littlefield, 2002), 29-44.

15 Stephen Gould, *The mismeasure of man*. (New York: Norton, 1981).

the same.[16] If one agrees that race is a social construct,[17] there is then the invitation to explore the wisdom behind the reliance on physical markers to support antiquated definitions of race and racial categorization in the United States and Europe. Despite the fact that race is socially constructed, and the reality that skin color cannot be used as the sole determinant of a person's group identification in the United States, it seems strange that a person's place in the racial hierarchy can come down to one drop and/or the accompanying color or racial stereotypes that the person reinforces or debunks. These truths are highlighted by examining the "color story" of the nation's first president "of color"—Barack H. Obama.

Obama as the Litmus Test of Change

Not since the trial of O.J. Simpson for the murder of Nicole Brown Simpson and Ron Goldman, or the Rodney King police beating—and the ensuing Los Angeles riots—has the nation gone back and forth about race quite as much as it did when then-Senator Barack Obama made a bid for the White House. Obama created a dialogue on race without necessitating the gathering of a commission on race or setting this issue as a part of his political platform. Simply by "being" and running for the highest political office in the land, Obama single-handedly forced the nation to grapple with questions of race, identity, and stereotypes often ascribed to people of color (particularly those ascribed to Black men). Without question, Barack Obama's campaign for the Presidency—and his subsequent election—underscored the influence one person could have on a nation's dialogue about race. Furthermore, it brought to light questions about the real degree of racial progress in the United States in light of the fact that issues of race still became a part of the campaign, despite Obama's attempts to run a race "above color."

A lesson in contradiction, President Obama is a well-educated person of color raised by a single White mother in Hawaii (and by White grandparents in Kansas). Having only limited contact with his Black father over the years, it is still his Kenyan father's blood coursing through the president's veins and coloring his skin that has made the subject of race take precedence for some parts of the voting populous more than others. In a country where skin color and racial identification have been so important, it is no wonder that when a person of color makes it to a level of prominence on both the national and international stage, that person then fosters even more conversations about color and race. Surely, the concepts of color and race—and the relationship between the two—deserve greater attention in light of the ever-changing landscape of America's demographic make-up and the reality that a biracial person's identity became a central part of the national discussion. This truth asks many to reconsider previously held notions about color, race, masculinity, and ultimately how these factors interact when it comes to decisions about the nation's political leadership.

---

16 Tasha N. Dubriwny, Benjamin R. Bates, and Jennifer L. Bevan. "Lay understandings of race: Cultural and genetic definitions." *Public Health Genomics* (2004): 185-195.

17 Michael Omi and Howard Winant, *Racial Formation in the United States: From the 1960s to the 1990s* (London: Routlege, 1994).

When it was confirmed that Barack Obama had secured the Presidency, media outlets across the globe announced it to the world.[18] However, one need only examine the headlines on the morning of November 5, 2008 to see that while Barack Obama had won the election, America's preoccupation with race was still apparent. A glimpse of what the world was thinking was captured by two major news outlets: The *New York Times* and MSNBC. The *New York Times* carried the headline, "Obama Elected President as Racial Barrier Falls,"[19] while MSNBC carried the headline, "Barack Obama elected 44th president: 'Change has come to America,' first African-American leader tells country."[20] The very fact that President Obama was not called the nation's first biracial president speaks volumes. It underscores the notion that his Blackness dwarfs his mixed-race ancestry. In fact, it almost seems the title of Obama's memoir, *Dreams from my Father: A Story of Race and Inheritance,* foreshadowed the nation's preoccupation with his ancestral lineage.[21] Thus, while Barack Obama's presidency is a story of triumph and progress, it is equally, "A Story of Race and Inheritance."

Theoretical Frameworks Undergirding this Discussion of Color, Race, and Obama

The American tapestry has a checkered past, and tense race relations have been a part of that. Color has been situated in a historical context, and a preliminary look at Barack Obama's part in the nation's dialogue on race has been offered. To now get a greater understanding of the influence that President Obama's color and ancestry has had on national conversations about race, a sound theoretical underpinning must be introduced. For that purpose, four related areas of theoretical distinction will be addressed. Notions regarding meaning, body politics, personal constructs/constructivism, and identity negotiation will help the reader better understand the debates surrounding Obama's identity, as well as speak to his ability to either mirror or challenge society's views about race in the twenty-first century.

Meaning

When examining the impact of color on how one understands race—particularly how race is understood in the United States—the introduction of a communication construct makes sense; in fact, it is essential that the concept of color be explored within the context of mediated messages and social influence. To understand the impact of using color to describe entire groups of people, there must first be the realization that language is indeed powerful. With the naming or the identification of a thing/construct/entity comes the recognition that meaning is attached to the named thing/construct/entity. Additionally, the possibility of

---

18 Jamese Dyrn, *Jamesedyrn's Webblog*. Noveber 5, 2008. http://jamesedyrn.wordpress.com/2008/11/05/world-headlines-immediately-after-barack-obama-is-elected-as-president-of-the-united-states-of-america/.

19 Nagourney, *Obama Elected President*.

20 Alex Johnson, *Barack Obama elected 44th president* . November 5, 2008. http://www.msnbc.msn.com/id/27531033/ns/politics-decision_08/t/barack-obama-elected-th-president/.

21 Barack H. Obama, *Dreams from my Father: A Story of Race and Inheritance* (New York: Three Rivers Press, 2004).

change or influence can come as a result of the act of assigning a name or word of description. Because words carry meaning—and each color represents a unique word— it logically follows that colors represent ideas and conjure emotions that often go beyond mere symbolism.

In their seminal text, *The Meaning of Meaning,* Ogden and Richards say that meaning comes from the intersection of a person's initial thought (or reference), a person's choice of words to represent the thing (or symbols), and finally, the actual object to which the thought and the symbol were referring (the referent). [22] A major premise of their semantic triangle is that there is not a direct connection between the symbol used to identify the object and the referent. The semantic triangle affirms that, "…meaning [doesn't] reside in words; [it] reside[s] in people."[23] For example, the word *dog* can be used to describe a beloved pet. However, most people would expect to be greeted by a cute little Yorkie Terrier—not a 70-pound Labrador Retriever. Thus, the thoughts that come to mind when the descriptor of "loyal companion" is offered might vary drastically. That is because as with any attempt at communication, there is the reality that symbols and words are arbitrary, abstract, and ambiguous.[24]

The arbitrary nature of language is further reinforced by West's reminder that "different languages use different signals to express the same idea."[25] Continuing with the last example, the word that comes to mind to describe one's "loyal companion" might be "dog" in English, but if the receiver of the message speaks French, they will think of "le chien" instead. In that same vein, the word used to identify a color in one language is not necessarily the word used to identify that same color in another language. Yet, whatever word is chosen, common images, emotions, and descriptors often come to mind when individuals are presented a color sample and then asked to identify both the color and the images that are conjured by those colors.[26]

Colors (whether used to describe objects or to identify a person's racial category) prove to be just as problematic as any other words, for they cannot be used in a vacuum devoid of meaning and emotion. If the power of words is evidenced by their ability to influence thoughts, actions, and even emotions, it follows that colors—as symbols of specific hues—can likewise have the same level of influence. This is true despite the fact that while colors carry meaning, there is nothing about the specific words that indicate what a color *should* represent. For example, the term that we know as "yellow" could just as well have been "red" because the terms themselves do not have meaning. It is the idea

---

22 Charles Kay Ogden and Ivor Armstrong Richards, *The Meaning of Meaning: A Study of the Influence of Language upon Thought and of the Science of Symbolism* (New York: Harcourt Brace and World, 1923).

23 Em Griffin, *A First Look at Communication Theory* (New York: McGraw-Hill, 1997), 57.

24 Julia T. Wood, *Communication theories in action: An introduction* (Belmont, CA: Wadsworth, 2000).

25 David West, "Language, Thought and Reality: A Comparison of Ferdinand de Saussure's Course in General Linguistics with C.K. Ogden and I.A. Richards' The Meaning of Meaning." *Changing English: Studies in culture and education* (2005): 329.

26 The tendency to associate characteristics with certain colors appears to cross cultural boundaries. There are exceptions, though. For instance, in Chinese culture, red wedding dresses are common, whereas white dresses are generally expected in Western nations. This association of characteristics in different cultures will be addressed in more detail in the discussion that follows.

associated with the terms "yellow" and "red" that have taken on (and continue to give) meaning.

Research about color often looks at the construct and its meaning where tangible objects are concerned. The traits generally ascribed to those colors are imposed onto the objects that bear those colors. This is exemplified by an advertiser's use of color specifically to influence the public's selection of products. Madden, Hewett, and Roth's findings, for example, show that blue, green, and white are colors typically associated with descriptors like, "peaceful," "gentle," and "calming."[27] While these colors tend to share similar meaning across countries, some cultures see these colors as representative of things that are "beautiful," and "pleasant." (The meanings associated with these colors, interestingly enough, are all positive, regardless of which country or culture is being considered.) The same authors also found that the colors black and brown are often associated with the descriptors "sad" and "stale" across cultures, though some cultures view the same colors as being representative of things that are "formal" and "masculine."[28] Following this line of thinking, it would be easy to see why certain colors become more widely accepted than others. If someone must choose colors for a logo, a product label, or a campaign surrounding a product, the individual involved in the decision-making process is likely to consider the commonly-held beliefs about specific colors when choosing the shades that will be used to appeal to the target audience. In other words, marketers and advertisers are going to be proactive in choosing colors that conjure positive emotions for potential customers. In essence, there is likely then the promotion of certain colors, often to the demotion or outright exclusion of others, simply because of the meaning that is created or conjured when certain colors are put forth. This reality may make more sense when color is understood as a descriptor of people as opposed to a mere description of inanimate objects. People in the United States have historically been assigned descriptive traits, and those traits often mirror the traits that have been associated with the color used to identify them. For example, the color white has historically been used to describe things that are good and pure, the very absence of color. The color black is often used to identify things that are bad and evil. In fact, according to the *Dictionary of Colour*, black is actually described as "the opposite of white."[29] Moreover, at least six definitions of the word "black" from the *Merriam-Webster Dictionary*[30] conjure negative ideas or images.[31]

If one then believes that words have power, and that the power or the traits generally associated with those words can be imposed on a person or a group of people, the problem of identification by color becomes clear. When a color is used to identify a person's racial group, the meanings generally associated with the

---

27 Thomas J. Madden, Kelly Hewett, and Martin S. Roth. "Managing images in different cultures: A cross-national study of color meanings and preferences." *Journal of International Marketing* (2000).

28 Ibid.

29 Ian Paterson, *Dictionary of Colour: A Lexicon of the Language of Colour* (London: Thorogood, 2005).

30 Merriam-Webster Dictionary. "black." n.d. http://www.merriam-webster.com/dictionary/black (accessed June 11, 2012).

31 Negative definitions for the word "black" in the Merriam-Webster Dictionary include the following: 1.) dirty, soiled; 2.) thoroughly sinister or evil; 3.) connected with or invoking the supernatural and especially the devil; 4a.) very sad, gloomy, or calamitous; 4b.) marked by the occurrence of disaster; 5.) characterized by hostility or angry discontent; and 6.) characterized by grim, distorted, or grotesque satire.

color are then transposed onto the person or an entire group. This is problematic for three reasons: (1) The objectification of people reduces their humanity, (2) many of the socially imposed ideas associated with the presence of color (as differentiated from Whiteness—or the absence of color) are often negative, and (3) the tendency to associate the same meanings to people that are used to describe objects is further complicated by the reality that these meanings are often enduring, frequently lasting across generational and geographical divides. With the understanding that the meanings associated with color are shaped by a number of variables over an extended period of time, it becomes vital to consider some of the other elements that influence one's beliefs about color and race. Analyzing the body as a text helps in that mission because the color of one's skin can be viewed as a message—or a rhetorical artifact that is being read by the observer.

Body Politics: Obama as a Rhetorical Text

When many think of the term "politics," they think of Democrats or Republicans, social platforms, speeches, and super PACs. Most do not immediately think of the body as political. However, the black body is—and has been—politicized. This has been true from the days of slavery, with decisions like the Three-Fifths Compromise, and this politicization continues today. In fact, President Barack Obama manages to bring together "the political" in a unique way. With his election to the highest position in the land, he, like none other before him, has managed to move from his political platform to a constant reminder that his very body is political.

The study of body politics centers on the belief that the body is a rhetorical text that can be analyzed to get clarity on the unspoken messages that are being both sent and received. Thus, the concept of body politics provides yet other platforms through which one might gain a greater understanding of how color is perceived in the United States by providing a glimpse into the way meaning is assigned to the body, and specifically how skin color is problematized by Whites. A number of communication scholars (including Dangerfield[32], Jackson[33], and Hopson[34]) have contributed to a still scarce literature on the politics of the Black, masculine body. This work is important to one's understanding of just how Obama is perceived as his color and gender intersect when he is being "read." As a Black male, both in terms of self-identification and in terms of how he is identified by others, President Obama provides a unique text for evaluation. He is a high-profile Black man who is recognized globally, and because of his position, he has arguably become the most powerful Black man of all time. Yet, the very fact that he is often described as a Black man, and not a biracial man, speaks to the beliefs about skin color and the body politics at work in this country. As it relates to col-

---

32   Ronald L. Jackson II and Celnisha L. Dangerfield, "Defining Black masculinity as cultural property: Toward an identity negotiation paradigm," in *Intercultural Communication: A Reader*, Larry A. Samovar and Richard E. Porter (Belmont, CA: Wadsworth, 2003), 120-131.

33   Ronald L. Jackson II, *Scripting the Black Masculine Body: Identity, Discourse, and Racial Politics in Popular Media* (Alabany, New York: State University of New York Press, 2006).

34   Ronald L. Jackson II and Mark Hopson, *Masculinity in the Black Imagination: Politics of Communicating Race and Manhood* (New York: Peter Lang, 2011).

or, gender, and power, Jackson and Crawley find that color or race "is a powerful preverbal communicative cue that may shift students' perceptions of an otherwise qualified and credible Black male instructor, because with it comes presumptions about what it means to be Black and male in the United States."[35] While President Obama is not a professor, the power differential between an instructor and a student is similar to that of a politician and his public. For those who choose to look only at color for ideas about how a person is likely to act, President Obama's skin color trumps his mixed ancestry and his upbringing.

The literature on body politics proves especially important for those who take meaning solely from the color of another's skin. At face value, it appears that one's character could be summed up, not by the reality of his/her behavior, but rather by the color of the person's skin—and the behavior or actions stereotypically associated with an entire group of people. Since skin color carries meaning, especially when that color is black and is present on the male body, it affirms that the body is a text that can be read by the observer. As with any text, some are immediately turned off by the cover, while others take the time to look deeper. One wonders if the deeper look into the ancestry of President Obama is what allows him to cross racial boundaries that few have been able to so skillfully navigate. So while Obama possesses the phenotypic features of a Black man, it may be his White ancestry that somehow purifies some of the "stain of his blackness," thus making him an acceptable leader to those who may have otherwise dismissed his potential based solely on the color of his skin. This argument goes beyond merely reading the body, and it calls for another theoretical construct that might explain why some people are able to see beyond skin color by resisting the existing scripts and creating their own meaning.

Personal Construct Theory and Constructivism

Personal construct theory and constructivism[36] are offered to provide an understanding of the influence of skin color on the concept of race, and as an extension, the influence of color on how people are viewed in society. Jesse Delia's theory of constructivism reveals an apparent juxtaposition at work that allows people to see the same thing, yet have a completely different idea of that thing, person, or even color. An off-shoot of George Kelly's personal construct theory, constructivism seeks to explain just "how the interpretive process works."[37] Thus, this theory is yet another avenue through which the influence of skin color might be explored, specifically as it relates to the way President Obama is viewed racially.

Personal construct theory and constructivism seek to explain just how humans tend to move from symbol to meaning. There are four areas that, once considered, provide greater insight into how people come to understand a particular idea, concept, or descriptor. The four areas can be categorized as prototypes, personal

---

35 Ronald L. Jackson II and Rex Crawley, "White Student Confessions about a Black Male Professor: A Cultural Contracts Theory Approach to Intimate Conversations about Race and Worldview," *Journal of Men's Studies* (2003): 25.

36 Personal construct theory and constructivism are related theoretical perspectives that both explore the way people "construct" or manage meaning. While often viewed as psychological in nature, these theories actually take a communicative stance in that they help explain the way meaning is conveyed and understood.

37 Wood, *Communication theories in action,* 158.

constructs, stereotypes, and scripts. Discussion of these categories merely expands on the previously highlighted literature on body politics, and in a more detailed way, provides an explanation of why color may have different meanings that are dependent on the sum of one's experiences, beliefs, and teachings about color and race.

Each of the areas outlined by Kelly, Delia, and others will now be explored, and President Barack Obama will be used as the common denominator for each construct. Introduction of this theory using a person of mixed ancestry shows what happens when a person falls outside of generally accepted beliefs about a racial group. Yet, this section also reminds the reader just how much stock people put into skin color and hierarchical placement within society.

The first area of constructivism that can be explored is that of the prototype, which refers to the "…ideal or optimal example of a category of people, situations, objects."[38] No matter a person's racial affiliation, socio-economic status, or political beliefs, few would deny that someone who aspires to the position of the President of the United States must be one who displays an array of positive characteristics. It is not challenging to envision a "presidential prototype," a "leadership prototype," or even a "familial prototype." For some though, developing a racial prototype might be a bit more challenging, not to mention the fact that it may seem downright unethical. One might recall Hitler's Aryan race and its accompanying promotion of a master race, and thus, one might shun all attempts at identifying racial prototypes. All of this is further complicated when one looks to a biracial person to serve as the prototype of Black masculinity.

Despite his skin color, some might argue that by virtue of the fact that President Obama is biracial, was raised by a White parent, spent time living in rural Kansas with his White grandparents, and was a product of the most affluent institutions of higher learning in the country, that he would be barred from being elevated to the level of prototype to which all Black men should aspire. When the then-Senator Obama burst onto the scene as a potential presidential candidate, some Blacks raised questions about his ability to operate as an authentic representative of Black manhood in the United States—or as noted in the often used colloquialism of the culture, they questioned Obama's ability to "keep it real." Obama's upbringing notwithstanding, his blackness is forever reinforced by the color of his skin in conjunction with his own self-identification with Black culture. So whether by choice or circumstance, President Obama and his family have become the real-life version of the Huxtable family from television's *The Cosby Show*. Ultimately, for those who rely on skin color and/or in-group membership (along with high levels of personal and public success) to tell the story, President Obama has become the prototype of Black manhood, the prototype of Black fatherhood, and the ultimate success story of what a person of color can do if only given the chance to excel. An article in *Essence* magazine highlighting the twenty-five most influential African Americans of 2009 masterfully affirms the idea of Obama as prototype noting, "For the world at large, the Nobel laureate represents America's best chance at polishing its global image and policing

---

38 Ibid.

its excesses."[39] The article says of the Obama family, "[They are] a captivating portrait that's changing hearts, minds and perceptions about Black men, Black women, Black children and Black love."[40] Only an effective prototype can change perceptions by raising the bar of expectation, and President Obama (and the First Family) are doing just that.

Constructivism especially encourages the exploration of a second area, personal constructs, since personal construct theory serves as a springboard for constructivism. Personal constructs refer to the placement of a concept along a continuum. Often described using the term "bipolar," personal constructs help situate ideas with regard to how they rate when compared between two opposing descriptors.[41] Since the subject of this entire text is color, it makes sense to look at President Obama in terms of this placement on the color scale. It is noteworthy to remember here that the president is racially identified as Black, although he is biracial. In the United States in particular, it is quite interesting that there is not a racial continuum. White plus anything else equals non-White. As a result, a biracial designation does not work for some because in their minds, there is only White and only Black; gray is not a possibility.

In the *Time* magazine article entitled, *Is Obama Black Enough*, another personal construct is highlighted: "good black" versus "bad black."[42] However, within the African American community, other personal constructs exist, especially as they relate to color. When considering the issue of colorism[43] or the practice of treating people within the same racial category differently based on the color of their skin, it is clear that personal constructs certainly exist. Descriptors such as *redbone, high-yellow,* and *light-skinned* are all used to refer to those of a lighter shade along the color continuum. On the other hand, descriptors such as *dark, chocolate, mocha,* and *ebony* describe those who occupy the darker end of the spectrum. People are then compared and labeled as one of the aforementioned descriptors, or judged to determine where they might fall within this broad scale. Interestingly, this practice is common, and quite reminiscent of the slave-era differentiation between house slaves and field slaves. In fact, because this practice is so common within the African American community, and because many African Americans are of mixed ancestry (even if it is several generations back), President Obama's biracial identity/skin color allows him to fit along this continuum without any challenges whatsoever.

Another personal construct identified by Young is the idea of "keeping it real" versus "keeping it proper."[44] The first end of the spectrum, keeping it real, is very important within the African American community. It is the belief that a person

---

39 Angela Burt-Murray ed., "25 Most Influential African-Americans." *Essence* (December 2009): 131.
40 Ibid.
41 Wood, *Communication theories in action,* 158.
42 Ta-Nehisi Paul Coates, *Is Obama Black Enough?* February 1, 2007.http://www.time.com/time/nation/article/0,8599,1584736,00.html.
43 Colorism refers to the in-group hierarchy of members based on the distance one is color-wise from another person on an invisible color line.
44 Alford A. Young Jr., "The Black Masculinities of Barack Obama: Some Implications for African American Men," *Daedalus* (2011): 206-214.

should be one's authentic self, avoiding the trappings of the stereotypical norms of the mainstream. To the contrary, keeping it proper

> ...refers to the social practices of African Americans (and most often to those of upper-income or professional status) that promote the most sanitized and, therefore, most acceptable public face to both white and black America...A remarkable aspect of the public black masculinity of Obama is found in his incorporation of these two styles in ways that, like [...] being biracial, make him appear at once different from many black American men[,] yet also seemingly just like one of them.[45]

The editors of *Essence* capture the dichotomy of the president by noting, "Whether he's executing a free throw or examining free markets, gracing the halls of the G8 or the pages of GQ, his substance and style are evident."[46] It appears that Obama's strength may lie in his ability to fit perfectly within the posted ranges, whether in terms of the identification of good black or bad black, in terms of the broad range of skin tones of African Americans, or in terms of his ability to simultaneously keep it real and keep it proper.

Still another area of constructivism for thought is the idea of President Obama as a stereotype. It is impossible to deny that the president is of African ancestry. One need only look at his brown skin to see that truth. It is telling that his White ancestry and upbringing are usually negated in favor of considering (skin) color, often to the exclusion of other things that have undoubtedly shaped him into the person that he has become. This third area of consideration, the stereotype, is particularly useful when deciding the meaning associated with one's skin color. It asks for reflection on the images envisioned as individuals are compared to the general beliefs about the majority of people similarly classified. Right or wrong, stereotypes exist, and they are often present as humans formulate their ideas about people, places, events, and concepts. For one seeking to judge President Obama as compared to often-held images of Black men, the task might prove daunting. That may be because President Obama's life and persona seemingly defy attempts to be stereotyped in that regard. However, despite the fact that he has excelled personally and politically, his skin color forever keeps him lumped into the racial category with some others that could be labeled "unsavory characters" by some people. This statement is not to suggest that all Black men are pathological, but the images often presented by the media are usually negative.[47] In fact, my research has found that people were likely to over-exaggerate phenotypic features that are deemed stereotypically more Black when recounting images observed in the media.[48]

---

45   Ibid., 208.
46   Angela Burt-Murray ed., "25 Most Influential," 131.
47   See the following articles for more information about the portrayal of Blacks in the media: Travis L. Dixon, "Schemas as Average Conceptions: Skin Tone, Television New Exposure, and Culpability Judgments," *Journalism and Mass Communication Quarterly* (2006): 131-149 and Travis L. Dixon and Daniel G. Linz. "Overrepresentation and Underrepresentation of African Americans and Latinos as Lawbreakers on Television News," *Journal of Communicaiton* (2000): 131-154.
48   Mary Beth Oliver et al., "The Face of Crime: Viewers' Memory of Race-Related Facial Features of Individuals Pictured in the News," *Journal of Communication* (2004): 88-104.

Jackson and Dangerfield outline many of the common stereotypes associated with Black masculinity, condensing them into three categories: (1) the Black masculine body as violent/criminal, (2) the Black masculine body as sexual, and (3) the Black masculine body as incompetent/uneducated.[49] Whether considering his educational achievements, his political career, his marriage, or his active presence in the lives of his two daughters, President Obama does not fall into the negative cast typically associated with many Black men and other people of color.[50]

Constructivism's fourth area of delineation is referred to as scripts. Wood asserts that "Scripts are our understandings of how particular kinds of interactions are supposed to proceed—what happens…"[51] Instead of scripts being read as a completely separate category, they should be read as the sum of the preceding categories: prototypes, personal constructs, and stereotypes. In line with this way of thinking as it relates to color and race—one could argue that the scripts are actually messages or cues sent forward as influenced by one's racial prototype, one's personal constructs, and the stereotypes held of people of a particular race or skin color. With this in mind, it becomes easier to understand why some might have completely divergent views about the color of one's skin, and so this influences the way a person ultimately feels about those of a particular hue. In short, the way a person "reads" another's skin color is "colored" by the way they view that person when compared to others lumped into the same group. If, in a person's mind, the President reinforces existing historical beliefs about people of color, the negative beliefs about African Americans in particular will prevail in that person's mind. To the contrary, if a person sees that the President counters long-held beliefs about Black people—or that person does not have the negative stereotypes in place and believes that Obama is more in line with the view of a racial prototype—one is less likely to be moved by the President's body politics. Instead, this person will be influenced more by Obama's social and financial platforms.

Color and Negotiated Identities

Nothing exists in a vacuum void of societal influences, personal experiences, and belief systems. Our identities are socially constructed, just as notions of race and color are also socially constructed. Cushman and Kovacic assert,

> "Reality is socially constructed in a creative and emergent interplay between the individual's interpretive process and the historically constituted contexts and processes of the community. Thus, the individual is confronted with a world that is already meaningful by virtue of the existing community's creation of reality. In the process of socialization[,] the individual incorporates the community's universe of shared meaning, engages in an ongoing interpretation process, and accommodates to the social reality of the lifeworld."[52]

---

49 Ronald L. Jackson II and Celnisha L. Dangerfield, "Defining Black masculinity."

50 The post-election possibility of stereotyping President Obama as incompetent may have more to do with political differences. As a result, this concept will not be discussed further since it would be difficult to determine whether the motive behind this sentiment is racial or political in nature—or some amalgam of the two.

51 Wood, *Communication theories in action*, 160.

52 Donald P. Cushman and Branislav Kovacic. *Watershed Research Traditions in Human Communication Theory*

The socially-constructed reality of race and color can have a distinct impact on both those within the group being labeled, and those outside of the group doing the labeling. Research, however, suggests that African Americans tend to have a "more fluid understanding of race that incorporate[s] ideas of self-definition and an emphasis on culture, while European-Americans [are] more likely to rely on physical characteristics to understand race."[53]

The sad truth is that once the element of skin color is considered, the ideas, images, and emotions associated with those colors are directly transferred to individuals by virtue of overtly-expressed (or subtly-implied) notions of race. These factors coalesce to create a portion of one's identity that is based solely on others' perception of skin color and race. Such is the case with body politics. In essence, since the shaping of one's identity and sense of self can be highly influenced by the way others view a person's skin color and/or race, a person cannot be completely separated from society's view of color. President Obama even underscored this in a *60 Minutes* interview in 2007 after his decision to check "Black" on his census form. When asked how he had decided he was Black, the President replied, "Well, I'm not sure I decided it. I think if you look African-American in this society, you're treated as an African-American."[54]

In line with that thinking, society's influence on identity can be seen in the negative images often associated with African Americans of darker hues, especially if those hues operate in tandem with other "African" phenotypic markers. Arguably, much of this can be traced to perceptions of difference associated with skin color, but it has continued far beyond that in the United States. As a result, there has arisen the long standing tradition of associating one's skin color with intelligence, propensity for indecent behavior, and as a marker of one's potential to excel financially. As Featherston notes, "Color is the ultimate test of 'American-ness,' and black is the most un-American color of all."[55] When Obama was elected to the Presidency, he was identified as a Black man by most, despite his racial lineage. It makes one wonder if the power behind some of the most common stereotypes of Black men is diminished for the President because of the public knowledge of his biracial ancestry. That is, while he is well-educated and has assumed a level of wealth and influence, for some, it may be that education and wealth—in conjunction with the white part of his ancestry—make him more palatable than the average Black man that one might encounter. No matter which has the greatest impact—being biracial, well-educated, or of a higher-socio-economic status, the negotiation of Obama's identity assists some in being more open to the reality of a Black man in the White House. When it comes to knowledge of ancestry's having an impact on acceptance, it appears that this may be the equivalent of "passing in reverse." That is, historically, it was knowledge of ancestry that worked against biracial Blacks. Intellect, education, financial affluence, and White ancestry could not overcome one drop of Black blood. Maybe it is the knowledge

---

(Albany, New York: State Univeristy of New York Press, 1995).

53 Tasha N. Dubriwny, Benjamin R. Bates, and Jennifer L. Bevan. "Lay understandings of race."

54 Adam Serwer, "In the Mix: Being Biracial in America," *Essence* (May 2011): 86.

55 Elena Featherston, "Preface - Musing on race and color in America," in *Skin deep: Women writing on color, culture, and identity* (Freedom, CA: The Crossing Press, 1994), iii.

of the President's ancestry that makes him acceptable to serve as President in a way that other Blacks before him could not. It is important to note that "passing" was not always intentional. That then would suggest that "reverse passing" may not be intentional either. In all truth, this is likely more a statement of a person's need to make others "acceptable" by reflecting on the part of a biracial person's color story that has fewer negative stereotypes. Yet, this offers another idea as to how some people may justify voting for a person of color, particularly when their personal constructs about people of color have been negative.

Considering that meaning associated with words can conjure different ideas when trying to describe a referent, it is interesting to note that the ability to process that meaning beyond the traditionally-held beliefs about color leads not only to a new understanding of the concept, but likely forces the revaluation of an entire nation's view of race. This raises the question as to whether the intellectual process at work—when one stops to consider prototypes, personal constructs, and stereotypes—has not only changed the associated scripts on race, but has also been a fundamental reason behind the shift that led to a Black man's becoming President of the United States of America.

Conclusion

A Gallup poll from October 1963 reviewing the reaction to a hypothetical Black President found that even on the heels of a major push for racial equality, half the voters surveyed said "that they would reject a candidate simply because he was a Negro."[56] Though some maintained this viewpoint forty-five years after that Gallup poll, enough Americans changed their minds to get Barack Obama elected as the forty-fourth President of the United States on November 4, 2008. Obama campaigned on the platform of change, and left millions chanting his campaign slogan, "Yes we can!" His election proved that America could—if only for a brief moment in time—put race and color aside to give a person the chance to ascend to the highest elected position in this country. While this feat was clearly a testament to America's attempt to put race and color aside—or to at least see beyond the stereotypes generally associated with Black men—it was simultaneously a reminder that so much more needs to happen. Obama desegregated the US Presidency, but it will likely take far more to integrate the collective memory. As Steinhorn and Diggs-Brown note, "Desegregation may unlock doors, but integration is supposed to open minds…"[57] The certainty that President Obama is only the first US President of color reminds us that while progress has been made, there is more work to be done. Amanda Ripley, a reporter for *Time* magazine, may have said it best: "Ironically, the person who mattered most in Obama's life is the one we know the least about—maybe because being partly African in America is still seen as being simply black and color is still a preoccupation above almost all else."[58]

---

56 Ellis Cose, *Color-blind: Seeing beyond race in a race-obsessed world.* (iNew York: HarperCollins, 1997), xx.
57 Leonard Steinhorn and Barbara Diggs-Brown, *By the Color of our Skin: The Illusion of Integration and the Reality of Race* (New York: Dutton, 1999), 5.
58 Amanda Ripley, "The Story of Barack Obama's Mother," *Time Magazine U.S.* April 9, 2008. http://www.time.com/time/magazine/article/0,9171,1729685,00.html.

In 1903, W.E.B Dubois noted that "The problem of the twentieth century [was] the problem of the color-line, —the relation of the darker to the lighter races of men in Asia and Africa, in America and the islands of the sea." No one can argue that the world has changed since the dark days of American slavery. Nevertheless, it appears that the racial/color categorization that was in place during that time is still alive, even if it survives only marginally for some. Dubow puts it eloquently in noting, "The stubborn survival of racial categories attests to the enduring power of the old race paradigm, as well as the fact that new insights and methodologies take time to be fully incorporated and internalized."[59] Unfortunately, the continued presence of archaic ideas about racial identification and categorization evidenced during President Obama's campaigns and during his terms in office remind us that not only is the one-drop rule still in play, but hate associated with color is still very real.

Suggestions for Future Research

While the election of the nation's first Black President took center stage of the country's discussion of race for a number of years, the death of a teenager in Florida captured the spotlight in the discussion of just how much skin color influences how people are perceived in the United States. When neighborhood watch captain George Zimmerman went weeks before being arrested for the death of Trayvon Martin, national outrage grew. That outrage turned to disgust for many when George Zimmerman was acquitted of the charges against him. While Zimmerman's lawyers successfully argued that he had merely "stood his ground" when he thought his life was in danger, civil rights groups claimed that Martin's "crime" was merely walking home as a young, Black male.

The stories of Barack Obama and Trayvon Martin intersect in a peculiar way. For as the nation celebrated the progress of race relations to the degree that a Black man could ascend to the Presidency, many were harshly reminded that merely being Black could cost a person his/her very life. In the time leading to the arrest of George Zimmerman, President Obama was asked to comment on the death of Trayvon Martin. In a press conference on March 23, 2012, the President ended with a powerful statement to the parents of Trayvon (and essentially to the entire world) saying, "You know, if I had a son, he'd look like Trayvon." After the court ruling was handed down acquitting George Zimmerman of the charges against him, President Obama once again made remarks about the case—remarks that tied his experiences to those of Trayvon in an almost poetic fashion. On July 19, 2013, President Obama said, "You know, when Trayvon Martin was first shot, I said that this could have been my son. Another way of saying that is Trayvon Martin could have been me 35 years ago." In that moment, questions of group membership and identification were cast far away. The President's self-identification triumphed over any attempts to be labeled by outsiders. Furthermore, it solidified in-group membership because it reminded African Americans—as the world looked on—of the similitude of the President's negative experiences as a Black man. Finally, in an indirect way, the President asked the nation to consider

---

59 Saul Dubow, *Scientific racism in modern South Africa* (New York: Cambridge University Press, 1995), 106.

what may have been lost because Trayvon Martin did not get to live thirty-five more years merely because the color of his skin created enough fear in someone that actions were taken that caused his very life to be snuffed away.

This chapter takes a look at the way a nation showed its true colors as a Black man endeavored to triumph over color barriers to become President of the United States. Going forward, it seems appropriate to analyze the impact of skin color and race on the experience of the average American, as he/she goes about life. It could provide clearer insight into whether it is President Obama's biracial identity, socio-economic status, political clout, or merely timing that made him the subject of discussions of race in the same way that Trayvon Martin has become the subject of discussions of race. At the very least, President Obama's remarks about the death of Trayvon Martin are deserving of deeper analysis; they appear to offer a unique point of comparison between two Black men who have had the entire nation talking about race and equality. Moreover, President Obama's speeches speak volumes about identification with—and connection to—community groups based on color and shared experience. This chapter began with a discussion of the role of people of color in shaping America. It is cathartic to now see a person of color at the helm of a country that once would not have even deemed Obama a "whole" person. Still, a study conducted soon after the fiftieth anniversary of Dr. Martin Luther King, Jr.'s March on Washington (and shortly after the court ruling on the death of Trayvon Martin) found that most Blacks are not as optimistic about progress as they were just five years earlier—in the time right after the election of Barack Obama to the Presidency.[60] So while some solace comes in knowing that a sliver of racial progress has been achieved, that peace is uneasy. That is especially true considering that even during Obama's Presidency, the stories behind the deaths of unarmed Black men like Trayvon Martin, Oscar Grant, Jonathan Ferrell, Jordan Davis, and Michael Brown made national headlines. It seems that as long as there is a sustained preoccupation with race and color (as highlighted by the need to categorize a person by the color of one's skin) in tandem with the use of archaic scripts when encountering a person of color,[61] this country is unlikely to experience the true integration needed to judge people by character—instead of color—as Dr. Martin Luther King, Jr. envisioned.[62] Indeed, the campaign slogan for Barack Obama's second term in office was "Change We Can Believe In." Only when color no longer plays such an important role in the categorization of men and women—and body politics become less powerful than national politics—will this country reach a point where there is genuine "change we can believe in."

---

60 Pew Research Center, "King's Dream Remains."

61 The article, "When it Comes to Politics, Are We More Racist than We Think" suggests that internet searches using archaic scripts are indicative that there is more racism at play than most would openly share. This article refers to the dissertation of a Harvard doctoral students to show that this nation's private Google searches for racial epithets might give a more accurate picture of the sentiments regarding race than a survey might provide—simply because people do not censor themselves as much when they think they are "privately" searching for information on the internet.

62 Lylah M. Alphonse, *When it Comes to Politics, Are We More Racist than We Think.* June 11, 2012. http://shine.yahoo.com/work-money/comes-politics-more-racist-think-185600847.html.

Bibliography

Alphonse, Lylah M. "When it Comes to Politics, Are We More Racist than We Think." June 11, 2012. Accessed June 11, 2012. http://shine.yahoo.com/work-money/comes-politics-more-racist-think-185600847.html.

Bowker, Geoffrey C., and Susan L. Star. *Sorting Things Out: Classification and its Consequences.* Cambridge, MA: MIT Press, 1999.

Burt-Murray, Angela, ed. "25 Most Influential African-Americans." *Essence* (December 2009): 129-140.

Censky, Annalyn. "Black unemployment: Highest in 27 Years." *CNN Money,* September 2, 2011. Accessed January 14, 2012. http://money.cnn.com/2011/09/02/news/economy/black_unemployment_rate/index.htm.

Coates, Ta-Nehisi Paul. "Is Obama Black Enough?." *Time,* February 1, 2007. Accessed February 24, 2012. http://www.time.com/time/nation/article/0,8599,1584736,00.html.

Cokley, Kevin. "To be or not to be Black: Problematics of Racial Identity." In *The Quest for Community and Identity: Critical Essays in Africana Social Philosophy*, by Robert E. Birt, 29-44. Lanham, MD: Rowman & Littlefield, 2002.

Cose, Ellis. *Color-blind: Seeing Beyond Race in a Race-Obsessed world.* New York: HarperCollins, 1997.

Cushman, Donald P., and Branislav Kovacic. *Watershed Research Traditions in Human Communication Theory.* Albany, New York: State Univeristy of New York Press, 1995.

DeMente, Boyce. *NTC's Dictionary of Mexican Cultural Code Words.* Lincolnwood, IL: NTC Publishing Group, 1996.

Dixon, Travis L. "Schemas as Average Conceptions: Skin Tone, Television New Exposure, and Culpability Judgments." *Journalism and Mass Communication Quarterly* (2006): 131-149.

Dixon, Travis L., and Daniel G. Linz. "Overrepresentation and Underrepresentation of African Americans and Latinos as Lawbreakers on Television News." *Journal of Communicaiton*, (2000): 131-154.

Dubow, Saul. *Scientific Racism in Modern South Africa.* New York: Cambridge University Press, 1995.

Dubriwny, Tasha N., Benjamin R. Bates, and Jennifer L. Bevan. "Lay Understandings of Race: Cultural and Genetic Definitions." *Public Health Genomics* (2004): 185-195.

Dyrn, Jamese. *Jamesedyrn's Webblog.* November 5, 2008. http://jamesedyrn.wordpress.com/2008/11/05/world-headlines-immediately-after-barack-obama-is-elected-as-president-of-the-united-states-of-america/

Featherston, Elena. "Preface - Musing on race and color in America." In *Skin deep: Women Writing on Color, Culture, and Identity*. Freedom, CA: The Crossing Press, 1994.

Glenn, Evelyn. *Shades of Difference: Why Skin Color Matters.* Palo Alto, CA: Stanford University Press, 2009.

Gould, Stephen J. "The Geometer of Race." *Discover* (November 1994): 65-69.

—. *The Mismeasure of Man.* New York: Norton, 1981.

Griffin, Em. *A First Look at Communication Theory.* New York: McGraw-Hill, 1997.

Jackson II, Ronald L. *Scripting the Black Masculine Body: Identity, Discourse, and Racial Politics in Popular Media.* Alabany, New York: State University of New York Press, 2006.

Jackson II, Ronald L., and Rex Crawley. "White Student Confessions about a Black Male Professor: A Cultural Contracts Theory Approach to Intimate Conversations about Race and Worldview." *Journal of Men's Studies* (2003): 25.

Jackson, Ronald L., and Mark Hopson. *Masculinity in the Black Imagination: Politics of Communicating Race and Manhood.* New York: Peter Lang, 2011.

Jackson, Ronald, L., and Celnisha L. Dangerfield. "Defining Black Masculinity as Cultural Property: Toward an Identity Negotiation Paradigm." In *Intercultural Communication: A Reader*, by Larry A. Samovar and Richard E. Porter, 120-131. Belmont, CA: Wadsworth, 2003.

Johnson, Alex. "Barack Obama Elected 44th President." *NBC News*, November 5, 2008. Accessed September 6, 2011. http://www.msnbc.msn.com/id/27531033/ns/politics-decision_08/t/barack-obama-elected-th-president/.

Lassiter, Sybil M. *Cultures of Color in America: A Guide to Family, Religion, and Health.* Westport, CT: Greenwood, 1998.

Loury, G. *Race, Incarceration, and American Values.* Cambridge, MA: MIT Press, 2008.

Madden, Thomas J, Kelly Hewett, and Martin S. Roth. "Managing Images in Different Cultures: A Cross-National Study of Color Meanings and Preferences." *Journal of International Marketing* (2000): 90-107.

Marger, Martin N. *Race and Ethnic Relations: American and Global Perspectives.* Belmont, CA: Wadsworth (Cengage Learning), 2011.

Merriam-Webster Dictionary. "black." n.d. Accessed June 11, 2012, http://www.merriam-webster.com/dictionary/black.

Nagourney, Adam. "Obama Elected President as Racial Barrier Falls." *New York Times*, November 4, 2008. Accessed September 6, 2011. http://www.nytimes.com/2008/11/05/us/politics/05elect.html .

National Association for the Advancement of Colored People. *African Americans and Education Fact Sheet.* n.d. Accessed January 14, 2012. http://naacp.3cdn.net/e5524b7d7cf40a3578_2rm6bn7vr.pdf.

Obama, Barack H. *Dreams from My Father: A Story of Race and Inheritance.* New York: Three Rivers Press, 2004.

Ogden, Charles Kay, and Ivor Armstrong Richards. *The Meaning of Meaning: A Study of the Influence of Language upon Thought and of the Science of Symbolism.* New York: Harcourt Brace and World, 1923.

Oliver, Mary Beth, Ronald L. Jackson II, Ndidi N. Moses, and Celnisha L. Dangerfield. "The Face of Crime: Viewers' Memory of Race-Related Facial Features of Individuals Pictured in the News." *Journal of Communication*(2004): 88-104.

Omi, Micheal, and Howard Winant. *Racial Formation in the United States: From the 1960s to the 1990s.* London: Routlege, 1994.

Paterson, Ian. *Dictionary of Colour: A Lexicon of the Language of Colour.* London: Thorogood, 2005.

Pew Research Center. "King's Dream Remains an Elusive Goal; Many Americans See Racial Disparities." August 22, 2013. Accessed September 17, 2013. http://www.pewsocialtrends.org/files/2013/08/final_full_report_racial_disparities.pdf.

Ripley, Amanda. "The Story of Barack Obama's Mother." *Time Magazine U.S.* April 9, 2008. Accessed September 6, 2011. http://www.time.com/time/magazine/article/0,9171,1729685,00.html.

Serwer, Adam. "In the Mix: Being Biracial in America," *Essence Magazine, May 2011.*

Steinhorn, Leonard, and Barbara Diggs-Brown. *By the Color of our Skin: The Illusion of Integration and the Reality of Race.* New York: Dutton, 1999.

West, David. "Language, Thought and Reality: A Comparison of Ferdinand de Saussure's Course in General Linguistics with C.K. Ogden and I.A. Richards' The Meaning of Meaning." *Changing English: Studies in Culture and Education* (2005): 327-336.

Wood, Julia T. *Communication theories in action: An introduction.* Belmont, CA: Wadsworth, 2000.

Wuthnow, Robert. *American Mythos: Why Our Best Efforts to Be a Better Nation Fall Short.* Princeton, NJ: Princeton University Press, 2006.

Young Jr., Alford A. "The Black Masculinities of Barack Obama: Some Implications for African American Men." *Daedalus* (2011): 206-214.

12

Aversion to the Color Gray: The Monochromatic Nature of Turkish Domestic and Foreign Policy

Jonathan S. Miner

We loved a man, the founder of our country [Ataturk]. No, we did not love him; we worshipped him. We jailed anyone who did not worship him. Now we jail anyone who still worships him...we intimidated the pious because 'those uncivilized creatures contaminated our Western culture with their strange habits like praying and fasting.' Now we intimidate the non-pious 'because those infidels contaminate our Islamic culture with their sins like drinking alcohol and not fasting'...once we signed government cables that led to the deaths of over 1 million Armenians. One day we marched upon the killing of an Armenian [Hrant Dink], shouting "We are all Armenians!"[1]

A summer 2011 editorial by Turkish journalist Burak Bekdil depicts modern Turkish politics in terms of contrasts as extreme as black and white, regardless of whether the issues are domestic or foreign, secular or religious, or pertinent to relations with Armenia and Cyprus. Bekdil also suggests that the Turkish proclivity for an all-encompassing endorsement of leader, policy, neighbor, or political position is eventually rejected completely and endorsed in the opposite, leading him to posit that Turkish schools ought to "teach various shades of gray at painting classes."[2] Bekdil echoes a common concern among scholars of politics in Turkey, namely that democracy is far from consolidated, and that deep divisions in society and flaws in governance remain significant problems. Bekdil's editorial also hints at a possible cause: an intentional lack of subtlety in domestic and foreign policy on the part of Turkish politicians and elites.

Exploring this issue is all the more intriguing when taking into account the positive developments in Turkish society in the twenty-first century. Many observ-

---

1 Burak Bekdil, "The Turkish Hate-Affair with the Color 'Gray'," *Hurriyet Daily News,* August 4, 2011, accessed February 22, 2012, http://www.hurriyetdailynews.com/default.aspx?pageid=438&n=the-turkish-hate-affair-with-the-color-8216gray8217-2011-08-04.

2 Ibid.

ers see the last fifteen years as evidence, not of a retreat, but of an imminent consolidation of democracy in Turkey. First, a smooth and peaceful transfer of power from a military-backed, secular, Kemalist regime to a moderately Islamist, Anatolian-based, conservative political movement in 2002 provides evidence of democratic consolidation.[3] Second, the Turkish economy grew on average six percent from 2002 through 2007,[4] and continues to expand while weathering the recession-based storm which has engulfed its European neighbors.[5] Turkey's economy has reached the global top twenty in gross domestic product, which brings economic power and influence.[6] Third, Turkey has expanded its regional and global influence. On issues from the Israeli-Palestinian conflict to uprisings in Egypt and Syria, it has championed human rights, international norms, and its own emerging "Turkish model" of a Muslim democracy, providing a generally positive global position and increasing international influence. On the surface, logic dictates that such positive, profound political and economic changes would likely result in a further consolidation of democracy and a more nuanced set of domestic and foreign policies due to the expansion of equal rights for all citizens. Yet the violence that engulfed Turkey in the summer of 2013 has brought into question these societal improvements and suggests a reassessment of the positive trends in Turkish politics.[7]

What domestic themes can help in making sense of these incongruities? What realities explain the inability of the Turkish state to consolidate its democracy under these positive conditions and the obvious problems that remain after the violence of 2013? This paper seeks to answer these questions, and tests the hypothesis that the contest for power among the entrenched Sunni Turkish majority stunts the growth of Turkish democracy and subordinates its importance.

The research suggests that Bekdil is correct in his assessment of Turkish politics, and the violence which began in May 2013 derives from the inherent flaws of a political system and society driven by an exclusive rather than inclusive Turkish nationalism. The lack of subtlety, nuance, and "gray" that moderates between "black and white" extremes in political discourse is a product of the factional power struggle among the majority constituency and its desire to remain the dominant source of political authority. Kurdish, Shia Alevi, Christian, Greek, Jewish, Laz, and other minorities comprise between twenty-five and thirty percent of the Turkish population of almost eighty million, and continue to be intentionally and effectively shut out of the political decision-making process.[8] As a result, nec-

---

3   Juan Linz and Alfred Stepan, *Problems of Democratic Transition and Consolidation* (Baltimore: Johns Hopkins University Press), 14.

4   "Background Note: Turkey," United States Department of State, accessed August 19, 2012, http://www.state.gov/r/pa/ei/bgn/3432.htm.

5   Martina Bozadzhieva, "Growing Opportunities behind Turkey's Soft Landing," July 31, 2012, accessed August 19, 2012, http://blog.frontierstrategygroup.com/tag/turkey/.

6   "Economy: Turkey," The CIA World Factbook, August 19, 2012, accessed August 19, 2012, https://www.cia.gov/library/publications/the-world-factbook/geos/tu.html.

7   Justin Vela, "As Turkey Changes, So Does Its View of Founding National Hero, Ataturk," *The Atlantic*, July 14, 2012, accessed July 20, 2012, http://theatlantic.com/international/print/2012/06/.../258802/; Muhammad Ali Saddiqi, "Polarisation in Turkish Politics," *Dawn*, August 20, 2012, accessed August 20, 2012, http://dawn.com/2012/08/20/polarisation-in-turkish-politics/

8   "People and Society: Turkey" CIA World Factbook, accessed August 12, 2012.

essary checks and balances and equal participation in society do not operate to push Turkish society forward; instead, it continues to stagnate. Turkish foreign policy is a direct reflection of the domestic power struggle and it lacks in-between shades of gray in its international relations.

The foreign policy of any modern state is directly related to, and "entangled" with, the goals of its domestic policy.[9] International, human, and economic security are policy goals of all states regardless of system type or style of governance.[10] While policy goals can to some degree be reached through actions within the state, significant efforts must be undertaken abroad due to the interdependence of the modern state on the global system.[11] This interconnectivity suggests that, in order to understand the foreign policy of any state, a study of its domestic political goals and actions are useful. A notable scholar of international relations, Robert Putnam, characterizes this interplay as a two-level game in which the domestic policy goals of a given state are also pursued on the level of the international system, and that states compete to realize these goals through their publicly-stated policies and privately-conducted actions at both levels.[12]

An important part of the domestic policy of any state is the nationalist identity that encompasses the aforementioned international, human, and economic security goals. Scholars of international relations continue to examine the development of nationalism as the driving force of policy in the state-centric period from its beginning at the end of the Thirty Years War in 1648 to the present day. For instance, in his 1998 volume, *National Collective Identity: Social Constructs and International Systems*, Rodney Bruce Hall utilizes the constructivist[13] theory of international relations to examine continually emerging state nationalisms and their collective impact on a changing global system. Hall claims that "nationalism brought with it the abstract notion of 'citizenship,'" and that each state necessarily needed to construct a specific identity to survive and flourish in a new modern state-based system:[14]

> As classes and other actors attained civil and political citizenship, the state became 'their' nation-state, an 'imagined' community to which they developed loyalties. Its power, honor, humiliations, and even material interests came to be sensed as their own, and such feelings were mobilizable by the statesmen, pressure groups and militaries.[15]

---

9   Robert D. Putnam, "Diplomacy and Domestic Politics: The Logic of Two-Level Games," *International Organization* 42(Summer 1988): 427-460: 427.

10 James M Scott, Ralph G. Carter, and A. Cooper Drury, *IR* (Boston, Wadsworth, Cengage Learning, 2013), 9.

11 Ibid., 13.

12 Putnam, "Diplomacy and Domestic Politics," 433.

13 Constructivism is an international relations theory which argues the structure of the global political system is socially constructed and created by humans over time. It is based upon the idea that human perception and interpersonal communication "construct" an appropriate reality for the current era. James Dougherty and Robert Pfaltzgraff, Jr., (New York, Longman, 2001), 38-39.

14 Rodney Bruce Hall, *National Collective Identity: Social Constructs and International Systems* (New York, Columbia University Press, 1998), 5.

15 Ibid., 6.

Nationalism is an extremely important component in the creation of modern Turkey, as it is for any other modern state. To explain the nationalism at the heart of dysfunctional Turkish politics, this research aims to trace the major themes in Turkish nationalism as developed since its modern founding in 1923, and to analyze how these faults and weaknesses prevent democratic consolidation at home as well as the creation of a "gray" or subtle domestic and foreign policy necessary to construct a diverse and healthy national identity. Unless and until Turkish leaders at home modify and expand nationalism to encompass a full incorporation of all ethnicities, and religious and cultural backgrounds of Turkish citizens, its domestic and foreign policy will continue to reflect only black or white extremist positions.

Although Mustafa Kemal (Ataturk) founded the modern state with the intentions of creating a western-style democratic society, scholars of Turkish nationalism and democratization in both international relations and history point to a continuation of political and social rules from the Ottoman period to the modern republic. Optimistic popular sources such as the media and proponents of Turkey's European integration of Turkey see the benefits of EU membership and look past the faults of the Turkish system and the inequitable aspects of nationalism that perpetuate it. Perry Anderson's 2009 study on the development and expansion of a unified European identity provides a convincing basis for making this general argument. Anderson argues that while much of the cosmetic nature of the empire was replaced—language and alphabet, dress, and secular identity, among many others—the Ottoman societal divisions among different religions and ethnicities remain intact to the present day.[16] Despite the Tanzimat reforms of the seventeenth century and Ataturk's forceful reorientation of the modern state, ancient social divisions remain the continuing political reality.[17] Divisions among religious and ethnic groups, believers and unbelievers, and men and women remain obstacles to a consolidation of democracy,[18] and have, in fact, been intentionally incorporated into the modern political and societal system.[19]

According to Anderson, the modern Turkish state incorporated this stratification into a new nationalism with "civic nationalism" open to all, and a "secret conclave… prepared for a more confessional or ethnic nationalism, restricted to Muslims or Turks."[20] Scholars including Morin and Lee,[21] Altan-Olcay,[22] Gulalp,[23] Adak,[24] and

---

16   Perry Anderson, *The New Old World* (Brooklyn NY: Verso, 2009), 398.

17   Ibid.; Erik J. Zürcher, *The Young Turk Legacy and Nation Building: From the Ottoman Empire to Atatürk's Turkey* (London: I.B. Tauris, 2010), 236.

18   Ibid.; Stephen Kinzer, *Crescent and Star: Turkey between Two Worlds* (New York: Farrar, Strauss, and Giroux, 2008), 8.

19   Ersin Kalaycıoğlu, "Turkey," Chapter 6 of *Introduction to Comparative Politics,* Mark Kesselman, Joel Krieger and William A. Joseph, eds. (Baltimore: Wadsworth Cengage, 2007), 378.

20   Anderson, *The New Old World,* 402.

21   Aysel Morin and Ronald Lee, "Constitutive Discourse of Turkish Nationalism: Ataturk's Nutuk and the Rhetorical Construction of the 'Turkish People'," *Communication Studies* 61, no. 5 (Nov/Dec2010): 485.

22   Ozlem Altan-Olcay, "Gendered projects of national identity formation: The Case of Turkey," *National Identities* 11, no. 2 (June 2009):166.

23   Haldun Gulalp, "Capitalism and the Modern Nation-State: Rethinking the Creation of the Turkish Republic," *Journal of Historical Sociology* 7 (June 1994): 175.

24   Hulya Adak, "National Myths and Self-Na(rra)tions: Mustafa Kemal's 'Nutuk' and Halide Edib's 'Memoirs' and 'The Turkish Ordeal'." *South Atlantic Quarterly* 102, no. 2/3 (Spring/Summer 2003): 509.

Poulton[25] agree with Anderson and argue that the founders of modern Turkey believed it was necessary to create a new national identity that was openly accepting of all, yet privately protected for a privileged confessional and ethnic group. The modern Turkish political system is therefore democratically founded, on the whole, but with significant reservations of power and legal omissions necessary to keep these privileged classes in seats of power. Anderson and many scholars argue that, rather than starting anew as a modern state in 1923, modern Turkey "accentuated" Ottoman traditions instead of replacing them with a fundamentally new system.[26]

A fundamental reason for this is a "perception of victimization"[27] among the Sunni Turkish majority that has existed since the founding of the modern state. From the headscarf issue in public schools to military dominance over politics, the acknowledgement of the Armenian "genocide" to the inevitable emergence of an independent Kurdistan, the majority say each issue will finally tear the Turkish state apart as European powers intended at the end of World War I with the 1920 Treaty of Sevres. Greeks and Italians, British and French, Armenians and Russians all conspired to gobble up the remnants of the Ottoman Empire, and control Istanbul internationally while leaving the new Turkish state a rump entity controlling only limited territory in central Anatolia. Continuously under challenge from both in and outside forces, the Sunni Turkish majority pays all costs necessary to protect and maintain its narrow, national political identity, one that may not be complex, nuanced, or fully democratic, but which ensures the continuation of the state and dominance of the Sunni, Turkish majority.

The development of this limited definition of Turkish nationalism is a work in progress and has evolved throughout each period in the modern state. During the authoritarian period (1923-1950) under Ataturk and his successor, İsmet İnönü, the myth and ideology attributed to Mustafa Kemal Ataturk created a Eurocentric society with a new Latin-based script purged of many Arabic and Persian words, western styles of clothing, and culture. Under Kemalism, the staunch, secular leaders and elites in Turkish society created a new system, but one which incorporated many old rules.[28] Public pronouncements of "Turkey for Turks" along with the intentional exclusion of Kurds, Alevi Muslims, and all other ethnic and religious groups in public discourse consistently characterized the "new Turkey":

> Only the Turkish nation is entitled to claim ethnic and national rights in this country. No other element has any such rights—İsmet İnönü, Prime Minister 1938-1950.[29]
>
> The Turk must be the only lord, the only master of this country. Those who are not of pure Turkish origin can have only one right in this country, the right to be servants and slaves.[30]

---

25 Hugh Poulton, *Top Hat, Grey Wolf and Crescent: Turkish Nationalism and the Turkish Republic* (New York: NYU Press, 1997), 4.
26 Anderson, *The New Old World*, 415.
27 Discussion with Dr. Hakki Gurkas, Assistant Professor of History, Kennesaw State University, August 8, 2012.
28 Anderson, *The New Old World*, 420.
29 Ibid., 428.
30 Poulton, *Top Hat, Grey Wolf and Crescent*, 120.

In response to World War II and European continental fascism, scholars traced the development and increasingly strident rhetoric of Turkish nationalism.[31] Due to the fragile nature of the young state and its place within the warring parties of Europe and expansionist Soviet Russia, Turkish elites created a voting system with a ten-percent threshold for parliamentary representation, restrictive laws on speech, and routine bans on political parties consistently enforced by the military, police, a pliant judiciary, and a culture of exclusion.[32] With alternating civilian political leadership through the 1950s by Adnan Menderes[33] and Turgut Özal in the 1980s[34]—interrupted by military interventions in 1960, 1971, 1980, and 1997—the primacy of the Turkish secular elite was maintained. A great deal of scholarly work exists on the different factors of this exclusivity in Turkish nationalism, as scholars have looked at problems of general society,[35] education,[36] language,[37] literature,[38] music,[39] news media,[40] gender,[41] and the ethnic exclusion of the Alevi,[42] Armenian,[43] Greek,[44] and Kurdish[45] communities.

Each exclusion protects the "secret conclave" of Turkish nationalism and continues despite the peaceful transition of government that so many view as evidence of democratic consolidation. The 2002 landslide election of Erdoğan and his Justice and Development Party (AKP), while significant for a peaceful governmental tran-

---

31   Ali Şahin, "The Results of Racism-Turanism Case Turkish Nationalism in Development Process in 1944," *International Review of Turkology* 4, no. 8 (2011): 31; Soner Çagcaraptay, "Citizenship policies in interwar Turkey," *Nations and Nationalism* 9, no. 4 (October 2003): 601.

32   Anderson, *The New Old World*, 428.

33   Ibid., 433.

34   Ibid., 441.

35   Baran Dural, "A Transformation of Social Life in Turkey: 1930-1936," *Electronic Journal of Social Sciences* 8, no. 29 (2009): 184-197.

36   Fatma Gürses, "Kemalism Model Lesson Book: Civilized Knowledge for the Citizen," *Journal of Gazi Academic View* 3, no. 7 (2010): 233-249; Kancı, Tuba, "Reconfigurations in the Discourse of Nationalism and National Identity: Turkey at the Turn of the Twenty-first Century," *Studies in Ethnicity & Nationalism* 9, no. 3 (December 2009): 359-376.

37   Yeşim Bayar, "The Trajectory of Nation-Building through Language Policies: the Case of Turkey during the Early Republic (1920-38)," *Nations and Nationalism* 17, no. 1 (January 2011): 108-28; Yilmaz Bingol, "Language, Identity and Politics in Turkey: Nationalist Discourse on Creating a Common Turkic Language," *Alternatives: Turkish Journal of International Relations* 8, no. 2 (Summer 2009): 40-52.

38   Ahmet Emre Ateş, "Istanbul, City or 'Castle for Nationalism'? Discussion on the Urban Interaction between Literature and Nationalism," *International Journal of Turcologia* 7, no. 15 (Spring 2013): 69-73; Duygu Koksal, "Fine-Tuning Nationalism: Critical Perspectives from Republican Literature in Turkey," *Turkish Studies* 2, no. 2 (Autumn2001): 63.

39   C. Hakan Çuhadar, "The Unchanging Symbol of Nationalism in Turkey: 10th Annual March," *Anadolu University Journal of Social Sciences* 9, no. 2 (2009): 199-208.

40   Howard Eissenstat, "How Happy to Call Oneself a Turk: Provincial Newspapers and the Negotiation of a Muslim National Identity," *Social History* 37, no.1 (February 2012): 111.

41   Ozlem Altan-Olcay, "Gendered Projects of National Identity Formation: The Case of Turkey," *National Identities* 11, no. 2 (June 2009): 165-186.

42   Markus Dressler, "Religio-Secular Metamorphoses: The Re-Making of Turkish Alevism," *Journal of the American Academy of Religion* 76, no. 2 (June 2008): 280-311.

43   Ayla Göl, "Imagining the Turkish Nation through 'Othering' Armenians," *Nations and Nationalism* 11, no. 1 (January 2005): 121-139.

44   Pınar Kenanoğlu, "Discrimination and Silence: Minority Foundations in Turkey during the Cyprus Conflict of 1974," *Nations and Nationalism* 18, no. 2 (April 2012): 267-286.

45   Cenk Saraçoğlu, "'Exclusive Recognition': the New Dimensions of the Question of Ethnicity and Nationalism in Turkey," *Ethnic & Racial Studies* 32, no. 4 (May 2009): 640-658; M. Hakan Yavuz, "The Kurdish Question and Turkey's Justice and Development Party," *Middle East Policy* 13, no. 1 (March 2006): 102-119.

sition between competing political parties, has taken place within a system that remains fundamentally flawed.[46] In reality, a different section of the very same "secret conclave" runs the state, and democratic consolidation has advanced very little.

The decade-plus rule of the AKP and the accompanying strong economic growth and prosperity has prompted a great deal of literature on the democratic consolidation of Turkey and questions whether the new leadership can shed Turkey of its imperfections and finally join the community of consolidated democracies. While many authors and public prognosticators extol the obvious symbolic importance of a Muslim-Turkey in the European club, the majority of scholars such as Anderson remain skeptical that Turkish society can escape the ingrained DNA of its history.[47] Many scholars see a further polarization among the "secret conclave" of Turkish nationalism and persistent in-fighting among nationalists,[48] Islamists,[49] and liberals[50] while continuing to exclude the rest of the population. The goal throughout the modern republic has been to amplify Turkish national identity in order to increase sovereignty in a world of states, and to drive Sunni Kurds, Shia Alevi, Jews, Greeks, Laz, Armenians, and Assyrian Christians to the "in-group" and join the majority of Turkish society, abandoning their desire for multiple political identities. This research aims to add to the literature and explain why it is unlikely that Turkey will further consolidate its democracy and produce nuanced domestic and foreign policy unless its public and private understanding of nationalism becomes substantially more inclusive.

As the basis for its conclusions, this study uses a content analysis of peer-reviewed journal articles, original scholarly texts, and news sources on Turkish domestic politics since the third consecutive election of the AKP on June 11, 2011. The literature review uses significantly older sources to establish nationalist identity in Turkey, but the bulk of research consists of recent articles and texts. The research draws primarily from sources detailing the policies of the AKP government and their relationship to the ongoing challenge to define Turkish nationalism among the Sunni, Turkish majority.

Content analysis as a methodological tool is described by Berg and Lune as "a careful, detailed, systematic examination and interpretation of a particular body of material in an effort to identify patterns, themes, biases and meanings."[51]

---

46 Anderson, *The New Old World*, 447.

47 Eylem Akdeniz, "The Historical 'Stickiness' of Nationalism Inside Turkey's Political Field," *Turkish Studies* 12, no. 3 (September 2011): 309-340; E.F. Keyman, and Tuba Kancı, "A Tale of Ambiguity: Citizenship, Nationalism and Democracy in Turkey," *Nations and Nationalism* 17, no. 2 (April 2011): 318-336; Stephen A. Cook, "Turkey's War at Home," *Survival* 51, no.5 (Oct/Nov2009): 105-120; Zafer M.Çetin, "Tales of Past, Present, and Future: Mythmaking and Nationalist Discourse in Turkish Politics," *Journal of Muslim Minority Affairs* 24, no. 2 (October 2004): 347-365; Tanıl Bora, "Nationalist Discourses in Turkey," *South Atlantic Quarterly* 102, no. 2/3 (Spring/Summer 2003): 433-451; Nergis Canefe, "Turkish Nationalism and Ethno-Symbolic Analysis: the Rules of Exception," *Nations and Nationalism* 8, no. 2 (April 2002):133.

48 Ioannis Grigoriadis, "M," *Middle East Policy* 17, no. 4 (Winter 2010): 101-113; Emrullah Uslu, "Ulusalcılık: The Neo-nationalist Resurgence in Turkey," *Turkish Studies* 9, no. 1 (March 2008): 73-97.

49 Diana M. Appelbaum, "Islamic Supremacy Alive and Well in Ankara," *Middle East Quarterly* 20, no. 1 (Winter 2013): 3-15; Cengiz Dinç, "The Welfare Party, Turkish Nationalism and Its Vision of a New World Order," *Alternatives: Turkish Journal of International Relations* 5, no. 3 (Fall 2006): 1-17.

50 Cevdet Yımaz, "Modernity and Economic Nationalism in the Formation of Turkish Nationalism," *Mediterranean Quarterly* 17, no. 2 (Spring 2006): 53-71; Fotios Moustakis, "Turkish-Kurdish Relations and the European Union: An Unprecedented Shift in the Kemalist Paradigm?" *Mediterranean Quarterly* 16, no. 4 (Fall 2005): 77-89.

51 Bruce L.Berg, and Howard Lune, *Qualitative Research Methods for the Social Sciences (Eighth Edition)* (Boston: Pearson,

The methodology is used here to identify "the patterns of language used in this communication [among Turks and scholars of Turkish politics] as well as the social and cultural context in which these communications occur."⁵² This paper is organized according to the following factors intended to identify the main problems in Turkish nationalism which result in a monochromatic domestic and foreign policy:

> A secular or Islamic state?
> The role of the military in government
> A stranglehold on political participation, the judiciary, and media
> Framing the new constitution
> The projection of nationalist discourse on foreign policy

With its origins in Bekdil's editorial, this study explores these themes in order to test whether they are a direct cause of Turkey's aversion to a moderating between extremes of black and white through the color gray.

A Secular or Islamic state?

The primary role of religion in public life is crucial to political identity among the Sunni Turkish majority. Kemalism, Ataturk's state-sponsored ideology, championed secularism above all else in order to break from the traditions of the Ottoman Empire and to reorient Turkey toward the developed west. As introduced in the literature review, rule by the Republican People's Party (CHP) and the military ensured that secularism was maintained. Leadership in a fused Sultan/Caliph was eliminated, and a Prime Minister was created with a Directorate of Religious Affairs to oversee religion, a concept labeled laicism. Under laicism, all religious leaders are employees of the state; as such, their termination was, and continues to be, subject to state approval. Religion was therefore never outlawed as under many communist regimes, but it was regulated and relegated to a subordinate status in Ataturk's Kemalism.

While Kemalism was dominant from 1923 through the late twentieth century, political Islam was legally permitted to reemerge in the 1980s. Part of the "Islamic-cultural thesis,"⁵³ the emergence of political Islam was intended to safeguard Turkey from the nearby ideological threat, Russian communism. In existence since the early 1970s, political Islam grew in opposition to the continued rule of the secular, military elite and coups in 1960, 1971, and 1980. Unfortunately for the secular ruling class, once communism faded from the scene, Islam emerged as the new challenge to Ataturk's vision of Turkey and quickly became the major cause of the split among the Sunni-Turkish majority. The rise of religious parties and their challenges to the CHP government have resulted in substantial and continuous tension that has been almost the sole focus of Turkish politics since that time.

2012), 349.

52 Ibid., 364.

53 Stephen Kinzer, *Crescent and Star: Turkey between Two Worlds* (New York: Farrar, Strauss, and Giroux, 2008), 60.

A legal ban on a series of Islamist political parties starting in the late 1970s and continuing with military coups in 1980 and 1997 kept such parties from controlling parliament. Borne of the father of political Islam in Turkey, Necmettin Erbakan, current Prime Minister Recep Tayyip Erdoğan, and President Abdullah Gül founded the Justice and Development Party in 2001. After narrowly escaping a legal ban—and Erdoğan's short incarceration for incendiary language—the AKP was overwhelmingly elected in the parliamentary elections of 2002. In the ten years since its election, the AKP has gradually loosened the restrictions on Islam in the public sphere, ending the ban on headscarves at public universities, increasing the opportunities for Koranic studies, and appointing AKP-affiliated individuals to key posts around the country. The AKP has recently imposed a selective ban on alcohol,[54] shortened the window for women's elective abortion,[55] and has advocated a more traditional role for women both inside and outside the home.[56]

During the summer of 2013, this debate hit a fevered pitch as a controversy over the redevelopment of a city park sparked weeks of violent confrontations among these two groups. As many secularists perceived an increasing movement toward conservative Islam,[57] the planned bulldozing of Gezi Park and the development of a commercial area ignited violent clashes between police and protestors in sixty of eighty-three regions around the country, killing five and wounding over four thousand protestors.[58] Through the use of tear gas and water cannons laced with pepper spray,[59] protests united intellectuals,[60] unions,[61] women, and other disaffected groups who took to the streets by the hundreds of thousands, causing the government's public confidence level to fall sharply.[62] Government responded

---

54 "Turkey Introduces Warning Labels for Alcohol," *The Sun Herald*, accessed August 25, 2013, http://turkishdigest.blogspot.com/2013/08/turkey-introduces-warning-labels-for.html; Dorian Jones, "Alcohol Apartheid: The New Turkish Laws that Segregate Drinkers," *The Atlantic*, August 18, 2012, accessed August 19, 2012, http://www.theatlantic.com/international/archive/2012/08/alcohol-apartheid-the-new-turkish-laws-that-segregate-drinkers/261290/.

55 Dorian Jones, "Turkish Women React to Proposed Abortion Limits," *Deutsche Welle*, June 4, 2012, accessed August 19, 2012, http://www.dw.de/dw/article/0,,15996913,00.html.

56 Semih Idiz, "Erdoğan's Crisis with Pregnant Women," *Al-Monitor*, August 3, 2013, accessed August 25, 2013, http://turkishdigest.blogspot.com/2013/08/erdogans-crisis-with-pregnant-women-al.html.

57 Lonna Lisa Williams, "Women Protest in Turkey," *Digital Journal*, June 19, 2013, accessed August 25, 2013, http://www.digitaljournal.com/article/352632.

58 Christophe De Bellaigue, "Turkey's Hidden Revolution," *Slate*, August 26, 2013, accessed August 27, 2013, http://www.slate.com/articles/news_and_politics/foreigners/2013/08/recep_tayyip_erdogan_and_turkish_liberals_turkey_has_a_diverse_irreverent.html; "Kask Numaralarını Gizliyorlar," *Hurriyet Daily News*, June 4, 2013, accessed August 25, 2013, http://www.hurriyet.com.tr/gundem/23430325asp; "Dayak Atarken Numaraları Gizlediler," *Turk Time*, June 5, 2013, accessed August 25, 2013, http://www.freenewspos.com/english/video/CNN/fePzOIQlHgY.

59 "Turkey: End Incorrect, Unlawful Use of Teargas," *Human Rights Watch*, July 17, 2013, accessed August 25, 2013, http://www.hrw.org/news/2013/07/16/turkey-end-incorrect-unlawful-use-teargas.

60 "Turkish pianist faces prisonment for anti-religious tweets," *Hurriyet Daily News*, May 28, 2012, accessed June 3, 2012, http://www.hurriyetdailynews.com/turkish-pianist-faces-prisonment-for-anti-religious-tweets.aspx-?pageID=238&nID=21702&NewsCatID=383.

61 Stephen Franklin, "Turkey Arrests Public-Sector Unionists under Broad Terror Law," *In These Times*, July 23, 2012, accessed July 27, 2012, http://www.inthesetimes.com/working/entry/13563/turkey_arrests_public-sector_unionists_under_broad_terror_law/.

62 Tom A. Peter, "Poll Shows Erdoğan's Popularity Rating Has Taken a Hit: Could He Lose His Mandate? *Christian Science Monitor*, June 18, 2013, accessed August 25, 2013, http://www.csmonitor.com/World/Middle-East/2013/0618/Poll-shows-Erdogan-s-popularity-has-taken-a-hit.-Could-he-lose-his-mandate.

by calling the protestors rodents,[63] looters,[64] and terrorists.[65] The unsubstantiated accusations against foreign news agents,[66] an international interest rate lobby,[67] and international Jewry[68] have dramatically increased tensions and have shown the ruling government to be unwilling or unable to respond in a constructive manner. A problem which should be solved through the political process has instead spread beyond expectation and continues to worsen. In May and June 2013, conservative supporters of the government emerged by the hundreds of thousands in support of the government and its policies,[69] and the government insisted that since it won three consecutive elections it had the mandate to serve its constituency.[70] Opponents have largely abandoned violent confrontation in Taksim Square and now meet weekly in parks across the city in open "people's forums" to discuss the next steps in their rebellion against a perceived tyranny of the majority.[71]

This is the central point of focus for the Sunni Turkish majority and is the issue from which all other political controversies emanate. Opposing sides to this debate distrust one another at a core level, and anyone living in Turkey is expected to take a side. While the vast numbers of the minority are expected to take a position on this issue, their status as Shia Alevi, Kurds, or Christian and Jewish minorities places them in the "out group," unable to maintain credibility in such a discussion despite their obligation and desire to participate.

The Role of the Military in Government

A second major factor identifying problems in Turkish nationalism is the role of the military in government. The Turkish military has carried out four coups

---

63   "PM Erdoğan Likens Gezi Protestors to 'Piteous Rodents'," *Today's Zaman*, July 24, 2013, accessed August 25, 2013, http://www.todayszaman.com/news-321702-pm-erdogan-likens-gezi-protesters-to-piteous-rodents.html.

64   Elena Becatoros and Susan Fraser, "Erdoğan Calls Turkish Protestors 'Those Who Burn and Destroy'," *Associated Press*, June 9, 2013, accessed August 25, 2013, http://www.csmonitor.com/World/Latest-News-Wires/2013/0609/Erdogan-calls-Turkish-protesters-those-who-burn-and-de stroy.

65   "Police to consider protesters in Istanbul's Taksim Square terror organization members: Minister," *Hurriyet Daily News*, June 16, 2013, accessed August 27, 2013, at http://www.hurriyetdailynews.com/everyone-who-enters-the-taksim-square-to-be-treated-as-terrorist-turkish-eu-minister.aspx?pageID=238&nID=48875&NewsCatID=338.

66   "Erdoğan's Divisive Language Invites Intellectuals' Ire," *Oman Tribune*, July 1, 2013, accessed August 25, 2013, http://www.omantribune.com/index.php?page=news&id=147422&heading=Europe.

67   Elena Becatoros and Susan Fraser, "Turkey PM's Party Rules out Early Elections," *Associated Press*, June 8, 2013, accessed August 27, 2013 at http://bigstory.ap.org/article/turkeys-pm-convene-party-leadership.

68   Daniel Greenfield, "Islamist Turkey's Government Media Blames Protests on 'Free Enterprise' Jews," *Frontpage Mag*, June 21, 2013, accessed August 25, 2013, http://frontpagemag.com/2013/dgreenfield/islamist-turkeys-government-media-blames-protests-on-free-enterprise-jews/?utm_source=feedburner&utm_medium=feed&utm_campaign=Feed%3A+fpm+(FrontPage+Magazine+%C2%BB+All).

69   "Erdoğan Supporters Rally after Turkey Protest Violence," *Al-Arabiya*, June 16, 2013, accessed August 25, 2013, http://english.alarabiya.net/en/News/middle-east/2013/06/16/Erdogan-supporters-rally-after-Turkey-protest-violence.html.

70   "Zombie Democracy," *The Economist*, June 22, 2013, accessed August 27, 2013, http://www.economist.com/news/leaders/21579850-note-turkeys-prime-minister-among-others-winning-elections-not-enough-zombie-democracy?fsrc=scn/tw/te/pe/zombiedemocracy.

71   Dorian Jones, "Turkish Protestors Take to Turkey's Parks," *Voice of America*, July 23, 2013, accessed August 29, 2013, http://www.voanews.com/content/turkish-protesters-take-to-the-countrys-parks/1707689.html; Arsu, Sebnem, "After Protests, Forums Sprout in Turkey's Parks," *The New York Times*, July 7, 2013, accessed August 25, 2013, http://www.nytimes.com/2013/07/08/world/europe/after-protests-forums-sprout-in-turkeys-parks.html?pagewanted=all&_r=0.

(1960, 1971, 1980, and 1997) since it created the state in 1923. A reduction in the influence of the military on politics is crucial to the consolidation of democracy as well as to acceptance into the European Union, both long-time goals of the Turkish government. This issue is closely tied to the secular/Islamist factor in the previous section because, as the traditional guarantor of secular Turkey, the degree of military influence in politics is seen as an indicator of who is leading that contest: the secular or Islamist factions. The weaker the military becomes, the greater the perception that Islamists will control politics and policy going forward; it is a zero-sum game played by both sides of this secret conclave vying for state power.

It is an inordinate worry among secular forces that since 2002 the AKP government has effectively reduced the power of military politics in the name of democratization through a series of questionable, high-profile trials. Using longstanding state security courts, the AKP government has cited the so-called "Ergenekon" and "Sledgehammer" trials to charge hundreds of military and secular leaders with crimes against the state. On August 11, 2011 the four heads of the military branches simultaneously resigned in an effort to expose the class-action trials as politically motivated.[72] The failure of this final effort by the military seems to have signaled its death knell as a factor in contest for power, as the result was neither a public uprising in their favor nor a military coup by secular loyalists; the AKP merely replaced the leaders of the four branches of the military with appointees of their own.[73]

The final phases of the removal of the Turkish military from politics occurred in the summer of 2013, when government used the police to quash the protests, flying in dozens from around the country claiming it was its duty to crush the protests, and that "nobody can intimidate us. We don't take orders from anybody but God."[74] It also threatened to bring in the army if protestors did not give up their efforts.[75] Verdicts in the Ergenekon trials were announced on August 5, 2013 and resulted in maximum sentences for hundreds of detainees convicted on slim and weak evidence.[76] No significant popular protests have occurred in response, and the protest movement has added this mistreatment to a long list of grievances.

In effect, the Islamist leaders of the AKP have stepped into the role occupied for decades by the secular CHP and the military. They are vying to represent the

---

72 Gül Tuysuz and Sabrina Tavernise, "Top Generals Quit in Group, Stunning Turks," *The New York Times*, July 29, 2011, accessed August 19, 2012, http://www.nytimes.com/2011/07/30/world/europe/30turkey.html?pagewanted=all.

73 "Turkey Appoints New Military Leaders," *Voice of America News*, August 5, 2011, accessed August 20, 2012, http://www.eagleworldnews.com/2011/08/05/turkey-appoints-new-military-leaders/.

74 Justin Huggler, "Defiant Erdoğan Tells Turkey: It's My Duty to End Protests," *The Independent*, June 16, 2013, accessed August 27, 2013 at http://www.independent.co.uk/news/world/europe/defiant-erdogan-tells-turkey-its-my-duty-to-end-protests-8659981.html.

75 Diane Sweet, "Erdoğan Threatens to Use Military to End Protests," *Occupy America: Crooks & Liars Blog in a Re-Post of Al-Jazeera*, June 17, 2013, accessed August 27, 2013, http://occupyamerica.crooksandliars.com/diane-sweet/erdogan-threatens-use-military-end-pro#sthash.X3UBkqwU.dpbs.

76 Joe Parkinson and Ayla Albayrak, "Turkey Court Gives 17 Life Sentences," *Wall Street Journal*, August 6, 2013, accessed August 27, 2013, http://online.wsj.com/article/SB10001424127887323514404578649533741512610.html; Daniel Dombey, "Turkey's Ergenekon Trial: Q&A," *The Financial Times*, August 5, 2013, accessed August 27, 2013, http://www.ft.com/intl/cms/s/0/4a9e370a-fdbc-11e2-a5b1-00144feabdc0.html?siteedition=intl#axzz2dDNITFDU.

rising Anatolian middle class, which is more conservative and traditional than secular Turks, but still a part of the secret conclave of Sunni Turkish citizens. While rise of the AKP and a future Islamic state is far from reality for many scholars and ordinary Turkish citizens, a combination of these two factors dominate social and political discourse to the exclusion of needed political and social reforms.

A Stranglehold on Political Participation, the Judiciary, and Media

A vigorous political climate in Turkey deepens the interplay among the Sunni Turkish majority and is yet another factor limiting the development of an inclusive nationalism and preventing democratic consolidation. As stated earlier, the People's Republican Party (CHP) is the traditional Kemalist and secular champion while the Justice and Development Party (AKP) represents conservatives to an increasingly middle-class Anatolian heartland. These two parties dominate politics along with representation from the Nationalist Movement Party (MHP), an ultra-conservative and xenophobic movement with a relatively small but virulent following, and which is also Sunni and Turkish. Together these parties comprise more than ninety-three percent of the seats in the Turkish Grand National Assembly and they contest the many important issues among their constituent base.

One might ask how seventy to seventy-five percent of the population controls over ninety-percent of the parliamentary seats? The answer is found in the constitutional engineering that is creating a stranglehold on political participation in favor of the majority. The most useful factor is a ten-percent threshold of votes for representation in parliament, which is justified as necessary to keep extremist groups at bay. However, the real effect of the electoral threshold is to keep out Kurdish political parties and to channel the remaining population into the three established parties. The vast numbers of minority voters in Turkey therefore have only three choices, all of which are Sunni and Turkish and none of which represent their complex political identity: a secular party (CHP), an Islamist (AKP), and a nationalist party (MHP).

Kurdish parties have attempted to enter the political arena, but are consistently declared illegal by a pliant judiciary. Whether historically dominated by the CHP—now the AKP—the judiciary has consistently thwarted political participation by regularly banning the political parties.[77] The current Kurdish parties, the Peace and Democracy Party (BDP) and the Participatory Democracy Party (KADEP), are only the latest in a line of political representatives to have narrowly survived a government ban but whose representatives cannot exceed the ten percent threshold and so run and are elected as independents. Tellingly, the Islamist AKP is as likely to prevent Kurdish and minority representation in parliament as the secular CHP, a clear indication that the Sunni Turkish minority will retain power despite their differences. In the summer of 2013, a Turkish parliamentarian walked 280 miles from Ankara to Istanbul to protest the threshold and convince

---

77   Robert Tait, "Turkey Bans Main Kurdish Party over Alleged Terror Links," *The Guardian*, December 11, 2009, accessed August 25, 2013, http://www.theguardian.com/world/2009/dec/12/turkey-bans-main-kurdish-party.

lawmakers to reduce it to five percent[78], but this viewpoint is not widespread among the majority of Sunni Turks.

Traditionally the bastions of secularism under the control of the CHP, the Presidency and media are new arenas in which the Justice and Development Party have made inroads and come into conflict with secular forces. Chosen by the majority party in parliament, the Turkish president has always been a secular leader and one who exercises a reasonable degree of power that both complements a strong prime minister and steps into a stronger role during times of political unrest. Since the rise of the AKP, its co-founder Abdullah Gül has become Turkey's first religious-conservative president. A constitutional amendment mandating a popular election for the position rather than a parliamentary appointment has enabled this transition and given the AKP majority the upper hand.

Historically a pliant branch of government for the secular CHP, the judiciary is now utilized in the same manner as the former ruling party to carry out its political program; it has rarely been an independent actor.[79] The vast majority of controversial issues in Turkish politics–terrorism, free speech, religious freedoms, ethnic language, and cultural rights—are played out publicly for the entire state to see through a public and politically motivated judiciary. While Gül has mainly brought grace and moderation to the position of president, the judiciary has drawn fire from all sectors of society. The Turkish constitution makes it illegal to "insult Turkey, the Turkish ethnicity, or Turkish government institutions" (article 301), denigrate the memory of its founder, Mustafa Kemal Ataturk (article 52), and provides for a series of state security courts to protect the sovereign state from security threats, terrorism, and any force that threatens the "unity of the state."

During the summer 2013 protests, politically-motivated courts protected the "unity of the state" in the following ways: they interfered in the Gezi Park development issue[80] stripped oversight in development, business and tax issues, inhibited social media freedom, and jailed dozens of activists while failing to prosecute police officers for excessive brutality.[81] Courts even released a man arrested for attacking protestors with a machete; he is now abroad in Morocco safe from prosecution.[82] Dozens of journalists have been fired,[83] and professional

---

78 Ayla Albayrak, "Woman Walks Hundreds of Miles to Protest Turkey Election Law," *Wall Street Journal*, July 16, 2013, accessed August 27, 2013, http://blogs.wsj.com/emergingeurope/2013/07/16/woman-walks-hundreds-of-miles-to-protest-turkey-election-law/?utm_source=feedblitz&utm_medium=FeedBlitzEmail&utm_content=23327&utm_campaign=0&mod=wsj_valettop_email.

79 Cansu Çamlibel, "Turkish Judges Wear Political Glasses: Euro Court Judge," Hurriyet Daily News, July 29, 2013, accessed August 27, 2013, http://www.hurriyetdailynews.com/turkish-judges-wear-political-glasses-euro-court-judge.aspx?pageID=238&nID=51653&NewsCatID=351.

80 "Turkish court annuls stay of execution on Istanbul's Gezi Park construction," *Hurriyet Daily News*, July 22, 2013, accessed August 29, 2013, http://www.hurriyetdailynews.com/turkish-court-paves-way-for-construction-at-istanbuls-gezi-park.aspx?pageID=238&nID=51164&NewsCatID=340.

81 "Hundreds March In Istanbul to Denounce Release of Police Officer Suspected of Killing Protester," *Countercurrents.org*, June 25, 2013, accessed August 29, 2013, http://www.countercurrents.org/cc250613A.htm.

82 "Court Releases Suspected Machete Attackers," *Today's Zaman*, July 8, 2013, accessed August 29, 2013, http://www.todayszaman.com/news-320276-court-releases-suspected-machete-attackers.html.

83 "Turkish Journalists Fired over Coverage of Gezi Park Protests," *The Independent*, July 23, 2013, accessed August 25, 2013, http://www.independent.co.uk/news/world/europe/turkish-journalists-fired-over-coverage-of-gezi-park-protests-8727133.html.

medical staff that assisted protestors have been arrested.[84] A social media law is being drafted,[85] and the government has aimed to suppress protests by any means, including denying loans to student protestors[86] and firing and raiding sympathetic businesses and social leaders.[87] Turkey has jailed more journalists than any other country worldwide, a distinction it claims over Iran, China, North Korea, and Eritrea,[88] and has fully brought the mainstream media under its control.[89]

It is likely that minorities in Turkey prefer its flawed democracy over the governmental systems of its neighbors. While a free and independent state for twenty-five million Kurds across the region is surely appealing, redrawing borders and likely conflicts with Iraq, Turkey, Iran, and Syria encourage the choice of increasing minority protections, limited autonomy, and deepening democracy *inside* Turkey.[90] The likelihood of the failure of a new Kurdish state and relegation to a life in disintegrating Syria, authoritarian Iran, or contentious Iraq is not an enticing option.[91]

The same can also be said of Turkey's approximately twenty million Shia Alevi; overwhelming in their support for a pluralist system, this large minority does not wish to be compared to its Alawite cousins in Syria or to appear supportive of its authoritarianism.[92] Lastly, Jews and Christians of all varieties also likely prefer the Turkish political system to those societies under stress in the Arab Spring such as Iraq or Egypt.[93] What has always been the desire of all Turkish minorities has been integration into the Turkish political system and the protections to speak their

---

84   Athena Yenko, "Istanbul Protest: Police Arrested Medical Staff and Denied Giving Details of the Arrest," *International Business Times*, June 18, 2013, accessed August 29, 2013, http://au.ibtimes.com/articles/479794/20130618/istanbul-police-gezi-park-taksim-square-prime.htm#.Uh95QRvVBqE.

85   Curt Hopkins, "Turkish Government Working on Plan to Censor Social Media," *The Daily Dot*, June 26, 2013, accessed August 29, 2013, http://www.dailydot.com/news/turkey-social-media-censorship-plan/.

86   "No loans for students who engage in protests, chant slogans: Loan board," *Hurriyet Daily News*, July 30, 2013, accessed August 29, 2013, http://www.hurriyetdailynews.com/no-loans-for-students-who-engage-in-protests-chant-slogans-loan-board.aspx?PageID=238&NID=51732&NewsCatID=341.

87   Piotr Zalewski, "In Turkey, Critics of Erdoğan's Government Claim Familiar Pattern of Reprisal," *Time*, July 30, 2013, accessed August 29, 2013, http://world.time.com/2013/07/30/in-turkey-critics-of-erdogans-government-claim-familiar-pattern-of-reprisal/?iid=tl-main-mostpop2.

88   Pandaya, "Media freedom remains major challenge in Turkey," *The Jakarta Post*, June 16, 2012, accessed June 17, 2012, http://www.thejakartapost.com/news/2012/06/16/media-freedom-remains-major-challenge-turkey.html; Peter Kenyon, "For Turkish Journalists, Arrest Is A Real Danger," *National Public Radio*, January 26, 2012, accessed June 1, 2012, http://www.wbur.org/npr/145844105/for-turkish-journalists-arrest-is-a-real-danger; Matthew Brunwasser, "Leading the World in Jailed Journalists, Turkey Cracks Down on Free Expression," *The World*, June 25, 2012, accessed June 30, 2012, http://www.theworld.org/2012/06/turkey-democracy/.

89   Zeynep Alendar, "Turkish Media's Moral Bankruptcy: An Interview with Haluk Sahin," *Jadaliyya*, June 10, 2013, accessed August 29, 2013, http://www.jadaliyya.com/pages/index/12158/turkish-medias-moral-bankruptcy_an-interview-with-.

90   Denise Natali, Henri J. Barkey, Marina Ottaway, "Iraqi Kurdistan Today: Between Autonomy and Dependency," *Carnegie Endowment for International Peace*, September 27, 2010, accessed August 20, 2012, http://www.carnegieendowment.org/2010/09/27/iraqi-kurdistan-today-between-autonomy-and-dependency/4ib.

91   Irem Karakaya, "Turkey, Iraqi Kurds to act against Kurdish rebels," *Associated Press*, August 2, 2012, accessed August 20, 2012, http://www.boston.com/news/world/europe/2012/08/01/turkey-military-drill-syria-border-eyes-kurds/H3VKTzlDCXCcXCQVT0tfaO/story.html.

92   Stephen Schwartz, "Alawites in Syria and Alevis in Turkey: Crucial Differences," *Gatestone Institute*, August 17, 2012, accessed August 19, 2012, http://www.gatestoneinstitute.org/3284/alawites-syria-alevis-turkey.

93   "Turkish Christians Subject to Discrimination, Attacks, Report Says," *Christian Post World*, February 15, 2012, accessed August 20, 2012, http://www.christianpost.com/news/turkish-christians-subject-to-discrimination-attacks-report-says-69526/#0kTlxGe0bQbXaAOm.99; Max Blumenthal, "Being Jewish in Turkey, before and after the Mavi Marmara," *Blog*, July 17, 2011, accessed August 20, 2012, http://maxblumenthal.com/2011/07/being-jewish-in-turkey-before-and-after-the-mavi-marmara-part-1-of-2/.

native languages and practice their ethnic and religious customs.[94] The demands of approximately thirty percent of society are not to be ignored, yet the Sunni Turkish majority has done just that and set up a system in which all citizens are not equal.

Framing the New Constitution

A final domestic problem that brings together each of the previous factors concerns the drafting of a long-overdue new constitution. Turkey has been a functioning semi-parliamentary system since free elections began in 1945, a republic in which the Prime Minister is chosen by the party receiving the most seats but which also has a President with not-insignificant powers. Throughout the twentieth century, the president filled the gap in times of political instability and strengthened the hand of the secularist forces when necessary. As mentioned earlier, the AKP introduced a constitutional amendment to choose the president in a direct, popular vote. Since the AKP's election to a third term in 2012, Prime Minister Erdoğan has made it known that he wishes to be the next president of Turkey, possibly extending his rule until 2024.[95]

Alongside his desire is a campaign promise of the AKP to at long last replace the 1982 constitution written in the aftermath of the 1980 military coup. Seen as an impediment to democracy in Turkey, the AKP tapped into a strong desire by the entire population–Sunni Turks and all minorities–to strengthen democratic protections.[96] The specter of the 2013 summer of unrest also hangs over this issue and a truce between the government and Kurdish terrorists which went into effect in May, just weeks before the Gezi Park violence broke out.

The possibility of an independent Kurdistan strikes deepest at the heart of insecurities among Sunni Turks, perhaps the largest contingency uniting the Sunni Turk majority. The Kurdistan Workers Party (PKK) continues to wage a Marxist-inspired war against the Turkish state, one that has caused over 35,000 casualties in a thirty-year conflict.[97] In 2012, the CHP and AKP agreed to work together to find a solution to this "Kurdish question," and with much fanfare they invited the nationalist MHP and the Kurdish Democracy Party to work toward a final settlement of these issues.[98] The MHP flatly refused and the BDP hesitated to the point that the initiative stalled. A truce between the Turkish government and the Kurdish rebel group known as the PKK did materialize and has placed additional pressure on the issue of national identity as outlined in a promised a

---

94   Ali Aslan Kilic, "Turkish minorities: We want a constitution that embraces us all," *Today's Zaman*, April 16, 2012, accessed August 20, 2012, http://www.todayszaman.com/news-277658-turkish-minorities-we-want-a-constitution-that-embraces-us-all.html.

95   "Turkey: Erdoğan has no rivals in 2014 presidential vote: First constitutional reform for US-style presidential system," *ANSAmed*, July 17, 2012, accessed July 17, 2012, http://ansamed.ansa.it/ansamed/en/news/sections/analysis/2012/07/17/Turkey-Erdoğan-has-rivals-2014-presidential-vote_7196315.html.

96   Ihsan Dagi, "What do the Kurds want?" *Today's Zaman*, April 29, 2012, accessed August 20, 2012, http://www.todayszaman.com/columnist-278970-what-do-the-kurds-want.html.

97   "Over 35K Dead in Turkish-PKK Conflict," *Press TV*, January 30, 2013, accessed August 29, 2013, http://www.presstv.com/detail/2013/01/30/286352/over-35000-dead-in-turkishpkk-conflict/.

98   Murat Yetkin, "Turkey's main parties converge on the Kurdish problem," *Hurriyet Daily News*, June 7, 2012, accessed June 8, 2012, http://www.hurriyetdailynews.com/turkeys-main-parties-converge-on-the-kurdish-problem.aspx?pageID=238&nID=22590&NewsCatID=409.

constitutional document which has not yet materialized. The constitutional future of Turkey dovetails with the other factors previously outlined and further supports the hypothesis that the Sunni Turkish majority remain too focused on their own internal struggles to advance democracy at home.

The Projection of Nationalist Discourse on Foreign Policy

These domestic preoccupations directly affect Turkish foreign policy. Whether dealing with Cyprus, Armenia, proposed French or American legal bans on genocide-denial, Kurdistan, or involvement with the European Union, Turkish foreign policy often lacks nuance and takes on a black or white character due to the limitations placed on it by its domestic politics. If we revisit the scholars of nationalism such as Hall and Putnam, mentioned in this study's literature review, they remind us that nationalism is an imagined community, created domestically through politics and society and used internationally in a two-level game intended to accomplish the domestic goals of international, human, and economic security.

Statements by Foreign Minister Ahmet Davutoğlu and President Abdullah Gül frame the connections between Turkish domestic and foreign policy:

> Foreign Minister Ahmet Davutoğlu:
> "...the principle of *zero problems towards neighbors* has been successfully implemented for the past seven years. Turkey's relations with its neighbors now follow a more cooperative track. There is a developing economic interdependence between Turkey and its neighboring countries. In 2009, for example, we achieved considerable diplomatic progress with Armenia, which nevertheless remains the most problematic relationship in Turkey's neighborhood policy.[99]

> President Abdullah Gül:
> ...Turkey has become a model of success that many countries around us now seek to emulate. And yet, until a year or two ago, some political pundits were asking, "Who lost Turkey?" or "Whither Turkey?"—the assumption being that Turkey had shifted its foreign-policy axis away from the West. In fact, Turkey's external orientation has remained constant, because it rests on the values that we share with the free world. What has changed is our increased assertiveness in our efforts to ensure greater stability and human welfare in our region, evident in our advocacy of freedom, democracy, and accountability not only for ourselves, but also for others.[100]

---

99   Ahmet Davutoğlu, "Turkey's Zero-Problems Foreign Policy," *Foreign Policy*, May 20, 2010, accessed August 20, 2012, http://www.foreignpolicy.com/articles/2010/05/20/turkeys_zero_problems_foreign_policy?page=0,1&hidecomments=yes; Richard Falk, "Turkey's Foreign Policy: Zero Problems with Neighbors Revisited," *Blog: Citizen Pilgrimage*, February 8, 2012, accessed August 20, 2012, http://richardfalk.wordpress.com/2012/02/08/turkeys-foreign-policy-zero-problems-with-neighbors-revisited/; Hamid Reza Emadi, "Turkish zero-problem policy in tatters as tension escalates with neighbors," *PressTV*, August 6, 2012, accessed August 20, 2012, http://www.presstv.ir/detail/2012/08/06/254781/zeroproblem-policy-really/#.UDLb2qllRuc.

100   Abdullah Gül, "Turkey Tacks New Foreign Policy Course," *The Japan Times*, May 24, 2012, accessed August 20, 2012, http://www.japantimes.co.jp/text/eo20120524a2.html.

This positive spin on Turkish foreign policy has caused a great deal of pushback both at home and abroad, the argument being that rhetoric does not match action.[101] Indeed, if the frozen relationships with Armenia and Greek Cyprus are to be used as benchmarks, the "zero problems towards neighbors" policy cannot be substantiated even on the surface. In 2012 Turkey flatly refused to attend any EU meeting chaired by the rotating president from Cyprus, and attempted to diminish Greek Cypriot leadership on all matters during the six-month rotation.[102] While there have been occasional meetings between Turkey and Armenia, each side is steadfast in its refusal to compromise, sit down, and discuss their unpleasant past and move forward.[103] Academic efforts to establish a national dialogue must begin at private universities, as public or state efforts to do so are either empty of content or flatly rejected.

This lack of positive foreign policy is also seen in the Turkish response to French and American government proposals to legally outlaw the denial of the 1915 Armenian massacres as genocide. When interest groups in either France or the United States manage to propose a bill on such matters, the Turkish government threatens to cut off all ties[104]; this is exactly what happened in 2012 when France, under President Nicolas Sarkozy, passed such a law.[105] The Turkish response was to suspend all relations with France immediately. When Francois Hollande was elected president and the law was struck down by the French constitutional court, all was forgiven; yet mere months later Hollande promised a new genocide-denial and the Turkish state reverted to its prior stance.[106]

This pattern continued throughout the protests of summer 2013 as the Turkish government continued to deny any wrongdoing or admit responsibility for a perceived disproportionate force.[107] Turkey accused the US of hypocrisy in criticizing its police response to the riots,[108] while also directly attacking the

---

101 Steven Cook, "Why Turkey's Dream of Regional Leadership Failed," *The Atlantic*, November 18, 2011, accessed August 20, 2012, http://www.theatlantic.com/international/archive/2011/11/why-turkeys-dream-of-regional-leadership-failed/248696/.

102 "Schulz rejects Turkish boycott of Greek Cypriot presidency," *Today's Zaman*, May 29, 2012, accessed August 20, 2012, http://www.todayszaman.com/newsDetail_getNewsById.action?newsId=281896; Szymon Ananicz, "Cyprus presidency and Turkey's relations with the European Union," *Centre for Eastern Studies*, June 26, 2012, accessed August 20, 2012, http://www.osw.waw.pl/en/publikacje/osw-commentary/2012-06-26/cyprus-presidency-and-turkeys-relations-european-union.

103 "Turkey rebuffs US call on thaw with Armenia," *Hurriyet Daily News*, June 6, 2012, accessed June 12, 2012, http://www.hurriyetdailynews.com/turkey-rebuffs-us-call-on-thaw-with-armenia.aspx?pageID=238&nID=22491&NewsCatID=338.

104 "Turkey Recalls Ambassador to U.S. Over Armenian Genocide Bill," Associated Press, October 11, 2007, accessed August 20, 2012, http://www.foxnews.com/story/0,2933,301221,00.html#ixzz248f7CBAP.

105 Thomas Seibert, "Turkey Suspends Ties with France Following Passing of Armenian Genocide Bill," *The National*, December 23, 2011, accessed August 20, 2012, http://www.thenational.ae/news/world/europe/turkey-suspends-ties-with-france-following-passing-of-armenian-genocide-bill.

106 "French President Hollande Vows New Armenia 'Genocide Law'," *BBC News*, July 7, 2012, accessed August 20, 2012, http://www.bbc.co.uk/news/world-europe-18758078.

107 Serkan Demirtaş, "EU Envoys Respond to Bağış's Comparison of Turkish and EU Police," *Hurriyet Daily News*, June 25, 2013, accessed August 27, 2013, http://www.hurriyetdailynews.com/eu-envoys-respond-to-bagiss-comparison-of-turkish-and-eu-police.aspx?pageID=238&nID=49482&NewsCatID=338&utm_source=feedblitz&utm_medium=FeedBlitzEmail&utm_content=23327&utm_campaign=0.

108 "Turkey protests: Erdoğan rejects EU criticism," *BBC*, June 7, 2013, accessed August 27, 2013, http://www.bbc.co.uk/news/world-europe-22817360.

European Union, Germany and other EU member states who spoke out.[109] Prime Minister Erdoğan publicly declared that protests in Brazil and Turkey were part of an international conspiracy to destabilize their governments.[110]

Conclusion

The monochromatic nature of Turkish domestic and foreign policy is directly caused by the limits of its national identity. These self-imposed limits have been ingrained in the Sunni Turkish character since Ottoman times and have been intentionally carried forward to the modern Turkish state. While publicly and internationally declaring an equal and open concept of citizenship, the "secret conclave" of Sunni Turks have developed a political system and accompanying social climate specifically designed to maintain this dominance.

A content analysis of the domestic political issues in Turkish politics and the international implications of Turkish foreign policy has shown the monochromatic nature of politics in modern Turkey. The lack of nuance in governmental policy and aversion to a moderation of extremes in the color gray is necessary in order to preserve the system and status quo of the confessional majority. Unfortunately, the realities of a multi-ethnic and multi-religious majority and the interconnectivity of modern politics, economics, and security expose the flaws in the Turkish system. As discussed at the outset, the themes outlined in this study remain hurdles to a truly pluralist national identity, the consolidation of democracy, and the international credibility necessary for Turkey to take its place within the democratic family of states and the European Union.

These conclusions help explain why the peaceful transition from a secular to an Islamist government, long seen as necessary for democratic consolidation in Turkey, is not indicative of true progress. The 2013 summer protests covered on international media and the Turkish government's violent response illustrate a continuation of the contest for power among the major factions in the Sunni Turkish majority, which inhibits authentic change to the exclusion of millions of minorities. The monochromatic nature of domestic and foreign policy in Turkey is a necessary device to maintain this supremacy, and the nuance, or gray, necessary for a fully democratic system will be possible only if the majority expands nationalist dialogue to include not only Sunni Turks, but Sunni Kurds, Shiite Alevi, and the Armenian, Assyrian, and Greek Christians, all of whom are part of this sizable minority.

---

109   Andrew C. McCarthy, "Erdoğan Exploits the EU-Integration Charade," *National Review Online*, July 8, 2013, accessed August 27, 2013, http://www.nationalreview.com/article/352886/erdogan-exploits-eu-integration-charade-andrew-c-mccarthy.

110   Susan Fraser and Amer Cohadzic, "Erdoğan: Turkey, Brazil Protests Part of Same, Foreign-Led Conspiracy to Destabilize Governments," *The Huffington Post*, June 22, 2013, accessed August 27, 2013, http://www.huffingtonpost.com/2013/06/22/erdogan-turkey-brazil_n_3483639.html.

Bibliography[111]

Adak, Hulya. "National Myths and Self-Na(rra)tions: Mustafa Kemal's 'Nutuk' and Halide Edib's 'Memoirs' and 'The Turkish Ordeal'." *South Atlantic Quarterly* 102, no.2/3 (Spring/Summer2003): 509-527.

Akdeniz, Eylem. "The Historical 'Stickiness' of Nationalism inside Turkey's Political Field." *Turkish Studies* 12, no. 3 (September 2011): 309-340.

Altan-Olcay, Ozlem. "Gendered projects of national identity formation: The Case of Turkey." *National Identities* 11, no. 2 (June 2009): 165-186.

Anderson, Perry. *The New Old World.* Brooklyn NY: Verso, 2009.

Appelbaum, Diana M. "Islamic Supremacy Alive and Well in Ankara." *Middle East Quarterly* 20, no. 1 (Winter 2013): 3-15.

Ateş, Ahmet Emre. "Istanbul, City or 'Castle for Nationalism'? Discussion on the Urban Interaction between Literature and Nationalism." *International Journal of Turcologia* 7, no. 15 (Spring 2013): 69-73.

Bayar, Yeşim. "The Trajectory of Nation-Building through Language Policies: the Case of Turkey during the Early Republic (1920-38)." *Nations and Nationalism* 17, no. 1 (January 2011): 108-28.

Berg, Bruce L., and Howard Lune. *Qualitative Research Methods for the Social Sciences (Eighth Edition).* Boston: Pearson, 2012.

Bekdil, Burak. "The Turkish Hate-Affair with the Color 'Gray'." *Hurriyet Daily News*, August 4, 2011. Accessed February 22, 2012. http://www.hurriyetdailynews.com/default.aspx?pageid=438&n=the-turkish-hate-affair-with-the-color-8216gray8217-2011-08-04.

Bingol, Yilmaz. "Language, Identity and Politics in Turkey: Nationalist Discourse on Creating a Common Turkic Language." *Alternatives: Turkish Journal of International Relations* 8, no. 2 (Summer 2009): 40-52.

Bora, Tanıl. "Nationalist Discourses in Turkey," *South Atlantic Quarterly* 102, no. 2/3 (Spring/Summer 2003): 433-451.

Cook, Stephen A. "Turkey's War at Home." *Survival* 51, no. 5 (Oct/Nov2009): 105-120.

Çagcaraptay, Soner. "Citizenship policies in interwar Turkey." *Nations and Nationalism* 9, no. 4 (October 2003): 601-619.

Çetin, Zafer M. "Tales of Past, Present, and Future: Mythmaking and Nationalist Discourse in Turkish Politics." *Journal of Muslim Minority Affairs* 24, no. 2 (October 2004): 347-365.

---

111 To conserve space in an overly long reference section, journalistic references used in the content analysis for this research have been removed and are available by request. Footnotes referencing these same journalistic sources remain in the body of the paper.

Çuhadar, C. Hakan. "The Unchanging Symbol of Nationalism in Turkey: 10th Annual March." *Anadolu University Journal of Social Sciences* 9, no. 2 (2009): 199-208.

Dinç, Cengiz. "The Welfare Party, Turkish Nationalism and Its Vision of a New World Order." *Alternatives: Turkish Journal of International Relations* 5, no. 3 (Fall 2006): 1-17.

Dougherty, James, and Robert Pfaltzgraff, Jr. *Contending Theories of International Relations.* New York: Longman Publishers, 2001.

Dressler, Markus. "Religio-Secular Metamorphoses: The Re-Making of Turkish Alevism." *Journal of the American Academy of Religion* 76, no.2 (June 2008): 280-311.

Dural, Baran. "A Transformation of Social Life in Turkey: 1930-1936." *Electronic Journal of Social Sciences* 8, no. 29 (2009): 184-197.

Eissenstat, Howard. "How Happy to Call Oneself a Turk: Provincial Newspapers and the Negotiation of a Muslim National Identity." *Social History* 37, no. 1 (February 2012): 111.

Göl, Ayla. "Imagining the Turkish Nation through 'Othering' Armenians." *Nations and Nationalism* 11, no. 1 (January 2005): 121-139.

Grigoriadis, Ioannis. "M," *Middle East Policy* 17, no. 4 (Winter 2010): 101-113.

Gulalp, Haldun. "Capitalism and the Modern Nation-State: Rethinking the Creation of the Turkish Republic." *Journal of Historical Sociology* 7, no. 2 (June 94): 155-177.

Gurkas, Hakki, Ph.D., Assistant Professor of History, Kennesaw State University, a discussion, August 8, 2012.

Gürses, Fatma. "Kemalism Model Lesson Book: Civilized Knowledge for the Citizen." *Journal of Gazi Academic View* 3, no. 7 (2010): 233-249.

Hall, Rodney Bruce. *National Collective Identity: Social Constructs and International Systems.* New York: Columbia University Press, 1998.

Kancı, Tuba. "Reconfigurations in the Discourse of Nationalism and National Identity: Turkey at the Turn of the Twenty-first Century." *Studies in Ethnicity & Nationalism* 9, no. 3 (December 2009): 359-376.

Kalaycıoğlu, Ersin. "Turkey." In *Introduction to Comparative Politics*, edited by Mark Kesselman, Joel Krieger and William A. Joseph. Baltimore: Wadsworth Cengage, 2007.

Kenanoğlu, Pınar. "Discrimination and silence: minority foundations in Turkey during the Cyprus conflict of 1974." *Nations and Nationalism* 18, no. 2 (April 2012): 267-286.

Keyman, E.F., and Kancı, Tuba. "A tale of ambiguity: citizenship, nationalism and democracy in Turkey." *Nations and Nationalism* 17, no. 2 (April 2011): 318-336.

Kinzer, Stephen. *Crescent and Star: Turkey between Two Worlds.* New York: Farrar, Strauss, and Giroux, 2008.

Koksal, Duygu. "Fine-Tuning Nationalism: Critical Perspectives from Republican Literature in Turkey." *Turkish Studies* 2, no. 2 (Autumn 2001): 63.

Linz, Juan and Alfred Stepan. *Problems of Democratic Transition and Consolidation.* Baltimore: Johns Hopkins University Press, 1996.

Mann, Michael. *The Sources of Social Power, Vol. II: The Rise of Classes and Nation-States, 1760-1914.* New York: Cambridge University Press, 1993.

Morin, Aysel, and Ronald Lee. "Constitutive Discourse of Turkish Nationalism: Ataturk's Nutuk and the Rhetorical Construction of the 'Turkish People'," *Communication Studies* 61, no. 5 (Nov/Dec 2010): 485-506.

Moustakis, Fotios. "Turkish-Kurdish Relations and the European Union: An Unprecedented Shift in the Kemalist Paradigm?" *Mediterranean Quarterly* 16, no. 4 (Fall 2005): 77-89.

Poulton, Hugh. *Top Hat, Grey Wolf and Crescent: Turkish Nationalism and the Turkish Republic.* New York: NYU Press, 1997.

Putnam, Robert D. "Diplomacy and Domestic Politics: The Logic of Two-Level Games." *International Organization* 42 (Summer 1988): 427-460.

Saraçoğlu, Cenk, "'Exclusive recognition': the new dimensions of the question of ethnicity and nationalism in Turkey." *Ethnic & Racial Studies* 32, no. 4 (May 2009): 640-658.

Scott, James M., Ralph G. Carter and A. Cooper Drury. *IR.* Boston: Wadsworth, Cengage Learning, 2013.

Şahin, Ali. "The Results of Racism-Turanism Case Turkish Nationalism in Development Process in 1944." *International Review of Turkology* 4, no. 8 (2011): 31-40.

Ülker, Erol. "Contextualising 'Turkification': Nation-Building in the late Ottoman Empire, 1908-18." *Nations and Nationalism* 11, no. 4 (October 2005): 613-636.

Uslu, Emrullah. "Ulusalcılık: The Neo-nationalist Resurgence in Turkey." *Turkish Studies* 9, no. 1 (March 2008): 73-97.

Yavuz, M. Hakan. "The Kurdish Question and Turkey's Justice and Development Party." *Middle East Policy* 13, no. 1 (March 2006): 102-119.

Yımaz, Cevdet. "Modernity and Economic Nationalism in the Formation of Turkish Nationalism." *Mediterranean Quarterly* 17, no. 2 (Spring 2006): 53-71.

Zürcher, Erik J. *The Young Turk Legacy and Nation Building: From the Ottoman Empire to Atatürk's Turkey.* London: I.B. Tauris, 2010.

About the Contributors

Renee Pilette Bricker is associate professor of history at the University of North Georgia. Her research interests include those of identity, expressions of citizenship, loyalty and violence in early modern England. She is revising for publication a larger project that examines the role of violence as a mediator in shaping identity and creating loyalty in late Tudor England. She has published biographical sketches of early modern English women, and on Tudor social history.

Celnisha L. Dangerfield is a speech instructor at Chattahoochee Technical College in Marietta, GA. While her research broadly addresses issues of race and culture, it is specifically geared towards aspects of intercultural communication, African American communication, and identity negotiation. Ms. Dangerfield is a co-author of the journal article, "The face of crime: Viewers' memory of race-related facial features of individuals pictured in the news" (*Journal of Communication*). Additionally, she has several book chapters to her credit including, "Lauryn Hill as lyricist and womanist," (in *Understanding African American rhetoric: Classical origins to contemporary innovations*), and the co-authored chapter, "Defining Black masculinity as cultural property: Toward an identity negotiation paradigm" (originally published in *Intercultural communication: A reader*). Her most recent work—a chapter that explores the life of rapper/actor/activist Tupac Shakur—appears as a co-authored contribution to the text, *Icons of hip hop: An encyclopedia of the movement, music, and culture*.

Amy Hagenrater-Gooding is assistant Professor of English at the University of Maryland Eastern Shore where she teaches courses in creative writing, poetry and drama. She obtained her Ph.D. in Literature and Criticism at Indiana University of Pennsylvania where she conducted research on masculine maternity and the subversion of gender roles through gender construction. She was recently awarded a $10,000 grant from the Bill and Melinda Gates Foundation to study the use of MOOCs in the traditional classroom. She is currently working through another grant project at her home institution to establish a cross-curriculum reader to engage multiple disciplines and subjects and foster a collaborative learning environment. Her most recent project involved collaboration with the art department where students in her graphic novel class had the opportunity to team up with advanced art students and write, sketch, storyboard, and illustrate a portion of their own graphic novel.

Victoria Hightower is assistant professor of Middle East History at the University of North Georgia, Dahlonega campus. She graduated from Florida State University in 2011 with her doctorate in History and holds two Master's Degrees in History (Florida State University 2004) and Near East Studies (University of Arizona, 2006). Her research focuses on the relationship between history and heritage in the United Arab Emirates and has published articles on pearls, sustainability, gender, and political power.

Christopher Jespersen is Dean of the College of Arts and Letters at the University of North Georgia. He is author of *American Images of China, 1931-1949* (1996), which was published in 2010 in Chinese by Jiangsu People's Publishing House. He is editor of *Interviews with George Kennan* (2002) and author of articles in *Diplomatic History* and *Pacific Historical Review*, among other journals. Jespersen focuses on American diplomatic history, especially in East Asia. He has served as a Salzburg Seminar Fellow twice, is an alumni of the East-West Center and the West Point Summer Seminar in Military History, was a recipient of an Organization of American Historians-Japan Association for American Studies Residency in Japan award, and has served in the editorial boards of *Diplomatic History* and *Pacific Historical Review*. In addition to various teaching awards, Jespersen is his university's only three-time award winner of the Pie-in-the-Face contest, held by Staff Council to raise money for Relay for Life.

April Conley Kilinski is professor of English and Literature at Johnson University in Knoxville, Tennessee. Trained at the University of Tennessee, her academic interests include Caribbean, African, African American, and Multiethnic literatures. She has recently published on Richard Wright's *Uncle Tom's Children* as well as on Judith Ortiz Cofer's short story, "By Love Betrayed."

Sungshin Kim is associate professor of history at the University of North Georgia. Her most recent publication is "The Great War, the Collapse of Civilization, and Chinese Visions of World Order," in *Peace & Change* (2015). She is currently working on the themes of civilization and race in liberal internationalist thought in late nineteenth- and early twentieth-century China.

Robert Machado is assistant professor of English at Lebanon Valley College, PA, where he teaches courses in US literature, Film Studies, Interdisciplinary Arts, Writing, and Theory. His research involves the study of color across verbal and visual media, postclassical narrative theory, and 19/20-C US literature. He also has published work on early cinema and early photography, multimediality in literature, and the avant-garde. As an early member of the "lowercase sound" movement, since 2001 his experimental sound art under the name Civyiu Kkliu has been performed in galleries on the West and East Coast, and published in the US, the UK., the Netherlands, Belgium, and Austria. His most recent art involves small format Polaroid photography, and monochrome noise.

Timothy May is professor of Central Eurasian and Middle Eastern History at the University of North Georgia. He is also the author of *The Mongol Art of War: Chinggis Khan and the Mongol Military System (2007); Culture and Customs of Mongolia (2009),* and *The Mongol Conquests in World History* (2012).

Jonathan Miner is associate professor of Political Science at the University of North Georgia. Dr. Miner is a scholar of International Relations, specializing in United States Foreign Policy and Middle Eastern Politics. His dissertation, "Spokes of a wheel? Assessing combined efforts of government and civil society to stop terrorism in the United States, Indonesia, Turkey, Spain and Russia" was completed in 2007.

Michael Proulx is a specialist in Roman history at the University of North Georgia. His research examines the emergence of new forms of authority in the Roman imperial period. His publications include *"Patres Orphanorum:* Ambrose of Milan and the Construction of the Role of the Bishop," in *The Rhetoric of Power in Late Antiquity: Religion and Politics in Byzantium, Europe, and the Early Islamic World.* Edited by Elizabeth DePalma Digeser, Robert M. Frakes, and Justin Stephens. London: Tauris Library of Classical Studies, 2010; "In the Shadow of Anthony: History and Hagiography in the Works of Sulpicius Severus and Paulinus of Milan." *Studia Patristica* 39 (Leuven: Peeters Publishing, 2006): 423-429.

Thomas Radice is associate professor of history at Southern Connecticut State University, specializing in early Chinese intellectual history. He has published articles and book reviews in *Asian Philosophy, Dao: A Journal of Comparative Philosophy*, and *Sino-Platonic Papers.* Currently, he is completing a book manuscript on ritual performance in early Chinese thought.

Pamela Jane Sachant is professor of Art History and Head of the Department of Visual Arts at the University of North Georgia. Her research interests include American folk and self-taught art, especially the work of Texas artist Eddie Arning, and the work of George Seeley and F. Holland Day, photographers associated with the Pictorialist and Photo-Secession movements. Her current work in progress includes articles on J. Alexandre Skeete, who modeled for both Seeley and Day, and the 1940s Chinese portrait dolls of Vivian Dai.

www.ingramcontent.com/pod-product-compliance
Lightning Source LLC
Chambersburg PA
CBHW041312240426
43669CB00023B/2967